Comin

Coming Full Circle

A Memoir

Anne Ibbotson

Ashgrove Publishing
London

In memory of Arthur and Elsie Ibbotson
and Sarah Maria Groves;
the three who gave me so much.

PART ONE

Chapter One

I have started this story many times in my head and always at the same place, only this story is not a fantasy or a piece of fiction, it is the story of a child born in London but who grew up in a small village in Derbyshire, and it is a story which, even now, does not have a proper beginning. But we must begin where memory dictates on the main road of that small village in the Peak District. I could take you back to the exact place today and we would find that a lot there has not changed for many years – though some things, I know, are very different.

There is a woman walking up this main street, my mother, and I am with her. A plain child of about six or seven years old, bright auburn hair scraped back into a bow which is always sliding off and getting lost. A source of enormous irritation to me then, as it inevitably involved a telling off of a considerable severity. I can see too the hand-knitted Fair Isle cardigan I was wearing, predominantly beige with some hints of kingfisher blue and yellow. There was a grey pleated skirt and I'm sure there were socks, sliding down around my ankles into, of course, Clarks or Start-rite sandals. My mother would have been neatly dressed, hair naturally curly but cut into a style which made it appear permed. She wore glasses and would have her purse with her, though probably not her handbag.

We are walking along the left hand pavement just past Hancock's grocery store and opposite Hancock's Garage that in those days always had a showroom with large glass windows. There was a black car in there, but the one I remember clearly was an apple green one, unusual for its time and not often seen even now.

I remember the sun was shining that day, though it was a winter sun, for I remember too the smoke curling into the sky from the chimneys of the old granite stone built cottages which lined themselves along the road leading to the centre of the village, the neat little front gardens still bright with flowers; so this was very early winter, or maybe only autumn. Where were we going? I've no idea but we were probably coming from the second of my father's two shops. It had a little bow window filled with boxes of sweets (removed every night for reasons of hygiene), a few yellowing paperback books and bottles of lemonade or dandelion and burdock. Inside there were more of the same, together with the chocolates and biscuits that could not stand the hazards of the shop window. I remember we made our own ice-cream then, my father churning it in a large tub, and it was delicious. I remember too one hot summer Saturday 'helping out' in the shop and standing on an upturned lemonade crate (Eardley's of course) to serve the ice cream, scooping it into the cornets or pressing it into the wafer press, which I still have. We were busy that Saturday and the level of the ice cream slipped lower and lower down the inside of the barrel until, finally, I had to reach right to the bottom and fell in head first. I rather think they pulled me out and carried on selling the rest, for money was short in those days and I don't suppose I had done it much harm. Later we were to be taken over by Wall's Ice-Cream and a lot of the fun went out of the job.

But to return to that village street, we were having a conversation about my ballet lessons. I wanted a special practice tunic like the other students all wore but it was available only from one expensive shop in Sheffield. My mother, as always, was insisting she would make me one – she was very clever with her hands and a good seamstress. I, of course, wanted the bought one and was already experiencing the pangs of bitter disappointment.

My mother spoke with a strong Derbyshire accent, we all did. (I remember, after I had started school, being asked to read the only poem written by a local poet. It contained the phrase 'tap o' th' 'ill' and when I read it everyone laughed and I nearly died of shame. My grandmother had scraped together the funds to send me to a private school in the village, one which was way beyond our means and where everyone else arrived at the school gates on groom led ponies or in chauffeur-driven cars while I walked, my school hat covered by a plastic rain hat in case it rained. We were a careful family, not one to take unnecessary risks, erring indeed on the side of serious caution.) So when my mother spoke in her normal voice, the word 'dancing' came out with a flat 'a'. What came next surprised me as much as my mother, for I replied, very gently I seem to remember, that in future I was going to say 'darncing', not 'dancing', and although my mother only smiled, that phrase more or less changed my life. I don't quite know why it has always seemed such a turning point, and there must have been some snobbery attached to it somewhere, but from then on I never really fitted into the local village life and I never belonged to the 'so called' rich set either so I ended up spending many hours alone … And that is the real point of this beginning.

I was never a lonely child, though of course there were times when I longed to be a part of something, especially at school where I was always the last to be chosen for the team games, sometimes even forced on my reluctant team mates by an insensitive games mistress. And I was not a lonely teenager, for by then I had a dog and a horse and I had learned to build my own daydreams and to an extent create my own reality. Inevitable, I suppose, but really not healthy and something that was to cause me real problems in the future. So perhaps now we have some hint of the character beginning to emerge from that small Fair-Isle-clad figure and it is time to go back to another beginning.

This one, of necessity, comes from other people's memories though it does include another row of terraced houses. But these are rarely bathed in sunlight and stand in a small back street off the Old Kent Road behind the Elephant and Castle in London. It must have been a slum area all those years ago, and in a lot of ways it hasn't changed much. Today, part of the street is given over to a high-rise block of flats, built presumably after the war, and there is a modern pub, the watering hole for some small-time local villains, or so I'm told. I have only been there once and then only briefly, so the images are vague and the impressions dark. It is nevertheless one of the landmarks in my life, for it is the street where I was born. At this stage my biological parents must stay in the shadows for I knew nothing of them until much later. Indeed my father still remains a mystery, for I know nothing of him at all and am not even sure if the name on my birth certificate was his real name. But I am a fact, a proof of their existence if you like, though I gather a pretty much unwelcome proof at the time, especially with my flaming red hair. I made my appearance on a day in November in one of those tiny terraced houses and there my mother and I lived together in uneasy proximity for five months. At five months she brought me, late, to a small office in central London where a village lady and the local district nurse were waiting to take me to St Pancras station and the train to a new life. At this point the woman who brought me there ceased to be my mother. My father, whoever he was, was not present that day, so he, too, must relinquish his title of 'father', if indeed he ever knew that he had acquired it in the first place.

They were to meet, those three women, though they shouldn't have done, and I often wonder what they said to one another. All her life my new mother was to keep the dress, bonnet and little shoes I was wearing that day, and I wonder what her thoughts were every time she saw them, for we never talked about our first meeting, though now I wish we had.

The other woman, the one who gave birth to me, fades from the picture after this meeting, just as she must have wanted to do. She re-emerges many years later in photos and a letter but she is dead by then and although her story is not an easy one, I can have no feelings for her, though I have never wished her harm. But let us leave her at the Elephant and Castle and travel north to Sheffield and the local train to the small Derbyshire village of Hathersage that was to be my home for the next eighteen years of my life. There my parents and I slowly learned to live together and we were happy. They were strict parents in some ways, especially my mother, and the first word I ever spoke was 'No.' But I quickly learned that my father was the softer one of the two and it was to him that I usually ran when I wanted something. He used to read me a bed-time story every night before I went to bed and I felt very safe curled up on his knee as he spoke of witches and bad fairies and terrible hobgoblins. I was fascinated by books and I think it nearly broke his heart when I learned how to read for myself long before I went to school. When I was about three years old I discovered I could delay my bedtime by entertaining them by singing nursery rhymes and dancing across the floor and I was given a miniature wheelbarrow and used to help in the garden at weekends.

In many ways it was an idyllic childhood. My father ran the village post office and had a lease on the little shop farther down the street. My mother didn't work as such, though she was somewhat involved in the ordering and running of the two places; and she was heavily concerned too with the Women's Institute, the Mothers' Union, and many another good works group, besides playing the piano for the Sunday school at chapel and keeping an immaculate house. In some ways I came after all these activities, though I never felt threatened by all this. I had never known anything else so it all seemed quite normal. I'm sure she was around while I was very small and later I developed a liking for my own company and anyhow by then I had my dog.

We went to the next village to choose him and I was told I could have the one I wanted, but of course it was not to be for I chose the weakling, the runt of the litter, and had to be persuaded to take one of the stronger puppies, a sturdy, wobbly lump of Cairn terrier, the brindle kind. We called him Scampy and put him into a tall-sided box he soon learned to climb out of. I adored him and Gracie, my traveller's sample doll and, until then, my constant companion, soon began to feel the pangs of rejection. But Scampy and I were inseparable and could do things Gracie considered boring, like taking long walks on the moors or braving the wrath of my mother and paddling in the icy cold winter water of the local stream.

Water of any description seemed to hold a terror for my mother. A local philanthropist had given the village a sort of early sports centre. It included tennis courts, a bowling green, playing fields and a swimming pool. I loved water and longed to join the other village children at the swimming pool but for a long time permission was refused. Eventually, however, my constant pleading met with success and it was announced that I was to have swimming lessons. My mother bought wool and a crotchet needle and produced a monstrosity in grey and dark blue. Still it was a swimsuit of sorts and the lessons began. I found them exceedingly difficult and even floating didn't come easily. I never connected this with the swimsuit that quickly became waterlogged and pulled me down. So I soldiered on and eventually reached the point of swimming along on the end of a rope held by the instructor. He was very handsome and my ever present mother seemed to enjoy talking to him. One day I was ploughing across the pool, endeavouring to stay afloat, when I noticed that the rope had become slack. I immediately panicked and sank to the bottom of the pool. I was completely disorientated and had no idea of which way was up. It seemed hours before anyone noticed and I was dragged coughing and spluttering from the water. I was terrified and can remember the feeling of the weight of that water on me quite clearly. I did try to keep swimming but the panic always returned and does to this day if I find myself out of my depth. A great pity this, for I still love being in the water and spend a lot of time trying to swim in a few inches of sea, not an easy exercise. So swimming was abandoned, Scampy and I resumed our paddling and Gracie, with her wardrobe of clothes identical to mine, stayed mostly at home and shared the drearier events of life, like trips to the dentist or Sunday-school outings. Eventually, of course, I was to outgrow her completely but I still have her today and part of her wardrobe survives, lurking in the bottom of an old tin trunk.

When I remember those summers now I often think back to a particular walk Scampy and I took time and time again. Of course the sun was always shining and they had just started the haymaking. In those days there were still cornflowers in the hedgerows, scarlet pimpernel hiding among the corn stalks, hedge parsley and ragged robin, speedwell and wild garlic. Scampy ran ahead of me, following a hundred different scents until he was running round in circles and had to give up, returning to me, tongue lolling from the side of his mouth, his tail wagging in happiness.

We were heading for the river, the Derwent, which wound itself along the outskirts of the village and was generally placid except in the depths of winter, and even then it was incapable of summoning up much rage and just peaceably flooded its banks until some rather cross sheep were left standing on a frozen slick, bereft of grazing. They used to hold sheep auctions there in the autumn and we used to walk down, my mother and I, for they were exciting in a rural sort of way. One time we were all three of us there and I found a coal black lamb among one of the flocks. It was love at first sight and I cried hard and long when my father wouldn't buy him for me as a pet. But in my summer memories there is no hint of the winter that must always have come for the sun always shone as Scampy gambled along the riverbank hopeful of a rat, and I strolled along the dappled path with one wary eye on the great bull grazing in the bordering field. I was not scared of large animals for we were a farming community and I grew up surrounded by them, but this particular bull had an evil reputation and was often to be found roaming free. In this memory, however, he is safely behind his fence and grazing quietly.

The riverbank was always a world of its own, conjuring up pictures of *The Wind in the Willows* and hinting at a secret life full of intrigue and gossip. There were kingfishers flitting along the banks, flashes of vivid colour in a shadowy world of greys and dark greens. There was a heron too, rarely seen unless you sat quietly for a while, restraining a panting dog who was eager for the next adventure. Swallows and swifts abounded, and always, in the background, the lonely cry of the curlew could be heard, warning off some unseen enemy, probably me.

That river path was an essential part of my childhood. Well away from the road and the sound of the traffic, there was little to disturb that peace which Henry Miller, quoting St Paul, so graphically described as one 'which passeth all understanding'. He was to find it at Epidavros in Greece, and many years later I was to find it there too. Was it close to God? Maybe, but if so then some superior deity this, not one locked in the arguments and obsessions of the earthbound churches. I was to come across it many times in my life and in many places, and it was always a source of strength, but nine-year-old children are not aware of any of this and so Scampy and I raced our way along the sun-drenched footpaths until the buildings of one of the old Halls came into view.

The valley seemed to be full of these ancient mansions, built of the local stone with clear lines and mullioned windows, and often sprouting turrets and parapets too. Romance clung to them, for who knew what intrigues and liaisons had gone on within those walls? There must have been secret conspiracies surely, and abductions too ... then the stuff of dreams for a small child with a vivid imagination, and a whole summer in which to indulge it. There were seven Halls, all built on hilltops by a father for his seven sons. They must have had enemies galore for I was told that vantage points were chosen so that fires could be lit by the brothers to warn each other of approaching danger in a time of crisis. Those times were long gone but they were still inhabited then and within the walls there was a strong sense of a way of life that had been lived by my grandparents and great-grandparents, one that had been changed irrevocably by the aftermath of World War I.

Some of these old buildings were more intimately connected with my childhood. One I remember visiting as a small child was inhabited by a stern black-bonneted aunt who subscribed to the adage that said children should be seen and not heard. Scampy was never taken on these visits and I was always dressed in my Sunday best, clean white ankle socks and polished shoes, a small bored child sitting in a too large chair, swinging her legs and waiting for release. There were other visits to this Hall, however, always in September and always for the blackberries. Then Scampy ran free and my mother and I, sturdily shod and armed with baskets and walking sticks, would leave home early and head for the estate on the edge of the moors. Sometimes my grandmother came too, or a friend of my mother's, and then we would take a picnic and spend the day there, lying in a grassy meadow and drinking the clear water from the stream that ran alongside its bottom edge. Occasionally for a change we went to the moors behind North Lees and there drank the waters from the Leveret Croft, said to be especially clear and contain a cure for chicken pox I think. North Lees was a different place with boisterous cousins and half cousins farming the rough moorland pastures and living in an old Hall only half restored, with its huge log-burning fireplace and hints of a link to Charlotte Brontë and Thornfield Hall.

That Charlotte visited Hathersage regularly was an established fact, for her friend Ellen Nussey lived in yet another Hall across the valley, behind the church where her brother was the parson. Later, at university, I was to research all this and, book in hand, follow the path from the old Moscar Cross down to the village. For this, it seemed clear, was where Jane Eyre descended from the coach after running away from Rochester. She made her way across the moors and into the village of 'Morton' where she collapsed in the cake shop. Every twist and turn is described in the novel, even the 'cross', (in reality a square stone pillar with a cross etched onto each surface,) is still standing at the meeting point of the old coach roads and when I went to find it many years ago it had only recently been put back after being buried during the war. In the village the 'cake' shop is still there too. It was a butcher's shop when I was a child and owned by family friends, and I knew it well. And Eyre is a village name; there is one buried in a tomb in the local Parish Church, for the family had gained its name and lands after the Battle of Hastings when, so it is said, the first knight prised open King Harold's visor after it had jammed in the fighting, thus giving him 'air' and enabling him to fight on until he fell, pierced through the eye with an arrow. Most of these facts are generally accepted today.

I also believed for many years that the old family residence of North Lees was the one on which Charlotte based Thornfield, for I even remember being shown the room she made the padded prison where Rochester's unfortunate wife spent most of her days, but this I now think is probably false. Still the most conclusive piece of evidence that Charlotte did use our village as a background for one of the great British classics is the reference to a needle factory. At the time Charlotte was writing, this was an industry found in Southern England, – with the single exception of the needle factory that was working in Hathersage at the time of Charlotte's visits, the shell of which was still standing when I lived there.

All fascinating stuff, but for me these interests were far away as, stopping only to take off my shoes and socks, Scampy and I raced across the moors where the granite rocks formed stark silhouettes against the blue sky, the rich green bracken of the summer months lapping at their feet. I loved the moors too, and it was here that I saw my first ghost.

In one of the really hot days of summer we had gone up there early, Scampy and I, armed with sandwiches and lemonade for me and water for him. As we lay in the warm heather, half asleep, both of us squinting into the sun, I turned my head and saw a figure walking towards the rocks about a hundred metres away. I thought it was a hiker at first but something about the shape was wrong. I moved my head and twisted over on to my stomach and saw her more clearly. A bonneted lady, dressed all in grey, a short cape across her shoulders. I watched as she walked slowly away from me, reached the rocks and vanished. I went back many times after that but I never saw her again; though there were others by the old paper mill and in various old Derbyshire houses.

So now, although the riverbank was important to me and an essential part of my summer, I think, no I'm sure, that as I grew older I was happiest on the moors. We ran free, my dog and I, a dog with no lead and a wild child without shoes, my hair blowing in the inevitable wind, sometimes singing 'Oh What a Beautiful Morning' at the top of my voice for the sheer pleasure of it. And we knew every inch of them, where the bogs and marshes were, where to find the first bluebells, primroses and violets. Often we spent the whole day up there, some unseen cord pulling us both along the cart track which led past friendly farmhouses until the rich grazing turned into bracken and the first sprigs of heather pushed their way between the granite rocks. Then our steps grew light and there was an eagerness to arrive there and, once there, a sense of belonging, of everything being all right and the world a good place to be. It has never left me this need for the moors and I was to return time and time again when my world fell to bits, sometimes driving through the night in order to see the sunrise, returning down the motorway in time to start work. It was my only constant, the one place I needed to be, the one thing that never turned away or let me down. Now I have left it behind for I have moved to a new country and found something else, but there will always be the memory of it and perhaps I will never quite be able to let go of it completely. Perhaps, I don't want to. I rarely look back, but sometimes my memory takes me there and I can still feel the wind in my hair and that sense of belonging.

We knew these moors in every season but they were most beautiful in autumn. Then the light had a transparency rarely found anywhere else, the purple of the heather, the rich gold of the dying bracken after the first frosts and the dark of the rocks made for a natural beauty I took for granted then, and only began to appreciate and understand much later when I had almost left it behind for ever. But I do remember one morning while I was still at school. I was working in the holidays as some sort of maid in one of the local hotels and that morning I had got up at dawn to start the breakfasts. It was bitterly cold, a heavy frost lying across the moors and keeping an icy chill in the little scullery where I was working, but I looked up out of the tiny window just as the sun touched the horizon and flooded the moors with the warm light of dawn. The sight took my breath away.

Autumn was the most beautiful season for me throughout my childhood, and not just on the moors, for as you dropped down into the valley the colours grew, if anything, deeper and richer. Once the harvest was in and we had all been to church or chapel to celebrate it, the fields were re-ploughed and the brown earth stood in deep furrows. They were shadowed by the deciduous trees whose leaves now slowly turned from green, to yellow, to orange and burnt sienna, until they were finally shed to herald the start of winter. They made a rich carpet before the wind blew them into piles and, a few years later, provided a constant source of delight and terror for my prima donna horse, Benny, who took great pleasure in trampling through them, convincing himself that some terrible animal lurked in their midst. It was at this point that he usually went up on his hind legs and I made an undignified descent to the ground. He was trained to stop and wait when his rider came off and so he stood there staring in amazement at my stupidity. He snorted in derision and fluttered his highly feminine eyelashes, as much as to say: 'Why are you down there? Come on, get back up.' And, usually unhurt, I would clamber back on and we would set off again until the next time. Scampy never accompanied us on these trips, for by this time he was approaching his middle years and Benny and I ranged far, a slightly uneasy friendship this one, neither of us too sure of the other.

But autumn never lasted long in Derbyshire and usually well before Christmas the icy winds blew across our valley and brought the first snows. It was the silence that told you it was a white world beyond the heavy curtains. There was something in the weight of the air too, even inside the house. On these mornings I would creep out of bed, cold little feet not bothering to find slippers, and peer through the windows. Across the front lawn there would usually be the tracks of the early morning birds and often a convenient robin would be perched photogenically on a branch, a Christmas-card scene. If the snowfall had been a heavy one, perhaps the snowplough would be passing along Station Road. No high-tech mechanism this, just two long planks of wood shaped like a V and pulled by a local tractor driven by Mr Dalton who ran the farm where I was soon to stable my horse, but it was an efficient way to clear the snow nevertheless. On these mornings it was important to get dressed quickly and race downstairs to feed the birds, whilst an ecstatic Cairn terrier charged through his new all white world returning to the house only when he was covered in melting snowballs, his moustache caked with ice; and later there was Benny to feed too.

The acquisition of my horse had not been easy to achieve and had involved a certain amount of strategy on my part. We were a very 'horsey' community but my first real experience of riding one was when I became friends at school with a girl who owned a rather fiery pony called Jester. We used to meet on the moors and I would gallop him over the heather in great delight. One day he stumbled and threw me. As I landed I hit my head on an inconvenient rock and staggered to my feet feeling dazed and dizzy. This feeling stayed with me for several days and I really didn't feel well. I was probably concussed but didn't dare say anything at home. It certainly didn't put me off riding. I longed for a horse of my own, but my parents showed no sign of weakening on this one. My mother wanted me to have piano lessons but I didn't like the instrument much and I refused. Then I hit on the idea of agreeing to the piano lessons if I could have a horse. The result was an impasse, so I went on hunger strike. It caused me no great problems for it was term time and I simply stocked up on school dinners and refused anything at home. This fact didn't seem to dawn on my poor parents and I could see that they were getting worried. Eventually my grandmother capitulated and agreed to buy me one and Rouchan Ben joined the family.

One Sunday morning I collected him from a meeting point high on the moors and rode back in triumph. He was beautiful, but very strong willed and rather temperamental – we were a well-matched pair. So, after Benny's arrival, I had to go to the farm every day. He was quite a highly bred horse with some Arab blood coursing through his veins, and so he spent the worst part of the winter in a loose box, going out into a small paddock if the weather was not too bad. This meant that every morning of the really bad weather I had to get up with my father around 5.30 a.m. and muck him out and feed him before going to school. Being the prima donna he was he would not eat hay and so had to be fed exclusively on a mixture of bran, apples and carrots. He cost us a fortune and was always getting us into trouble with the RSPCA. Local do-gooders saw him in his paddock hay-less and reported us as starving him. The fact that he was as round as a barrel most winters, with a long, shiny coat, obviously escaped their notice and in the end the RSPCA inspectors begged us to leave a hay net full of hay in full view for the whole winter. It quickly became inedible but seemed to do the trick and the complaints stopped; only to be replaced with those of the local churchgoers. These started arriving at our door because Benny's not so secret passion in life was Polo mints. Somehow he knew that many of the elderly parishioners used to have a supply in their pockets to help them through the often lengthy Sunday sermon, so he took to meeting them at the small gate to his field and following them up the hill to the church, nudging them gently until he got what he wanted. For him it was a game, but to them he was a big, powerful animal and he obviously terrified them. So, on Sundays he had to be contained within the small field where he stood, head hanging over the five-bar gate, looking longingly for the unobtainable peppermints. Then my grandmother took pity on him and all was well.

He was also an escape merchant. He had been bred by the Masserella family to be a show jumper, but he had not made the necessary height and so had been sold on as a riding horse. His genes had given him a talent for jumping though his experiences somewhere along the line had given him a hatred of show rings. So, while he could jump out of almost any field you put him into, he would refuse the first jump in any show ring and on the rare occasions I took him into the local gymkhanas I almost invariably ended up on the ground in front of several hundred people. Unsurprisingly I soon stopped that game but had to resign myself to being woken in the middle of the night to go and retrieve him from some alien location, often the chapel grounds, where I would find him, lost and frightened, waiting to be rescued. But these escapades were dangerous for him so we replaced the gate with a higher one and watched in amazement as he took the bolt between his teeth and slid it open. Finally we chained the bolt and that seemed to work.

Meanwhile, my friend Joyce was having problems with her pony Tommy escaping from his field, too, and taking his Shetland pony friend with him. So one summer night we settled ourselves into a cosy bush with a couple of sleeping bags and waited. That night and for three nights more nothing happened and we were about to give up – and then we saw them. This field was fenced with barbed wire, so it was with considerable attention to detail that the larger pony took the bottom strand in his mouth and lifted it high, enabling the Shetland pony to roll under it to freedom. Tommy then jumped over the wire and they trotted off together.

But to return to the winter, we went sledging, of course, and sometimes we skied down the packed snow of the main road. Trekking up to the Surprise Gap, we had a long run down to the village centre but this could really only be done with safety when the Surprise Gap itself was packed with snow and the road closed to traffic. So on other days we took to the local hillsides, hopelessly inept and heading into a convenient tree when we needed to stop. Our skis were old and our boots borrowed and usually the wrong size but it made a change from tobogganing and it was fun.

My father made me a sledge – one of his rare ventures into woodwork – and together we used to polish the runners at the first sign of snow, dragging the dusty steed from its summer refuge in the coalhouse. One of the fields behind the village school was the main meeting ground for all the village children. It covered a large area and had in it several runs varying from gentle to steep – one of which was out of bounds as it ended in a ditch at the bottom of the field, this ditch being fenced off with the ever popular barbed wire. Of course it was this run that quickly became a magnet for our local tearaways and you were regarded as 'chicken' until you had negotiated it. I was banned totally from going near this particular part of the field, but somehow or other I had to escape parental supervision and sledge it at least once. At last my opportunity came and I threw myself on my sledge and pushed off from the top, flying faster and faster down the slope. It was an exhilarating feeling – at least it was until I saw the barbed wire racing towards me. Something made me throw myself back on the sledge just in time and I sailed under it, dropping heavily into the ditch. I pulled myself out, thanking whatever instinct had thrown me backwards, for if it had not I would have ripped open my face.

Then one day, I would wake up to find a watery sun dancing hesitantly outside the bedroom curtains. In the garden, the Christmas roses drooped, withering on their stems, and the first snowdrops and crocuses pushed their little heads through the still hard earth. Spring was on the doorstep. In Greece the word for 'spring' is virtually the same as that for 'opening' and I suppose that that is exactly what it is, although we never thought of it like that in Derbyshire. There everything revolved round the farming calendar and spring was the time of planting. But it also meant that Scampy and I could start our extended wanderings again, and we had different haunts for this time of the year.

Primroses were our first source of treasure, then the violets and later still the bluebells. We knew of a bluebell wood where the flowers grew thick like a carpet nestling close round the silver birch trees and the occasional knarled oak. On the warmer days we used to lie dreaming amongst them, the sun streaking through the branches of the trees, the little white clouds scudding by, the perfume turning your head with its intensity. Sometimes I walked home my arms full of these luscious flowers that seemed to come from a child's book of fairy tales. Later I had them in my garden in London and friends now have them in the South of France. Without realising why, I bought a rug in Poros, that same deep blue colour, and when I put it down in winter here the whole room looks fresh and alive, though until recently I had never made the connection. Spring brought energy with it too, not just from the first sprigs of the new crops, but all the leaf buds and the busting lilac flowers and the daffodils. It also brought with it my mother's mad passion for spring cleaning. Everything had to come out, be turned around and put back. Curtains must be changed for the lighter summer ones. Loose covers too and cushion covers and countless other things I no longer remember. My services were required and so for two or three weeks my wanderings were curtailed and I became the dutiful daughter. Restless I was, and resentful, but nevertheless I helped to do these mundane chores which seemed so important to her and so insignificant to me. And they still do to this day, though I can occasionally force myself to go through the motions, usually out of concern for what people will think.

And then suddenly we were free again, my dog and I. Free to watch the frisking lambs and to stroke the wobbly-legged calves and grunting piglets. By then ducklings and goslings waddled round the farmyard pond and the occasional foal gazed, soft eyed with wonder. The house filled itself with bowls of primroses and heavy lilac heads stood in vases on the mantelpiece or waited transportation to graveyard or church.

When I was very young we lived in a house called The Gables. It was a large three storey, stone built house with an enormous, always cold bathroom we hardly ever used, even though it had its own fireplace. There was a front room too, again hardly ever used, but always opened with some ceremony on Christmas Day, although I don't think anyone ever felt very comfortable in there. We lived mainly in a sort of extended kitchen with another fireplace that needed black-leading regularly and had a side-oven that baked the most delicious bread and I remember being bathed in front of it, a fire blazing in the grate. My earliest memory is of this room and of climbing out of my high chair while my mother talked to someone at the back door. I remember the chair rocked alarmingly as I climbed down and almost toppled over and my mother was horrified when she returned and found me wandering around delighted with my achievement. I've got a feeling that was the end of the high chair. And there was a time not long afterwards when my mother was at the back door again and returned to find I had emptied the coal bucket on to the carpet, covering myself in coal dust in the process. Then, too, I distinctly remember sitting in my pushchair boxed in by the waterproof, and having my view of the world restricted to about six inches by fifteen. I hated this sense of being contained and I have hated it all my life.

In my early years I was rated a 'delicate' child, for, having got me safely back to Derbyshire, my parents had to nurse me through a bout of double bronchial pneumonia. There were to be two more of these and in the middle one I nearly died. I must have been quite young because I was still in my cot. It was night when Dr Jago came, smelling of whisky, and warned my mother that I was very ill and might not make it through till morning. I swear I remember thinking, 'Oh yes I will!' And of course I did, though I was to go on to have just about every childhood ailment there was. Chickenpox was the worst, for my hands were bound in cotton gloves, and to this day I can't bear to have my hands restrained in any way, and I rarely wear gloves. But on the whole these were only interludes in an exciting childhood, though one that was nearly always spent alone. I have a dramatic image of myself around this time, one still vivid today. I was in our front garden wearing some old things I had found in the attic; clad in a long white dress with a Union Jack around my shoulders and a paper crown on my head, I stood on an old wooden box in a high wind which was causing the dress and my hair to stream behind me. I felt like a queen and it was a good feeling. I stood tall, not moving until my mother found me and asked what on earth I was doing. But I had no answer then.

It was also around this time I made friends with Mr Birkenshaw, a grandfatherly figure who worked as a caretaker at the local swimming pool. Before I was considered old enough to go wandering with Scampy I spent many happy hours helping him to paint the empty pool ready for the summer. I had a very small paintbrush of my own and worked long and hard to cover a tiny patch of wall. He was also in charge of our village hall that stood next door to The Gables. On summer evenings I used to slip out of the garden and sit on the steps that led up to the main doors. The reason for this was that strange voices and sometimes music could be heard coming from inside and I was curious. One evening Mr Birkenshaw opened the door and beckoned me inside. It was very dark but at the far end by the stage I saw moving pictures and a blonde, curly-haired child playing with bricks. I stood open mouthed for long minutes until my mother appeared and dragged me outside. But the memory stayed and my world widened that day. I had discovered cinema and Shirley Temple and I wanted both.

I loved animals and was fascinated by the wild life in the gardens and the neighbouring fields. I used to collect the dead moles, all of them Mouldy Warps, and bury them by the front steps, each grave having its own little wooden cross, until that part of the garden resembled one of the great World War I cemeteries. Snails, too, intrigued; at one point I collected a hundred of them in a cardboard box and smuggled them into one of the attics. Of course they escaped and set off down the staircase walls in search of freedom. My mother, the DIY expert in the house had just re-wallpapered those same walls and was less than pleased to find the army and its shiny trails adding further decoration to the new wallpaper. I was in serious disgrace for that one, though I swear I heard laughter behind closed doors when, officially in bed, I crept back downstairs to try to hear what was being said by the grown-ups.

Then I made friends with Mr Pearce. He and his wife ran a clothes and household-goods shop on Station Road. Twice a week he went off in his car to visit some of the more isolated villages in the area, taking a selection of his stock with him. One day he asked if I would like to go with him. Parental permission was sought and given and we left one morning on what was to be the first of many trips. They were fun, those days away from the village, sitting in the car and watching the world go by, and being spoilt rotten by many of his customers. I developed an insatiable curiosity for what lay around the next corner, something that was never to leave me. And I loved too the stories he used to tell about his experiences during the war when he made several trips to Russia in the naval convoys. I became fascinated by the thought of Russia, at that time a country closed to visitors, and I became determined to go there one day.

Of the war and its aftermath I remember little. My father joined up within weeks of war being declared and had been sent to a training unit in south east London; but when his uncle died he was quickly sent back to the village as he was needed to take over the running of the post office there. He was around throughout my childhood, something I never questioned. Only afterwards did I come to understand how recent that war had been, and that I had lived through it without understanding that it was happening. I don't remember being hungry or going without anything. True we grew a lot of our own vegetables and there was often a bag of apples or plums my father brought back from the post office but we had meat too and perhaps the fact that my father had a sweet shop was not unconnected with this. After the war was over I was certainly familiar with the two words 'black market', the whole village was and it was mentioned quite openly. Once there was a gift from America of a summer dress, one that was very pretty and soon became a favourite of mine. We christened it my 'gum chum' dress and I wore it only on special occasions; and I remember a street party and the whole village decked out with flags and streamers; and ration books, but that was all. Hathersage was only eight miles from Sheffield but the village saw little of the terrible bombing that reduced areas of the town to rubble and killed many people. I was still very young and war was a word whose meaning I could not comprehend.

I thought the world a wonderful place to be then but I was often in trouble of one kind or the other, a natural inquisitiveness meant I pushed the boundaries perhaps further than I should have done and these adventures often ended in disaster. In vain did the grown-ups exhort me to 'stop and think' but I was very strong willed and something of a natural born rebel and it simply wasn't and never has been a big part of my make-up. Or perhaps there was another reason. I was born left handed but from the very beginning this was discouraged and I was made to use my right one – something that caused complications that were to dog me all my life. As I got older I certainly did begin to think things through but whereas most people's logic went from twelve o'clock to six o'clock via three o'clock I invariably went from twelve to six via nine. Although I usually got there in the end there were many delightful diversions on the way and it was these diversions that often produced consternation and misunderstanding from parents and teachers alike. Much later my 'upside down' logic manifested itself most aggressively when I embraced technology and the internet and to a certain extent shows up in the pages of this book.

Chapter Two

Somewhere in the middle of these memories I went to school. The aforementioned Private school was situated in what used to be the local manor house, yet another of these romantic Halls mentioned before. But this one was even more exciting for it was known to have a secret passage leading to the local church, built during the days of religious persecution for the priests to escape through in the event of a raid. Its main entrance was also known to be down in the cellar, but it had been bricked up for years and very much out of bounds, though visiting dignitaries were taken to view it from time to time. The long school lunch break often found me wandering around, alone and somewhat bored, and one day, with my sharp eye for detail, I noticed that a certain paving stone in the somewhat decaying conservatory was higher than the others and somehow rather odd. A tool was improvised, a piece of pipe probably, and after a few days of careful prising the flagstone came up, revealing a flight of stone steps descending into the darkness. I was just easing myself through the gap when the headmistress hove into view and that was the end of that. Several weeks later, when I was lurking in the shrubbery up by the boundary wall, I stumbled upon another entrance but was discovered almost before I got started on excavating that one. The third time I was foiled in an attempt to gain access to the passage down a drain. After that enthusiasm waned and I concentrated on spreading rumours that the headmistress had murdered a recently departed games mistress. The evidence for this was some dug-up bones, probably those of a rabbit or pet cat but resembling finger bones, to my eyes at least. One of my rare moments of popularity this and I thrived on it. I was also briefly popular when I organised my first concert. The costumes were one of the highlights for a simple request had brought forth from several mothers ball gowns and furs of a type previously unseen by us except in picture books. It was my first taste of theatre but the magic was to stay with me and in the long summer holidays I organised other concerts, using a convenient wall in a neighbouring yard as a stage. My unfortunate playmates were cast mainly in the role of audience but they were allowed one turn each, Norma Cottrell being, to my eyes, nauseatingly cute in whatever she chose to perform.

I was nearly expelled twice once from this second school –

after I threw a metal chair in a fit of red-haired rage and nearly hit the headmistress – and once from the previous, as yet unmentioned, private school which comes first in the education section of my CV. As I said, I was a delicate child (or so they thought, for I was to prove them all wrong later), so I'm sure the first school I was sent to was chosen for its proximity to the house. It was literally next door and every break-time, whenever I tried to do anything remotely interesting, my mother's voice could be heard admonishing me to 'get down from that tree' or 'button up your coat', all stuff I found acutely embarrassing, especially when at its height during the winter. But the expulsion incident actually took place during the summer holidays.

I seemed to do rather better for friends at this school, in fact the school photos of the time show me well in the centre of things, though I don't remember too much of what went on there. I do remember the offending tree and trying to climb it, and I remember stitching coloured laces, mainly lilac and a rather sickly green, into pieces of grey card with holes in them. Was there no formal teaching? There must have been but I could read and write a little before I started school so these classes probably had little impact. Miss Fawle and Miss Marriage ran the school, they were two lesbians I suspect, formidable ladies with close-cropped hair and severely tailored tweed suits and they terrified me. There must have been other teachers at that school – indeed the photos show a whole line of them, but today none of them looks familiar. Of the pupils, a few ring bells but only Molly, she of the fairy-tale cottage on Baulk Lane and remembered for *Milly Molly Mandy*, stands really clear in my memory, and Sheila of course. And it was Sheila who was to be involved in my downfall.

We had become friends during term-time, but her parents were in the army and she ended up spending one of the long summer holidays at the school. Living next door to each other it was inevitable that we spent a lot of time together. She was considered a nice child and good company for me; in fact, she was rather timid, and she was somewhat in awe of me and admired me greatly. Heady stuff. We ran pretty free and were having a great time; fields came right up to the school and our house in those days, the present housing estate then a mere bubble in the mind of some council architect. The only forbidden place was the railway line that ran at the southern end of the farthest field. Being banned, of course it presented an almost irresistible attraction. These were still the days of steam trains and they brought with them more than a hint of excitement. We had no car and rarely left the village so the other villages farther up and down the valley held for us the mystery that places like Bali or Peru hold for children today and the drivers were a friendly bunch and happy to wave to small children with an equally small dog attached to the end of a red lead. Though the railway line and embankment had been separated from the field by a sturdy fence, this presented no deterrent. What did, was the fear of the quite awful telling off which would result from any disobedience in this matter. It was also trespassing, of course, but this was a long word with little meaning for one headstrong child and her cohort.

We were after moon pennies on that particular day. There were plenty in the field but those on the railway bank looked bigger and fresher. I can't remember now whether Scampy was with us or not, though I suspect not, for if he had been he would have been tied to the fence and barking, and I have no memory of that. Anyhow over the fence we went, scrambling up the bank to where the daisies bobbed in the light breeze and warm sunshine. We were bare-legged and bare-armed so when Sheila slipped and started sliding down the bank she was sure of scraping her arms and legs. What happened was immeasurably worse. There were really no vandals in the village in those days but I suspect some of the local boys had been throwing stones at glass bottles for a section of the bank was littered with broken glass, and that just happened to be the area down which she slid. She cut herself to ribbons, the blood running down into her clothes. Looking back now I think she was lucky not to cut a vein or artery, but it looked terrible and I was horrified. I left her screaming and ran back across the field to get my mother.

Sheila survived, though she was left with a lot of fine hairline scars. Meanwhile, I don't think I have ever been in such trouble before or since. I seem to remember being restricted to the house and garden for months, though it was probably only days. Pocket money was stopped and, once Sheila was returned, bandaged, to the bosom of the school, I was forbidden to speak to her. It passed eventually – of course it did – and by the time the autumn term started the memory was beginning to fade, though it has never ever completely left me. I can't say, however, that it ever really stopped me from breaking the rules again, often with similar, disastrous results.

The building that first school was in was grim and forbidding, with gardens filled with hydrangeas, and enclosed in ivy covered walls. Gloomy, even in summer, the inside was the same, high ceilings and dark paint and rooms where the sun somehow never managed to penetrate, I think it prided itself on being somewhat progressive, but to me it was a remnant of the Victorian age and when it went bankrupt and I was moved to that new school in the old Hall there seemed to be an enormous lightening of everything, though I don't think I was ever really happy there either.

It was around this time that I discovered I was adopted. I don't remember what I was doing exactly but I was in a group of about eight other children. Whatever it was we were doing, we were doing it quite happily together, so the shock, when it came, was all the more painful. Suddenly one of them, I don't remember who, said: You're not like us, you're different.'

'No I'm not,' I replied, already on the defensive for I sensed somehow they were right. 'Yes, you are,' I heard them say. 'You're adopted, you don't have a real mother and father.'

This came as a bolt from the blue. To be different was bad enough, for no child wants that, but to have to live with something as momentous as not having a real mother and father was a prospect that put my whole world in question. I rallied as best I could and shouted that I would ask my mother and prove them wrong; but they had lost interest by then and walked away, leaving me alone. But my world had shattered, for somehow I believed them, though it was to be several days before I could summon up enough courage to ask.

Once again I could take you to the exact place where my mother and I were walking; strangely enough, just past the school gates. I stopped and my mother stopped too. From somewhere came this odd little voice: 'Mummy,' it said, 'who's adopted in this village?'

There was quite a long pause before she named two others and then, finally said, 'And you are.' She started to say something else but I stopped her short.

'I don't want to talk about it,' I said, 'not ever.'

And we never did. She should have broken me down, of course, but she didn't. Something changed for ever at that point and for a long time after I could not bear to think about it. It was the start of a divorce from the reality of the whole situation and for many years after I was unsure as to whether or not we'd had that conversation. What I did decide was that if the world saw me as different, then different I was going to be. And so I was. But my belief in my parents had received a shattering blow too.

Why had they not told me before I went to school? We lived in a small village where everyone knew everyone else's business and they could not possibly have thought to keep it a secret forever. Now I think they meant to tell me but just left it too late, for I remember that for several years I had two birthdays, one must have been on the date they first adopted me and the other was on the date of my birth. I never questioned this then for it meant an extra present but now I recollect that this stopped happening after that conversation outside the school gates. From that day on and without realising what I was doing I began to build a protective wall around myself and, although there were still to be many happy times I never completely trusted them again.

The rest of my junior school days remain something of a blur, but in due course I passed the eleven plus, much to the relief of all concerned, for a considerable financial burden was thus lifted, and I gained a place at grammar school. Before I took the exam my parents promised me a bicycle if I passed but they reneged on their promise and, though I waited every day in anticipation, it never appeared and I never quite forgave them for that either.

My mother's inherent snobbery reasserted itself at this point and, with the help of the headmistress, she obtained a place for me at Lady Manners Grammar School in Bakewell. An excellent choice academically, no doubt, but everyone else from the village went up the valley to New Mills while I travelled alone to Grindleford, one train stop away in the opposite direction and then onwards by school bus. So, every morning the other village children and I faced each other across the railway line, they in their green uniforms, I in my navy-blue and white. Though there is no question that I was to benefit from this decision for the rest of my life, the immediate effect was to isolate me even further. Still, grammar school was new and exciting and I loved it, though I don't think it ever totally loved me, for it wasn't long before we seemed to get off on the wrong foot. I really did see it as a new start for no one knew me there but events soon conspired against me.

The journey was quite difficult and involved a train ride, a ten-minute walk and then a half-hour bus ride. For the first part I was on my own and only as the bus started travelling through the grey-stone villages did other similarly clad boys and girls emerge from the shadows of the roadside and clamber aboard. Peter Crossland was the first. Funny how I remember that name for he was much older than I and already close to leaving school.

He was a farmer's son, impatient to work full time on the land he loved so much, and he had no interest in academic life. We spoke rarely and he had little impact on my days, but his name comes easily to mind while others of those who were to be closer to me do not.

We had paid a visit to Grindleford a few weeks earlier, my mother and I. The purpose of this visit was to introduce me to a friend with whom to break the ice of this new experience I suppose. My parents had come up with a girl who seemed to them to be a potentially eminently suitable companion. She shall remain nameless – for I'm afraid I cannot think of her with a great deal of affection. She always came nearly top of her class and could best be described as serious and conscientious, both good qualities, but for me her blood ran thin and we soon ceased to sit next to one another on the school bus. Anyhow, by then Carol had appeared on the scene and within weeks we had become inseparable. In those days biros were not allowed in school and all lessons and homework had to be written with a fountain pen. Although mine had been bought with great ceremony and was something of a milestone in my life, inevitably it leaked, they all did, especially on to your index finger, and the stains were difficult to remove. Both Carol and I had a notoriously slapdash approach to most things and we were careless of such matters. We became known as the inky twins, and Miss Smith, our form mistress quickly despaired of us, though there always seemed to be a hint of laughter in her eyes when she told us off.

So the days sped by and for a while it really did seem as though this was a new beginning and I loved it all. The new environment, the wider range of academic subjects, the new friendships, tennis, (I was good at that); in fact the general stimulus I felt of being challenged on almost every level. It was an excellent school with a new, progressive headmaster. It was mixed, of course, all Derbyshire grammar schools were and they were all the better for that. Later, I was to realise how right my mother had been and how lucky I was to have a place there. The only disadvantage was the journey. For that first year, unless I went back on the specially chartered school bus at four o'clock, I couldn't get back at all and this meant I was excluded from the after-school activities and so from a large part of the school life itself. But I had learnt that exclusion seemed to be an inevitable part of my existence and so I soldiered on totally unprepared for disaster when it struck.

The school was divided into houses, three or four, I can't remember now. Barker was green I think, Glossop was red, and Taylor, my house, dark blue. There may have been a yellow one but I'm not sure. Anyhow, that first autumn term, produced news of an arts and crafts festival, the main feature of which was to be the inter-house competitions; the aim was to earn points to ensure that your house came out top. When I saw the range of categories available to first years I was delighted for, as I think I have already said, my mother was brilliant at making things and had taught me well over the years. So I carefully sorted out the skills that suited me best and set out a plan of campaign. For several years my mother had made and iced wedding cakes, christening cakes and birthday cakes, and I had helped her. So I was delighted to find just such a category there and set about baking a cake and eventually icing it. I was proud of my achievement and was not surprised when I won first prize, but I was disconcerted when almost immediately afterwards I was called to the headmistress's study. My cake sat on her desk and I was accused of cheating. The cake was judged to be too professionally iced to be the work of an eleven-year-old girl and I was informed that my mother had done everything, I nothing.

I went home and told my mother but she was reluctant to interfere. Eventually the headmaster intervened and I proved my innocence by baking and icing another cake under the close scrutiny of Miss Smith. My prize was re-awarded and an announcement made in the hall at morning assembly, but the pleasure and sense of achievement had been blighted and was never to return. Despite the public apology people seemed only to remember I had been accused of cheating and somehow or other I had been put out of the mainstream of life at the school, so from then on I stopped involving myself in very much and became the original 'rebel without a cause'. I fought the system on every level, making life very difficult for myself in the process. I simply could not let myself conform. If school berets were to be worn, I took mine off. When knee socks were ordered to be just that and reach up to the knee, mine barely climbed above my ankles, homework was often not completed and I ran around the corridors usually late for class. And so my name was often on the detention list, to be read out in hall and bring shame on my house.

The detention punishment lacked any sort of imagination and consisted mainly of hundreds of lines which one wrote, zombie like, while dreaming of other things. Because I could not be kept behind in detention, I was allowed to take the task home but this presented something of a problem for me as my parents were firmly on the side of the teachers, and so I used to go to enormous lengths to keep my misdemeanours secret. We still lived at The Gables at this time and for some reason I have never been able to fathom I slept in the 'best' bedroom. This room had all of my mother's prize furniture in it, plus the cut glass ornaments and the most expensive carpet. It was no bedroom for a child, and with two empty attic rooms smaller and cosier, only a flight of stairs away, it seems odd that I should have to sleep in a large double bed with only Gracie for company. But this room did have large windows with a windowsill almost wide enough to call a window seat, and, so, once my parents had gone to sleep, I crept behind the curtains and, by the light of the street lamp I would labour away until the lines were finished. Then I would clamber back into bed and grab what was left of the night for my sleep.

I hated that bedroom when I was young, for the street lights threw weird shadows and when it was windy there were creaks from both outside and inside the house and I used to lie afraid in the centre of the bed and long for morning. There is one night scene that has stayed clearly in my mind, though I was not alone for this one. There had been some sort of terrible row and I can clearly see both my parents standing by the bed. Now I only remember the end of the conversation and what had brought us to that point remains a mystery, but I heard myself say, 'It isn't that I hate you, it's just that I don't love you.' And my mother said to my father, 'No, don't hit her.' Whatever that was all about I really don't know now, but I think I must have nearly broken my mother's heart. There was fear there too, and it stayed with me for years. But this was an isolated incident for there was no violence or abuse in our family. I only remember being slapped once and I must have sorely tried mother's patience over the years. Still that evening left its mark, for today I still hate people shouting and, though never averse to a good argument of the intellectual kind, I always avoid a confrontation wherever possible.

There was nothing of mine in that room, even my clothes were kept somewhere else and of course I was forbidden to play in there. In fact I was forbidden to play almost everywhere in the house. Once, as a small child, I found Scampy's tennis ball and was bouncing it in our extended kitchen. My mother was in the garden hanging out some washing, and I suppose I had got bored. Of course it bounced out of control and knocked off the framed photo of my recently dead grandfather, shattering the glass. I was petrified, and put myself to bed for I was sure that was to be my fate. When my mother returned and found me I think she was shamed into rescuing me and I escaped further punishment that time. The lesson from all this was to prove useful and from then on I almost always owned up to my crimes, often taking the blame for other people who were less honest or perhaps just less brave. It has made life very difficult sometimes but I can't say that I have ever regretted it, though I must confess that I am extremely intolerant of people who don't do the same.

Lady Manners Grammar School was situated high on a hill outside Bakewell. When I was there I heard a rumour that the building had been originally destined for the South of France, but its delivery had been altered by the outbreak of World War II. Trapped in Britain by the hostilities, someone, in their infinite wisdom, had decided that the ideal place for it would be on this windy, cold, and often snow-clad hilltop. Whatever the validity of this rumour, it was certainly an odd building for that location.

It was made up almost completely of glass with French windows facing onto an open corridor. We had to wear special 'house' shoes once we had arrived at school but in winter we were often authorised to wear our outdoor shoes when ploughing through the drifting snow or crossing rain drenched tiles. At the height of the winter we also used to don coats and scarves to change classrooms and huddle in the cloakrooms against the warm water-pipes if we thought we could get away with being a few minutes late for the next class.

On the rare hot summer days, however, it was delightful there, for we were in the heart of the country and the various breaks and games lessons found us playing hard at tennis or basking in the sunshine, girls illicitly holding hands with their various boyfriends.

It was a highly democratic school under the guiding hand of our new headmaster. We all went cross-country running (I hated that) and occasionally the girls played rugby against the boys (badly) and the boys played hockey against the girls (viciously, leaving us with large bruises). Inside the classrooms we were all treated equally and told that, career-wise, the world was our oyster and we should get on and do what we wanted to do and blame no one but ourselves if we didn't make it. For one term the girls did woodwork and the boys cooking, though my teapot stand was hardly more successful than the boys' shepherd's pie. The heyday of that grammar school provided a rare atmosphere indeed and I was lucky to participate in it.

I mixed my subjects at school for it was science orientated and I was definitely arts. I came effortlessly top in English and though I was no good at art itself, I got on well with its relatively freethinking teacher Mr Woolley who used to play jazz records during our classes. But Mr Taylor, the English teacher, was my main ally, followed by the biology master and the games mistress. Secondary games suited me much better than their primary counterparts. I was good at tennis and my inky twin and I soon made it into the junior team. I hated the gym, but made the school second team in hockey. I was proud of all this but couldn't quite let it rest there, so my tennis dresses (made by my mother to my specifications) were always more flamboyant than anyone else's and I used to arrive complete with games bag and matching accessories. To this day I am not sure if I was born a drama queen or simply turned myself into one, but from my earliest memories right up to the present day, I have a great love of being centre stage and a great need to hide in a corner peering shyly from behind a heavy curtain, total ego and no self-confidence – in many ways a lethal combination.

But life rumbled on through those first few years, good terms and bad terms, in and out of trouble. While our headmaster, who joined at the same time as I did, was progressive in his methods and rather well known in the field of botany – he had written a school textbook and used to go off and give lectures – our headmistress was a rather remote figure who stood severe and correct at Mr Dale's side at all official functions. In some ways we pupils were a mixed bunch but I was proud of my school and, despite the shaky start and all the rebellion, thrilled to be a part of something at last.

The academic standards were excellent on the whole, the teachers specially chosen and often successful in their own fields. But there were exceptions and I remember one unfortunate French teacher who simply could not control a lively bunch of teenagers. We hit on a way to make her life miserable, and every time she tried to teach us, one by one we would ask to go to the lavatory. Once there we would sit in our respective cloakrooms and giggle, leaving her to teach an empty classroom. This probably went on for a couple of weeks, until one day, just before the bell was due for the end of class, we returned, still giggling, to find the headmaster standing silent in front of the blackboard. When we had all slunk back into our seats, he spoke quietly for several minutes about good manners and sensitivity to other people's feelings and kindness, until we all felt about two inches high. But we noticed that the French teacher left at the end of term and was replaced by one with a stronger personality. We were never punished for that particular misdemeanour, there was no need, we had learnt our lesson and never did anything like it again.

Then scandal hit. Our much loved biology master eloped with the pregnant games mistress towards the end of the summer term. As students we were agog but though I'm sure the staff room rocked with gossip, little reached our ears and eventually things quietened down. By the time we returned in September the matter seemed closed and we had new teachers. Of the games mistress I remember little but our new biology master came from Bradford and was blessed with a strong northern accent. We quickly picked up that he was highly sensitive about this and used to imitate him behind his back. His favourite injunction was, 'Arrrh shurrup,' uttered loudly whenever he found us too boisterous. But he was an excellent teacher and we had a lot of respect for him. Then, one day I was sent to the biology lab during the lunch-break, and finding the stockroom door unusually open, I peered round to see if anyone was there. It was empty, but Nimrod, the school skeleton, was hanging from his hook and sir's cap and gown were there next to it. It was too good an opportunity to miss. I positioned Nimrod on his stand in the main classroom, dressed him in the cap and gown and stuck a notice coming out of his mouth that read, 'Arrrh, shurrup.' Then, chuckling happily to myself, I walked down the corridor to rejoin my classmates.

Biology was first period after lunch and of course we were all there early, sitting silent and still in anticipation of … what? Nimrod had gone – someone must have found him. I had considered myself something of a star, but not anymore. Funny, I can't remember his name now, but he was furious. Of course I owned up immediately and was sent to wait outside the headmaster's study. I sat, filled with apprehension, awaiting the arrival of my victim, but it was the headmaster who arrived first and wished to know exactly why I was there. He was suitably serious while I told him about my prank but I swear his mouth twitched several times. I was told to write a letter of apology, after which the matter would be considered closed. Later that day as I settled down to write my letter I found my heart was not in it. I did not feel I had committed such a terrible crime and it had really only been a joke – in bad taste maybe, but hardly a crime. So I wrote a careful letter apologising for the fact that I had obviously upset him but failing to apologise for the joke itself. The next day I placed this in his pigeonhole and went on my merry way. Only it wasn't his pigeonhole, I had mistakenly chosen the wrong pigeonhole and put the letter into that of Mr Shooter, the head of the science department – and Mr Shooter's daughter Lesley attended the school and was a friend of mine. She told me that the rest of the teachers had known nothing of the incident until her father opened the letter under the impression it was for him, and promptly informed the rest of the staff, who found it all very funny. In a strange way I had won.

At the start of my second year at Lady Manners the catchment area was widened to include more children from Hathersage, and others from farther up the valley. Then a new bus route was announced linking Bakewell directly with the Hope Valley and I was able to join in some of the after school-activities. I joined the Bee Club, a strange choice this as I am allergic to bee stings but it was run by our beloved headmaster and that, I think, was the main attraction. In the short time he had been at the school he had gained the respect of staff and pupils alike, both as a headmaster and as a person. I thought he was an incredible man and longed to impress him. Within the space of a few terms he brought the whole school into the twentieth century, rather to the annoyance of some of the older members of the staff. He encouraged us all to think for ourselves and welcomed energetic argument. He formed the lunchtime debating society where we all took turns to speak. If you were chosen to lead the debate he would give you the proposed motion and ask you whether you were for or against it. If for, he would make you argue against and vice versa, and to this day I dive head first into an argument or debate and relish every word, often leaving my opponent sprawled, helpless, in defeat. But there is nothing personal or vicious in my arguing and I expect my opponent to give back as good as he or she gets, and I also expect us to be friends again once the matter has been resolved. Only rarely do I lose my temper and that is another thing altogether. A true Scorpio, I find myself extremely straightforward, but apparently other people do not. I also see myself as pursuing a simple logic in whatever I do, though this is something that is rarely a perception shared by other people.

Our school journeys were often difficult in winter and if there was thick snow it was not unusual for the school bus to fail to get through. In that event we traipsed into Grindleford to get another bus back home. On one particular winter's day we had waited some time for the bus and I became convinced that it was unlikely to come. We had grown tired of snowballs and catching up on homework and so Fishy Haddock and I decided to take the matter into our own hands and walk back through the woods to Hathersage. The others were reluctant to join us, so Fishy and I set off together and soon found ourselves walking through the magical fairyland that was the Padley Woods. The next day I set out again and joined my fellow students only to discover that they had all reached school safely on the previous day, the bus arriving a few minutes after we had left. In assembly that morning Fishy and I also discovered we had been put on detention for lack of initiative. I was furious, not so much by news of the detention – I was used to that – but rather the reason given for it.

Next year we found ourselves in a similar situation, only this time the snow was slightly worse and word quickly came through that the bus would not come, I returned home, donned my jodhpurs and hard hat, saddled Benny and hacked the eight miles to Bakewell, leaving Benny at the hunt stables next-door to the school. My entrance caused quite a sensation but the school was furious, especially when I pointed out that I had done it as I had no intention of being put on detention for lack of initiative a second time. They fed me and sent me home early and I seem to remember trotting back into the village just as daylight faded. I had ridden to Bakewell several times and knew the local hunt people well enough to ask for stabling so for me it was really not a big deal. I thought I was showing a considerable amount of initiative but it seemed that I had got it wrong yet again.

There were some high spots however and Carol and I were chosen to sing in a school carol concert that was broadcast to America. This involved being in Bakewell church quite late at night and seemed very exciting. I sang a solo in one of the carols and had my first experience of stage fright. And one summer the touring Australian test cricket team stayed in the hotel in front of which we waited for the school bus. Desperate to meet them I wrote a poem about them and left it at the reception desk there but next morning they were gone. I was so disappointed, until, that is, the manager of the hotel came out carrying a sealed envelope with my name on it. Inside were two sets of autographs of the entire team. I gave one set to Fishy Haddock and took the other one proudly home. My father was stunned but delighted at my audacity and soon the whole village knew what I had done.

Alas though, eventually the teenage hormones began to bite and I became, if anything, more difficult. I gained a part in the school play, the lead, and I was thrilled, but I ruined any chances of repeating the success of that particular achievement by not learning my lines until the day before. Once on stage I was word perfect and a considerable hit; but the school rated responsibility, conscientiousness, and consideration highly and I had been swept away by all the attention and had not spared a thought for the needs of my fellow thespians.

It must have been a similar bid for attention which had me walking out of classes and going to sit under a hedge for a while, returning when I felt like it I suppose. Today I am not totally sure whether these latter events were fact or fiction, for no comment was ever made when I left the classroom or when I returned to it, but I am pretty sure they are real.

I also perfected the art of fainting to order and did this so many times in assembly that I was ordered to see a doctor. The fainting bit was almost real except that I never quite passed out. It really is quite simple to hype yourself up to it, depriving yourself of oxygen until you just 'go', without really blacking out. It is another very useful bid for attention as, however well people know you, they can never quite bring themselves to ignore you and so you can get a good half-hour centre stage if you know how to play the ensuing scene – and there are quite a few choices there. But although I continued to be difficult, in my own way I enjoyed school and took a pretty active part in it all. My school reports, however, left a lot to be desired and featured the words 'is capable of better' rather a lot.

I was still pretty much of a loner though; my friendship with Carol had foundered when we went into separate classes, and although others took her place, it was about this time that I embarked on the dangerous practice of forming a relationship and then systematically pushing it to the limits and destroying it. I think I knew what I was doing even then but I couldn't stop myself. Push people so far that they have no choice but to walk away and you can then turn round and say, 'See, I told you so, I knew you'd go in the end, no one can really like me.' Once you are on that treadmill the wheel turns endlessly and you are lost. But I often wonder if it wouldn't all have been very different if a person I loved hadn't just told me to shut up and then put their arms around me. No one ever did that and so the walls grew thicker and stronger and within my prison I felt safer and safer.

My first teenage love was called Michael, and he and his sister lived at the top of a steep hill at the far end of Grindleford. I thought it very daring and exciting but looking back now it seemed only to involve lots of puppy-dog eyes and rather heavy sighing on my part, though there was the odd stolen kiss or two. He used to cycle over to Hathersage in the long summer evenings and we met secretly and held hands but that was about as far as it went and 'passionate' is not a word I would use to describe this, my first great love. Once I had managed to escape from the house we used to sneak away to the deserted playing fields on our way to the little shop in Back Lane that sold spearmint ice lollies for 2d. Delicious these were but for some reason high on the list of banned substances issued by the Life Police at the Gables. We often had no money and so would check the return button on the nearby phone box, successfully retrieving the few necessary coppers on more occasions than seemed logical.

Money always seemed at a premium in my childhood and when I was around eight or nine years old I used to steal from the cupboard in the living-room. My father kept change for the shops there and it came straight from the bank in the blue and beige moneybags. By taking only one two-shilling piece from each bag, or one half-crown for variation, I escaped detection for a long time. The money thus acquired was spent in a shop at the bottom of Station Road, a child's paradise of cheap trinkets and long-forgotten packets of cotton wool, and paper cups – and one I was forbidden to enter. I don't know why I got such a kick out of buying so much of this stuff, all of which was quite useless anyhow, but I did. We had made houses under the hawthorn bushes in the fields by the house and a lot of the stuff went there, and I suppose we bought sweets and biscuits from the large open tins that stood in front of the counter.

Of course I got found out eventually and there was a terrible fuss. Norma Cottrell had been involved in the spending though not in the stealing and we were forbidden to play together. It was also pointed out that I had made Mrs Beresford, the village lady who worked in the shop, look dishonest, and then there was a lot of talk about 'bad blood'; the first time I was to hear that expression, but not the last. 'Bad blood', the words terrified me for I took them literally and thought there was something seriously wrong with me. Later, when I understood them better, I think it hurt even more. Still, somewhere along the way lessons were learned, though the spearmint lollies troubled no consciences, except perhaps slightly in the matter of defying the Life Police. After about a year the friendship with Michael faded away, though I remained friends with his sister for the rest of my schooldays.

In the school holidays I mostly returned to my more solitary existence, except for a fortnight in the summer when my parents and I went to the seaside. Like thousands of others we went for the same two weeks in the month of August, changing our destination from year to year. At first it was Blackpool, later Scarborough or Bridlington and once, Whitby. My memories are of cold, windy promenades and deserted beaches, and I have photos to prove my memories are reliable. Alan Bennett has described these resorts and the boarding houses we all stayed in far better than I can, but I do remember developing a dread of tinned peaches and these and ham salads revolt me to this day. And of course salad cream has been off my shopping list for years.

Blackpool was donkeys and the place where I found one called Gracie. I fell in love with her and wanted to take her home at the end of the holiday and cried when I had to leave her behind. Scarborough is memories of gazing up at the Grand Hotel, watching the, for me, elegant guests come and go. I dreamed of staying there and subsequently did though that all comes later and was not quite the experience I had anticipated. Bridlington was fishing boats and maybe it was there that we walked every day round the small harbour. And then there are other memories that belong nowhere and everywhere, like paddling and building sandcastles, often in the thick sweater necessary to combat a bitter wind. But suddenly, as I reached my teens, we decided to travel south for our two-week, ritual. This, somewhat radical decision, was occasioned by the Festival of Britain, and I think we planned to go on to Clacton on Sea afterwards. The trip seemed to involve the sort of planning that would take an army half-way round the world.

I remember little of events on the South Bank in 1951, though there are photos and a programme to prove that we were there. It was predominantly educational and probably all the fun things were deemed too expensive or 'not suitable'. I'm sure we stayed for two nights in London, and there was one glorious evening when we ate in a restaurant in Leicester Square. Once safely seated we discovered, 'shock horror', that they were licensed premises and no fit place for the likes of us. I was secretly delighted and tried hard to persuade my father to order some wine, mainly so that we would all appear fully at home in such sophisticated surroundings. I failed and we ate quickly, not really happy until we found ourselves crossing the sinful pavements around King's Cross and St Pancras to the small, unlicensed hotel where we were staying. Here we slept fitfully until we were able to negotiate the tube to Victoria or Charing Cross station for the train that would take us to the less daunting locations of the rural south. And there was an enormous excitement about these new destinations where the sun seemed to shine most of the time. One of the railway stations opened directly on to the street and, once safely arrived, you stepped down into a world where people wore bright clothing and carried buckets and spades. I remember my father changing into his holiday outfit as soon as we reached our latest bed and breakfast hotel. Grey-flannel trousers and short-sleeved grey and green checked shirts were now the order of the day. Sandals too, brown leather and always worn with socks. My mother's wardrobe was extensive for she had been sewing for weeks. Remnants bought from the material departments at Cockayne's and Walsh's (only Sheffield's best would do), had been carefully and lovingly turned into a series of what looked like the same dress but with different, matching buttons to add a slightly reckless touch to the whole ensemble. I have virtually no memory of my own 'frocks', for such they were – dresses and gowns came later into my world. The photos show me in a collection of flower-patterned affairs obviously mother-made at some stage earlier in the summer.

Whether or not the weather was really any better is debatable, but the memories and the photos too, seem to indicate that it was. And we seemed to respond to it too, my father took to drinking a lunchtime shandy and my mother hit on ginger ale. My treat was originally a strawberry milk shake, though later on I achieved the giddy heights of independence and was allowed to choose for myself between chocolate, banana and raspberry.

We started going to the theatre too, for the traditional, end of the pier variety shows were still very much a part of the life of the seaside resorts. I loved the excitement as the curtain went up and the dancers burst on to the stage. The Kendals were on the bill one year and when they finished their act they introduced their mother, 'the great Marie Kendal', who was sitting in the audience. I turned to look at a small, very old lady, sitting near to us in the stalls and I had no idea who she was. But a wave of excitement spread through the audience and people rose to their feet and applauded. My mother whispered that she had been one of the great stars of the music hall. It didn't mean much to me until years later, but I certainly knew that she was special.

The guest houses too seemed to have a lighter approach to life. We were still locked out after about nine in the morning and not supposed to return until six in the evening but we did tend to pop back for things we had forgotten and there was often a lounge at our disposal selling such exotic drinks as Babycham at highly inflated prices. Of course we didn't succumb to these temptations of the devil, but negotiated for late-night Horlicks or perhaps 'just a cup of tea'. Still, I enjoyed these holidays in the south, though before they could begin there was always a lengthy interlude of tears at leaving Scampy behind in the tender care of my grandmother, or the responsible daughter of a neighbour. I was secretly convinced that something terrible would happen to him while I was away, but happily nothing ever did and I was always treated to an ecstatic welcome on my return.

My grandmother has been mentioned rarely in these pages so far but she was a large presence in my life. Widowed when I was about three, she appears in my early recollections as a black clad figure, someone who sniffed into a handkerchief a lot of the time. She told me she had spent her early life in service – as a ladies' maid, she insisted – and married my grandfather who was a groom and later a chauffeur. My mother was their only child and I was always led to believe that they had never wanted her to marry my father, though I am not sure why.

Recently, however, a cousin sent me a copy of the 1911 census and in it I found my grandfather described as an assistant caretaker to the Derwent Valley Waterboard where his mother was caretaker. Maybe he worked at several jobs during his life but this new revelation explains a very clear memory of being taken to the Ladybower Dam on the day of its opening by Their Majesties King George VI and Queen Elizabeth. My mother and I were taken into a large reception hall where there was a long table decorated with crystal glassware and what I was told were real gold plates. I was deeply impressed and excited but when, a little while later, a large black car pulled up and two people got out I suffered bitter disillusionment. I stood in disbelief clutching my small Union Jack, for neither of the two people who were the King and Queen of Great Britain were wearing a crown and there was no sign of a long dress covered with diamonds.

Grandad had died of a burst duodenal ulcer, something that could have been dealt with only a few years later, and Gran was obviously devastated by the loss. I first remember her as living in a bungalow just outside Bamford and my mother and I used to visit, taking a bus ride and a lengthy walk before being fed the invariable lunch of corned beef, mashed potatoes and baked beans – at that time for me, food for the gods. My grandmother's mashed potatoes were like no others I have ever tasted, so light they almost seemed to float off the plate. The secret, she claimed, lay in the fact that the milk and the butter were always heated together first, before being mashed into the potatoes. Well maybe, but I have tried that and mine still don't taste as good. But she seemed rather a remote figure in those early days; locked into her grief she had little to offer a small child and it was only when she came to live in Hathersage that we became really close.

She bought one of the old stone cottages that stood almost opposite the scene of my near disaster on the sledge. I was in my teens by then and used to be sent to her cottage by my mother, bearing cakes and Bakewell tarts. Slowly we built up a friendship, and when she took to lending me her copies of classic literature under the guise of racy modern novels, we became friends for life. By doing this she did me an enormous favour for in the future I was never to be put off reading anything and books became one of the mainstays of my free time. Amongst these books were the complete works of the Brontë sisters and I devoured them greedily. I could quote long sections of *Jane Eyre* and Jane herself replaced *Anne of Green Gables* as my role model. I believed myself to be an expert on the Brontës and was convinced that no one could really understand their books unless they knew the moors as I did ... but more of my grandmother later.

Of my other grandparents I knew little then. My father's mother had died only a few days after giving birth to him, and his father seemed somehow to hold him responsible. Dad was brought up by an aunt and uncle and for all my childhood we never spoke to his father or to any of his numerous half brothers and sisters. Our second house faced a row of their cottages across the main village street and I used to walk on the footpath that passed through their farmyard; just a small girl, but we never spoke. In fact they rapidly grew to be monsters in my imagination and Uncle Harold, who had never left the village in his entire life and was somewhat reclusive, became an ogre of quite alarming proportions. They were mostly farmers, these shadowy relatives, but their names were rarely mentioned in our house though there is one story I remember clearly and I have the evidence to prove that it was true. Besides farming my great grandfather had also run a small business, travelling to Sheffield by horse and cart and selling his farm produce to some of the big houses there. One of these was the home of the Cockayne family who owned a prestigious shop in the centre of the town. They were soon to open a new modern store on the old site and asked my great grandfather to be their first customer, telling him he could have anything in the shop for sixpence. He chose a length of patterned muslin and had it made up into a dress for his wife. Unfortunately his wife died a few years later and their two grown-up daughters fought over who should inherit the dress ... where-upon their outraged father took a pair of scissors, cut it length-wise into two halves and threw one at each of the daughters. I have no idea what happened to one half but the other one is here with me and when I was still a child we lent it back to Cockayne's for the fiftieth anniversary of the store where it was proudly displayed in one of the shop windows. Meanwhile my father grew up estranged from most of his relatives and took over the running of the village post office after his Uncle Tom died.

As I grew older Dad became a more ill-defined figure in my life. He worked long hours at the post office and often came home tired in the evenings. I was frequently told by my Mother to 'let him be' so eventually I did. He was an excellent amateur cricketer and I still have some of his cups and trophies and a small collection of newspaper cuttings and he told me he was once offered a trial for the Yorkshire County cricket team. Although he was technically born in Derbyshire we were only three miles outside the Yorkshire border and some of the Ibbotson farmlands were in Yorkshire too. Indeed the family name itself came from the nearby town of Sheffield where, I found out later, there were some rich industrialists and émigrés to Russia and Italy.

Photographs of my father in his twenties show him to be exceedingly handsome, and it is easy to understand why my mother fell for him. My mother on the other hand looks rather lumpy in these photos and she wore glasses even then. The fashions of that time didn't suit her and everything drooped, but my father adored her, and only later did I begin to understand just how much. I think she must have been everything to him – mother, sister, wife, maybe, even, daughter and I'm sure he would have preferred to have her to himself; my arrival was almost certainly at her insistence and he would have agreed to the adoption for her rather than for himself. But he was a kind man and generous too. He had a bevy of old ladies who came to him for help with their income tax and children rarely went sweetless from the post office.

Chapter Three

The post office itself was in one of the old stone cottages in the middle of the village. You went into it through a large, heavy door and walked across stone slabs to the long wooden counter. To the right as you entered was the area where post office matters were dealt with. I can't remember now if there was any sort of grille, probably not, though if there was it was there to give the counter a more dignified air rather than for any security reasons. In the middle of the shop, starting more or less opposite the door, there were boxes of sweets and a set of brass scales for weighing out the two ounce and four ounce bags as required. Every Sunday I was allowed a quarter of sweets and, being of the house as t'were, I was allowed to dip and choose, a few from here, a few from there. Quality Street was often favoured with my attentions, the one in purple foil – a sort of runny toffee with a nut, being my favourite. Luckless customers buying a quarter themselves were unlikely to find any of these included in their bag. Liquorice Allsorts too came high on the popularity list, especially those you could unroll, separating the liquorice from the fondant. Mint imperials were there and treacle toffee, which made you terribly thirsty; the rest I forget. But I was allowed only three sweets a day after the midday meal in those days so my four ounces lasted all week. Later, when I was asked to work in the other shop, I used to gorge myself on the Quality Street, not realising that my father knew exactly what I was doing and operated a policy of 'let her get on with it she'll soon get sick of them and stop'. He was quite right of course and today I hardly like sweet things at all and much prefer a handful of olives to a quarter of sweets, though I do overdose on a bar of chocolate occasionally.

At the far end of the post office came the stationery, the birthday cards, cardboard horse-shoes for newly weds and such exotic things as greaseproof paper and string. Another room, known as the back room, led off this area and in it was found the telephone and the benches for sorting the mail. For several early years of my life I was convinced that the telegrams popped out of the telephone receiver, rather as money and bills travelled across the older shop floors in the cylindrical containers on the criss-crossing ceiling wires. It was a bitter blow to learn that they came by word of mouth.

There was always something mysterious about that back room –

the odd-shaped packages and the letters with the foreign stamps and the Finnegan turkey arriving every Christmas from Ireland, badly packed and already smelling high. All these things gave me, as a child, a first glimpse of a world outside the boundaries of Hathersage and Sheffield, though quite what that world was to be, I wasn't sure.

The postmen who came to sort the letters were all middle aged men, avuncular types who had spent their lives tramping the few village streets and the moorland sheep tracks to reach the remote farmhouses, often with some long-awaited letter from a missing son or daughter. We always employed students at Christmas, two or three, to help with the extra mail, and when I was finally at university I became one of them. It was hard work, for my father, not wishing to be accused of favouritism, gave me the route that included all the remotest farms and so I finished long after the other two, often tramping through snow and bogs even on Christmas morning itself. I remember once finding a library book reminder card that was the only thing to be delivered to a farm high on the moors, only to be told when I got there that the book had been returned the day before. It had involved about an hour and a half's detour across rough tracks and through deep snow, so I had asked if I could leave it until the next day, but had been told no. The Royal Mail was the Royal Mail and there was a commitment to deliver every item the day it arrived, whatever it was. My father was proud of his good standing within the Post Office organisation and his uncle had taken and delivered the first telegram ever sent in England. The king, George V, had inaugurated the whole service by sending good wishes to his prime minister, Stanley Baldwin, when by chance he was shooting on the grouse moors outside the village and staying in the hotel where, many years later, that early-morning scene across the moors was to take my breath away. I have letters too, relating to an occasion during the war when King George VI was to stop in the Hathersage railway sidings. My father was informed that he would be expected to deliver and collect the king's mail from the train and that it must be specially sent under tight security, and I think there is a follow up letter thanking him for the efficient way in which the matter had been handled. So commitment and self discipline were introduced into my life at an early age and, although I often rebelled then, later they were to stand me in good stead, and I came to value those early lessons.

In many ways everyday life in that small village where I grew up still had vestiges of feudalism about it. During one Sunday evening stroll when I was about three or four years old and attired in my best coat and bonnet, I remember stopping at a very small cottage with a tiny front garden packed tight with growing vegetables and flowers. There a bent, elderly couple came to the door, Mr and Mrs Schofield if I remember correctly. They greeted us like visiting royalty, shaking my hand and addressing me as 'little Miss Ibbotson', and Mrs Schofield all but curtsied. My mother would have loved this of course for it would have fitted in nicely with her hopes of a middle-class status which were oh so evident in the hats and the Sheffield shops patronised or left alone. She also eagerly sought acceptance within the ranks of the Women's Institute, eventually reaching the giddy heights of Handicraft Secretary. And she spent long hours sewing dresses and organising the chapel-equivalent of the Rose Queen – only recently I found the velvet cloak and gloves carefully preserved in tissue paper. There are photos too of these events; in one my mother, carefully dressed and obviously in control, is bustling around the dray sorting out some last-minute detail while my father stands there scratching his head. She desperately wanted me involved in these events and although part of me longed to join in there was always something that stopped me and kept me sulking at home or sent me stomping, solitary, across thc moors, dog at heel.

Every year while I was growing up the village held a week-long summer pageant. Looking back this was highly ambitious for such a small village, for the competitions ranged from a swimming gala and a cricket match to various exhibitions and dances. Inevitably, a carnival queen and four attendants were chosen to grace the events and give something of a formal air to the whole proceedings. These five local maidens were chosen weeks in advance at a beauty contest held in the village hall, and for the period of the pageant they wore beautiful crinoline dresses hired at great cost from Sheffield. They also received bouquets and presents and were generally treated as celebrities. Of course I longed to be one of the chosen ones and the first year I was eligible I set off fully confident – well, I think I was – on the night of the selection and then returned home un-chosen and dejected, later spending the whole week of the pageant wracked with envy. A physical pain this that manifested itself in a refusal to join in any of the proceedings and was to find me brooding in my bedroom for their duration. For the next two years I refused to risk rejection again but in the third year the pressure from my mother was enormous. Even so she left the house without me on the crucial evening, and it was my father who persuaded me to 'do it for your mother'. So finally I donned my favourite green-and-white-striped dress and went. Of course I was chosen as one of the attendants. My mother had worked hard and long every year and I'm sure my selection had been guaranteed, though I didn't think that then. I was secretly delighted but pretended it was all of no importance.

The week of the pageant was one of the highlights of my teenage years. Though the dress was not the crinoline I had dreamed of, it was pretty in a Charlotte Brontë sort of way, and my mother was so proud. Again there are photos and one with my mother and grandmother sitting in the front row of the audience. Even my father was present that evening though in fact he rarely attended any event, not even funerals, claiming tiredness and early rising as an excuse not to do so. Of course I wanted him there, I wanted him at school events too, but it was not to be. It was always my mother who donned some highly inappropriate hat and coped as best she could.

What was it about English ladies and hats in those days? I hate the things and rarely wear them, but in our village they were a badge of respectability, favoured particularly by the church and chapel going matrons. My mother had a vast selection, kept in the best wardrobe and ritually taken out, brushed and stuffed with fresh tissue paper. Hats seemed to be something she could not make herself so they were bought with an uncharacteristic disregard for cost and brought home like trophies to join the others in the wardrobe. Brought up as a highly polite child, I somehow managed to be courteous even to the parish paragons, though I disliked most of them and avoided contact whenever possible.

In the few months before my father died and when he was rapidly going senile, I found myself working at Yorkshire Television and commuting between London and Leeds. I used to stop off and spend one or two nights in Hathersage with my father, cleaning and cooking and generally sorting out the house. On one particular occasion I found the house in a worse state than usual. So I started early on a Sunday morning and was cleaning the kitchen, putting the scrubbed chairs and table, etc. outside in the garden to dry. At the moment of greatest domestic chaos one of the Chapel ladies walked past on her way to the Sunday-morning service, hat firmly on head. On seeing me she stopped in her tracks, a look of horror on her face. 'Oh, Anne,' she said, 'does it have to be done on a Sunday?' 'No, of course not,' I replied. 'When can you come and do it?' And that got rid of her. On the whole, I can honestly say that I don't trust women in hats.

I don't know why we went to chapel. I found out later that my mother had promised to bring me up in the Church of England but although we went to the parish church occasionally this was one of the rare instances of her failing to keep her word. There must have been a good reason for she was not a woman who broke promises lightly and religion was important to her. Whether or not it is important to me, I am not sure. I certainly went along with it as a child, for I had no choice, and I remember a highly charged scene at a Billy Graham rally where I sank to my knees in near ecstasy and a spirit of conversion, but I suspect that was due more to teenage hormones and mass hysteria than anything else and the effects soon wore off.

My first break with conventional religion came when I was still very young. We had a much loved cat called Ginger but he became very ill with a mysterious skin disease and lost all his fur. My mother made him a coat to keep him warm but he just got sicker and sicker and I resorted to prayer and asked God to make him better, promising to believe in him for ever if he did. Alas Ginger died and the beginnings of disillusionment set in. Years later and when I was judged by the chapel to have achieved womanhood, I received a book prize at the annual presentation, a sort of farewell to childhood. It was an unreadable compilation of religious tracts and I was bitterly disappointed. So that was me and the earthbound churches more or less finished for the time being anyhow. From then on I sorted out my own gods and we lived peacefully on a rather more equal basis. But certainly my childhood hitherto had been bound by religion. We peeled vegetables on a Saturday night and no work was done on a Sunday. Only weeks before she died my mother did an unthinkable thing – she hung a tea towel out to dry on the line after washing up the dishes from Sunday lunch. I almost had to sit down from the shock. By then I think she knew she had cancer (though my father and I did not) and her faith had probably been pretty much shaken. She certainly seemed to change in many ways around that time.

These joyless Sundays gave me a dread of the Sabbath which has never left me, the only good part of those hours in Chapel was the music, for we had a fine organist and I sang in the choir from a very early age. Once a year we performed the whole of

Handel's Messiah and I loved the feeling of singing and the discipline of the music – but there were many other hours spent just waiting for release from the often cold ambience of that bare and dimly lit building. Every Sunday I used to wake up with a sense of emptiness, of a long day stretching ahead, governed mainly by the rules and regulations of a church that seemed to regard any form of pleasure as a sin. So, most books were banned and to chapel we went, and to Sunday school and to evening service, and after Sunday school we walked the dog and that was just about it. No cards, no games of any kind, no homework even. Laughter, never a regular visitor in our house, was firmly excluded; radio and television stood silent until Monday morning. Only on holiday were the rules slightly relaxed, and then, when Benny arrived, I was excused the Sunday morning ritual in order to exercise and groom him. Many years later I watched *Oranges are Not the Only Fruit* on BBC Television and could recognise so much of that stagnant Sunday life.

Was it what they wanted, my mother and father? Or were they really only following the strict rules of behaviour laid down by the churches and especially powerful in such small rural communities? Was it my arrival that brought on a suffocating sense of responsibility? How could laughter be such a sin? For me laughter is as essential as the air we breathe. I love to laugh, the physical sensation of it and the sound of it. Once at Epidavros in Greece, I saw a production of *The Frogs* by Aristophanes. It was excellent and I went both evenings. The theatre was packed, the audience international and the laughter a physical presence. At one point it spread like a wave from one side of the auditorium to the other, a great surge of joy. Strangers touched one another, held on to one another, I have never experienced anything like it before or since, and it happened at the same moment both nights. This was the laughter that came deep from the psyche – no girlish giggling, or the false staccato you hear at cocktail parties. This laughter was a life force, it regenerated and fed the very people who laughed, and some nights at Epidavros, even now, its echoes seem to be lurking within the marble stones of the theatre, longing for a chance to re-emerge and spread out again, a living presence.

Inescapably, Sundays loomed at the end of each week and I learned to cope with them by inhabiting my other world where Scampy and I ruled supreme. But the religious influence went deep and when I was at Goldsmiths' College in London, and together with a group of other girls took myself off one Sunday to see Danny Kaye in *The Five Pennies*, I really thought the heavens would open and I would be struck dead as I left the cinema. I remember that real sense of fear even now and it stayed with me for most of the rest of that day. In time, however, the inhibitions began to fade and Sundays took on a more general aspect as I became more deeply involved in college life.

Only my grandmother seemed uninfluenced by demands of chapel or church, though I think she was religious in her own way. I remember her as being tall, though I'm not sure now that she was. She was quite big-boned, with sharp features, and in my opinion she should have worn her hair in a bun instead of wearing it in rigid, corrugated waves. Strangely enough I hardly ever remember her wearing a hat. She had an incredible natural stature and dignity, did not suffer fools gladly or in any other way, and later in her life had a deep horror of anything that stood the remotest possibility of coming under the heading of charity. Every Christmas when all the old-age pensioners in the village were given a food parcel, my grandmother always firmly refused to accept hers despite many attempts to explain it away as her 'right'. She was stubborn, of course, but broadminded in a way I've only ever found in the older generations, whether in England or Greece or almost anywhere in the world. I don't think it is anything to do with age, more a reflection of the way the world was during the early part of their lives. Perhaps, in many ways I was like her, we were certainly both very good at fighting battles where no war existed, but she was intensely loyal and I like to think that perhaps I take after her in that way too. I don't know whether or not she had a hard life with my grandfather but somehow I think not. I've no idea exactly where they worked but there were plenty of big houses around and their status within the hierarchy should have been quite good – and later of course, there was that job at the Water Board. Certainly she came originally from a poor background for in one early document her sister is described as a pauper. Anyhow, when she and my grandfather retired they bought their own detached bungalow with a large garden, so there must have been money around somewhere.

The houses we lived in then were cold in the winter, cool in the summer, and almost always slightly damp. So there are certain smells that belong to this time, rarely found now, but when they are they bring memories of childhood flooding back. Rare moments of true happiness mingle with others, a sense of waiting perhaps or a sense that life had not yet really begun? I certainly knew something was missing and my grandmother's attitude and the long conversations I was to have with her only enhanced this feeling.

They did well with their lives, my adoptive family. My father told me that when he was at school it was a struggle to find the necessary sixpence each week. He left when he was only fourteen and yet he was a literate man and quite brilliant with figures. I used to watch him doing the daily post office accounts, his pencil flying up and down the columns of numbers as though he were simply drawing a line. Practically his only form of relaxation was his interest in sport. As I've written before he was a keen and good amateur cricketer, and I was the best eleven-year-old over-arm spin bowler in the village, though my batting left a lot to be desired. My father on the other hand was a more than useful batter, often saving the day with his last-minute stand. He loved football too, and went every winter Saturday to either Sheffield United or Sheffield Wednesday, often taking me with him. I used to love those trips and hated it when I was left behind for some reason or other. If I was sick, he usually came back with a book for me, a schoolgirl fantasy of some kind, and I lay curled up in bed reading until either it was finished or my mother tore it from my hands with some words about eye strain or making myself sick with 'too much reading'. There were no books other than mine in our house but I was always encouraged to read and if I spent my weekly pocket money on a book the price was often, though not always, returned to me by my father. He was always broad minded and interested in world affairs and I think he was thrilled when I did well enough at school to go to Goldsmiths'. He rated education very highly in the order of things and believed it to be of greater importance than religion or politics and I know he deeply regretted not having the opportunities to study that were now available to my generation. He never complained about his life and he certainly had the respect of the village, but cricket and football remained his only sources of relaxation and he took an avid interest in both. I think he loved taking me to the matches and explaining to me the finer points of the game and I loved accompanying him but later I turned against football and now I hardly ever watch it. It is so very much a television sport these days, whereas before it was a spectator event, the crowds, the cold fingers and feet, the hot cup of soup at half-time – real soup, not something from a machine – my father with his 'Saturday friends', all contributed to a sense of occasion. Now the big televised matches isolate where once they united and so much of it is about money.

Those Saturdays at the football were probably the closest I ever got to my father, for as I grew older I began to be ashamed of being in his company, and ashamed of my mother too. Is this something a lot of people go through; is it part of growing up? I somehow don't think so. They used to say they had educated me above them and in some ways it was true, but these were good people and I should have been proud of them, alas, I never was. Only a long time after they had both died did I begin to know and understand them, and by then it was far too late.

My mother was no intellectual but she was a good cook and, as they say, clever with her hands. She was quite brilliant at dressmaking. I remember a party dress she made for me when I was about thirteen. For days I had been vaguely aware that she was making something, but there was nothing unusual in this and I paid little attention. Then one evening I came home and saw a vision of floating pink tulle hanging from a hook in the living-room. For a thirteen-year-old it was a dream come true, mauve taffeta and pink net. I tried it on and floated around the room. For once she had got it more than right. But in other ways she had her shortcomings. Her spelling was atrocious, 'their' and 'there' remaining a mystery until the day she died, and she never read a book or newspaper. Still, I think she was happy with her lot and saw herself as rather successful. I'm sure she would have liked my father to be more sociable but there came a point when she simply gave up and got on with things without him. Just before she died she started talking about getting a divorce, but I doubt she ever would have done – my grandmother was still alive, for one thing, and the Women's Institute would hardly have approved, for another.

I'm not sure exactly when I began to be ashamed of them both. My mother certainly came first and it may have been something to do with the hats. She came rarely to school events, for it was difficult to travel to and from Bakewell, but on those rare occasions she did turn up for speech day or sports day, however she dressed, it was wrong. She even asked me what to wear on several occasions, but other children had glamorous mothers, some who arrived looking like film stars even, and my poor homely mother had no chance. Years later the daughter of one of these glamour mums told me how she envied me mine, all round and cuddly and ever present at home, and I learned what I should have always known.

Around this time I made friends in the village with Angela. Her family were rich by our standards and came to live in Hathersage when they moved from one of the more prosperous areas of Sheffield. Originally from Ireland, the whole family were great fun and a refreshing addition to the village. They built a large house on top of the hill behind Westmoor – our new home – and it seemed enormous and extremely luxurious. We had moved from The Gables by then for my father had bought a piece of land behind the post office and built a detached semi-bungalow on it for my mother. It was her dream house, modern and easy to run, the rooms were small but quite well planned. It was situated in the centre of the village and everything about it was worthy of an upwardly mobile member of the Women's Institute. I, of course, hated it, especially after I saw Angela's home.

Angela's family was a generous one too. She had an older half-sister who was married and lived in Ireland, so Angela was virtually an only child. She had studied agriculture at college and her father had set her up with a small farm close by the River Derwent and that favourite walk of mine. It was a small livestock holding with some hens, occasional pigs, but mainly Jersey cows. The herd varied in size but each animal had its own name and character and some days they resembled a group of mischief-making elderly ladies out on a spree. They had wonderful, soft faces, enormous eyes with long lashes and were extremely skittish. The farm was quite a distance away from Angela's home but one morning she woke up to find them all on the front lawn of the house, greatly enjoying her father's newly laid turf. How they got there we could not imagine for it was a complicated journey and getting them back to their field was no easy task.

I'm not sure how we became friends, I do remember looking longingly across the river on one of our summer walks, Scampy barking at some turkeys she had, but I think we may have been quite formally introduced. Anyhow, it doesn't matter now, the memories that remain are all happy ones and I quickly became involved in the running of the farm and then, not long afterwards, in Angela's rather exciting social life. My mother was delighted with this turn of events and I think she saw her daughter as definitely moving in the right direction.

Thanks to life on the farm I was allowed to wear trousers, until then strictly forbidden and life with Angela also brought a freedom unimaginable before. She had her own car for one thing, and also a small green van she used for collecting hen feed and bales of hay. I loved travelling around the country lanes in this old banger and envied Angela for owning both it and the car. Driving looked so easy, that, one day, when Angela asked me if

I could manage to take the van up the lane to collect the empty milk churns, I unhesitatingly replied, 'Yes.' 'Go then,' she said, so I did. I leapt into the driving seat, started the engine, put it in gear, and drove straight into the nearby barn wall. Fortunately I did little damage, some dents and a smashed headlight, I think. Angela was not best pleased but we concocted some story and her father paid for the repairs. After that, she taught me how to stop and start the van and so all of one summer I trundled happily around the village, very proud of myself, until the local policeman stopped me and told me for heaven's sake to go and pass my driving test or at least put L plates on the van, otherwise he was going to have to arrest me for illegal driving.

So I started saving up my pocket money and, despite my parents pointing out that I would never be rich enough to own a car, I resolved to pass my driving test as soon as possible. I was working at a temporary job in Sheffield when I finally had enough money for lessons so for a long time I pursued my new hobby in secret. I think my Instructor was called David but I'm not sure. He certainly seemed a David sort of person and he was quite a good judge of character, for somewhere around the third lesson he took me up onto one of the more remote moorland roads and told me to put my foot down and do a hundred miles an hour. It was great. Then, having got that out of the way, we settled down to the business of tuition. I failed my test the first time for 'improper use of the driving mirror', whatever that may have meant. Friends accused me of trying to put on make-up while overtaking an articulated lorry but I hardly think it could have been that. Anyhow I passed the next time and my policeman friend heaved a sigh of relief.

Just before I passed my test my instructor mentioned he was driving down to Cornwall to join his girlfriend for a short holiday and I hit on the bright idea of going with him. He wasn't too keen on this at first but I eventually talked him round, persuaded The Gables, heaven knows how, that a few days in Cornwall on my own was in both our interests, and one rainy morning we set off.

I don't think I'd planned much beyond the actual journey, for when he finally dropped me in the middle of the little town of Mousehole, I really hadn't a clue what I was doing there, and I was shocked to find myself in such a plight. We arrived late in the afternoon and I watched him drive off into the gathering dusk with something approaching panic. I don't quite know what I expected of him but it certainly wasn't that. Eventually I think I went into a shop to enquire about a bed and breakfast and they must have pointed me in the direction of the YMCA, because that is where I ended up. Not the YWCA, because there wasn't one, but there was a separate room at the men's house and I was offered this.

The next morning things looked slightly less grim, though the weather continued to be appalling. I set off to explore the area and almost managed to convince myself that I was having a good time, though food was limited to bread and cheese and my money seemed to be disappearing fast. I sent a postcard home every day and was desperately homesick, but could not allow myself to admit it. I also did not have enough money for my rail fare home, so unless I wanted to swallow my pride and phone my parents – I didn't – I had no choice but to sit and wait out the week until David picked me up and drove me back to Sheffield.

One day in the middle of the week I managed to avoid the ticket inspector both ways and have a free day trip to Exeter on the train. But Exeter was busy and expensive and difficult so I was pleased to be back in Mousehole and the YMCA, where my room by now was rapidly beginning to seem like home. Then, towards the end of the week, when funds were beginning to run so low that even the daily postcard to the Life Police was under threat, I wandered down to the harbour and met Gustav on his yacht. It wasn't a very big yacht and Gustav wasn't exactly the man of my dreams, but we got chatting and I went back the next day for coffee. It was during our second cup that he asked me to sail round the world with him. Over the next twenty-four hours it was touch and go as to whether or not I went. I really thought it a chance of a life time and imagined our glorious arrival in South America or the Caribbean. But the yacht was very small and I really wasn't very keen on Gustav, so eventually common sense, or maybe cold feet, won the day and I said no. I still have the newspaper cutting telling of how he was stopped by the harbour police and found with an under-age girl on board. But that was long after I had been safely returned to the Life Police in Hathersage.

Chapter Four

I was well into my teens by now and my social life had expanded considerably. A diary from that time, recently discovered amongst some old papers, makes perfectly clear that the long days on the moors had been replaced by trips to Sheffield and overnight stays with school friends. I seemed to be constantly busy and very much a part of village and school life. I played tennis in Bamford and joined the Hathersage ladies' hockey team, I also began to stay overnight with friends. Scampy must have missed his long walks.

Davina was a friend from school and lived in one of the tied cottages on the Chatsworth estate where her father worked for the Duke of Devonshire. I began to visit her for weekends, and because of her father's job we enjoyed unlimited access to the big house and wandered freely round the grand salons, then not yet opened to the general public. They gave a fascinating glimpse of another life, one of privilege perhaps, but also one that was fast becoming part of history. It all seemed far from anything I had ever known and quite removed from my reality. If we came across the Duke or Duchess they greeted us cheerfully and seemed to be very down to earth and quite unaware of their place amongst the aristocracy and I never saw them wearing crowns or long jewelled robes either. My ballet classes had been replaced by membership in an amateur dramatic society and the diary tells me that I had the lead role in one production and got good revues; and life on the farm continued to fill my days even when I was at school. Benny had reluctantly been sold by now and gone to live at a country pub where he quickly developed a taste for a daily pint of beer. But I was used to getting up early and so took to going down to the farm to help with the early morning milking routine before changing into my school uniform in time to catch the train to school.

They were always good days those days on the farm; working in the summer holidays into the long evenings and racing to bale the hay before the inevitable rain. All the family were roped in with Angela's mother preparing exotic picnics and ice cold, fresh lemonade appearing in thermos flasks at regular intervals. We often worked on by moonlight until dawn streaked the sky and we fell into our beds exhausted but filled with the satisfaction of a job well done. Other nights saw us sitting with a calving cow, holding a nervous hoof so to speak, until a living bundle covered in blood and mucus dropped into the hay and we left a delighted mother, whiffling softly as she cleaned her new calf, and went for breakfast. If we returned about an hour later the calf would be standing on wobbly legs, luminous round eyes gazing in wonder at its mother and in mock terror at us and the shadows that lurked in corners of the cow shed. Once there was a disaster, when for no known reason the calf died just before it was due to be born. We sat up all night with the cow but it was no good. The calf's hind legs were sticking out of its mother but we couldn't free it and the vet had to be called. Later that morning I watched as Angela and the vet put chains on these two hind legs and literally pulled the calf free. There was such a sense of failure, of emptiness, and later the same feeling as I watched the cow herself being destroyed. These moments were the downside of farming but mostly I found it fascinating and fulfilling.

As I got to know Angela better I began to be invited to the dinner dances and various events that made up the area's social life. My mother rose to the occasion, and by the time I was seventeen I had eight evening dresses of one kind or another. I joined the Young Conservatives, not out of any political conviction but simply because they had the best social life of any group in the area. Indeed, at that stage politics bored me. I was aware my mother and grandmother voted Conservative, more for reasons of respectability than anything else. My father would never say which way he leaned, though he was always very conscientious about voting. It was rumoured in the family that he was a secret Labour supporter, a scandalous thing to be in the village, though it would have made a great deal of sense if he was. But most of the young people I knew then were definitely of the Young Conservative group, though of a more modern and interesting kind than my mother's cronies at that time.

I loved Angela's life and very quickly took it on as part of my own. My mother was delighted of course but it alienated me even more from our more average lifestyle as I began to spend more and more time at her house. Sometimes we only called in at my home to collect an evening dress and the necessary underwear before the pair of us raced home and changed, giggling over the make-up and the perfume. Then, totally unrecognisable from our farming alter egos we would sit and wait in the elegant sitting room for two highly eligible but in retrospect totally honourable escorts to take us to some dinner dance or other.

Sex did not really have much of a role in my teenage years. I was aware of it of course, and surrounded by it on the farms, the mating of the horses being something of an alarming spectacle, though nevertheless fascinating in a basic sort of way. I was aware too, of some strange but not unpleasant sensations when I rode Benny but I wasn't too sure at all about these so I never thought about them too much. So, coming face to face so to speak, with my first erection, was something of a surprise. I knew the young man in question from our dinner-dancing days. He was extremely good looking and always appeared rather more sophisticated than the others. But I didn't know him well. I'm not sure how I ended up with him in his car alone but I was rather thrilled to find myself there and when he suggested we went for a drive, I quickly agreed, anticipating some romantic hand-holding and maybe the odd kiss. So, when he unzipped his trousers and placed my hand on this warm lump of flesh, I was completely surprised and not a little puzzled. He must have realised then that I was totally inexperienced for he quickly zipped himself up and drove me home. Only days later did I make vague connections between him and the mating stallions.

I'd like to write that it was all a shock, a traumatic experience, but it wasn't, still it did wake me up slightly and I decided I'd better start asking some questions, for the experience in the car hadn't quite matched up to the carefully edited cartoon film we had watched only recently in the biology class. Of course sex was never discussed at home. It must have gone on, I suppose, but not to my knowledge and I think it rated highly and probably close to politics and religion on the list of things regarded as private matters and not discussed openly by 'nice' people. Several years later I was to spend a good hour watching some male students dance naked around the fountains in the Place St Michel in Paris and all this improved my knowledge of the male anatomy considerably.

They were fun those dinner dances, the anticipation building up as we bathed and changed, and then the actual event. Did we pay for ourselves? I think we did. Although most of the boys came from families with a professional background and never seemed to be short of money, I don't think we went as girlfriend/boyfriend. On these occasions I was nearly always escorted by one Peter, he was a very pleasant and considerate young man who I'm sure found me as exciting as I found him, i.e. not a lot. I was always half in love with the 'bad' boys, the ones who drove sports cars and who had a slight reputation. But it was all very innocent and they were generally kind and considerate, most of them having younger sisters at home. I remember one evening going to a dance at the Rising Sun Inn where there was a swimming pool. After the dance had ended we all decided to go for a swim, mainly thanks to the Blue Nun served at dinner I think. It was hardly the scandalous affair described later by my mother – though how she found out about it I never did discover. The boys waited until we were stripped and in the water before coming into the pool area, turning out the lights and joining us. We may have brushed against the odd naughty bit but I don't remember it, I only remember the pleasure of bathing without a swimsuit, so much more liberating than when encased in crocheted cotton.

It was thus that the Young Conservatives spent most of their leisure hours. I have no memory of going to a political meeting of any kind, though there must have been some. I was politically naïve then. Brought up to enjoy the benefits brought in by a post war Labour government, I had little idea of how things had been in a comparatively recent past. We lived under what was an essentially a two party system with policies that moved a little to the left or right depending on which party was governing. With a strong opposition always in place, nothing seemed to change very much and there was a great feeling of stability. Margaret Thatcher was to change all that with, so I believe, disastrous results and Tony Blair was to blur the issues even further but all that was in the distant future and the 60's seemed a place where all things were possible. Later the television drama Kathy Come Home would shake the whole country but the general feeling then was that it had exposed a hole in the safety net of the benefits system and that now this hole would be swiftly closed.

Until I started to travel I never saw dire poverty – the kind without hope. I believed we had a system in place in Britain that prevented anyone from starving. I also believed that Britain would be amongst the countries that helped to spread this system throughout the world. It was to be a long time before I 'grew up' and I still remember my deep sense of shock when I saw my first beggar on a street in London and the sheer horror of the deprivation that I began to find in other parts of the world. Meanwhile, Angela and the rest of us split slightly from the group and just got on with enjoying ourselves.

This was around the time David and his family came to live in one of the big houses on Sheffield Road. Over their garage they had an enormous games room, originally the chauffeur's flat I suppose, and so we moved in there and the YC subscription demands remained un-answered, their leaflets quickly thrown into the bin.

These were the days of rock 'n' roll and reports of scandalous goings on in London. That summer I had that holiday job in Sheffield and used to meet up every day at lunchtime with a girl who worked as a waitress in one of the many Chinese restaurants in the city centre. I'm not sure now how we met and I can't remember her name, but we were great mates for a while. One day she came to me in a panic. Lonnie Donegan was doing a 'gig' in Sheffield, and somehow she had met him and was to meet him again later that night. But she had nothing to wear, could she borrow my dress? The one I was wearing that day was pink with white spots. Mother-made, of course, but it was pretty, with a dropped waistline and highly fashionable then. Thrilled at being so close to celebrity, I quickly agreed and we changed in the ladies loo of the restaurant when she finished work. Alas we were not quite the same size and she swam slightly in my pink while I struggled in her regulation black skirt and white blouse. I have no idea how I explained this to my mother but I must have got away with it somehow. My big disappointment came the next day when my friend returned the rather crumpled and unwashed dress but refused to give me any of the details of what had gone on during the evening. Many years later I told the story to Lonnie himself when we were both working on *The Six O'Clock Show*. He laughed a lot and said it was a nice story but he had no recollection of the evening. There were so many girls, he said, and so many frocks, it would be impossible to remember.

Meanwhile, at the house on the Sheffield Road we rocked the evenings away. I was a good dancer and had been classed as good enough to enter the auditions for the Royal Ballet School, but the Life Police had banned all thoughts in that direction. So I turned to ballroom dancing and was classed as good enough to enter for the ballroom competitions until once again the Life Police intervened. Nevertheless this did not stop beautiful long dresses being produced to wear to the local village-hall dances, though I was banned from even the local competitions and not allowed to go to dances in nearby Sheffield. But rock 'n' roll was not ballroom dancing, though whatever it was, it was great, and we took to it like ducks to water.

Still there was no way it came under the heading of 'nice' and the Life Police were dead against it, but for us it had such energy and it gave us an identity all our own. The catchphrases which came out of it, the clothes, the very music itself, bound us together in a sort of secret society. 'Rock Island Line' was like 'Wow!' and 'Funiculi, Funicula' was left standing. To be fair my mother tried to keep up. She made me a circular red felt skirt which swirled beautifully and revealed a glimpse of white 'knickers' from time to time, a fact of which she was certainly unaware and would have wholeheartedly disapproved. But I had good legs and enjoyed showing them off, still at that stage pretty much unaware of the sexual allure of white socks, long legs and that glimpse of 'knicker'.

Angela's family had friends from Sheffield who had come to live near by. I never really got to know them very well but they had two sons; one, the elder, was called Michael and was extremely good looking. He was also an excellent dancer and I loved dancing with him and I'm sure I fell in love with him in a teenager sort of way. You could see his garden from our kitchen window and he often worked out there wearing a gorgeous blue sweater. On the days he was working in the front garden, quite often it seemed, Scampy would be dragged across the park and up the hillside until we both arrived breathless but casual at the stile opposite his driveway. Benny, too, often found himself taken on the ride that ended up on the road that went past his house. But, alas, it remained a one sided affair and never went further than the dancing.

And the dancing got better and better as we watched *Six-Five Special* (away from the eagle eyes of the Life Police, for we didn't yet have a television set) and copied the routines of the professional dancers on the programme. And it was in the middle of one of these routines, at a point when my legs were in the air somewhere, that Mick's hold on me slipped and I went skidding across the floor and into the leg of a billiard table. I crashed into it, the hollow of my neck and shoulder fitting neatly round the leg. Something snapped and the pain was epic. I nearly passed out for real. I went home early that night and didn't sleep at all. Next morning I got through breakfast somehow and took myself off to Sheffield as usual, but instead of going to work, I went to the hospital and discovered I'd broken my collarbone and dislocated my shoulder. They put my shoulder back to the sound of an outraged howl but the collarbone disaster could not be hidden from the Life Police who shouted a lot and I was in trouble again. Still, it wasn't long before we were back dancing and even my mother began to take a certain interest in it all.

We were totally unaware we were living through some sort of revolution, but with the advent of 'Rock Island Line' and Billy

Haley and the Comets life in England changed, and with that change many of the traditions and values of early twentieth century Britain went out of the window for ever. Some parts of this were good but not all. The last dregs of the British Empire slipped away and a lot of the pink drained out of the world map. The old India hands, struggling to survive in an England they no longer either understood or could afford, symbolised the passing of a way of life that would never return. At that time my friends and I understood none of this, we knew only that we were having fun and everything in life seemed ours for the taking. So the immediate problem was only to decide exactly what it was we wanted.

By this time I was in my final year at school. Academically I was doing all right but not brilliantly. I had also achieved the dubious honour of being the only member of the sixth form not to be made a prefect. I was at home studying for my 'A' levels when the list of prefects was put up on the school notice-board. Joyce, our neighbouring bank manager's daughter, brought me the news and I was incredulous. I had longed to be a prefect and had secretly resolved to be a good one, but the school, tired I suppose of all my pranks, must have decided it just wasn't worth it, though no explanation was ever given. When I finally checked the list for myself and reality hit, I allowed no one to see how devastated I was.

I had a new boyfriend by then and for the first time I experienced the agonies and sleepless nights of being in love. It was very much an on/off sort of non affair but it was to go on for several years and Gary was to become one of the very important people in my early life. He bred budgerigars and so I persuaded my mother that our family was not complete without one and finally set off on the somewhat complicated journey to his house to collect one. I'm not sure I wanted a budgie at all but this little bundle of yellow and green feathers had a huge personality and rapidly made his presence felt around the house. My father adored him and Pip (for so we named him) was soon to be found sitting on my father's shoulder where he learned to talk and say such embarrassing things as, 'Anne's courting,' and, 'Who's a pretty girl?' He and Scampy had an uneasy relationship at first but they soon learnt to tolerate one another and so Pip's cage door remained almost permanently open and we learned to enter the room carefully until we had ascertained exactly where he was. They must have learned to communicate somehow, for later, when my mother was recovering at home from an operation for the removal of gall-stones, I came home for a visit and watched a somewhat amazing morning ritual. I was sitting in the dining-room one day with Scampy lying at my feet when he suddenly got up and went to the door. He pushed it open and stood half in and half out of the room waiting for something. Pip then flew down from his cage and walked out of the half-opened door. Together they walked along to where my mother lay in the downstairs bedroom and Scampy went through his door routine again. I heard my mother say, 'Oh, good morning, there you are.' I was astounded. My father stood there laughing and told me that they did the same thing every morning.

Gary had an old sports car named Ava – there are photos somewhere, and this gave him an added cachet, though I don't ever remember spending a great deal of time in it alone with him. I see it full of people like Hancock and Jones and Murdock and the dreaded Mavis who once scattered whatever scraps of self-confidence I still had by informing me that everyone had one good point and I had my hair; she also definitely saw herself walking into dreamland with Gary in the not too distant future, (she didn't).

Gary was a good Rugby player and played hooker for the junior county side. And so I seemed to spend several Saturdays standing on the sideline with the other sixth-form 'wives', slowly freezing to death and shouting, 'Go, go, go,' and, 'Kill, kill, kill' from time to time. In summer there would be the double fixtures, tennis and cricket, and so we would get to travel on the coach together and occasionally hold hands while the games master sat in the front seat with the games mistress, smoking and being careful not to look behind him.

Of course we managed some outings alone and apart from all the 'love' bits we became great mates and had a lot of fun. 'Magic Moments' became 'our song' and we sang it non-stop as we sped around the countryside, but there were rows too. I remember a spectacular one up on the moors near Stanage Edge. In the middle of it all I demanded he stopped the car so that I could get out and walk back to Hathersage. He did. I was not wearing shoes at the time and had been sitting with my legs hanging over the side of the car, so, shoeless I set off towards the Surprise Gap, hobbling slightly from the stony road. After a few minutes the car returned (I had been confident it would) but to my surprise it didn't stop. My shoes (pink ballet-type pumps, I remember clearly, though I couldn't tell you what else I was wearing) were thrown in front of me and Gary drove on. I left the shoes where they were, eventually arriving home with bleeding feet. The next day I went back to find the shoes, for they were my favourites at the time, and they were still there. It took us several days to get over that one.

Gary was a year ahead of me at school so he was already applying for places at university, predominantly Oxford or Cambridge. He was not academically brilliant like some people I was to meet later, but he was a conscientious student and eminently likeable in a gauche sort of way, for he was decidedly clumsy then and the butt of most of the sixth-form ragging. I remember sitting in the midst of some sort of after-school activity in Room 2 with Miss Schofield whilst Gary, fresh from the showers, raced up and down the opposite corridor in his underpants looking for the rest of his school uniform which had obviously been well hidden by his team mates after rugby practice. In fact, now I come to think of it, Gary seemed to spend an awful lot of time in his underpants, much to the amusement of his many and various observers. But he was a kind boy and eventually became a respected and much loved paediatrician. I really was in love with him then, a sort of all consuming and completely uncritical form of worship. Not particularly healthy as love goes but very real. I spent one sleepless night while he was away on a climbing holiday; all night long I was in a state of considerable agitation, though I had no idea why, for only that morning I had received a letter from him telling me that all was well and that he was having a great time. But days later, when he was safely back among us, he told tales of spending that night on the mountain in a snowstorm and in considerable danger. That was the first time I became aware of an instinct that has served me well over the years but I never thought of it as anything other than intuition then. Later the word 'clairvoyance' came into my vocabulary and I was to be told several times that I have that gift, but whatever its title, it is certainly something that I value and rely on still.

So I was happy with Gary, life was fun and I was beginning to feel secure and look forward to the future. Things were going well so I suppose I should have expected a setback, but I could never have imagined the form it would take. Gary's father was a small, round, quiet man and for the life of me I can't remember what he did. His mother was a large boned lady, a local magistrate and a formidable woman on all levels. Gary was an only child and had arrived late in their lives; so to say he was the focus of all their attention would be to give in to gross understatement. They lived in a lovely old stone cottage in the village of Monyash, high on the moors behind Bakewell, staunch Conservatives I suspect, and between them the probable owners of a vast selection of hats. Nevertheless they were generous in their public service and occasionally kind to their son's rather unpredictable girlfriend. So the invitation to afternoon tea thrilled rather than threatened, especially as Gary was to collect me in Ava. At first all went well. As I've said earlier, I was a polite, well-brought-up person and used by now to coping with my mother's WI friends and various elderly relatives, so I was on my best behaviour and quite relaxed when Gary was despatched to the village shop and the Monyash Life Police took over. He must have known what was going to happen for he never reappeared. His mother appealed to me 'to leave Gary alone'; his career and the Oxford scholarship for which he was about to apply were now the only things of importance in his life and he was too young for emotional commitment and could not afford to stay so involved with me. She was, of course, quite right in what she said but quite wrong, I think, in the way she went about it. I don't remember much of the rest of the afternoon; it was Gary's father who drove me back and I sat, silent, in the back of the old Bentley, unsure as to what had happened. In the event, it seemed to make little difference one way or the other and eventually after Gary's death, at a ridiculously early age, she was to write me a most conciliatory letter.

The last Christmas that Gary and I were at school together there was to be a special school party for every year group but our sixth-form party was the exception as it included the fifth form pupils too. It was to take the form of a dance and was to be held in the evening in a hall in Bakewell itself. It generated much excitement and great thought had to be given to clothes and make-up, etc., well by the girls anyway. A few weeks earlier I had seen a black V-necked top in the window of Mr Pearce's local shop and I had decided it would be perfect for the dance. So I talked about it long and often at home and eventually noticed that it had disappeared from the shop window. I was pretty certain that my mother had bought it as a Christmas present for me, but the dance was before Christmas, what to do? I pestered her long and hard until it was thrown at me with the words, 'Why do you have to spoil everything?' It was a bad start to what was supposed to be a special day, but it was to get worse.

The dance began well and looked like being a great success, at least until the interval. One of the boys there had a father who ran a pub a short walk away from the dance hall, and a group of the boys decided to go there for a drink. This was completely against school rules and some of us protested. The boys went anyhow and reluctantly some of the girls, I included, went with them. We might have got away with it but two of the boys stayed on and got drunk. They then made the mistake of coming back to the dance. They were quickly discovered and suspended on the spot. The rest of us were told we would be dealt with on the following Monday and the dance came to an abrupt end.

That following Monday the members of the sixth form were all called to the library where the headmistress stood accompanied by the science master. Alas, our beloved headmaster was away ill, seriously so, though we did not know it at the time. If he had been present things might have gone differently. In the event we were read the riot act and then the boys who had been at the pub were asked to 'own up'. Without exception they all did and were promptly suspended until further notice and asked to leave the school premises. Attention then turned to the girls, and the hope was expressed that none had been present. I looked around at three I knew had been there but not one of them would meet my eyes. Reluctantly I stood. There was a silence but still no one moved. Thus I was the only girl to be asked to leave the school and the meeting was closed. I went home and told my parents what had happened. The riot act was read and 'bad blood' reared its ugly head again.

It was a miserable Christmas. I was banned from speaking to Gary and his phone calls went unreported. The first day of the spring term came and went and I remained at home. Eventually a letter in a typewritten envelope arrived at the house. It was from Gary telling me that we were all allowed back at school. I returned the next day and found that all those suspended had been permitted to return a week ago but the school, knowing that I was adopted and not being sure of my home circumstances, had asked Gary to tell me of the decision. Once again, though with the best of intentions, the fact of my adoption had separated me from the rest of the crowd.

I found that two of the other girls had finally owned up, though one never did and got away with it. We were a subdued group for the first few days, but our headmaster had returned and word got around that he was far from pleased with the way the matter had been handled and felt it should all have been dealt with in a less dramatic way. The matter faded into the past and other things occupied our minds. Pressure was put on us to study hard and our futures became a matter of concern. Gary would take his entrance exams for Oxford and, with the help of a casual meeting with the mother of the provost in Corpus Christi quad, where they chatted about squirrels, he gained a place at that college and would go on to fulfil his parents' ambitions to the full. For his twenty-first birthday I bought him a chrome squirrel to sit on the radiator cap of Ava and after his death was told that it had been one of his most prized possessions and would be handed on to his newly adopted son.

The rest of us ploughed on with our studies. My subjects by now were botany, zoology and chemistry, all subjects I disliked, but had been persuaded into prior to entering the sixth form. Why did I agree, rather than specialising in English literature and the other arts, all subjects I had a talent for and secretly longed to study? Probably because Gary was studying the same subjects one year ahead and was always ready to help me write the necessary essays. It was another way to spend more time together.

Still, I was growing up and beginning to appreciate the value of an extended education and I did make up my mind to try hard to settle down and study once I entered the sixth form. Alas my school record by then was hardly exemplary and I must have had a reputation as an unreliable and somewhat rebellious student and looking back over some of the more recent events in which I had been involved I had to admit that I had hardly emerged as a star pupil, though there were some positive bits.

Earlier, and one year prior to taking O levels and before entering the sixth form, our class had dropped English literature as one of its subjects. As this was the one thing at which I excelled I was considerably put out and eventually found the courage to approach the headmistress about it. For once she appeared to be sympathetic and promised to talk to the headmaster. They came up with the compromise that I should study for mock O level English literature on my own, and if my results were good, they would reconsider the situation. So with help from Mr Taylor, the English teacher and my form master for that year, I set about doing just this. When the results finally came out I was top of all the year, beating even Fox who was our token swot and usually came top in everything. The powers that be kept their promise and I was transferred to the other class where I studied hard and long, took the exam and, to everyone's amazement, failed. Even the headmistress was surprised, while I was bitterly disappointed, especially as they would not let me sit it again in the September. My other results were OK – good enough for me to pass into the sixth form anyhow. We all passed at O level chemistry, something not entirely unconnected with the fact that Mr. Poole had made an extremely accurate prediction of what exactly would appear on the examination paper. For those of us rather dodgy in this subject it had been a real blessing, for all we had to do was revise the things in his breakdown and even Belfield managed this.

'All I'm doing is giving you a chance,' he said. 'Academically, they'll sort you out later.' Unconventional to say the least but I've always admired him for it.

I failed Maths of course, and in fact was to fail it three times in all. French I passed at the second go, on Friday 13th I seem to remember. The French mistress was in a state of total shock for a week though she had the grace to congratulate me.

Miss Wheeler had taken over our French classes and she was a superb teacher, but she had the reputation of being something of a tyrant. She was a chapel lay preacher, and a strict disciplinarian. A small round figure, with her hair scraped back into a tight bun, she commanded our respect. French was hated by most of us then for none of us could see any reason for speaking it but she hammered it into us anyway, a fact for which I have always been grateful. She was also the star at the centre of one of our more memorable lessons. Usually she made us work hard and our forty minutes with her were not regarded as likely to be a bundle of fun, but there is one that stands out and makes me laugh at the horror of it even to this day. We always sat alphabetically in class, irrespective of gender, and it was my misfortune to sit next to Belfield and in front of Jones, the two bad boys of our year. Their speciality was flicking ink pellets when no one was looking, and also feeding me with Polo mints in the certain knowledge that they always made me sneeze repeatedly.

Of course it was totally forbidden to eat in class, except that is, for some rather strange, Horlicks-tasting tablets which the government in its wisdom took to issuing daily in place of the usual quarter-pint of milk. These were something of a success with us for they had to be sucked slowly and the regulation twenty tablets could not possibly be consumed in the break and therefore these had to be eaten during lessons. This of course opened the way for all sorts of other things to be eaten during lessons too, hence the Polo mints.

This particular French lesson must have taken place in the spring for the classroom was full of spring flowers, distributed in an assortment of vases, about the room. One particular vase of daffodils was balanced, rather precariously, on the little ledge above the blackboard where Miss Wheeler stood writing. The lesson was in full swing when Jones took it upon himself to launch an ink pellet. His rubber band must have been less than reliable for the pellet went badly adrift and hit the vase balanced above the blackboard. It was a direct hit, and the vase, water and flowers descended rapidly on to Miss Wheeler's head. She stood there, daffodils on head, water running down her face, the vase in pieces at her feet, and her facial expression did not change. The class sat transfixed, not daring to laugh, but my stomach was in knots. Slowly she removed the flowers, collecting them into a bunch, and then, taking a handkerchief from her pocket, she dabbed her face dry. She then sent Jones for a mop and bucket (she must have known) and me to fill a new vase with water. Alas, the only vase not in use was a huge mauve and grey Victorian thing far too large for the flowers. They sat in it, their heads poking miserably over the top. She took this vase and balanced it back above the blackboard in the same place as the other one and where the very sight of it kept our nerves on edge. Not a word was said on the subject as we struggled desperately to cope with the rest of the lesson. I have never been so glad to hear the bell.

In the months ahead Gary went on to do well in his A and S levels, and for some reason I still have his certificates. Mrs Hampson's actions were justified and Gary would eventually go up to Oxford on a scholarship and that glorious life of the Oxford undergraduate, while I struggled on in my school uniform in the sixth-form. We wrote, of course, and I think there was the occasional phone call and then, joy of joys, I was invited down for Eights Week. I rushed out and bought a highly unsuitable and far too tight dress and jacket from Coles. It would have been perfect for a married lady of forty and definitely required a hat.

Oxford was everything I had ever imagined and it more than lived up to the highly romantic image I had culled eagerly from the books taken from the Hathersage Village Library. Later, when I was working at the Oxford Playhouse I heard Frank Hauser say that he had always felt a total misfit until he went to university and found whole groups of people there with the same interests as himself and he began to realise that he was not the freak he had considered himself to be for so many years. Although only a visitor, it was to be the same for me.

We had such fun that week, lolling in punts and falling in the water, dancing until dawn, strolling among the 'dreaming spires' and all the other things you read about. I met Gary's new friends of course, David and Pete, Eric and Taffy and I fell half in love or in love with all of them. Most were destined for personal success of one sort or another, my favourite for a long time being Taffy who came down from Oxford with a double first in classics and then went on to handle the Tampax advertising account. Three became physicians or surgeons, with one going into research and becoming highly influential in the treatment of cancer. Pete would one day marry my inky twin, Carol and join the BBC as a producer; and we all stayed close for a number of years. But most of these people pop in and out of the following pages and I am rushing ahead slightly.

That weekend was just a taste of others that were to come, but it gave me a glimpse of a privileged society and a way of life that had been going on for generations. None of our group would have fitted in at Brideshead exactly, but they opened doors for me and changed my thinking for ever. There was such energy there, all things seemed possible and most were, even for those of us who were only visiting. To sit up until the early hours of the morning discussing politics, art and theatre, philosophy and literature with other people equally passionate about these subjects and keen to share their knowledge of the latest avant-garde films from Sweden and France was heady stuff indeed. We felt we belonged to the intellectual elite and if it all went slightly to our heads, well, perhaps it wasn't too surprising. The enchanted hours passed all too quickly and I soon found myself travelling back to Sheffield and the impending Advanced level exams. The inappropriate dress and jacket were consigned to the back of the wardrobe and never worn again. I re-adopted my schoolgirl persona and wished I had worked harder so that I could join Gary at Oxford.

In the meantime Hathersage post office suffered a surge in letters from Oxford, for Pete began to write to me regularly too, in fact far more regularly than Gary and the Life Police became increasingly curious. Pete came from Ilford and was far more original than most of Gary's friends. He was studying history and came close to getting a first. Unlike Gary, who had to work hard to achieve success, it seemed to come easily to Pete. He had a razor-sharp mind, used words like daggers and roamed at ease between Socrates and Sophocles. He was like no one I had ever met before and we had quickly formed an alliance. He wrote wonderful, funny letters, creating characters called Dreebs and Krids – his alter egos or characters from some imaginary subterranean kingdom – he related their stories in detail, often illustrating them with drawings I thought excellent. Of course I still have a bundle of them, tied up with the lace of a tennis shoe in lieu of the red ribbon I thought to be hardly appropriate. He professed to have fallen in love with me and I, flattered by it all, thought myself a little in love too.

At home for the summer holidays, I started to receive phone calls on the post office telephone and the antennae of the Life Police were fully alerted. Then one day Pete walked up our garden path and completely ruined my mother's afternoon in the garden. On his way to the Edinburgh Festival, he had come to collect me, he said, having hitch-hiked from London. His plan was to stay the night with me and we would leave the next day and carry on hitch-hiking to Edinburgh.

There was outrage in our small kitchen. Poor Pete! I think he was given a cup of tea and a biscuit before he was sent back to the A1. I desperately wanted to go with him, but my experiences in Cornwall and nineteen years under my mother's thumb made a confrontational rebellion out of the question. I watched as Pete retraced his steps down the garden path and sat regretting my lack of courage for the rest of the summer. His letters arrived thick and fast, revealing details of his evenings spent working with the Oxford University Drama group and sharing beers with Jonathan Miller, Alan Bennett, Peter Cook and Dudley Moore – names only at first but they were already making news in the Arts pages of all the newspapers. Later I was to work with them all but at the time it seemed like an opportunity missed for ever. And maybe in some ways it was. I longed to be up in Edinburgh but Pete's visit had done nothing to impress my mother to his suitability as a suitor and the arrival of a badly wrapped and decaying haggis from Scotland only completed his absolute fall from grace.

Later that summer the Advanced Level exam results came out and my future hung briefly in the balance. The sixth forms at Lady Manners were small in those days, only fourteen or fifteen pupils each year and the academic standard was high. The year I left school I think eight students went on to Oxford or Cambridge, four to various London colleges, two to provincial universities. As for me, I finally went to the University of London Goldsmiths' College. But first I had to spend the rest of the summer working in Sheffield with one of the top insurance companies of the time.

My memory of these few months is a little hazy. I know I had applied to Bristol University – to study, for some bizarre and unfathomable reason – psychology. I had been for an interview and gained a place there subject to certain grades in my exam results but I didn't quite achieve these grades and so the place was not forthcoming. I applied to do a third year at school but was firmly rejected. Thus it was that the eminently respectable and highly boring job at the insurance company was found and applied for and my life seemed to go into the doldrums. But I secretly wanted to be an actress and somewhere around this time I took to walking around Sheffield with a copy of *The Stage* under my arm, pondering the idea of applying for a place at RADA. I think this idea must have been germinating for a long time for I had stolen away from the hotel on one of our overnight stays in London, found my way to Gower Street and gazed in awe at the rather unimposing door of the Royal Academy of Dramatic Art expecting to bump into Lawrence Olivier as I turned to walk away. Derbyshire County Council encouraged anything to do with the Arts and I had spoken to their senior representative several times about the possibility of going to Drama School. He had been most encouraging but not a great deal of practical help, nevertheless I had somehow managed to secure an audition in London; the only problem still remaining was that of escaping the clutches of the Life Police. I had to plot my weekend away with care.

I had made a friend of the sister of one of the boys at school and had spent several happy weekends at their home over the years, for she had liberal parents and an extremely good-looking older brother. They lived in a beautiful old stone house and the family tended to throw parties at the drop of a hat. What more could a teenager want? Carol, the second Carol in my life, had recently gone to live and work in London, and so I contacted her and secured a place on the floor of her flat for the two nights. This also provided me with my excuse to go to London. The Life Police were less than enthusiastic but as I was now technically working there was little they could do about it. So, on the appropriate date, audition pieces ready, I set off more or less prepared to take London by storm. The audition went, but I don't now remember whether I thought it had gone well or not. On the Saturday night we went to a club, which seemed to me to be both exotic and glamorous. It was in a little slip road off Regent Street and not far from Piccadilly Circus and I felt it to be rather risqué and not a little dangerous. In fact it was. I went home and told my mother all the details of my exciting weekend and a week later saw the club exposed in the *News of the World* as a den of vice and drugs!

The results of the audition were not quite what I had wanted, I got a place but not the scholarship I had hoped for, and naïve as I was, I couldn't see myself working all hours of the day and night in order to pay the tuition fees. Later I found out that by gaining a place I was eligible for a full university grant – for Derbyshire County was one of the few who accepted RADA as a legitimate place of further education – but by the time I found out all this, it was far too late. So the letter from Goldsmiths' College, when it finally came in late September, seemed like a reprieve from a life of penal servitude and I grabbed the opportunity with both hands. London was suddenly within my grasp. I think my parents were pleased too, though they never actually said so. With that letter, all things became possible again and it was with great relief that I said goodbye to the eminently respectable insurance company and, largely, to Sheffield itself.

We did pay it one last, momentous visit, my mother and I. It seemed we had to buy 'one or two essential things', mainly underwear I guessed, correctly, as it turned out. It was then that my mother surprised me as never before by producing a large wad of notes from her bag and proceeding to take me on a spending spree of unprecedented proportions, whispering the equally surprising caveat, 'Don't tell your father.' When we eventually caught the bus back from Sheffield to Hathersage we were laden with packages containing beautiful things. Several days later we packed an enormous trunk with what seemed like all my worldly possessions and sent it off to London. Three days after that I followed behind it. The rest of my life had finally begun.

That letter from Goldsmiths' opened a door on the rest of the world and a way of life that was to prove exhilarating, exciting, heartbreaking, demanding and ultimately rewarding. I quite literally stepped through it to freedom. As I took my seat on the British Railways service to St Pancras, I started the journey away from Hathersage and I was never to belong there so completely again.

Chapter Five

As the train sped southwards, leaving behind all that was familiar, I was aware of a growing feeling of excitement. Anne Ibbotson from a small village in Derbyshire slipped slowly into the past and I decided to create a new persona. In my suitcase was a letter from my so-called 'house mother'. It seemed she was supposed to introduce me to life at the college and generally be responsible for me during the first few weeks of the new term. But her letter had been less than enthusiastic about my arrival and I had decided largely to ignore her and go my own way. We had to be in the hall of residence by 7.00p.m but I had caught an early train from Sheffield and as it sped through the outskirts of London I found myself with a large part of the day still stretching ahead.

As the Eurostar terminus, St Pancras may have been restored to its former grandeur, but in the days of the steam engine it still had the sort of romance about it that only belonged to the great Victorian railway stations. Certainly that day as I walked down the platform to the ticket barrier, I thought it one of the most exciting places I had ever been. The steam from the now quiet engine hissed its way across the platform and drifted in ribbons to the street outside. The original colours in the station had become drab, but they still had a sort of beauty, the blacks and greys, the sunlight fighting to shine through the grimy glass ceilings and casting a greenish tinge across the shadowed reaches of the platforms. I let the other passengers leave and walked slowly out of the cathedral-like building, savouring these few moments on my own before I walked down the steps and out into the busy street. I had been to London before, of course, but this time everything seemed heightened – the colours, the noise, and the smells. The memories of other visits faded and I created a whole new set for myself alone. I realised that at that moment no one who knew me had the slightest idea where I was. The world was mine, I could go anywhere, do anything. I was free, so I turned and walked down the steps to the tube and, laden with various bits of last-minute luggage, entered a hot, noisy, carriage and headed for Victoria! I was almost on the platform for my south London connection when rebellion set in and I entered the nearest hairdressers. Nearly two hours later I emerged, my head covered in auburn curls, held in place by a 1920's style headband. Having got so far it seemed silly to stop there and so I investigated a row of shops in a nearby street. I came out from there with packages this time and made my way to the station's toilets. The young lady who finally boarded the train for Brockley bore little resemblance to the one who had waited impatiently on Hathersage station only a few short hours before. In one of the shops I had found a black dirndl skirt with huge patch pockets and a blue-and-white-striped shirt blouse. On my feet I wore the T-strap shoes I had travelled in. Thus attired, and clutching a college-banned transistor radio, I marched up the road and into the hall of residence just as the local church clock struck seven. Inside I was shaking but I was subsequently to learn that my arrival had caused something of a sensation, and had definitely set me apart from the rest of the students. No bad thing, as I was quickly to discover.

My first impressions of the house that was to be my home for the next year were hardly edifying. I don't know what I expected, but the building was a large part-converted villa that greatly resembled a seaside boarding house. In charge was a retired university lecturer from Oxford, an imposing figure on our first meeting, but she turned out to be more broadminded and understanding than she looked and the rules were considerably more relaxed than those laid down by the Life Police. This was my first stab at communal living and I was highly nervous at the thought of sharing a bedroom. Still, I overcame my fears and found myself busy assessing my fellow students and wondering what, if any, was to be my role among them. We ate in college before being shown to our rooms where, attempting to undress without revealing an inch of unnecessary flesh in true Ibbotson tradition, I slipped into my pyjamas, crawled into my designated bed and fell asleep faster than I thought possible.

The first few days were a blur of introductions to college activities all aimed at providing us with an exciting few years in academia – or so it seemed to me anyhow. With London apparently at my feet and Gary, Pete and their friends suddenly more accessible in Oxford, I found myself contemplating a range of possibilities hitherto undreamed of. My new image paid dividends, for during the first few days at Goldsmiths' people kept their distance from me and I was able to sort out my feelings and reactions before I dived into all that was on offer. What I hadn't realised was that everyone else was feeling as nervous as I was, but they rushed into friendships and joined societies without bothering to think too carefully. Later some spent weeks trying to get away from clinging violets while others found themselves co-opted on to the committee of a fading poetry society when they had only joined because they thought it would look good on their college record.

I found to my delight that the College had an Art School upstairs and a thriving drama department. I joined the drama group and the fencing society and the sailing club. Then, as I went about collecting all the literature for my biology course I realised that I was like a fish out of water in the science department. To mix my metaphors hopelessly, the chickens were coming home to roost. Something had to be done. I plucked up all my courage and went to see the dean. He was courteous and listened carefully as I pleaded to switch to the English course.

'But your background reading?' he queried.

So I started to talk about the classics and that concept of them as 'racy' novels given to me by my Grandmother, and slowly I saw his attitude change.

'When you walked in here,' he said, 'I had every intention of turning down your request, but now that I have talked to you I accept totally that you are on the wrong course. You will have to work hard on your background reading but I believe you'll do that, I'll arrange for you to change courses on Monday. Good luck! As I walked down the corridor away from the dean's office I was three feet off thc ground and rising and I rushed out to buy a copy of Dylan Thomas to celebrate.

In the next few weeks I discovered how to enjoy studying and for the first time to approach learning as pleasure. I resolved that this was the way it was going to be from now on and so it was. Life became fun and I started to make new friends and began to find a role for myself amongst them, even a new identity. I simply bounced through the days that first year, skipping minor lectures to go to art exhibitions and chatting up the commissionaires who still manned the entrances to the theatres. Mostly these were kind but lonely old men who welcomed the chance of a chat over a cup of tea, and they were soon smuggling me into matinée performances free of charge. This was something I didn't solicit but nevertheless it was welcome, for it helped to stretch the budget a little further as money was tight. It was for most of us, so it didn't really cause too many problems.

I was fairly lucky in my room-mates too, though one was serious, the studious type, and liked to go to bed early, the other one, Lorna, was more adventurous. A couple of years older than the rest of us and engaged to be married, she was still determined to make the most of her college years. Between us we began to drive the other inhabitant mad. The first source of irritation appeared to be my radio. Transistors were banned in college hostels but I had walked openly into the hall of residence with mine and no one had said anything. So of course it got used, mostly late at night and very softly but always to the accompaniment of many sighs and much tossing from the third bed. The other source of annoyance was the phone calls from Lorna's fiancé. Often coming through around the eleven o'clock deadline, they again found our unhappy room-mate usually in bed and half asleep. Originally we had all been studying biology, and I think she had envisaged cosy evenings all working together on the same essay, but of course I had messed all that up too. This would never have happened anyway, of course, for Lorna and I much preferred to gossip away and leave college work to the last moment. So one day our room-mate announced she was moving out, to the relief of all concerned.

I slightly envied Lorna her elevated status as 'engaged woman' and so throughout that first year I wrote long, loving letters to Gary and Pete in Oxford. At first they and their friends came down to London quite regularly and were unusually warmly welcomed by the head of hall. The Oxford link formed a bridge, and they were unfailingly polite and courteous. I went up to Oxford too, delighting once again, in the atmosphere of the university and finding it easy to write my overdue essays sitting on the floor of Gary's room or in one of the libraries.

Only a few days ago I found a cache of letters from that time. They had been lying forgotten in that old tin trunk and I was amazed at the revealing and tantalising glimpse they gave of those halcyon days. Oh, how in love with being in love we were then. We agonised over our feelings and our futures, together or apart, but love was all and our relationships rarely became affairs. Eventually we all began to move on and broken hearts recovered and friendships formed, friendships so strong that they have never been really broken, though time has slackened the ties. These letters covered Gary's first year at Oxford and carried on right through to my leaving Goldsmiths'. There was also news of old school friends, many of whom seemed to have settled for early marriage and children. Lesley, once a brief love of Gary's life and a girl who at school had seemed seriously academic had done just this; the dreaded Mavis ended up in Borneo, also married and with children, but not before she had been involved with David, one of Gary's Oxford friends. Gary's letters ranged from calling me 'old girl' to 'darling' and with a certain predictability he fell in love with me just as I apparently fell out of love with him.

Rather to my surprise I found myself considerably more popular at college than I ever had been at school and though I still thought of Pete and Gary as the two rivals for the role of my boyfriend, it probably didn't stop me from indulging in a few innocent flirtations with some of the male students. This had rather unexpected results and during the time I was at Goldsmiths' various prospective spouses were to find themselves 'just passing through' a tiny village situated in a remote and difficult to reach part of Derbyshire. Once there they would then find themselves the recipients of a biscuit, a cup of tea and a cold reception from the Life Police who must have been bewildered by this strange and varied procession and wondered what on earth their daughter was really getting up to in London. But it was all so innocent then and, kept at bay by the terrible and shameful consequences of an unwanted pregnancy, sex barely raised its head. So we continued to fall in and out of love, examining in detail our feelings or lack of them, and embracing our own particular angst as we embraced Sartre, Kierkegaard, T.S Eliot, Dylan Thomas, every note of music from Ella Fitzgerald to every obscure Elizabethan quartet and, in my case, every theatre production in or around the West End. We bought paperback editions of Robert Carrier and learned to cook. We occasionally drank too much, smoked exotic cigarettes, dressed as bizarrely as we dared and laughed and suffered in equal proportions. Oh, but it was good to be alive!

Meanwhile Gary and I came to accept that our relationship was one of those becoming more a friendship than a love affair and Pete's reception in Hathersage had turned out to be something of a setback for Pete and me too, though we still wrote long, ardent letters full of unfulfilled desire. Money was always a problem for us and romantic meetings were rare, I thus found myself rather more footloose and fancy free than I had intended and London appeared to be full of interesting and attractive young men. Eventually our relationship floundered through lack of opportunity and not long after this he met Carol, my ex-inky twin, and they quickly became an item.

My erstwhile 'inky twin' was, by then, also in London at university and one evening I met up with a group of her friends and went to the Freemasons Arms in Downshire Hill in Hampstead, I little realising at the time that this, my first pub in London, was to become my local for over twenty years. I met Robin that evening; tall, dashing, rich and highly intelligent he seemed the epitome of every girl's secret dream. We got on well, but alas he remained a dream and soon faded from the scene. Still I was beginning to wake up to some of the possibilities waiting in this new life of mine and Jones and Belfield, ink pellets and Polo mints were relegated firmly to the past while even Oxford lost some of its allure.

Next to appear, at a party I seem to remember, was an art student from the Slade, David by name. He was painfully thin, dressed all in black and given to agonising over Sartre and the Existentialists. I thought him wonderful and felt life had taken on yet another dimension. Then he told me that we could not go on seeing one another for I made him laugh too much and he could only paint when he was suffering. Heartbroken I again retired from the lists for a while and allowed life at college to fill my time. I also was determined to remain a virgin, something that in retrospect may have affected David's decision over our future.

I think it was Lorna who suggested we get a part-time job, and accordingly we went to work in Selfridges in the Food Hall every Saturday morning. Even that came under the heading of 'fun' for we were soon serving famous actresses and politicians and the money was certainly useful. Only the early rising was a problem.

I had grown up in Derbyshire more or less untouched by racial prejudice. When I had gazed in astonishment at my first black man, my mother had gently explained that he came from a distant country where the sun shone all the time and was very hot, so he was really only sunburnt. After my own torturous hours in the sun trying to shed my pallor I was supremely envious of the man's deep rich brown and accepted the explanation completely. And so it was something of a shock to discover that many of the Oxford Street shops operated a covert system of racial discrimination. Even the black superstars from America found it difficult to open any sort of an account in them. Many years later I was to find the same bigotry firmly entrenched in the licensing trade. I was incredulous at first and hated the system but there was little I could do to change it. I settled for being especially sweet to the unlucky customers and hoped they didn't realise what was happening, though I suspect they did.

So the college scene continued to get better and better, and by the time I went back to Derbyshire for the second Christmas I was very much the pushy student, complete with duffle coat and London University scarf. It was about then that I began to realise that Angela and our old group had been getting on with their lives just as I had with mine. Angela had started going out with David and was all but engaged to him. One or two of the others had also grouped into serious pairs, and although I was welcomed, all the dramatic accounts of events and excitements I had again saved up to tell them fell upon stony ground and I soon stopped talking and settled for listening instead.

There was a village dance in the Memorial Hall just before Christmas, so I added a pair of black stockings to my still favoured London-debut arrival ensemble and made my entrance. There was an audible gasp and it seemed that all heads turned in my direction. I held my ground and loved it. Was it during this dance or another, earlier, one that I went with friends to the pub, had one drink and ended up singing with the band? All very daring, for pubs were still high on the list of no-go areas issued by the Life Police, but it was fun at the time. And then maybe it was more than one drink for I seem to remember waking early with a slight hangover. As I walked into the kitchen my mother greeted me with the words, 'And what do you think you were doing, singing with the band last night?' Proof, as if I needed it, that a village grapevine is more efficient than the telephone – for we still didn't have one. Indeed, it was privations like this which, many years later, made it possible for me to survive on a small Greek island.

My love of the village and the moors still held sway and the holidays always passed quickly until it was time to head south again; and by now it was no eager fresher who stood regularly on the Hathersage platform, but a slightly world weary and all knowing undergraduate and the burgeoning gap between me and my Hathersage friends continued to get wider. There were growing differences at home too; even that Christmas had been something of a disaster. With my hard-earned cash from Selfridges, I had bought a bottle of wine, sweet Sauterne because I thought my mother would like it, but at the Christmas dinner table, proudly produced and opened, it sat rejected. I swallowed down a small glass laced with tears of disappointment.

London was becoming increasingly familiar to me, and, once there, my world always seemed to settle quickly back on to its axis. Friendships were renewed and I was soon in the West End once more, drinking tea in dark stage-door cubby holes and slipping into already darkened theatres as the curtain rose and actors made their first entrances. It was an exciting time for the British theatre, those first years I was in London. Look Back in

Anger had brought a sea change which was attracting worldwide attention. Almost every week there was a new first night and it was a marvellous time to be going to the theatre. I still have the programmes to prove it, two plastic bags filled with a thousand memories, some of never-to-be-repeated performances such as that of Peter O'Toole in *Baal*, of Patrick McGoohan in *Brand* and of the whole, rebellious cast in *The Long, The Short and The Tall*. Some actors were already reaching the peak of their careers, others, now famous, were taking their first supporting roles and beginning to attract the attention of the critics. While a whole wave of new drama was thus already exploding in the West End there was also Joan Littlewood, working out in Stratford East, who made long journeys on the tube well worth while.

To write about those days now would be to write another book for there was such excitement in the air, that whether I was queuing at the Royal Court (no friendly Doorman there) or watching the magnificent swish of the crimson curtains at Covent Garden there was never any other place I wanted to be at that moment in time. I began to take all these privileges more and more for granted and I was increasingly aware of how much I wanted to become part of it all, on stage that is, not sitting in the audience.

The college drama group had seemed the obvious place to start, so I had got heavily involved and played a minor role in that first summer's major production. I also took to walking around in an orange cloak, with a stuffed toy koala bear on the end of a green lead. Later I added a Red Riding Hood-style cloak that swished beautifully and was on permanent loan from the college theatrical-costume store, and I knitted a long, black tube with sleeves and posed, serious and intense, for a photo at a poetry reading. To complete the image I hugged my copy of T.S Eliot's collected poems to me like a child hugs a doll, and quoted large chunks of *The Waste Land* at every opportunity. Of course there were lighter pleasures too – the half pints of bitter sipped slowly over an hour at lunchtime, and the cigarettes bought on a Saturday and expected to last all week – a packet of ten Gold Leaf at first I seem to remember, and later twenty Balkan Sobranie, the coloured papers of which were carefully matched to my wardrobe. And then the discovery of those long cigarettes from Manila that were mostly cardboard with a little sweet-smelling tobacco at one end. Oh, how we tried to be different, to stand out from the crowd, but in doing so simply succeeded in becoming part of another one.

As one of the colleges of London University, Goldsmiths' had access to all the student groups and activities within the whole university, so the Students' Union just down the road from the much yearned for RADA became a useful base in the West End. To be truthful I had found it all a little overwhelming at first, as I pursued my policy of 'alone is best' and never thought to do very much in a group, eventually though I became friends with another student called Dawn and sometimes we went out together. Central London was a delightful place to be then and we enjoyed it to the full. Our lectures were not compulsory and few of the so-called 'fringe' subjects interested me enough to command my attendance. We cheated British Railways of many fares by not buying a ticket and simply walking off the train at London Bridge claiming we were changing platforms for Waterloo. We then descended to the tube or simply walked across the bridge itself. Did the ticket collectors know? I think so, for they often wore a knowing smile or gave us a conspiratorial wink as we passed and we all wore our college scarves and often travelled in groups. We did the other usual student things too – took part in CND marches and others for causes I no longer remember. We argued with people on boxes at Speakers' Corner in Hyde Park, spent long hours in Soho coffee bars, visited museums and art galleries and one weekend Dawn and I became pavement artists for two days to raise money for World University Students (WUS). We mounted rather simplistic paintings on cardboard and propped them up along the railings outside the National Portrait Gallery and collected a surprising amount of money. People stopped to chat and amused policemen strolled by and asked us how we were doing. Students were indulged then and people often bought us those coffees in Soho, or a beer when we sat in one of the old pubs in the Old Kent Road.

I loved these pubs on a Saturday night. They were always packed and the evening usually ended with a sing-along as the atmosphere grew heavy with smoke and the old grannies tottered slightly and changed their tipple from stout to 'a drop of the gin'. I felt remarkably comfortable there, though I had no idea that my birthplace was within walking distance of where I sat. In fact my adoption, although always at the back of my mind, played little part in my new life, and perhaps for the first time I had a sense of being completely involved in something bigger than myself and enjoying every minute of it.

There was plenty of opportunity for a social life within the college too and every year the Art School upstairs threw a pre

Christmas fancy dress ball. The first year I was there it took place on a bitterly cold evening and at first I had no intention of going for I had an essay to write, long overdue as usual. But Lorna persuaded me that I should go and so the essay was postponed yet again and together we concocted a rather dashing outfit of ruched petticoat, strapless bra, black stockings and suspenders and the ever present T-strap shoes. Lorna's long evening gloves and a rose on a velvet band at my throat completed the ensemble and off I went, freezing under the Red Riding Hood cloak. It was a great night, a live jazz band and cheap drinks kept us on a 'high' all evening and I danced most of the night away. Anne Kilcoyne and Freddie, her boyfriend, were resplendent in their pyjamas – Anne's baby doll and rather see-through, Freddie's the more conventional, striped variety. There were a few pirates and ghosts and all the usual costumes you can make out of a sheet and a multitude of safety pins. One or two had hired something more exotic, but on the whole I felt good in my outfit and totally forgot the waiting essay.

A few weeks later, at home with her parents, Anne Kilcoyne was sent out for fish and chips. She handed them, still wrapped in newspaper, to her mother and went into the dining-room. About two minutes later her mother rushed in, waving the greasy centre pages of an old copy of the *News of the World* in which a full length photo of Anne and Freddie in their pyjamas, drinks glasses in hand, had caught her attention. Accompanying the photo was a lurid headline which added to the parental distress and the next few days, Anne said later, were alarmingly uncomfortable.

Gary and I had agreed that we should both enjoy our student days to the full but there were still occasional trips to Oxford and, Pete notwithstanding, we went to the Oxford and Cambridge rugby match together and afterwards to the Twickers Ball. (I still have the ticket), but by the time of the May Ball in Oxford, he had found someone else to take and I was not invited, much to my disappointment. Still there were other things to look forward to.

By the end of that first summer term my friendship with Dawn had become a close one. She was in the same hall of residence, but a year ahead of me. An ash blonde with a peaches-and-cream complexion, she was a natural beauty and made me feel gauche and clumsy, but we got on well. From somewhere came the idea of hitchhiking on the Continent during the long summer holidays. In those days hitchhiking was quite safe and an accepted way for students to travel. I leapt at the chance without stopping to work out the logistics of the situation, and so we poured over maps and discussed train timetables *ad nauseum*. That I didn't possess a passport was a drawback that didn't actually occur to me until I was back in Derbyshire for the early weeks of the holidays and earning some money by working at a local garage.

This garage, near Bamford, had for some time been one of the mainstays of my holiday occupations. I was employed as a petrol-pump attendant and had first worked there while I was still at school. I was busy at the pumps the day after passing my driving test when they suddenly asked me if I had a driving licence. 'Yes.' I replied proudly. 'Good,' they rejoined. 'Take that car, drive it to Derby, pick up a Hillman they have there and bring it back.' The car in question was a Mini, parked inoffensively on the forecourt. Without thinking too much about the fact that I had not driven on main roads alone before (we did not have a car) and I only had the vaguest idea how to get to Derby, I nevertheless set off fearlessly towards my destination. Somehow or other I got there safely, my confidence growing with the passing miles and the sighting of a signpost to Derby. When I finally reached the garage they signed my receipt and pointed to the Hillman. It was at the back of the main depot, parked tightly against the back wall and surrounded by other new and expensive cars. 'Just edge it out, they said, and walked away. So, heart in mouth, I did just that and then set off back. Just before Grindleford, about five miles from home, the light began to fade but I searched for the switch that operated the car lights in vain. So I ended up driving fast behind a Jaguar and using his headlights until I was safely back. From then on I enjoyed driving more and more and became committed to the notion that leaping into the deep end before discovering whether or not I could swim suited my temperament. I did a lot of driving for that garage and slowly built up my confidence until I considered myself a good driver. And I never have lost my love of speed, or indeed my love of the open road.

But now my holiday with Dawn grew ever closer. Dawn wrote excited letters from Reading and as the days sped by the question of my passport became more and more pressing. Finally I broached the subject with the Life Police. As this involved a request for my birth certificate it could turn out to be a potentially tricky moment, even so it had to be done. In the event it proved comparatively easy. There was some initial opposition to the idea of 'going abroad' and my father pointed out that, according to the *Daily Mirror*, if Paris was on the agenda then a cup of tea on the Champs Elysées was going to cost me most of my summer earnings. But finally the objectionable certificate of adoption was produced without comment, the necessary forms filled in and all sent off – only to be returned. Apparently, the large red, stamped certificate of adoption was no longer valid. A new, shortened version of all such documents had been introduced in order to save we adopted and illegitimate children embarrassment. But, in order to obtain this, we had to wade through bureaucracy and suffer – a large amount of embarrassment. Anyhow, by the time this new, shortened version arrived things were getting desperate. But, to my astonishment, help was forthcoming, for my father paid for me to go to Liverpool, where passports were issued on the spot, and my mother suddenly started sewing an alarming variety of lightweight nightdresses and sun tops. And so it came to pass that on the appointed day I was waved off by a surprisingly supportive Life Police, and I left for London suitably equipped with the new passport and a totally inappropriate wardrobe. The adventure had begun.

Few memories remain of the journey until we arrived at Amiens in the middle of the night. Then suddenly I can hear the clashing of the carriage couplings and the shouting of the porter and the engine driver, the French voices sounding strange and exotic in the warm night air. The smells too, Gauloise and garlic, still so evocative of a country I was to fall in love with and visit again and again, convinced that one day I would live there, maybe even marry a Frenchman. But I rush ahead. That night Dawn and I sat sleepless in the carriage as it sped onwards to the dream that was Paris.

Arriving at the Gâre du Nord early in the morning, the sense of excitement continued, moderated perhaps by a touch of fear as we suddenly realised what we had done. Surprisingly, Dawn took the initiative and produced a list of youth hostels near the centre of the town. We sorted out the Metro and found ourselves in a less than glamorous area of Paris where we were lucky to get two beds. The 10.00 p.m. curfew was carefully explained to us and then we were shown how to climb in over the wall once this deadline had been reached and the front gates closed. Suddenly things started to be fun; feeling considerably reassured we dumped our bags and set off for the Paris experience.

I have visited this magical city so many times now that it is impossible to recollect where we went and what we saw on this first visit, but the impressions made then were never to change. That it was beautiful was not in dispute, but there was for me at that time and on every subsequent visit something about the city that is pure delight. They say New York is a fast and fun city (though I think Athens is faster), but Paris, has an energy like nowhere and a sense of style and elegance all its own. But many of these impressions were to come later, for the moment we were two excited, first-time tourists, with very little money and an enormous appetite for experience.

We gazed enchanted at the wide avenues, the superb buildings and the stylish shops of the Right Bank, then we went in search of Sartre and some of the literary images so fresh in our minds from those late night conversations in London and Oxford. I like to think we actually glimpsed Sartre and Simone de Beauvoir, but it may have been later. Anyhow, for two days our intellectual and emotional needs were satisfied, though not so much our material ones, for Paris was expensive and if our money was to last, then eating out would have to become a luxury. So we hit the supermarkets and, along with bread and cheese, attempted successfully to smuggle a bottle of white wine into the YWCA, thus defying the basic rule of the whole organisation. Later that evening, giggling at our audacity, we opened it, only to discover that we had bought an excellent bottle of sparkling water.

But Paris was too expensive for us by far and so, on the third day, we took ourselves to the outskirts and began hitchhiking. Again the memories are patchy. My O level French coped with most situations and improved as the days passed. Everywhere we were treated with kindness and generosity, with people going kilometres out of their way to deliver us to the youth hostel doors. Sometimes they bought us meals en route, nearly always we got out of the car with fruit and chocolate, and every evening there was the youth hostel and the easygoing companionship of other young people from a wide range of countries. Once we even met a recent escapee from East Berlin.

So we basked in all this warmth and friendship and our finances improved alongside the generosity. But there were other moments that stand out from this background of goodwill, like the moment I discovered Dawn's reluctance to thumb a lift. Dawn had insisted that we walk while hitching and would not allow us to sit at the side of the road like everyone else, so we walked in single file. It had also been decreed that the person behind did the thumbing, and that we took it in turns to walk behind. Only after several days on the road did I discover that when it was her turn to walk behind she was simply not thumbing. Of course, this had slowed our progress considerably and I was exceedingly put out by the discovery. So we had our first row. I don't know that it was properly resolved but Dawn did start thumbing and I had discovered that her sensibilities were a whole lot finer than mine, a fact that lead to incident number two.

The hitchhiking was going well and we soon found ourselves in Switzerland, sitting by Lake Lucerne considering our options for the night. Dawn consulted her Youth Hostel Association book and discovered there was a hostel on top of a nearby mountain. Romanticism took over and she began to insist that we stayed there for the night. There was a ski-lift she said, so we set off in search of it, not too clear as to how we were going to get there, but anticipating a long walk at the very least. As nearly everyone we met seemed to speak fluent German and only halting French, we spent quite a while going round in circles but eventually ended up at a farm on the outskirts of the lake where, we had been told, we were sure to find the man who would 'help' us. Well we did, and he led us confidently away from the farmhouse and opened the doors of a large barn. Feeling a little nervous by now, we entered the gloomy interior and found ourselves looking at an impressive ski-lift. He opened the door at the far end of the barn and gestured for us to climb onto the high platform and get in to the car. We did, and almost immediately it lifted off its base and began its slow, swaying journey upwards.

At first it all seemed rather pleasant as we slowly travelled across fields and low, rocky outcrops. But then the ground fell away dramatically and we found ourselves looking down into deep gorges and skimming the tops of enormous fir trees. I have never had a head for heights and suddenly I was terrified. I fought back the desire to scream and closed my eyes, but even this was not enough, and I ended up sitting in the middle of the carriage floor, trying to stifle the feelings of panic that were welling up inside me. After what seemed an eternity we stopped. 'Are we there?' I asked Dawn. 'No,' she said, 'don't look.' It seemed we hung suspended and swaying for another age, until the carriage finally jerked into motion again and we arrived at the top of the mountain. I still feel slightly sick at the thought of it all, and it certainly was with enormous relief that both of us found ourselves in another shed with the ground only a little way from our feet. Then someone arrived to open the doors and help us down off the platform and it was all over. Once out in the open we felt that we were, quite literally, on top of the world.

We were taken into a farmhouse and then upstairs into a long room under the roof of the building. In one corner there were five beds, curtained off from the rest of the room, and here we put our bags and collapsed in relief. After a few minutes curiosity drew us back downstairs where we found our host. Dinner would be in two hours we were told – an unexpected luxury this, as we had begun to anticipate a hungry night – and so we headed out into the fading sunshine and stepped on to the set of *The Sound of Music*. The views were exceptional. Mountain peak after mountain peak was etched against the blue sky, and somewhere far below them sparkled the waters of Lake Lucerne. We wandered along the sheep paths; the tinkling of the sheep-bells and the goat-bells the only sounds to disturb the profound silence that surrounded us. We found gentians and edelweiss and pockets of still frozen snow. Dawn was ecstatic and even I began to be glad we had come.

Supper was a thick stew, eaten with chunks of freshly baked bread, accompanied by a glass of cold beer. It seemed a meal fit for a prince. We scoffed it down and then, already half asleep, we climbed to our loft and into bed. Perhaps an hour later we were awakened by the sound of many footsteps ascending the bare wooden stairs. In my sleep-drugged state I could think only of jack-booted Nazis, and I sat upright in alarm. But these invaders of the night turned out to be only workmen intent on occupying the beds outside the curtains and then, throughout the rest of the night, making frequent use of the metal buckets at the far end of the loft. Once all this was obvious I quickly went back to sleep, but Dawn remained awake and in a state of outrage for the rest of the night. At first light, when the workman had coughed and spat their way out of our lives, Dawn leapt from her bed and quickly got dressed. 'We are leaving now,' she said. 'No, we're not.' I replied, 'There's breakfast first, and anyhow, I'm not going back into that car for all the tea in China.'

Dawn conceded breakfast, but continued to insist we left immediately afterwards in the cable car. I remained adamant. The coffee and rolls were delicious but not fortifying enough to make me change my mind, so a compromise was reached and we set off to walk down the mountain. Nearly two hours later, after walking through the pine forests, breathing in the crystal-clear air, delighting in the views, the countryside and the bird- song, we finally met an English-speaking Forester and stopped for a chat. 'How far to the bottom?' we asked. 'About another six hours,' he replied. So we turned round and walked back and somehow or other I got myself into the cable car and in ten terrifying minutes I found myself falling into the understanding arms of the farmer's wife at the bottom of the mountain, with my feet once more on terra firma.

Dawn's sense of outrage finally faded as we walked on the shore of Lake Lucerne and sat down by the edge of the lake in a small park. Our equilibrium restored, we had begun to discuss what we would do next, when there was a rustle in the bushes behind us and we turned round to see a man standing there exposing himself. We fled, I practically speechless with laughter, and Dawn horrified and totally disillusioned with all 'foreigners', the Swiss in particular. (Only a few days later, however, when we were walking through the outskirts of Folkestone, more bushes parted to reveal another man in a similar state, and Dawn was forced to reassess her opinion of 'foreigners'.) So we left the Swiss behind and returned to Paris.

From Paris I think we crossed into south-east Belgium and then into Germany. I remember clearly that we found ourselves in Koblenz, staying in a converted castle on the Rhine. We arrived at the start of a three-day festival that included a boat trip down the Rhine and exciting evenings around bonfires. The all-day boat trip was unexpected and particularly delightful, the scenery stunning. We passed the Lorelei rock and having survived her charms spent most of the day lazing on deck, drinking cold beer and eating the snacks provided. The three days passed quickly but we saw far more of this famous area than we would have been able to do by ourselves and we met many of the local people too. They came to entertain us with music and dancing and often stayed late into the night just talking. We were sorry to move on but ahead lay a walk in the Black Forest and a hostel in Luxembourg, where we discovered the delights of a whole wall of loos that flushed automatically every few minutes and took you totally by surprise as you sat, sleep-dazed, in the early morning.

Then, inevitably, we began to run out of time. Dawn had to be back in England a week earlier than I and the days started flying by. With only three days before her deadline we found ourselves in a corner of France on one of those long, straight roads edged with poplars. On the first day we covered more than half the distance back to Paris, but on the second day, as we started our early morning walk, we gazed along a deserted road. By mid-morning we realised we had seen fewer than six vehicles go past and none of them had shown the slightest interest in stopping. Uncharacteristically, Dawn decided that we should sit and thumb rather than walk too far away from the refuge of the hostel, and so we did, idling the afternoon away by nibbling the inevitable bread and cheese and draining the last of our lemonade because it was still so hot. We surveyed a picture- postcard scene with nothing moving except our spirits as they slipped slowly downhill. Dawn was seriously worried now, for all our plans centred on catching the night boat- train from the Gâre du Nord, and by late afternoon this was becoming more and more of a remote possibility.

Around 5 p.m. we started reluctantly to walk back to the small town where we had spent the previous night. I was second in line, and when I heard a car coming up behind us I stopped walking and raised my thumb more in habit than hope. Unbelievably the car stopped and its driver asked where we were going and when I said it was to Paris, he told us to get in. And so we were soon reclining in the soft seats of the large Citroën as it sped through the kilometres back to the capital, the sun beginning to slide gently below the horizon to the sounds of a Bruckner violin concerto. As we reached the outskirts of the city the music changed and the notes of the Blues challenged the flashing neon on the buildings. We pulled up outside the Gâre du Nord as the last notes died away. It had been a near perfect journey back and there was still an hour before the train was due to leave. Plenty of time for some last bread and cheese and a café crème.

Safely returned to the relieved but astonished bosom of the Life Police, I felt I was now a seasoned traveller. The last few days of the holiday sped quickly by and it was no time before I stood once more on the familiar Hathersage station platform, ever the more sophisticated student and, now woman of the world.

Chapter Six

It was towards the end of my second college year that I acquired a fiancé, whose name was Colin. He was one of the mature students at the college and therefore a few years older than I. He said he had been in the Air Force and told daring stories of flying coffee into Germany, East or West, I don't remember now. He certainly spoke with the accents of the British RAF and wore a flying jacket most of the time, a silk scarf tied round his neck to complete the image. He was studying drama and I suppose we met on one of the productions that year. I was impressed and rather in love with the idea of being engaged, but when I went back to Derbyshire bearing the glad tidings to the Life Police they simply dismissed the idea as 'ridiculous' and refused to talk about it. This was a bit of a body blow but I wasn't quite sure what I could do about it; clutching engagement presents from Angela and her family I returned to London to give the matter some thought.

For reasons now unknown I had agitated to leave the easy familiarity of the hall of residence and after bringing considerable pressure to bear had been accepted as part-sharer of a flat in the house of two eminently respectable and highly protective schoolteachers. The aim was probably more freedom but apart from a certain laxity about lights-out and portable radios, the restrictions were, if anything, more all encompassing. Still, it was too late to change now and just had to be got on with.

My flatmate was Dinah, a third-year student of speech and drama and soon to be a dedicated teacher. As my sights were still set on International Stardom, our relationship was an uneasy one at first, but later we learned how to harmonise our different personalities and we became good friends. She was engaged to be married to someone her parents found totally unsuitable and they had virtually stopped speaking to her. It all sounded very fraught at the time and rather familiar, especially as Dinah appeared to be the most conventional of women. She stuck firmly to her man, however, and was later to marry him and have a very happy life indeed. Once the first baby was born, the family relented, thus making complete nonsense of all the objections in the first place. I was still smarting over the reception of the news of my engagement and so we shared a common bond and long discussions were to take place over endless cups of instant coffee during the ensuing months. Meanwhile we both defiantly wore our engagement rings and professed an interest in sheets and towels and other such nonsense.

Dinah was tiny and slightly built. She had long hair down to below her waist that she wore plaited and wound into a tight bun. She had the figure and stature of a ballet dancer and a strong sense of discipline. Formidable at times in the classroom, she also had a delicious sense of humour and unlimited kindness. All in all, our flat sharing went well.

The house was still in Brockley, not far from the Lewisham High Street in a road lined with ornamental cherry trees that were a delight in spring and cool and shady in the summer. It was only two streets away from the hall of residence so one always had the option of popping back there if a little extra company was required or, more likely this, one needed help with some essay or other. It seems odd but I have no recollection of my fiancé ever setting foot over the threshold, although we often entertained Dinah's for some highly respectable afternoon refreshment.

So life settled into a different routine though at the first opportunity I still raced to Shaftesbury Avenue to renew my connections with the theatre commissionaires and their over-strong, milky tea. This second year in London started well and was to become one of the first really happy ones of my life. As a second-year student I now thought I knew everything. I was a leading light in the college drama society and was all set to overdose gloriously on the new productions in the West End. I sported a highly eccentric dress style, all my own, and had a reputation at college of being something of a 'character'. I revelled in it all and wanted it to go on for ever.

In the middle of the autumn term I was given permission to return to Derbyshire for my twenty-first birthday. This I was reluctant to do, but I knew that a cake had been baked and that a stack of presents awaited me. So I became the dutiful daughter, toned down my wardrobe and headed for St Pancras. It was the right decision for great efforts had been made to do things 'my way'. There was no party as such but Miss Dior perfume awaited and, something that really touched me, my parents presented me with a cheque for twenty one pounds, a pound for every year of my life. It was a fair amount of money at that time; I was impressed, and also very moved that they should have taken the trouble to build up this small fortune year by year. I turned away to hide the tears in my eyes and gulped down the lump in my throat. The next day Angela came to drive me into Sheffield for my return to London, and as we piled the luggage into the car, I placed my handbag on its roof. We drove off, forgetting it completely, and it gently slid down into the road, precious cheque inside. Fortunately my rather tearful mother, who was waving us goodbye, saw it fall and halfway to Sheffield we were overtaken by one of my father's cricketing friends, gesticulating wildly for us to stop. The rest of the journey was singularly uneventful but once back in the college pub my birthday celebrations continued in a manner rather more uninhibited than those at home.

Having safely achieved my majority, I set about considering most carefully something that was already a source of concern and debate amongst the female contingent at college. Namely, whether or not it was a good idea to be a virgin after we had reached the age of twenty-one. By now most of us had fiancés or boyfriends and it was pretty well known who was sleeping with whom. I was under some pressure from my tentative fiancé, but opportunity was rare and it was easy enough to defer this major event if that was what I wanted. So the debate raged on for the time being until, eventually, it ran out of steam of its own accord.

For the autumn one-act drama festival I had been chosen to play Alison in an excerpt from *Look Back in Anger*, I was thrilled, especially as 'Jimmy' was to be played by the heartthrob of the third year. In the event it all went well and I received good reviews in the university press. I also fell a little in love with my leading man in the time-worn tradition of leading ladies with handsome co-actors. Then it was time to return to Hathersage for a while.

I had dreaded this visit for Scampy had died a few weeks earlier and the house was sorely empty without him. I had warned my mother that I didn't want to speak about his death and so we didn't, something else bottled up to come out later.

The return to London brought with it the threat of future exams, together with the deadlines for our special studies and theses and we were given permission to absent ourselves from the college in order to research and prepare the latter of these. Lorna and I found ourselves singularly ill prepared until she had the bright idea of our going to her family's caravan in Scotland, cutting ourselves off from all temptations and working solidly until we were finished. The general idea worked well and we did indeed catch up with our work but I have only dismal recollections of one of the most beautiful parts of Scotland. For a start it rained constantly, dense sheets of rain that soaked through the thickest macintosh and trickled coldly into our walking shoes. To be outside for more than half an hour was to end up chilled to your very bones and soaked to the skin. But we had some fun in the oil-lit caravan in the evenings over bacon and eggs and warm white wine and there must have been the odd day of sunshine because I have a vague memory of purple heather, bracken and granite rocks all on a scale larger than anything I had known in Derbyshire. We finally returned south, our consciences clear and bulky written files in our luggage. The climate improved immediately and our spirits lifted accordingly. Once back in London, college life surrounded us again and all was well.

With the Easter holidays looming my fiancé became fixated on a visit to Paris. His airborne-coffee-smuggling stories were still an essential part of his persona and he claimed to have ex-accomplices and money owed in France, so the trip had to be made and one Thursday morning we set off from his grandmother's house in Surrey.

Money was really tight this time, for the Easter holidays were short and there had been no time to earn very much, so we hitchhiked our way down to Dover and caught the night ferry across to Calais. From there we hitch-hiked on to Paris and arrived on the Friday evening, both of us tired, hungry and extremely irritable. My dashing ex-RAF fiancé seemed in worse shape than me, so, as we drifted across the city, I took charge and insisted we went to find his friends and collect the money he still assured me he was owed. I was also hoping we might receive the offer of a bed for the night or at least some food. So, after a lengthy perusal of the map, a street was settled on, and we set off across Paris on foot to find it. By the time we got there, tempers were even more frayed and serious doubts were beginning to enter my somewhat gullible head about the truth of the whole story. But for the moment, I went along with it, more in hope than conviction, for there was little else to do. In those days there appeared to be no free seats in Paris, even the benches in the little parks had to be paid for, so I wandered wearily up and down the street and watched my fiancé disappear into just about the only building without a concierge guarding its entrance. I was longing for a summons to join him so I was glad when he quickly reappeared and crossed the street towards me. But the news was not good; his contacts had 'disappeared' and there was no money. He hinted at 'dark dealings' and said that we should leave the street immediately. 'And where exactly are we to go?' I asked, but he seemed to have no answer to that one.

We spent a miserable night, our second without sleep, for if we were to eat at all, then a hotel was out of the question. I think we found some sort of workman's café and ate pasta with tomato sauce, sitting over the empty plates until a stream of market porters forced us out of our seats and back to pounding the pavements. As the first light of dawn streaked the sky we found ourselves huddled together for warmth on the embankment down by the Seine. There was no romance to be found there, the water rats plopped in and out of the water and the lights of passing police cars flashed across as we shrank back into the shadows. The arrival of the sun brought only a little warmth and I could have come close to killing for a coffee. From somewhere my now-less-than-dashing companion recollected a memory of another rendezvous, one he said must be kept alone, so we dragged ourselves back on to the streets, and I found a miraculously free seat in the gardens of the Louvre while my fiancé disappeared on his mysterious mission. When he returned it was with a ten franc note, useful money for it meant that we could eat and afford the ferry back to England, but it was hardly, I thought, recompense for dangerous coffee-smuggling missions into East Germany. Still we ate and drank coffee, and then, when Colin fell asleep after expressing his opinion that he had no idea what we should do next, I woke him roughly and insisted we started to hitch our way back to Calais. Somehow we made it in time for the night ferry, and after losing most of another night's sleep, we started to thumb our way back to Woking.

We walked, or rather hobbled our way around the South Circular road, but it was now Easter Sunday and no one was stopping for hitchhikers. The cars were all on family outings, grandma and the 2.4 kids filling the back seat with mum regal and important in the front. It was a hot day too and by now I was almost hallucinating from lack of food and sleep. When we reached a small market town (I forget which,) I snapped and led us to the railway station. By lucky chance there was a stopping train to Woking in about an hour, so I marched us on to the platform past the curious but non-challenging ticket collector and sat us down on only the second free seat we'd found throughout our disastrous travels. It was a struggle to stay awake but we just about made it. At Woking station I marched us off the train, out of the station and away, again the ticket collector somehow just didn't see us. There was a bus waiting that would take us to the door of Colin's grandmother's house and we got on although we had no money; but no one came to ask us for our fares. In no time we found ourselves standing at the door of the little house, and Colin's grandmother was exclaiming at our sorry state. Food was produced and eaten, and then, after a long bath, I sank into the soft layers of the feather bed in the guest room and slept on and off for nearly two days.

Recovery was fast but the engagement was never the same again and was later to founder on the rocks of disillusion. And to this day I have no idea whether or not the stories he told me were true. It was, however, only the beginning of the end for we went along with the pretence for the rest of our time at Goldsmiths' and for some time after that, I carefully removing my engagement ring every time I went home. Did I ever seriously consider marrying him? I certainly thought so at the time, but everyone was getting engaged and maybe I just wanted to be part of it all. I was not the only person ever to get engaged for the wrong reasons, though I should have thought about it all more carefully.

But for the moment, more important things were happening. I had the lead in the drama society's production of *The Flies* by Jean Paul Sartre, and I was also directing a one-act play for the college drama competition. Playing 'Electra' was my first experience of being cast in a leading role since my disastrous debut at school, and this time I learnt my lines in good time. I loved the rehearsal period for *The Flies* and sank myself hook, line and sinker into the role. First-night nerves were terrifying, but once I was on stage I felt I was in complete control and enjoyed every minute. I received good revues in the college newspaper, revues that were carefully cut out and preserved, together with some rather dramatic photos.

The play I chose to direct was a Japanese Noh play called *Hanjo*. Written by Yukio Mishima, it was a rather obscure piece, full of symbolism. Suddenly the days were not long enough and non-essential college lectures disappeared from my schedule completely. Only the one on sex drew a full auditorium, but alas we learned little we hadn't already culled from various late night discussions, or, others, more raunchy ones, in the bosom of 'our' pub, the 'Rosie' (the Rosemary Branch), over half a pint of bitter. So, for the moment, sex and drugs and rock 'n roll could not be said to feature largely in our lives at all. The one act play festival came and went and the entries were judged by Clifford Williams, a professional actor/director. To my total astonishment *Hanjo* came first and was chosen as Goldsmiths' entry for the University Festival later that year. My cup 'ranneth' over and I was pretty much overwhelmed. Suddenly walking around with a copy of *The Stage* tucked under my arm seemed less of an affectation than before, and I began to dare to dream.

Then H walked into my life and turned everything upside down. Basically he was fun and made me laugh a lot, ever my downfall this. At first we were always in a group of friends but I started spending more and more time alone with him and we were always laughing. He was good-looking in a raffish sort of way and heavily involved in the theatre, and it was through him that I became a stage manager on a production of a play called Wiley. This was staged at the Royal Court Theatre one Sunday evening in July. It was the first time I worked in the professional theatre and should have stood out for that reason, but somehow it doesn't. Far more vivid is the day I walked on stage at the Old Vic. This was organised by a friend on the third-year drama course and still rates as something very special. As I moved across that empty stage, the ghosts of great actors from the past seemed to step out from the wings. Many of the most famous names in British theatre had performed, and were still performing on these very boards, and the spirit of Lillian Baylis was omnipresent. It was quite an experience.

That last term now seems bathed in sunshine as all youthful memories seem to be. Of course there were final exams hanging over us and with them the awful possibility of failure, but it really didn't stop us from revelling in every moment of our undergraduate existence. Despite the need to revise, my visits to the theatre were still an integral part of all this and I spent every spare moment there, regardless of whether the production was a musical comedy or a classical drama.

By winning the one-act play competition I had caused something of a furore in college circles. Noses, I think, had been put out of joint and people were a little huffy. Then I suddenly started receiving more and more offers of help with the Festival production. I was given a small grant for set design and this was the start of my undoing. My original concept, startling in its simplicity (mainly through lack of cash), had worked really well and was a statement in itself. Now it became smothered in other people's ideas and I lost track of it all. I should have been firmer, I should have insisted on hanging on to my production, but the people offering help were several years older than I and one or two had even worked in the theatre professionally. The play got through to the last three and got good reviews, but it didn't win. Ironically the main criticisms were directed at the changes I had not wanted. A lesson had been learned but that didn't mean I never again made the same mistakes.

Then suddenly it was all over. Trunks had to be packed, theatre programmes carefully filed, posters peeled off bedroom walls; Che Guevara carefully transported by hand to Derbyshire. Faces started vanishing from the lunchtime crowd at the Rosie and promises of eternal friendship were made, only to be broken a few weeks later. I was one of the last to leave, but, inevitably the time came when, clutching the green-collared koala bear but not quite daring to wear the Red Riding Hood cape, I headed for St Pancras and the train to Sheffield.

Once back in Derbyshire, I was surprised to be told that there would be no need for me to work that summer, I was to have a last few months of freedom; a treat indeed. September was the deadline, then I must start earning a living for real, but in the meantime I idled away the days and pretended not to be watching the post for that little brown envelope with the exam results. With little to fill my days except the prospect of another hitch-hiking holiday with Dawn, I really became convinced that I would fail. The worst part was the thought of having to break the news to the Life Police, especially as I felt it was only what they were expecting.

Inevitably the dreaded morning arrived. I strolled down to breakfast and there was the envelope sitting expectantly by my coffee. I pretended not to notice it and picked up the cup, but my mother was not to be so easily deterred.

'Is it your exam results?' she asked brightly.

'No, I don't think so,' I muttered, 'I think it's a book I left behind in London.'

'Ah!' she said diplomatically, and let the matter drop.

I finished my coffee and solitary piece of toast and went back to my room, the envelope glaring banefully at me from the dressing table where I placed it.

I finally plucked up the courage and opened it. It was of course, the results. I turned to the list of thirds, but my name was not there. So, I had failed. There was no way that I could have passed any higher and 'bad blood' would probably be seen to be responsible again. I looked idly at the firsts. All the predictable names were there, including that of my early roommate. Then I started checking the names of friends in the list of second- class passes. Lorna was there and Freddie and Anne Kilcoyne and, unbelievably, ME! I was stunned. I had had a marvellous time at Goldsmiths' but I had thought the work easy and had given it little attention. Only English literature had been treated seriously and there I had worked hard. And somehow I had done it. I sprinted back downstairs to tell my mother. She seemed really pleased – there was little doubt about that – well, so was I, though I played it all down of course.

I went down to the post office to tell my father and he was pleased too and produced a rather large sum of money from his back pocket. 'Now about this next holiday.' he said.

So a postcard was despatched to Dawn and my mother got out the sewing machine and embarked on yet another series of inappropriate tops and nightdresses. For the few days before it was time to leave I basked in the warmth of success – and also the glow of affluence, for Gran too had come up with a 'little something' and my mother slipped ten pounds into my hand at the last moment.

My erstwhile fiancé was waiting in London. He must have been working, for he insisted on buying me a pale-blue bikini, a yellow blouse and some beige trousers. My image improved tenfold and Dawn was impressed. We left for Belgium that night, just Dawn and I, by now seasoned international travellers.

I remember less of this trip, though I know we crossed to Belgium and pressed on into Germany and Holland and finally into Denmark, just not quite able to find the time to make it into Sweden. It was nothing like our previous summer's trip. Dawn enjoyed the colder climate and the spotless loos; I yearned for the chaos of hotter climes and wished we were heading towards the Mediterranean. The people were very kind again and often with the lifts came food or at least a ride all the way to the youth hostel door.

There were some amazing experiences too, like our drive through Holland and up to the German border with an ex RAF pilot who had flown in the Second World War. Being something of a maverick, he had taken up smuggling Scotch whisky into Germany, but he was delightful company and treated us to lunch before dropping us off just before the border and speeding on his illegal way. We walked across the border on foot and stopped to hitch again at the start of the autobahn. The first car stopped and we were offered a lift by another nice man who later revealed that he had been a Luftwaffe pilot, also in the Second World War, but now flew civilian aircraft for Lufthansa. He gave us each a model aeroplane before finally dropping us off in the middle of a still ruined Hamburg.

Nearly twenty years after the war large parts of the city lay in a state of desolation, with blasted buildings and bomb craters half filled with rainwater. I was reminded of the bomb damage still to be seen in Sheffield and found Hamburg a depressing place, with little to see. We paid a fleeting visit to the red-light district, shocked to our provincial cores by what we saw, and, later, saddened at the thought of the brutality and the wasted lives.

After Hamburg, where I have the impression it rained constantly, we headed onwards and into Denmark, carrying with us dismal images, but also memories of the warmth and generosity of many of the people. Copenhagen delighted Dawn, and even I found it pleasing to the eye. The shops were full of beautiful clothes and glass and pottery, many with designs as yet unseen in Sheffield or, indeed, London. We both fell in love with a casual macintosh jacket we saw and bought one each and I found a blouse in purple and green and had to have that. Later we headed out to Ellsinore and walked on the ramparts of the castle in the footsteps of Shakespeare's Dane, sad to have just missed a production of that great play.

We contemplated a trip to Sweden but time was running out so we regretfully headed for Esbjerg and the night ferry back to England. But this was no smooth, cross channel ferry. It was a stormy night, the sea rough and the boat pitching alarmingly. By midnight I was the only person left on deck, and even I was beginning to feel decidedly queasy. Reluctantly I took refuge in my bunk until the boat made it safely into Harwich harbour and all was well. Then with the last of the little extra money we had that year, we treated ourselves to egg and chips, before leaping on a train back to London. It had been an interesting holiday – we now knew all about Hans Christian Anderson, had seen the Little Mermaid and would cherish countless other memories, – but I had longed for the Mediterranean and vowed to go there as soon as possible. Meanwhile I had to find a job.

My much tried parents were pleased to see me but made it clear that the September deadline still held. I renewed my friendships in Hathersage but the gap between us was huge and I finally realised that I no longer fitted into a small village with, what I regarded then, as its limitations and constraints. London called, and so I packed up a smaller version of the college trunk and headed back.

Celia and Dawn, together with two other girls, had rented a flat in Harcourt Terrace, not far from the Earl's Court Road. Five girls in a one-bedroom flat would be cramped, but teachers' wages were low and my extra rent would be welcome. So we put mattresses on the floor and coped somehow. There was still the problem of a job and that was now pressing. In those days, you had to teach for a year to add a teaching qualification to your degree and so, reluctantly, I gave in to pressure from the other girls and applied for a position in a London school.

By now the school term had started and all the best jobs had gone, but teachers were in great demand and I was quickly found a supply-teacher's job in a Hackney school and assured that it would count as part of my final year. So I started my first teaching job to which I had to travel each day across a large part of central London on a no.11 bus -for many months the best part of the day. The Life Police seemed reassured by the news and I resigned myself to a year's wait before embarking on my true path to super stardom.

The job was horrendous. I was not qualified to teach Educationally Subnormal children (as they were classified then), indeed, had never really come across any, but I was assigned a class of eleven-year-olds and one of thirteen-year-olds who were waiting assessment and transfer to special schools. Forty percent of them suffered from epilepsy. I had never witnessed an epileptic fit before, and when I saw the first one I had no idea what was happening. Fortunately there was a friendly colleague in the next classroom and he came to help. But I was terrified and waited fearfully for the next one.

Meanwhile the classes were, for a first-year teacher, quite simply uncontrollable. Children literally climbed the walls, hung out of second-floor windows and in some cases were violent. I was filling in for their regular teachers who seemed to spend long periods on sick leave. Hardly surprising, I thought, and longed to do the same. I began to dread the sound of the alarm clock each morning and to live only for the weekends. Years later I learned that the school was considered one of the worst in London and that there was no way I should have been left in charge of those children with their multiple problems. But at the time I never thought to complain or ask for a transfer, though I did spend another two weeks at a nearby all girls' school, filling in again for someone on sick leave.

Helen Shapiro was at that school and was in the process of being 'discovered', but the children I taught were not destined for a glamorous future. They used to wait by the main doors in a large group and surround you as you left for the day. They then would walk silently with you to the main gates and the bus stop. They never spoke or were violent in any way but the threat of violence was almost tangible and the degree of intimidation was like nothing I have ever experienced, before or since. Then I was returned to the first school where each day things seemed to get worse and the pressure built until I was crying myself to sleep every night and was shaking uncontrollably towards the end of every Sunday evening. Finally, however my luck changed and they appointed a full-time, specialist teacher and I was transferred to another school to teach drama.

Life became a little better, though again the school was rough by any standards, and the children had no respect for either the educational system or its teachers. I still hated Mondays but there were now moments when I actually felt that I was making some progress. There was also a new headmistress there who went out of her way to be helpful and supportive. It was a mixed school, but I was used to that, and got on well with the boys. It seemed that drama was something of a catharsis for them and they particularly enjoyed acting out street arguments and domestic squabbles. I felt, however, that before starting on anything too controversial I had to find a way of persuading them to part with their flick knives and knuckle dusters, if only for the duration of the class. Surprisingly I gained their confidence enough for them to agree, and with one particular class it was the beginning of a rather special rapport.

In so many ways they were desperate kids, coming mainly from broken homes and already living on the edge of crime. There was little anyone could do; their lives were already set in a pattern they would never break and almost certainly didn't want to. One boy of fifteen decided he liked me and appointed himself as my protector. He was far taller than I am and, though not heavily built, had a reputation for violence that commanded the respect of the class. He was always there when the going got rough and would stand up and shout, 'Quiet for Miss,' whenever I needed the attention of the class. So sometimes we actually got something done – but, of course, only after I had stood at the door with my shoebox for the flick knives, etc, as everyone filed into the hall, (and at the end of the class stood there again handing them back.) Flick knives were totally illegal and also banned from the school premises, but, like so many things in these teenagers lives, the rules and the laws were regarded as one of life's minor irritations and simply ignored until the headmaster or the local police enforced them. They then became a rather more irritating aspect of life, at least for a little while.

My protector had a stall at a Saturday market in the East End and from this earned more money in one day than I did in a week.

Indeed, he frequently offered to give me some, implying that its source, if not exactly legitimate, was at least constant and lucrative. I turned his offer down, to the bewilderment of the whole class for neither he, nor they, could understand why I would want to teach for so little money. Well, neither could I really but there seemed few other options around at the moment so we ploughed on in mutual incomprehension and left it at that.

Then, one day our hall was needed for some event or other and I was told I had 'to hold a debate or something' in a classroom. Not quite sure what to do and forgetting to collect the flick knives, I decided to hold a question-and-answer session. To my amazement they were curious and not unenthusiastic.

'What shall we talk about?' They asked.

'Anything,' I replied. 'And I'll try to answer honestly.'

'Can we talk about sex?' They demanded.

'Yes,' I said. 'But I may refuse to answer if you get too personal.'

There was virtual silence and then some giggling, but finally the questions came, and with them pictures of home lives that almost defied description. Violence was endemic, homes an accumulation of broken furniture and rotting infrastructure. Sex was taken brutally after a night of drinking and was often witnessed by the kids. Love was a word they used without comprehension of what it meant and unwanted pregnancies were something to be lived through, the resultant babies just another inconvenience.

They asked about my experiences, and my fiancé, and we gazed at one another in mutual incomprehension again. I managed to get something across about contraception, the girl's right to say no and the Marie Stopes clinics. I also tried with such abstract conceptions as 'respect', 'restraint', and understanding each other's needs, but I think I lost them there. Still, it was the easiest class I ever taught and there were no discipline problems whatsoever. There were more long-term benefits too, for I never really had a problem with that class for the rest of my time there, and they had a reputation of being one of the toughest in the school.

I wish I could say that I began to settle in, but I didn't, and the pressures continued to mount up until finally Colin took matters into his own hands and went to see the headmaster and I was marched to a doctor and given a medical certificate for sick leave. I never actually went back, but I think the education authority knew they had used me in a way no first-year teacher should be used, and they gave me my graduation certificate anyhow. I heaved an enormous sigh of relief and decided life was worth living after all – then I started to consider the future.

In the meantime, life at Harcourt Terrace breezed on. The only things that had made life bearable that year were the weekend parties and the general fun of living away from home and hostel. Of course, there were the long, paid holidays too. Earl's Court was full of Australians, and our house was no exception. All the tenants were young people, all determined to have fun, and so the weekends became one long party. On Friday it started in the basement flat and usually went on all night with people crashing out anywhere. Saturday was often our turn and Sunday lunchtime belonged to the people upstairs. People brought their own drinks, usually beer, and I don't remember much food, though there must have been some. We returned the empties to the local pub on a Sunday evening getting enough money back on them to buy food for the rest of the week. This was often a substantial soup, eaten from empty jam jars, though we did have school meals during the term.

The parties were great fun but I don't remember people getting really drunk. I suppose no one could afford to. I don't remember much sex either, there were too many people around and the floating Australian population went for friendships rather than hot passion. There was one Sunday morning, however, when I found a friend's suspender belt with stockings still attached and pondered the logistics of it all. And there was a fight one night when Colin, still my fiancé, leapt in to defend my honour and someone's nose got bloodied, but mostly it was just fun. In the week there were still trips to the theatre and the Soho coffee bars, exhibitions and the Café des Artistes on the corner, where we all pretended to be creative, drank endless cups of cappuccino and felt that this was where life was 'at'. Then Colin made the decision that he would emigrate to Australia – having first ascertained that I would follow later when he had made a life for both of us out there. Did I ever really intend to follow? I'm really not sure even now, for how on earth did I intend to break the news back in Hathersage? I still have no idea how I would have done that and I certainly didn't then. It seems I simply had a 'Scarlett O'Hara' moment and pushed it all to the back of my mind. Then H came back on the scene, if only intermittently. Maybe that was the reason I decided to move out of Harcourt Terrace but I think it more likely that my Greta Garbo approach to life simply reasserted itself. So I found a rather basic and none-too-clean room with an Irish family in Bayswater where I lived in splendid isolation for a few months, though I still visited the weekend parties, and, with my fiancé now on a boat somewhere between England and Australia, relished my first taste of complete freedom.

That Easter Dawn and I embarked on our third trip abroad. Two Australians we knew from the parties were driving down to Spain, and we somehow talked them into giving us a lift as far as Barcelona. I don't think they were terribly thrilled to have us along but the idea of sharing expenses must have been tempting and they took us.

Although it was my first longed for experience of southern Europe I remember little of this holiday too, the memories that do survive are mainly ones of sun and heat and a blue, blue sea. But I do vividly remember crossing the Pyrenees after a rather long lunch, and, somewhere among the mountain peaks, a loo becoming a vital necessity. I looked around in desperation, but the road stretched before and after us with only bare rock rising up steeply and no sign of a petrol station or anywhere else where we could reasonably stop. The situation quickly reached crisis point, but what to do? Finally we just stopped the car and I clambered up the rocks, taking with me a beach umbrella from the car. Shielding myself behind this from the passing cars and other traffic, I somehow managed to solve the problem, and returned to the car a much happier person. During the teasing that followed I determined to write my first book and call it *Taken Short in the Pyrenees*, but I never quite got round to it.

I remember Barcelona only hazily and it was to take another visit, many years later, before I started to appreciate and love the city. But there was certainly an afternoon in an air-conditioned cinema where we had gone to see an American film (*Ben Hur*?); an afternoon that quickly filled with disappointment when we found the film had been dubbed into Spanish. And there was another memorable moment on the town beach, I in that first bikini, where I looked up to see at least a hundred male faces staring down at me from the promenade, wrapt, until the police came and moved them on. I was mystified by this ... until someone explained that bikinis were banned in Spain at that time.

I do remember us leaving Barcelona though and heading for the coast – the Costa del Sol in fact, then still relatively unspoilt. We found a small room in an old pensione, virtually windowless and full of mosquitoes, but the people were kind and when we overpaid one night in the local restaurant we found the owner looking for us the next day in order to give us our change. If we wanted to move along the coast there was the local train that used to arrive packed full, with people hanging from the open doors and off the back hand rail, but somehow or other they always pulled us in and helped to regurgitate us when we reached our destination. It seemed a delightful way to travel then. Alas, the rest has disappeared from memory, and how we got back to London, I have no idea.

Having left teaching, or perhaps teaching having left me, I had taken to working in the Oxford Street shops in order to survive. Perhaps not surprisingly Selfridges was the first and longest job I had at this time. There I met Jimmy, one of the team of window dressers working there. He was great fun and loved to go skating, so skating became one of the passions of that time and, rather to my surprise, my parents turned up trumps with a beautiful pair of boots for my birthday. Off we went, two or three times a week and I loved the freedom of movement, the coolness of the ice and the general feeling of exhilaration that came after one of the dance sessions when they cleared the ice of the beginners and we had the space to dance. As we got to know the staff there they often let us skate on the empty rink as they skimmed it ready for the night's freezing session. That was even better.

It seemed that nearly every shop in Oxford Street had a 'Staff Required' notice on permanent display so I joined quite a large group of itinerant workers who moved up and down the street more or less at whim. For something more long-term Dawn and I applied to Pan Am to work as air hostesses (considered seriously glamorous at the time) but she was successful and I wasn't so she didn't take up the post offered. Then I was accepted as a trainee personnel manager with ICI, but theatre still fascinated me and the thought of spending the rest of my life in an office appalled me, so that opportunity was rejected too. Stability was hardly more evident on the home-front either and I moved to another bed-sit. But this time Dawn too had tired of the over-communal living in Harcourt Terrace and she suggested we find somewhere together. She fancied Hampstead and by a lucky chance it all became possible. Carol and Pete had come back into my life and were married by this time. They were living in a small attic flat in South Hill Park and had somehow become friends with Diana, a double-dyed Hampstead eccentric. She was extremely extrovert, given to sudden rages and dressed exotically. She was married to a journalist who worked for one of the more left-wing newspapers and who exerted a restraining influence on Diana whenever possible, actually not often. I was a little afraid of both of them but Diana owned a house at the edge of the Heath and had a studio flat vacant and to let. Dawn and I moved in, and settled there happily, avoiding our landlady as much as possible.

Dawn was now deeply involved with Dr David, a friend of Gary's from Oxford, and she was intent on marrying him. I was somewhat envious of this seemingly idyllic relationship until one day I asked her if she loved him very much and got the reply that he was what she wanted. I waited for the rest of the sentence but nothing else came, and I have never known the answer to my original question.

Our days in Hampstead were fun. The no. 24 bus became an integral part of our lives and the Freemasons Arms in Downshire Hill filled the gap left by the Rosie in New Cross. More than filled the gap actually, for it had a big garden for sunny days and a large, wood-burning fireplace for the winter. And there was always company and things to do; the Everyman cinema, for instance, the music in Kenwood on summer evenings, and the freedom of the Heath. Life had definitely taken an upward turn. Then H came back from France.

He had been there for quite some time and I had heard nothing from him. Somehow he had talked his way into getting a grant from the Arts Council and had been studying the government subsidisation of the French theatres throughout the country and had now returned to write up his findings. These were subsequently published in one of the theatre magazines, Encore, and I still have a copy somewhere. But as always money was needed to live, and so he had quickly acquired a job as doorman at the Dominion Theatre in Tottenham Court Road. By then I was working in a handbag shop near Marble Arch where I was firmly resisting attempts to turn me into a manageress. Colin was settled in Australia and apparently out of sight was out of mind, for H and I saw quite a lot of each other, meeting for lunch whenever possible. This meant I spent a lot of time flying up and down Oxford Street, late for H or the afternoon shift at the shop until one day he told me he was leaving for Paris after he had been paid on the following Friday. I held my breath until he went on to ask if I wanted to go with him. Then I didn't even stop to think, just said yes and we started planning where and when we would rendezvous for our departure.

With everything quickly sorted the rest of the week dragged on, but Friday came at last and I waited impatiently for our wages to be paid at mid-day. I had already packed and had only to return to Hampstead to collect a small bag, meet H at the theatre, and we'd be off. But instead of my wages I found myself greeting my mother and father who chose that moment to arrive on a surprise weekend visit. They walked into the shop, were made extremely welcome by the manageress and, for one of the few times in my life, left me speechless.

We arranged to meet later and they went off to explore Hyde Park. Soon after my wages came I took my lunch break. I raced to the Dominion to tell H of the unexpected development and to plead for a two-day delay to our travel plans, but the pleas fell on deaf ears. He was leaving that night, with or without me, and I could follow later if I wished. I was not happy with the thought of arriving in Paris on my own, especially as the only way to find him appeared to be by turning up at the Maison Franco Brittannique (part of the Paris university complex) and asking for him. Anyhow I took the piece of paper with the address and phone number and trudged back up Oxford Street to finish the day's work and concentrate on spending the weekend as a dutiful daughter. We did it somehow, my mother liking Hampstead and taking to Dawn, but nearly in tears at the thought of my only being able to afford bacon bits and the smallest of eggs. I think I must have slightly exaggerated the poverty bit for I did well with last-minute presents when I finally waved them off at St Pancras and returned to giggle with Dawn and re-pack my Paris bag.

Monday found me leaving early, bag in hand, but by now slightly alarmed at what I was doing. I leapt on the much-loved 24 bus and demanded a ticket to Paris. The conductor, philosophical about the strangeness of his customers, merely laughed and said they weren't actually going to Paris, but would Victoria do as a start? It would and did. Once there, I was in good time for the boat train and as it slowly pulled out of the station I bowed to the inevitable and excitement banished all my qualms.

Chapter Seven

The Gâre du Nord was the same as always and the Metro held no terrors for me. Only when I emerged at Cité Universitaire did I start to get nervous and wonder what on earth I was going to do if I couldn't find H. But there was no problem for everyone said that they knew of him, and it wasn't long before he appeared, almost as startled by the sight of me as I was of him. My defences rose and I muttered something about only being there for a couple of days and needing somewhere to stay. Had I money? He asked. I had, and so a little later we set off back towards the Boulevard St-Michel and the Hôtel des Capucines in the Rue de l'Hirondelle and three delightful days during which we spent all my money, including my return fare to England.

The next few weeks were crazy. H had become involved in helping Algerian students, illegal in France, to join the university. Once they had registered they became legal and could stay in France for the length of their university course. There was a network set up to help them which was run by other students. Our job was to collect them in the outskirts of the city and travel with them in case of problems. It was the time of the Algerian War and in some ways what we were doing had an element of risk about it but we never thought about that. The police in Paris were hard men and something of a shock for me, for they were armed and quite prepared to shoot. The Algerians were not popular in Paris and there was one terrible night spent walking by the northern reaches of the Seine and seeing bodies floating in water that was red with the blood from their slit throats.

By this time we had no money and survived on student meal-tickets and the odd hand out. We slept in student rooms during the day – often in African halls of residence – and then walked the streets at night. Occasionally someone would let us have their room for the luxury of a night's sleep and a shower. On one of these occasions (we were in the Senegalese all male hostel), I went to the loo in the middle of the night and met a succession of white Y-fronts intent on the same mission. Only sleepy eyes were visible above these lumpy shapes. The Life Police would have been horrified, but it was all quite innocent, for after the glories of the Hôtel des Capucines nights of passion were rare indeed.

One night we spent over a coffee in a bar in the Place du Châtelet At one point I went downstairs to the loo and found it to be a communal one, men and women together. I emerged from my cubicle to find a man by the urinals, a man who seemed totally unconcerned by my presence. I affected a sophisticated air that I was far from feeling and returned upstairs to find H deep in conversation with a Moroccan. I sat back down and tried to follow the conversation but the man was staring at me and it was difficult to concentrate. Eventually I realised the point of the conversation – H was trying to sell me into the White Slave network. I dragged us out of the café and away, H laughing and protesting that he was only teasing even though he had been offered a good price for me. But I was deeply hurt and we walked across Paris in virtual silence. Still, somewhere in the middle of all this, Colin's ring was sent to Australia in an envelope and it was several years before I saw him again.

H then acquired the use of a scooter and also a friend with a motorbike, so our travels across Paris were greatly facilitated, though I have no idea where the petrol money came from. Food was less of a problem, and when all else failed there was always a plate of spaghetti and tomato sauce at the café bar across from the university, shared between us if times were especially hard. Then our fortunes took a turn for the better when we got the job of painting a flat in Montmartre. Of course we lived in it at the same time, and suddenly there was coffee and croissants for breakfast and nights spent in a bar on the Rue Blanche where flamenco guitar music was played into the early hours of the morning and professional musicians dropped in to 'gig' and buy us glasses of a red wine I can still taste to this day.

Paris at that time was like everything you've ever read about it and like two gipsy children we roamed its streets, delighting in each new experience. Jean-Paul Sartre and Simone de Beauvoir were again seen in the cafés of the Left Bank and exiled Russian princes and princesses roamed the streets, yearning for their vast estates and a way of life that had gone for ever. In Montmartre the ladies of the night and their pimps stood on street corners and the sound of the cancan leaked from the open doors of the Moulin Rouge. One night we somehow got tickets for Edith Piaf's last concert at Olympia. She had throat cancer and was dying and during the last few years of her life she had shocked Paris with her unconventional behaviour, her seemingly unprofessional attitude. That night the vast audience was hostile, somehow they wanted her to fail, but when this tiny figure in black came centre stage, stood in a spotlight and started to sing, hostility turned back to admiration and the audience rose to its feet. She sang her heart out that night, this woman of the streets with a musical gift like no other. 'No Regrets' had the whole audience weeping and they made a recording of it that night that I still have. Many years later there came another French singer with a voice similar to Edith's and I was to work with her for many weeks, but she had lived a sheltered life and that voice from the past could never be replicated. Edith was, and still is, unique; only Judy Garland belonged to the same genre, and she enters these pages later on.

On a more prosaic level we also haunted one of the bookshops of the Left Bank. Run by an American it was known for the tea and biscuits provided free on Sunday afternoons. Of course there was a price of sorts and this took the form of some patient listening on our part, for we had to sit there while our host told tales of his evenings spent with famous authors, and then gaze in awe at their books. These were all autographed of course but strangely all in the same handwriting and apparently with the same pen! Afterwards I seem to remember, we would dare to cross the Seine and enter the world of the Right Bank where we found a different life style, one where money could provide all that the heart could desire – and memories of Dawn and that very first visit lurked in odd corners down tiny side streets. This was not our world though and we soon returned to the more familiar streets of the Left Bank.

It was all so romantic, and the lack of money seemed but a minor inconvenience and perhaps only enhanced the image of starving artists in that most exciting of cities. In my memory of it, the sun is always shining, the streets of the centre full of fashionable men and women, the boulevard cafés packed with writers, painters, actors and musicians. Of course I began to write superbly bad poetry.

But we had finished painting the Montmartre flat and the university summer holidays were looming. When the students went home, with them would go our back-up support, so H found me a legitimate job. The advert was on the noticeboard of the Maison Franco Britannique, and it was for an au pair to spend the summer in the South of France caring for two small children. My heart sank but I went for an interview anyway and got the job.

The Paris home of the family was in Neuilly, that exclusive area of Paris, close to the Bois de Boulogne, where people lived rather discreet and sheltered lives. But my heart had sunk needlessly, as it turned out, for the family members were to become friends for life and I was to play a rather erratic part in their future, with all its ups and downs. For the moment, however, I was less than pleased at getting the job, for they were leaving Paris almost immediately and that meant no more H and no more carefree wanderings across a city I had grown to love. I rejoined H in a nearby café and imparted the news. I was somewhat taken aback to be told that he was moving on to Greece and I was not part of his plans. When I asked why not, I was told that I didn't make him laugh any more. I sat on in the café pondering the inscrutability of the male psyche. In London I had been sacrificed for art as I made David laugh too much, here I was guilty of the opposite crime. How was one supposed to get it right?

So I left for Générargues on the night train and the Paris idyll came to an end, but the day before I left H had said that I was to earn some money and then follow on – so there was at least a ray of hope for the future. Meanwhile I reconciled myself to life with two small children, and began at least to look forward to experiencing the South of France.

Madame C, the children's mother could not have been more kind or welcoming and I was made to feel very much a part of the family. I wrote to the Life Police who must have heaved a sigh of relief at the news but merely wrote back enclosing three razor blades for my lady's razor, as leg-shaving was soon to become a necessity in the southern heat. These razor blades were to continue to arrive throughout the summer, a sort of fragile link between two mutually incomprehensible worlds.

I slept fitfully on the night express and was quite glad when it pulled in to Alès at 7.00 a.m. We stepped off the train and waited for them to unload the car, then drove into the town centre for coffee and croissants. It seemed the whole adventure had got off to a good start. I remember leaving Alès and then travelling through the rocky area that turned out to be the beginning of the Cévennes. It was not at all as I had imagined the South of France to be, that I would only find later. The house, however, was wonderful, though, as I was later to discover, somewhat isolated. It had originally been the home of a silkworm farmer, and in those days consisted of two rooms, one on top of the other. The farmer and his family had lived downstairs, the silkworms above, and it stood in a vineyard with a terraced garden and lemon trees, roses and other exotica as yet without a name. As we stepped out of the car I was almost deafened by a noise that was close to but not quite that, of a swarm of bees. 'What on earth is that?' I asked my bilingual employer. She was obviously puzzled by this question. 'That noise,' I went on, 'it's everywhere.' 'Ah,' she smiled, 'the cicadas, I am so used to them I simply don't hear them any more.' And after a few days it was to be the same for me.

Madame B came down the steps to meet us. She was the children's grandmother and the house was actually hers. She and her husband had originally bought it and then enlarged it, buying up old local stone and tiles and transforming it into the six-bedroom house it now was. Later I was to get to know her well and like her very much. She was a strong lady who read *Le Monde* daily, and had no time for De Gaulle. Like my own grandmother, she suffered no fools and perhaps that is why we soon established a rapport and we were often to be found together in the kitchen where she gave me several useful culinary tips that I have used all my life. That day, however, she was just a welcoming figure in dark grey, bustling around preparing lunch and settling us all in. I had my own room and it opened on to one of the small terraces and smelt of the pine trees that came close to the little side window, giving an air of mystery to the encroaching countryside and, on dark days or stormy nights, were somehow threatening in their proximity.

My duties were not to start until the next day, and would be far from onerous. I was to speak English with the children and generally keep an eye on them, but the responsibility for their welfare was to stay with their mother or grandmother. I was to have one day off a week, a movable feast if necessary, and the money seemed generous. My only real problem was that of my clothes, for I had only one summer dress with me. It had something of *The Sound of Music* about it, though the skirt was only mid-calf in length, and was made of pastel-check cotton – mauve, pink and pale green, with inch-wide straps and a broderie-anglaise insert at the top. The bodice was laced and it was perfect for the summer, but I could have done with more than one. I solved this problem, however, by washing it each night, hanging it in the vineyard to dry and then creeping out in the early morning to retrieve and iron it before breakfast. This quickly became a routine, now as much a part of any day as the sunrise and the sunset and the air filled with the smell of the wild herbs and the delicious food that appeared from Madame B's kitchen. This latter was mostly prepared by the local, daily help who was almost as round as she was tall and never seemed to stop smiling. Life could have been a lot worse.

It was unfortunate that, to my mind the children were spoilt, especially by their mother, and the elder one I found very difficult. She was especially close to her father and he was not there, so almost every day we had a tantrum and it was difficult to find things that interested her. The younger one, however, was all charm and very quick to pick up English. They were clever children and already spoke some Spanish, learned from the Spanish maid in Paris. Later in the summer, I was to ask the six-year-old in English, how to ask for a packet of cigarettes in Spanish, and she told me.

Slowly the days settled into a routine and my first day off came as something of a shock. The little village consisted only of a bakery and a small general shop, but about half -an- hours walk away was the small town of Anduze. The walk was along the main road, but quite pleasant even so, for the road ran alongside the river until you crossed the old stone bridge into a central village square. It reminded me a little of Bakewell, the bridge that is, and in some ways the town too, though to my eager eyes it was altogether more exotic. In those early days of summer the local frogs crossed the road in hundreds to reach the river and spawn. Alas many never made it and were killed by the speeding motorcars and lorries. It was a sad sight to see them outlined on the road and I was glad when weather and car tyres had removed their flattened remains from the road surface and I could think of pleasanter things as I walked along.

My first visit to Anduze was the most exciting, for everything was new, but the town really was French provincial and any thoughts I might have had of adding to my barely adequate wardrobe, quickly faded. Still it had cafés and two antique shops, and, in comparison to Générargues, positively hummed with life. I soon exhausted its possibilities but there was a certain sense of freedom in sitting in one of the cafés and watching the world go by, especially if I had been sent there on some errand or other and was officially 'working'. There was one time when I sat next to a noisy and rather patronising group of mainly English people, only later realising that it was Gerald Durrell and his wife Jacqui together with friends. I was greatly embarrassed by their behaviour and very disappointed for I loved his books, the early ones about Greece in particular.

I also knew that Lawrence Durrell had a house in Sommières, a bus ride only from Anduze. I determined to visit the little town, for the Alexandria Quartet had almost cult status in England in those days and I had nearly got run over in Park Lane when I was walking along with my nose buried in *Justine*. The day I eventually went to Sommières, however, though pleasant enough in many small ways, did not provide a glimpse of my then idol. I explored every one of its small streets in high anticipation, but to no avail. I remember a rather parched landscape with a river running through it in which I bathed and beside which I ate my packed lunch from Madame B's kitchen. I remember the town as being set on a small hill, its houses huddling together giving the impression of dark secrets spread by black-clad gossipy village women: the harpies, the flies of Jean Paul Sartre, the witches of Shakespeare. But it was very hot that day and I saw no witches, only a few of their cats, dozing in shadows away from the sun.

And so the weeks passed. They were lazy days mostly, although we went to Alès sometimes or drove for swimming to the river Gard. The evenings were free but there was nowhere to go so I spent them reading and watching the sunset in the gap between the mountains behind Anduze. Then one day the gap opened and through it came Dawn and Dr David on their honeymoon, and with them also came some more, very welcome, summer clothes.

They only stayed one night but it was so good to see them. They brought news of friends and events in London, and we talked the night away. The next morning they left without my seeing them again, only the extra clothes sitting on a chair in my bedroom reminded me that they had even been there. Meanwhile I kept hearing talk of holidays, of going to Argentina, and I grew very excited at the idea of that, but in the event, we went to northern Spain, packing an exotic picnic into the boot of the car and spending the first night in Carcassonne at the most luxurious hotel imaginable. The next day we reached the Spanish border and I realised with something approaching panic that my three-month resident's permit was more than a little overdue. I froze as the Spanish immigration officer took my passport, but Monsieur C was a member of the Corps Diplomatique and with the slight raising of a Spanish eyebrow my passport was stamped and handed back and we crossed the frontier into Spain. I was safe for another three months. Later, much later, I learned that the family had some idea of what I had been up to in Paris, and were in complete sympathy with it all. (The final chapter of that particular story came when I was working as an actress and assistant stage manager at the Grand Theatre in Wolverhampton. I was interviewed by the local press who rather latched on to the story, and made me seem a very exciting person indeed. What they wrote made the whole Paris adventure sound highly romantic and very dangerous. Well, maybe it was, but it didn't seem so at the time.)

We finally reached the hotel in San Sebastian and settled in. The coast there was nothing like the Costa del Sol but it was very beautiful in a wild and rugged way. We took trips into the surrounding countryside and found tiny churches of crudely hewn stone with very little inside except a wooden crucifix and benches made from the local oak. The beaches were yellow sand stretching across wide bays, but the sea was the Atlantic and pounded the shore throwing up a white spray most days. We usually ate in the hotel and the food was good, but I longed to explore the countryside and stop in some of the small restaurants we saw from the windows of the car. It was a holiday for small children, of course, and Spain was judged more suitable than Argentina. Monsieur and Madame C could not have treated me better. I had my own room and always a small bottle of wine with the evening meal, but I was not sorry when it was time to start the drive back and I wished we had gone to South America.

Once back in Générargues we felt a hint of autumn in the air for the end of summer was rapidly approaching. In the mornings when I went down to the vineyard to retrieve my dress, I found the grapes icy cold from the night chill, the sun not yet high on the horizon. But the days were still hot and we hung on to the summer memories for as long as possible. For me it had been my first taste of a Mediterranean-style summer and in some ways it was to be another thing that would affect the course of my life. Still, inevitably, one day Madame C mentioned the return to Paris and the end of my job.

There had been no news from H but Fred, a college friend and he of the striped pyjamas at the Art School ball, had somehow re-entered the scene. He was teaching at a Berlitz School in Italy, so plans were started for me to join him there, but the timing could not have been right, for phone calls were missed and letters never arrived and instead I agreed to go back to Paris with the family.

By this time I had met Madame C's eldest daughter Catherine. She was the child of a first marriage to a well-known writer and a member of the Académie Française. Catherine was an even more rebellious spirit than I. Her current boyfriend was a Doctor, working with Médecins Sans Frontières in the middle of the Algerian war zone. She began insisting that she was going there on a visit and demanded the money for her fare. In the end, and after many stormy scenes, she got her way. I was appalled at how she spoke to her mother, but I suppose I secretly admired her too, for I would never have dared to speak to the Life Police in that way.

I was always more circumspect. We were to become close friends, and even in those early days there was a natural bond.

At the start of WWII Catherine's father was in Argentina visiting friends and fellow writers in an artists colony there and he was to remain there for the rest of the war. He sent for his wife and daughter to join him, travelling across the Pyrenees and into Spain where they would be able to get a boat to South America but Catherine was a tiny baby and there was no guarantee of fresh milk in Spain. This together with the other hazards of crossing the mountains made it too hazardous a journey for them both so Catherine's mother was left with the choice of her husband or her child. In the end she went, leaving Catherine with her grandmother and it was to be a very long time before they were re-united. That absence caused a rift that was never mended and it must have hurt Catherine very much. Together with my adoption we developed an initial bond and we talked long and often about our childhoods that summer. But the summer was over and everyone was returning to Paris, and as the daytime express sped northwards I was forced to address the problem of my immediate future.

Now I had money, for the generosity of my employers had meant that I had hardly touched my earnings. So, back in a Paris changed yet again by the autumn light, I bought a black-and-white wool skirt, a white blouse, some red shoes and a ticket back to London. I walked through our old haunts and searched for someone I knew but it was as though the people of a mere two months before had never existed. Of H there was no trace and I was only to see him once more before he disappeared completely from my life. It must have been months later that we met in London and by that time he was teaching, wearing corduroy trousers and a check shirt. The magic, the romantic idol, had disappeared. I was sorry to find it gone, but he had left me with exciting memories and in the last analysis there were few regrets.

This time my long suffering parents showed obvious relief that I had returned safely, though they were quick to point out that it was now time to start thinking seriously about a career and a more lucrative life-style. What to do? Hathersage friends had all got boyfriends or were about to be married and the gang was no longer together. In any case, I had acquired a taste for London and it was difficult to imagine working anywhere else. So I packed a large suitcase for the third time and, more or less with the family's blessing, I moved back to London.

My first contacts this time were Pete and Carol, happily still living in their attic flat in Hampstead. A bit of floor space was provided on a temporary basis and Carol came up with the news that they needed a games mistress at the school where she was teaching geography. I actually had the right qualifications, so I applied, got the job and proceeded to preside in splendour over my own fully equipped gym at Sarah Siddons Secondary school in Paddington. This unexpectedly quick solution to my financial problems made flat-hunting easier and I soon acquired a large, clean, if somewhat sparse bed-sit in Fleet Road, not far from Pete and Carol and the Heath. Life seemed about to enter an uncharacteristically stable period, but of course I was wrong about that.

My job at Sarah Siddons was well within my capabilities, though if truth be told I was a little nervous of all the equipment in the gym and the far from disciplined kids who were to use it. There were some bright pupils at that school, but a few came from even more disastrous backgrounds than my previous hard cases in Hackney. There was one class where the children were so severely disaffected that if I could get them to change from their ordinary clothes and back again during the forty-minute period then I spent the rest of the day congratulating myself on a successful lesson. Once, having them for a double period on a wet winter's afternoon, I put on some music and encouraged free expression. The music turned to rock 'n roll and when I ended the class I found one poor soul completely transported, and it was some time before I could get her back to earth.

I also remember another girl, older this time, one who smelt horrendously but could not be persuaded to take a shower. She was difficult too, and caused many problems in a reasonably steady class. Eventually I managed to approach her on the subject of why she would not shower. It took several weeks before I gained enough of her confidence for her to admit that her underwear was filthy and in ribbons and she was afraid of the comments of the other girls. So we hit on a plan that would avoid these problems. Twice a week, and at lunchtime when no one was around, I would lock her in the showers, and there, in total privacy, she could indulge herself with the plentiful hot water. I have no idea whether or not the underwear improved, for I never saw it, but certainly her life did. She continued to be sulky and surly but the other children learnt to tolerate her and life in the gym improved accordingly.

Then one week she was gone from school. I was not too worried at first, but by the third week I took her address from the school register and went exploring. In the dark back streets around Paddington Station, in the basement of a virtually derelict house, I found her. She was living with a senile aunt and uncle in incredible squalor. She had two black eyes and bruise marks all over her and I was certain she had been raped. But hard though I tried, she would have nothing to do with me and eventually I left. We never saw her at school again. I tried to interest someone in her case, but shoulders were simply shrugged and I was told not to get involved. The Headmistress at the school heard me out but her face showed her feelings quite clearly. I was told to leave it with her, but I am sure she did little, if anything, to help that desperate child. I reluctantly moved on, but still believed I should make efforts to help some of the children.

My final attempt was with a girl who was being brought up by her grandmother. There had been problems, but Heidi was a bright and attractive teenager though she was also headstrong and had a reputation for being difficult. She liked gym however, so I had no trouble with her and we developed a good rapport. She confessed to an interest in theatre, so I took her to a theatre matinée, after first asking permission from her grandmother. All went well, but the next time I suggested something similar, abuse was hurled at me and I was more or less accused of having an 'unnatural interest' in her. With the lesson finally learned, I got on with my own life.

On the whole, teaching at Sarah Siddons was a vast improvement on Hackney. Having my own gym and office helped and having Carol there for company helped even more. I was allowed to wear my tracksuit (complete with whistle) to morning assembly and there was no homework to mark in my free periods. The headmistress had an unfortunate habit of interrupting classes with so-called 'News Bulletins' that came out of the loudspeakers proudly mounted in each classroom. But Carol and I discovered that two pencils, strategically inserted, killed all communications, so although we missed out on one or two important announcements, the nuisance value of this was offset by the general improvement in the quality of life. There was the necessity of posting a child to give advance warning of a surprise visit by the said headmistress, but there was always someone who hated gym or had a letter from her mother and who could thus be happily prevailed upon to fill the role of sentry.

The staffroom was a bit of a nightmare for the uninitiated, for some of the staff had been with the school in the old building and were rather full of their own self- importance. There were certain chairs that could not be sat in and coffee mugs that you used at your peril. Still we survived rather well Carol and I, smoking illegally in my office at lunchtime and generally skiving off whenever possible. Many was the time I walked into morning assembly, unaware until the last moment that I had a lighted cigarette in my hand and obliged to stub it out in the nearby potted plant, which seemed to thrive on its nicotine supplement.

The London County Council, as it then was, had a somewhat unrealistic approach to its team-games curriculum. Our hockey pitches and tennis courts were situated halfway to Oxford, ridiculously far away from the school. But the government had decreed in its education policy that all children should enjoy the benefits of three hours of games a week and who were we to gainsay them? So two afternoons every week a large coach would arrive at the school and another teacher and I would fill it with apathetic children and we would edge our way through the western suburbs and out into the country. Without rushing the operation unduly, the journey across London, the time taken to change into games' kit, to take the obligatory showers and to change back into school uniform, plus the journey back meant that we had little or no time for the actual games themselves. And so the whole thing became an easy option for all concerned and my fellow teacher and I smoked far more cigarettes than were good for us. Thus passed what eventually turned out to be my final year as a teacher.

With no commitments outside of school hours I found myself with plenty of free time, so as well as resuming my ice-skating, I became involved with the Unity Theatre near St. Pancras. This famous little left-wing theatre was on the brink of going professional and often there were 'real' actors and writers there, trying out a first play or a classic role not available to them elsewhere. According to a note from a pre-war programme, the Unity Theatre came into existence in 1935, when a number of workers' theatre groups which had previously performed in small halls, at public meetings and on the steps of public buildings combined together to establish a permanent theatre with its own premises. They rented a very small hall in Britannia Street, King's Cross, and opened there in 1936. It had been a church mission hall and then a doss house and was a hundred years old.

An appeal was made to the workers of London for help in converting it to a theatre and the response was amazing. Scores of bricklayers, carpenters, plumbers, electricians, and unskilled volunteers set to work on the conversion, ready for the opening night of the first production in February 1937. Over the years, it continued to be supported by trade unionists. 'The aim of Unity Theatre was a simple one. It was to help in the struggles for world peace and a better social and economic order by establishing a form of drama which dealt with realities and reflected contemporary life.

When I discovered Unity there were still some highly politically motivated members, but the emphasis was more on theatre and achieving a high standard with each new production. There seemed to be a modest amount of money for props and sets, etc, and there was plenty of opportunity for a wildly enthusiastic, if somewhat inexperienced, stage manager to become fully involved. I remember my first show there quite clearly, but perhaps that is hardly surprising. On one particular evening I had found the whole theatre in a state of panic. The next production, due to open in three days' time, was a revue – left-wing in content, of course, but professionally mounted and well choreographed and costumed ... there lay the cause of the panic. The costume designer had just thrown an enormous wobbly, burst into tears and walked out. She had barely started and obviously found the amount of work involved was too much for her. I don't remember being asked to help, I think I simply took over, demanded some money, got it and steamed in.

I didn't see my bed for three nights, but with the help of some mild amphetamines, easily available if you knew someone in the nursing profession (and we did), and gallons of black coffee, I somehow costumed virtually the whole show. And it looked good too, though I say it myself, and got a separate round of applause on the first night. I was really high that night, a combination of the pills and adrenalin, and when the curtain finally came down I returned to my flat with double vision and an inability to sleep. Later I slept for thirty-six hours and after that life returned to normal. I never used amphetamines again, or anything else for that matter, I simply relied on adrenalin and grew to love the natural high that it produced. I was not alone, I think most people involved in theatre and television did the same in those days.

It was during the subsequent nights of the show that I got to know one of the actors taking part in it. I had better conceal his real identity, for he played a large role in the next two years of my life, and little of it was good. So let us call him Paul. He was actually a fully qualified chemist, though, like me, he was desperate to work in the theatre, and he had agents coming to watch his performance. I was impressed I think, and we soon started going for coffee, or for rides in his car. We met regularly at Unity and were often involved in the same productions. Programmes from that time reveal that I played several parts there, and Paul did too. Somewhat inevitably, I suppose, our relationship turned into an affair, and perhaps almost inevitably, for we were careless, I got pregnant. This coincided almost exactly with the news from Derbyshire that my mother was ill and had to go into hospital for treatment. During the previous winter she had fallen in the snow and hurt her back and I assumed that some legacy of that injury was now giving her serious problems. Well, I was right though not exactly in the way I thought. I went back to Derbyshire several times suffering from terrible morning sickness and spent a lot of time in the downstairs bathroom retching and praying that no one would hear. For my parents the pregnancy would have been just about the worst possible thing that could happen to me. The fear of my incurring this unmentionable disgrace had been ever present from the time I reached sixteen. There was no way I could tell them, so again I pushed a problem to the back of my mind and struggled on.

Paul was of little help, though he did offer to marry me 'if he had to'. I felt so rejected and alone. I didn't want this pregnancy to continue, I knew that, but I had no idea what to do. As a last resort I phoned someone I had known at college and asked on behalf of 'a friend' if she knew anyone who did abortions. Amazingly she did, and she gave me a phone number. At that time abortions were virtually illegal in Britain and you needed a letter from two psychiatrists before you could even be considered for one. I had heard a story of a young girl who had had a legal abortion in hospital a few months before and the experience was horrendous. A nurse there was said to have left the remains in a jar at her bedside so that she would see it when she came round from the anaesthetic and be reminded of what a naughty girl she had been. Such were the general feelings in Britain then. Sex was something you only did after marriage and a pregnancy out of marriage was a sin.

The woman whose phone number I had practised homoeopathy and was supposed to be a responsible person, but still I hesitated, hoping against hope that something would happen and the whole thing turn out to be the bad dream I still half believed it was. But gin and hot baths had no effect and even I couldn't face the thought of 'doing something' with a knitting needle, so one day I phoned.

The woman on the end of the phone was hardly reassuring and asked questions about whether I preferred cheese and bacon rinds to the cheese and bacon itself. I don't remember all the conversation but she agreed we should go ahead and an appointment was made for the following week. I told Paul and he reluctantly agreed to pay for half, though he made it clear that he felt it was very much my 'fault' and he regretted he would be unable to go with me as he had an audition that day. I felt close to panic but there seemed no option but to go on my own. I had told none of my friends and didn't feel that I could do so now. So I went sick from school and set off on the two-hour train journey to the little market town where the woman lived.

I felt I hated her as soon as she opened the door; she was small and fussily dressed and seemed completely uninterested in me, or my condition. She led me into a small room, like a study, and sat me on the edge of a long table and began. Later she said we must wait for a couple of hours, and she sat me down and left me. I sat there all afternoon, but nothing happened. About four o'clock she brought me a cup of tea and announced that I had to leave as her daughter would be coming home from school and it would be 'inappropriate' for me to be there. I got up to leave, terrified of what might happen on the journey back. She had taken the fifty pounds from me on my arrival, now she told me not to contact her again, and that was that.

I made it back to Hampstead, and put myself to bed. Paul was not back from the audition, and I had no idea what to do. I slept a little but woke sweating and started to feel very ill, then the waters broke and there was blood and a lot of pain. In desperation I phoned Pete and Carol up the road and they came and got me. I told them what had happened and they made up a bed for me in their little front room and phoned Gary. By then he was an intern in one of the big London hospitals and had a girlfriend who was a nurse and training to be a midwife. They came at once, both of them risking their entire careers, and somewhere in the middle of the night I aborted. They were both wonderful, and, I have since been told by one of our doctor friends, had they not been there I would probably have bled to death. When it was all over, they cleaned me up, gave me a sedative, and left me to sleep. I spent the weekend with Pete and Carol and on the Monday returned to Sarah Siddons considerably shaken. I think Paul phoned once, but I wouldn't speak to him.

Writing this has been painful, very painful, but I could not face the disgrace of it all and the distress of my parents, especially as my mother was so very ill. I have rarely felt as alone as I did during that time, but once I found the phone number of that woman in Suffolk, I really believed I had no choice but to go ahead with what I did.

Very few people know of these few months in my life, and I am only writing about it now because I believe that safe, medical abortion must be available under controlled conditions for everyone. If it is not it is naïve to assume that the alternatives will not be used by desperate people, whatever the consequences. I know because I was there. To those people who are against abortion I would point out that because something is legally possible it does not mean that it has to be used, counselling and support should result in each individual deciding for themselves. Contraception nowadays is freely available and must continue to be so. When I was young it was almost impossible for someone unmarried to get help and the Pill was yet to come. Pregnancy advice and support must be readily available too. I was fortunate, very fortunate, in my friends, without whom I would have been lucky to survive.

Still, the days passed and the memories faded a little. Back in Derbyshire my mother's situation stabilised and we were told, by the doctor that she had to get worse before she could get better. We believed him. Why did we not realise that she had terminal cancer? I don't know, but we didn't. We really believed she was getting better, and so, with the summer holidays looming and with lots of reassurance from my parents, Celia, two other girls and I arranged to go to Malaga and North Africa for a fortnight's holiday. And this time we were to fly. It seemed that life was back on course, but it wasn't. The holiday was only a break before the horrors that were to come.

To fly away on holiday was something new and very exciting. I loved the take off and the sense of speed, and I remember what seemed like a wall of heat that met us when we stepped down from the plane at Malaga airport. We stayed one night there and the next day moved out to what was then a small fishing village by the sea where we quickly found a large and very cheap flat. Out exploring on my own, I was walking down the main street when I literally bumped into a girl I used to sit next to on the school bus in my final year. It was my first experience of the serendipitous ways of the Mediterranean, but it was certainly not to be my last. I remember little of Algeciras, (for such it was), mainly because of the quarrels and disputes that were quickly to arise among the four of us. They were almost always about money. The other three earned far more than I and so I had suggested we all put the same amount into a communal float and bought all the basics from that. But they were always complaining to Celia that I drank two cups of coffee to their one, or that we ate extra slices of bread at mealtimes. They never seemed to want to do anything either, but sat lazing around the flat complaining of the heat. Celia was sort of stuck in the middle of us all, trying to keep the peace, largely unsuccessfully.

After a few days we crossed to Tangiers, always part of the plan, and I hoped for better times. Celia seemed excited by it all, but the other two girls hated it. They arranged for an early flight home, spent all their money on bad-taste souvenirs in the souk and left. Celia and I heaved a sigh of relief and moved into a small pensione. We roamed the souk, delighting in it all and being hustled good-humouredly by the merchants. We met a young music student who had started writing his own pop songs, and he took us home to meet his family. There we sat in the inner courtyard of one of the older houses of Tangiers, ate delightful aromatic food and drank the sweet lemonade of the Orient. He gave me a copy of one of his songs and begged help with the music companies in London. All things seemed possible that night and we assured him of his future success, but alas, events overtook me and the music was soon to lie forgotten among the other holiday souvenirs. Many years later it would surface, carefully wrapped, one of the many mementos lying at the bottom of that old tin trunk.

We spent lazy days on the beach, the sand soft and golden, the sea blue and inviting, and then Celia got sick. She was really quite ill, running a high temperature and unable to leave her bed. The hotel manager helped with tablets and bowls of soup, and I did any shopping that was necessary and sat by the bed whenever I could. Tangiers was not easy for a young European girl on her own, but the beach was the worst part. It was very hot in the hotel, (air conditioning was virtually unheard of), and each day I longed for the sea. But any girl alone on the beach would be quickly surrounded by a group of admiring men of all ages. I hit on the bright idea of sitting next to a family group, only to discover that as a potential additional wife I had an even more irresistible attraction for Islamic men. I gave up on the beach and wrote a postcard home, including, for some unknown reason, the address of the hotel where we were staying. A few days later I was astonished to receive an international telegram: MOTHER VERY ILL BUT BETTER NOW STOP COME HOME SOONEST STOP DADDY. I was alarmed but not unduly so, after all the telegram said 'better now' and we had been warned of a crisis still to come. Celia was barely well enough to travel, and I could hardly leave her there alone. Finally, when I did try to change the flight, it proved impossible. There were only four days left of the holiday, so I let things stay as they were and concentrated on getting Celia well again. I was completely unaware that my photograph was in all the English newspapers under the heading of 'Have you seen this girl?', that I was the subject of an SOS message on the wireless and that Interpol were searching for me. But our kindly hotel manager had not registered us with the Police as he was supposed to do, and no one could find me. My Mother was dying and they were afraid she would do so before I got home – and my Father had written she was 'better now' so as not to alarm me.

I got back to London to find that my father had been phoning my flat two or three times a day to see if there was news of me. I made a call to the post office (we still had no phone in the house) and he rang back, asking me to try and get to Derbyshire that evening, but it was already late and he still didn't tell me just how serious my mother's condition was, so I said I would go up next morning and started to unpack from the holiday. And next morning I did as I had promised and travelled to Hathersage. My mother was in the front sitting-room, in my bed that had been brought downstairs. She had lost a lot of weight and her eyes were barely focussing. She seemed delighted that I was there and took my hand, but her fingers were icy and her grip almost imperceptible. It was then I realised how desperately ill she was. After only a few minutes she appeared to be sleeping and my father motioned me outside.

'What is it?' I asked.

'Last night the doctor said it was cancer,' he replied.

I went as cold as my Mother's icy fingers. 'How long has she got to live? What did the doctor say?'

My Father looked at me as though I was mad. 'She's getting better,' he said, helplessly, but I knew, suddenly, that he didn't believe that, though I think it was only at that moment that he actually faced up to the reality of her illness and the fact that she was dying.

I had never seen anyone so ill before, and I was unprepared for the screams of pain that came every few hours when the morphine started to wear off. Perhaps she should have been in hospital, but she wanted to be in the home she loved so much, and my father wanted her there.

The doctor was amazing and always seemed to be there when the pain level grew unbearable, but she was rapidly becoming resistant to the morphine and needed more and more to ease that terrible pain. Finally he took me on one side and asked me if I could give her some of the injections, for he had other patients needing him and couldn't always guarantee to be at the house at the right time. I agreed, not knowing how I was going to do it. 'But I'm not a nurse,' I said, 'I might hurt her.'

'Anne,' he replied gently, 'you can't hurt her.'

Those words have echoed in my head all the years since her death and, I think, finally brought home the enormity of what was happening in that front sitting-room. They cut through me like a knife and still hurt, even today. He took me into the room where my mother was lying, restless and moaning softly, and he showed me how to give the injection. Then, leaving the next one ready on the sideboard, he left.

My father sat constantly with my mother and he hardly seemed to rest. She was slipping away from us, that seemed obvious to me, but he was in denial, convinced there was still a shred of hope. He longed for her to be conscious and rational, but lucid periods came less and less frequently and now only lasted a few minutes. When the doctor was there he was always polite and calm, but when I was giving the injections everything changed. He must have known they were running out of time together and he wanted to be with her so much, but without the morphine she was in agony, her eyes pleading for the next injection. He used to fight me away from her and I had to physically push him to the other side of the room before I could get the needle into her. I think this only went on for a couple of days, but it seemed so much longer. Then, one night I was sleeping fitfully, awaiting the next summons and when it came I clambered out of bed and put on my dressing-gown. I found him standing at the bottom of the stairs, a look of utter desolation on his face.

'She's gone,' he said.

I have no idea when it happened but I suspect he had sat with her lifeless body for most of the night. I didn't know what to do or say. I could only feel relief. Relief that she was no longer in such terrible pain, relief that it was all over, and, yes, relief that there was no longer any need for me to give her the injections. We neither of us cried then and it was to be many years before I could do so. If my father cried at all, I never saw it, but I think he must have done, alone and in despair. But what was I to do now? My father helped, though it didn't seem like help at the time.

'Go and tell your grandmother,' he said, 'she has to be told and I can't do it.'

I dressed and opened the back door as dawn was breaking. A cold, grey dawn this, in tune with the events inside the house.

Tell my grandmother that her only child was dead? How on earth was I going to do that? I walked slowly up the main road, oblivious of the early-morning workers already on the move. It is impossible to keep secrets in a small village and some already seemed to know of my mother's death and muttered words of condolence as I passed. I reached my grandmother's flat and opened the door with my key. I had expected to find her in bed but she was up and dressed. Before I could speak she spoke for me, 'It's your Mum.' She said simply, 'she's gone, hasn't she?'

'Yes,' I said.

My grandmother was so strong, we talked just a little and then she asked me to leave her. She said she wanted to be alone, but would come to the house later. I left, dreading my return to what used to be my home, but when I got there, I found that something had happened to my father. He was busy organising all the things that surround a death, but his eyes were dead and he was moving like a zombie. I never saw him come to life again after that day, and we moved farther and farther apart.

The doctor arrived, and then the undertaker, but I couldn't watch her leave. I started clearing away the signs of the sickroom and made my father help me move my bed back upstairs. I slept in it that night, one of the bravest things I have ever done. I put the sitting-room back to its usual self and then my father told me to stop. From that moment on nothing was ever changed. After his death, many years later, I found my mother's clothes and hats in the wardrobe where she had left them and her purse with a shopping list and housekeeping money was still in its usual place in the kitchen drawer.

Before I left Hathersage I took a walk along the cart track that led to the moors, and there I met our doctor in his car, bumping his way back from one of his patients. He stopped to ask me if I was all right, and then went on to say, cryptically, that he would never have let me give the last injection to my mother before she died. He talked of a time to die and the importance of considering the living, and when he finally drove off he left me convinced that on that last evening he had increased the morphine dose and 'allowed' my mother to slip away in peace. I will never be completely sure, but if I am right, then I will always be grateful to him for that.

Somehow we got through the funeral. I had to go to Sheffield to buy a winter coat, for I had nothing with me that met the requirements of our church-going community. I bought a beautiful one of black, grey and white tweed, with a high collar and flowing lines. I loved that coat and somehow it never became linked to my mother's funeral and I wore it happily for many years. Dawn, too, often borrowed it for special occasions for our wardrobes were still strictly limited and had really only worked when we shared a flat and pooled our clothes.

My father had worked a small miracle and persuaded members of the church and chapel to appear together at the graveside. This was something unheard of in those days and the village tongues wagged vigorously. I remember little of it all, only the village children falling silent and still as the hearse passed their playground – a playground that was next to the scene of my near fatal sledging disaster. And I remember, too, a shaft of sunlight falling across the coffin as they lowered it into the grave, and I feared for one awful moment that my father was going to throw himself on top of it.

When it was all over we dropped off my grandmother, as she asked, and went back to the house. We had invited no one back, even though it was the custom to do so, and anyhow there was little food in the house. My father and I stood awkwardly in the dining-room.

'What do we do now?' I asked.

'I want you to go away,' he said. 'I want to be here on my own.'

I had no money, no job, and nowhere to live. Friends had already packed up my belongings at the Hampstead bed-sit and an understanding landlady had released me from the contract. I had no idea what to do for I had assumed that I would be needed back at home, at least for a time. Finally I walked down the road to the public callbox and phoned Paul in Barrow- in – Furness where he was working a full season at the repertory theatre. He agreed I could join him there, reluctantly, I think, but there seemed nowhere else for me to go. I simply did not feel strong enough to start again in London.

Chapter Eight

The next morning I left early and travelled down to Hampstead to collect my things, from there I journeyed north to Barrow and whatever lay in wait there. I knew nothing about this town that was supposedly to become my new home – only that they built ships there – so I was unprepared for how remote it all seemed. Once Crewe had been left behind we entered terra incognita, cut off from the rest of England both geographically and culturally. It seemed that it was the end of the line in all senses. There was one main street, the docks and the half-built ships cutting jagged patterns into the skyline at the far end. There were small terraced houses crowded into one or two narrow side-streets, linked together in a thin network of domesticity. The overall colour was grey.

Paul had a flat at the residential end of the main street and a good walk away from the theatre. He took me back there, carefully introducing me as his 'wife'. He had warned me of this deception and told me to buy a Woolworth's wedding ring. I had done as he had asked but hated the lie, especially as it turned out to be totally unnecessary – we might as well have been brother and sister.

Why did he let me come to Barrow- in-Furness, and why indeed did I ask to come? I think it was guilt on his part, and desperation on mine, in any case it was a useless exercise. We bumbled along and I began to work part time at the theatre – unpaid, of course. Still I was good at making myself indispensable and could turn my hand to almost anything. So I built flats and painted scenery and made props and hoped for more. Finally someone left and I was taken on full-time. I was even paid a weekly wage – though not much, and it was often handed over half on Saturday and the rest the following Wednesday. Even so, it was a start, and I could hardly believe that someone was actually paying me to do the thing I most wanted to do in the whole world and would gladly have carried on doing for nothing. And so life slowly crept back on to a more even keel and the pain started to ease.

An actor called David Cook came to join us for one of the productions and we became good friends, and were to stay in touch after I left Barrow and returned to London. There were other friendships, too, and every day I woke up to the exciting thought that I was 'in' the theatre. That Christmas I was given my first professional role, the part of the hind legs in the pantomime cow. I put my all into it and got several laughs each performance. Then, after this most traditional of beginnings, I began to get other small roles as well. Inevitably the season came to an end and it was time to move on. Behind, in Barrow, I left a fine selection of hand- made props, goblets of pâpier mâché with glowing jewels made from half-sucked fruit gums and hand-painted sword handles and various bits of scenery and backcloth. I was told I was almost certain to be taken back next season but the new director never phoned and I had my first real taste of the unpredictability of work in the theatre.

Paul and I went back to London together, experiencing culture shock when we joined middle England at Crewe. Once back in London we simply drifted off in different directions, both of us filled with a sense of relief. I thought I would never see him again but after a while he began to phone me at the Hampstead flat and once, much later he came down to London from his home in Scotland and we met. He started to tell me how much he regretted not marrying me and felt awkward about talking about his wife and children to me ... and I longed to tell him to go away and leave me alone but never quite found the courage. Many years later I heard his voice in an advert on Greek television and I went cold.

Pete and Carol moved out of London to take up teaching posts in Rutland and I grabbed their attic flat with alacrity, unaware that I would live in that house for the next twenty-five years and eventually end up owning part of it. The house was one of those built to coincide with the opening of the new railway line to Hampstead Heath and was thus about a hundred years old. Designed for a middle-class Victorian family with a small retinue of servants, it had now been roughly sectioned off into five flats. My flat had the two attic bedrooms, a tiny kitchen and the use of a dilapidated bathroom on the half-landing, where the hot-water geezer threatened to blow up every time it was lit. But the wilderness of a garden was large and had a gate that opened directly onto the Heath itself. A bonus was that it was as close to living in the country as one could get in north London and from the back-bedroom window I could see only the green expanses of the Heath with just a glimpse of St Paul's and a hazy East End. I thought it was heaven, but couldn't afford it on my own, so it was converted into two bed-sits and Celia was co-opted to share it. At last it seemed that I could have my very own 'vie bohemian'. About once a month I cooked a huge pan of bolognaise sauce and held 'open' house. These events were always held on a Sunday and people knew to bring their own wine and pasta. We were a mixed bunch, though most of us were trying to work in the Arts and so believed ourselves to be rather special. I don't think anyone owned a suit or a hat. In the summer we would stroll across the Heath for the open-air concerts at Kenwood or simply spend long evenings in the wilderness of the garden at 99a. I seem to remember the constant laughter and a lot of rather bad guitar playing. I continued to stay close friends with Pete and Carol and they came down to London and I went to stay with them whenever funds would allow.

They bought an ancient Austin Seven, and one weekend we struggled to drive up the A1 to Derbyshire in it. They were to stay with Carol's parents and I was to visit my father. But we had hatched a plot. With the death of my mother the question of my adoption had come back into my life in a big way. So we decided that Carol would come over to Hathersage to visit, and while I went into the kitchen to make some tea, she would ask my father point-blank about my origins. I was shaking as I went into the kitchen and stayed there as long as I could. Finally I returned with the tea tray and looked curiously at the two people sitting there in silence. Something had obviously happened, but what? We drank the tea and made polite conversation until Carol got up to leave. I walked with her to the car, desperately wanting to know what had happened and afraid of what she might say. Finally she looked at me. 'He said you were found abandoned on some church steps in London,' she told me. 'He wouldn't say anything more.' It all seemed an anticlimax somehow. I was still missing the first five months of my life and all the other information that non-adopted children take for granted. Basically, who was I? I still had no idea and seemed no closer to finding out.

The next phase of my life has become a jumbled-up mixture of work and fun, interspersed with the three main theatre jobs that came along. Some ordinary jobs were better than others. I quite enjoyed working as a traffic controller with one of the big new mini-cab firms. The offices were filthy and the air stank of cigarette smoke, but the atmosphere was friendly, and at least you had to use your brain as you tried to co-ordinate cars all over London. And when you got the occasional nasty client you could always hang up and leave him or her stranded. After about 3 a.m. the work tailed off and there was time for a chat and coffee and sandwiches before the early-morning workers or the late-night revellers started phoning in again. I had chosen the night-shift there so as to be by the phone during the day, but it never rang ... except once when I wrote a short piece about just that and actually got it accepted by the BBC and went along to record it. I was employed fleetingly by some East End wide boys to wrap dud rolls of wallpaper in cling-wrap to be sold in a local market. But I felt so bad about doing this and duping little old ladies that I left after two days and went hungry for a week. Oxford Street and its shops must have filled some of the gaps but no memory stands out.

The first theatre job after Barrow was with the Huddersfield Rep, a theatre run by a unique character called Nita Valerie. Even among the flamboyant characters of the theatre she was without equal. For a start, the theatre was hers, inherited on the death of her husband, and had been privately run for years. The people of Huddersfield were fiercely proud of her and supported her to the hilt.

It was weekly repertory again, almost unheard of now, but pretty much taken for granted then, and a very useful training ground for people like me. We were a mixed bunch of actors and actresses but with one thing in common, the need to survive – and maybe even succeed – in a vastly overcrowded profession. And it was a bond we would not have had otherwise. On many occasions our affection for Nita's eccentricity gave us another common bond too, except that is when it came down to casting the plays. I swear Nita never read them. I remember one occasion when we were doing an Agatha Christie play and I saw from the notice board that I was cast as the male secretary; well, nothing too unusual there, not a part anyone could seriously covet. But after the read-through every single member of the company offered to swap roles with me, for I had been given the part of the murderer. For all her faults, Nita was nothing if not fair and she insisted I kept the part if I wanted it. I did, and so embarked on my first professional leading role, and thoroughly enjoyed it. The rest of the cast were a bit iffy at first, but they did come round and wished me luck and made a fuss of me on the first night.

I remember too, Nita's unpredictability backstage. One evening in midwinter, I was standing in the wings in a bikini, shivering and waiting for my cue to go on, when I felt a hand in the small of my back and was precipitated centre stage. I was about a page and a half of dialogue too early and received filthy looks from my fellow actors. Afterwards at the post-mortem in the green room, Nita just giggled and said that the pace was too slow and she had wanted 'to liven things up a bit'. On another occasion she physically held me off stage (she was a strong woman) so that I missed my cue and everyone else had to improvise until she released me and I finally entered, somewhat shaken, and we all tried to ad lib our way back to the script.

Jane Eyre provided one of the worst experiences. By the Monday night we were only just about able to get through it and hardly in a fit state for an audience. We had tried to rig up some sort of light sequence for the mad scene and our unfortunate assistant stage manager had been sorted out a flowing robe for her walk-on as the mad woman. So I was completely taken aback when, minutes before this scene was due, a green spotlight, not known to exist at the dress rehearsal, suddenly came on full strength and a great wailing sound issued from stage left. Then Nita appeared, looking like something out of a pantomime. She circled the stage continuously, but took care never to stray from the circle of green light. Eventually she exited, leaving the rest of us on stage stunned and bewildered and the ASM practically in a dead faint. Later she was to explain her actions with the simple statement, 'But, darlings, I always play the madwoman in Jane Eyre, my audiences expect it of me.' And they probably did!

There were days when I almost hated her and others when I admired her tremendously. She was virtually the last of that rare breed the actor-manager, and being a woman made her even more special. She taught me so many things about performance and stage presence, and after her mischievous sessions in the wings, I was hardly ever to 'dry' on stage. In fact I can only remember one occasion and that was in exceptional circumstances.

We worked hard in weekly rep. There was the play we were currently performing, the one in rehearsal for the following week, and the third one in the early planning stages for sets and costume fittings, etc. I loved it all. Every Saturday, allowing half an hour for the audience to clear and for us to grab a quick drink in the pub near the stage door, we moved in and started the 'strike'. This involved completely clearing the stage and setting the lighting grid back to its original plan. Then, anyone capable of wielding a hammer would start on building the next set. We flew what had to be flown, usually small pieces only, for the flies were not very high, and then we started the actual build. Once the shell of the set was up we went home to bed, returning on Sunday as the church bells peeled out for morning service. Then we dressed and propped the set, ready for the lighting crew to begin setting the lamps around early evening. Actors would begin to trickle in to check that moves, so carefully worked out in the rehearsal room, actually worked on stage. Monday was plotting, a full dress rehearsal and opening night. It all kept you on your toes.

Saturday night often meant a full house and several curtain calls. This was rather annoying in some ways for it only left a few minutes between the final curtain and last orders in the pub. On one particular occasion, we had been performing a rather freely adapted version of *Me and My Girl* and the whole cast ended up on stage in wedding dresses and morning suits. Now, for safety reasons, the front tabs (curtains) were powered by an electric motor while the obligatory and very heavy safety curtain was hand-operated. On this particular Saturday night we had done really well for encores, we were running well beyond our normal time, and in serious danger of missing out on our after-show drink. 'Only one curtain call,' hissed the stage manager, so as the tabs closed we turned and started stripping off our wedding finery on the way to the wings. By some quirk of fate, the ties holding both ends of the front tabs on to the electric rail snapped simultaneously and instead of stopping in the closed position they carried on travelling past each other to fall off the rail at each end into two tidy heaps on the stage. We were revealed in a motley array of brightly coloured underwear, and red faces. Needless to say, what was left of the audience was vastly amused, and we had written another page in the saga of Nita Valerie's life and times.

In the middle of the season we received the exciting news that two of the stars of *Coronation Street* were to visit us for a week and take the lead parts in a modern comedy. For us, this was close to the big time, and when I had to travel to Granada TV to meet them there my cup of happiness was close to running over. We were taken into the green room and suddenly surrounded by many of those famous and much loved faces from the series. In actual fact it was not unlike Sarah Siddons' staff-room, for everyone seemed to have their own special chair and coffee mug. Harry and Concepta Hewitt were 'our' stars (Ivan Beavis and Doreen Keogh in real life) and very friendly and co-operative they were too. Roy Barraclough made up the other member of the cast of this three-hander; then he was known only in the north and it was long before his double act with Les Dawson and his own role in the *Street* as landlord of the Rovers Return. We all got along amazingly well and the week in Huddersfield was a sell out. We stayed in touch too for quite a number of years and when *Rattle of a Simple Man* came down to London to play at the Whitehall Theatre I spent many happy hours with them, walking around London and gradually getting used to all the comments, some good, some bad, that were thrown at them by passers-by and shop-assistants alike. Roy and I stayed in touch, too, mainly by letter, some of which I still have, tucked away with the stuffed toy dog, Joxer, who had a rather large non-peaking part in the play. Then one day the Equity representative appeared at the theatre and set about persuading me to join the union. I did, more in love with the idea of being a 'proper' actress than for any other reason but it was one of the best things I did at that time, for shortly afterwards it was to become a closed shop and Equity tickets became like gold-dust.

Surprisingly, my father came to visit us, travelling on a series of buses in order to get there and leaving before the end of the Wednesday matinee in order to get back. He seemed to have shrunk in size and become a lost shadow of a man, struggling to find a safe spot in a life he no longer understood. He bought me two summer dresses and talked of my visiting Hathersage, but my mother's death lay heavy between us and when I mentioned her name he turned away and spoke of something else. As he left I saw a lonely man, locked up in his grief, but now I think perhaps he was reaching out to me. I didn't want to see it then, and was relieved when the bus took him away and my cosy world of fantasy closed back around me.

We did a production of *The Boy Friend* at some point and I played Dulcie, finding to my delight many years later that one of my closest friends had played the same part at Colchester Rep. We both broke into a far from smooth rendition of 'It's Never Too Late To Fall In Love', much to the deep embarrassment of her teenage daughter. The musicals were always the most fun, and they brought in the biggest houses too, but they were difficult to stage in a week and often produced slip-ups and mistakes that were to leave us trying desperately not to laugh – or 'corpse'. This was, and still is, one of the greatest 'sins' of the professional theatre, and one I really dreaded committing, for once I started giggling it was almost impossible to stop. There were always certain actors who delighted in trying to start you off too, and they were very good at it indeed.

The only other things I remember about Huddersfield are the rather run-down but cheap theatrical digs, the formidable landlady, retired from the theatre but anxious to chat, who stood guard in an almost warder-like way at the bottom of the stairs to make sure that no 'hanky-panky' went on, and the fact that someone stole my Christmas-tree decorations from my suitcase in the hall cupboard. I had helped myself to these from the house in Hathersage and they included those belonging to my grandmother when she was a child. They were very pretty and unusual and I can still remember most of them now. Not a Christmas goes by without my missing them, for in some way they were a link with some of the good times of my childhood. At the time I was deeply upset but there seemed nothing I could do about it for when I mentioned the loss to my landlady she flew into a rage and demanded to know if I was accusing her of stealing. I let the matter drop.

Then, inevitably, the end of the season arrived and once more I found myself London-bound and looking for work. But life was getting better; for one thing I had the flat to come back to in Hampstead, and I was now familiar with slipping in and out of part-time jobs in order to pay the rent. I also had a growing circle of friends, some lived nearby and many were connected with the theatre; life was fun. David Cook had taken over my flat while I was in Huddersfield, and we had stayed good friends. I was really very impressed with him, for he had already appeared in a Joseph Losey film and seemed to work quite regularly in good theatre. He was easily the most experienced of my theatrical friends and looked set for stardom. Somehow though, this never quite happened, and instead he went on to become a successful writer.

He had finished his education at sixteen, and when I met him in Barrow was hardly the most literate of people. He left the company before the end of the season and I insisted that he wrote to me. He was reluctant at first, and when the letters did start coming they were very short and full of spelling mistakes. He apologised, saying he didn't know how to write well. 'Just imagine we're talking,' I said, and the letters got better and better. I have always rather hoped that that was the start of his writing career, although there was someone else who was to have a far greater influence on him. This person was quite a well-known writer and they met when David was acting in one of his plays. He rapidly took over most of David's life, to the extent of calling on me one day in Hampstead and insisting that I 'leave David alone' as he was capable of great things and I was holding him back. I was pretty much speechless and deeply hurt and after that I saw less and less of David, though we always kept in touch and once he took me to a Barbra Streisand concert, a pro preview for which the tickets were virtually unobtainable.

When I came back from Huddersfield, David moved out of the flat, and for a while Celia and I reigned supreme. We got on well now that there were just the two of us and we both had our separate lives. She loved teaching, and was to do it all her working life, while I was happily climbing the ladder to Superstardom via ASM and weekly rep – and two happy people make for a happy home. Of course we did fall out from time to time, but these explosions were minor, and didn't happen very often.

Probably prompted by Celia, I took myself off to Somerset House in order to acquire a copy of my birth certificate. I spent hours searching the archives and eventually had to ask for help. I mumbled something about being adopted, and the lady behind the counter replied loudly that adoptions were in a special section 'over there'. I felt everyone was staring at me, though they almost certainly weren't. I was deeply ashamed and almost left the building. But I pressed on and a few days later the certificate arrived by post. I had glimpsed the one in Derbyshire twice before of course but never read it properly. I had had to take it into school when I was being registered for O levels and I remember the train and going into the loo. The certificate was in a sealed envelope and my hands were shaking but I managed to open it. All I remember seeing were the bright red words 'Certificate of Adoption'. I nearly passed out. Up until then I had believed my half-remembered conversation with my mother was something that I had imagined. But here was incontrovertible proof that it was fact. What on earth were my teachers going to say about me at school? I read nothing more and pushed the certificate back into the envelope and tried to re-seal it. Of course nothing was ever said but it was days before the incident slipped into the past and the world righted itself. The second time it appeared was when I needed it for my passport, but my mother had filled in the forms and I never saw it properly. Looking at the newly arrived certificate then, and indeed again now, I see that some of the information I so desperately wanted and yet dreaded finding had been available to me all along. Why had I done nothing about it? Partly I think, because I was in some sort of denial. I simply didn't want to believe it was true.

Now I had to really face up to the situation. My stomach was in knots, but I read on. I was born at 56 Barlow Street, Southwark. My birth mother's name was Violet May Chamberlain formerly Collet. My blood father was declared to be John Chamberlain, a hall porter of 124 Kingsbury Road, NW9. So my father had lied about the church steps – I was not the only one in denial. Then I read the final column. Here it stated that one was to omit the details referring to John Chamberlain and his address on the Kingsbury Road. It then went on to say that this correction was made by 'S.H. Little, Registrar, on the third of March, on the production of 'a Statutory Declaration made by John Kelly and Violet May Chamberlain'. So what did that mean? Was the mysterious John Kelly really my biological father? If not, who was he?

I decided to let the matter rest there for the moment but spent days thinking of nothing else and coming to no further conclusions but I think it was then that I started looking at the faces of people in the street and wondering if I was unknowingly passing by my father ... for it was always my father that I wanted to find. Many months later a friend drove me round the Elephant and Castle to Barlow Street. It was a cold, wet, winter's night. As we turned into the street I could hardly breathe. It was a strange place, there were very few lights and no one was around. About halfway along there was a pub. My friend stopped the car and suggested we went in for a drink. 'Someone might know something,' he said. 'No,' I shouted. 'Drive away, I want to go home.' He took me back to the flat and there the matter rested for many years, but it was not finished with, and there was a lot more to come.

Meanwhile life went on. My succession of part-time jobs continued to be many and variable and mostly forgotten. I do remember one rather long-term one when I worked for Kennings Car Mart on the Edgware Road as a driver. All day I drove their cars around London, often they were new cars from the factory, still un-waxed and with only three miles on the clock. Sometimes you would get to the depot in North London and find that the car you had been allocated had left the factory without a gearbox, or even, on one occasion, without an engine. And I remember once having to drive an Aston Martin for a whole week as I went from garage to garage and waited while it was custom adapted to the specifications of its new and obviously rich owner. That job necessitated the purchase of a white headscarf and some lengthy detours down fast roads. But maybe I was punished for my hubris when shortly after that I crashed and virtually wrote off a Morris 1100 on the last run of the day. It was not actually my fault, for a car pulled out of a side-road and went straight into me. I was unhurt but shaken. Kennings came out with the breakdown truck and took both me and the car back to the Depot where I sat drinking coffee waiting to be fired.

When the manager came out he surprised me totally. After checking that I really was OK, he demanded rather forcibly that I took a car back up to the other garage. It was wanted urgently, he said, and they were waiting for it. The last thing I wanted to do at that stage was drive another car but somehow I did it, arriving safely and being given yet another 1100 to return to base. By this time it was getting quite late and I was surprised to find the manager still there as I pulled into the forecourt. 'See you tomorrow,' he said, and left. Later a friend explained to me what he had done. It was the old story of getting straight back on the horse once you had fallen off. Driving was to become an essential part of my life in the future and I enjoy it still – I owed that manager a big thank you for what he did.

During all this time, I still continued to be involved with The Unity Theatre, and through them found myself working as an usherette for the big variety show organised for the last night of the old Metropolitan Theatre in the Edgware Road. This beautiful Victorian theatre was due to be pulled down to make way for a flyover. It had been one of the great homes of the music hall in its heyday, and all the stars of that era had performed there. Just to walk through the stalls was to step back in time and almost taste the atmosphere and hear the musicians tuning up in the orchestra pit.

The interior was predominately red – red plush seats and red velvet curtains – with gilt everywhere. There was a bar at the back of the stalls, with 20's glass embossed panels separating it from the audience so that you could sit with your drink and still watch the performances on stage without distracting the performers or paying public. I can't remember all the artists who appeared on that last night but amongst them were some of the last surviving music hall stars and Hettie King and Flanagan and Allen were certainly there. It was a very special evening, the audience was drawn mainly from the modern professional theatre, and I considered myself privileged to be there. After the final curtain, many left in tears, and I was nearly crying myself. I remembered watching the old Empire Theatre in Sheffield being knocked down a few years before. I had stood there horrified as this lovely old theatre, where I had first discovered the wonders of pantomime, was reduced to a heap of rubble in the street.

My only other memory of my Edgware Road period, was making friends with an Australian girl who was also working as a driver at Kennings, and through her discovering the wonders of the avocado pear.

What else was I doing? Well I would certainly have been buying a weekly copy *The Stage* again, walking around with it conspicuously under my arm in the optimistic hope that passers-by would realise I was an actress, and, more usefully, scanning it for open auditions or jobs in summer rep. The open auditions were dreadful, like a cattle market where you were herded through, briefly auditioned and mostly left feeling hopeless and rejected after waiting all day to be seen. Then, sometimes the phone would ring and a young, over-enthusiastic voice would urge you to turn up for something similar, claiming that you had been specially chosen by the director. I also remember one time going for a 'proper' audition at an agent's office in Mayfair. I spent hours getting ready and set out at last wearing the full-length suede coat, obligatory at that time for all would-be actresses and finally bought by Gran after much pleading. I got off the bus at Leicester Square and headed through the back streets of Soho. At that moment there was a crash of thunder and the heavens opened. There was a torrential downpour and in minutes I was soaked, even my shoes were full of water. I arrived at the office exactly on time and was shown straight into the inner sanctum where I proceeded to drip on to the expensive aubusson carpet. They couldn't wait to get rid of me. Needless to say, I did not get the part.

Chapter Nine

It was now becoming essential to have my photograph in the *Spotlight*. This was, at that time, the only casting directory in England and really did a first-class job. All directors, producers, and casting directors had a copy, so via its pages struggling actors could advertise their faces to a wide net of media professionals who would otherwise be unaware of their existence. It also saved the bother and expense of having photos copied countless times and endlessly writing letters. There was a stiff fee and photographic sessions were expensive too but on the whole it was worth it. There only remained the problem of a suitable photograph, and that was a big problem because I am not now, and never have been, photogenic. Something had to be done but I wasn't quite sure what so I put the matter on hold for the time being, convinced that a solution to the problem would present itself at some stage.

After Huddersfield I settled back into London life with alacrity and life moved on as I found myself in the middle of 'Swinging London' where all things were starting to seem possible – and in some cases they really were. It was the time of the Beatles, the Rolling Stones, Lenny Bruce and the arrival of the British satirists. The whole of middle-class Britain was thrown into disarray by the advent of sex and drugs and rock 'n' roll. As far as I was concerned it was quite a timid revolution, and, as I can remember most of it I almost certainly wasn't there in any depth. But there was an excitement electrifying London, and the shops were suddenly full of new and affordable fashions and anything went. The streets were full of it all too, large limousines, often a Rolls Royce or a Bentley, or a Mini Cooper with blacked-out windows usually signalled 'Famous Person;' they appeared everywhere, their occupants spilling out to buy fish and chips or special ice-creams and creating instant chaos and crowds as they did so. I mixed freely on the edge of all this, secretly convinced it would be my turn for the spotlight next. The world had turned itself upside down and the Establishment looked totally out of date and irrelevant.

I heard of a job working as an usherette at the fairly new Prince Charles Theatre just off Leicester Square. I went for an interview, got the job and found it fun. Everyone working there was an out-of-work 'something', mostly actresses but one was a trainee photographer. She was not exactly out of work, for she was apprenticed to one of the top photographic studios, but she was short of cash and needed the extra money. It was she who took me in hand that first night and she soon became another good friend.

The theatre was small and really only suitable for revue or something similar. At that time it was specialising in old-time music hall, something that fitted it like a glove. It was owned by Henry Fielding, one of the few impresarios still solvent in the 1960s and 1970s, possibly because the reputation he had for being tight-fisted was well deserved. Certainly we were not overpaid and it was often a struggle to find the money for the rent, but it always got found somehow and there was an element of security in the job. Mr. Fielding's policy of employing out-of-work actresses was deliberate and it worked well for him. We all wore Victorian outfits, a full length gathered skirt and a tight-fitting top with lace-up ankle boots. It was quite often a case of 'if the frock fitted' you got the job and this rule applied to the boots too, (though there were some spare ones). Fortunately I was pretty standard size and was quickly accommodated. We showed people to their seats, sold programmes and drinks and ice-creams in the interval and were on such friendly terms with the cast that we seemed to be a part of the actual show itself. I suppose we were really, for the master of ceremonies and the comedians often involved us in their repartee and we quickly learned to answer back, feeding their jokes and sometimes earning a round of applause.

I loved my new job and couldn't wait to get to work. For a group of girls who were working together but had surprisingly different temperaments we all got on very well. I especially remember the summer there, the heat and the city smells, the noise of the traffic and the bustle of Soho. All this met us as we arrived at the theatre, but when you left in the early hours of the morning, it was a different Soho, the streets still holding the heat of the day, the neon lights flashing and the pimps and the prostitutes lurking on the street corners. A problem for some people this, but for us they made the streets safer as we walked back to the all night buses that were to take us to our homes all over London. We used to hear the pimps calling across the streets, 'Leave those girls alone, they're nice girls. Go with one of mine if you want a really good time.' And so we soon got to know them by name and often stopped for a chat. It really did make us feel very safe and protected, though I don't think we were in any great danger for Soho was hardly the place it is today. There were drugs of course, and the Chinese mafia and goodness knows what else, but these things hardly touched us and in any case I had a pretty innocent view of life in those days and a great deal passed me by.

It was good to return home to Hampstead too. The house with its wilderness of a garden that opened directly on to Hampstead Heath, the street itself, full of small flats and bed-sits, often filled with out-of-work actors, artists and poets. Byron's great, great, great (?) grandson was to be found in the local pub (already infamous as the place where Ruth Ellis shot her lover), and actors, all currently becoming household names through the medium of television.

I made friends with the other people in the house and we took to sitting on the front steps in the late afternoon sun and drinking endless cups of coffee or indulging in the occasional luxury of a glass of wine. Those days now seem full of camaraderie and laughter. We had very little money, but it never seemed to matter. We lived for the day and hoped that tomorrow all things would become possible. There were occasional small professional successes, a radio broadcast here, a walk-on part in television, even the odd line. Gerry Pearson, met in Barrow, was now working for Rediffusion on a light-entertainment show presented from the carefully designed studio-set of a pub called the 'Stars and Garters'. This was recorded weekly and needed non-speaking equity members to fill the bars, and the trick if you were booked to appear was to keep out of the camera shots, (a near impossibility for a would-be superstar), for this meant that you could be rebooked week after week. Somehow I managed to keep a low profile for several weeks – a very useful source of tax free income for we were all paid five pounds cash in hand on the night. There were other plusses too, I handled my first snake and watched Chesney perform 'Underneath the Arches', tears streaming down his cheeks at memories of his recently dead partner, Bud Flanagan, and their years together on the great stages of British theatre.

In Hampstead village, while out shopping for bacon bits, I often found myself standing behind a familiar figure. Peter O'-Toole could be found drinking nightly in the hostelry then known as The Cruel Sea, Patrick Wymark lived round the corner from me and drank in the Magdala, and so on. But the Prince Charles Theatre provided most of my celebrities, for on the top floor of the same building was the Ad Lib Club, then the place to be. Every night as we were getting ready to close, the rich and famous started to arrive, so we got to know the doorman and he would tell us who was inside or expected to arrive within the hour. We loitered outside as much as we could, and gazed longingly at that mysterious staircase, but the world upstairs remained just outside our reach and I never went inside.

I was, however, developing a taste for the good life. For some unknown reason we received meal vouchers from our employer, entitling us to sandwiches and coffee in and around Soho. But most cafes and restaurants accepted them too, and one of these was the rather posh, to me, restaurant at the Academy Cinema in Oxford Street. So, one night, somewhat staggered at my audacity, I went in and ordered a luxurious meal. I don't remember what exactly but fillet steak featured there somewhere. After the final coffee I asked for the bill, and then proffered a bundle of vouchers. Eyebrows shot skywards but they were accepted, to my great relief, for I don't know what I would have done if they hadn't been, I certainly couldn't have paid. I left demurely but was aware of certain looks of amusement and admiration from the other diners.

Meanwhile, outside the theatre we continued to watch the seriously rich and famous come and go. Dirk Bogarde walked past with Judy Garland on his arm, we saw the Beatles and the Stones arrive – Mick Jagger as flamboyant as ever – and there were countless others whose names have slipped into the past. The theatre held a Charlie Chaplin film season with performances every Sunday, and that brought forth even more celebrities. One wet afternoon I turned to collect a ticket and found myself face to face with Rudolf Nureyev. My knees literally gave way and I had trouble staying upright. He had such a sense of magnetism about him that the very air around him seemed to vibrate. At that time I had not seen him dance and was not to do so for quite a while, but I knew who he was; even if I hadn't I would have known he was special. He walked like a panther, every part of his body totally under his control, and, mesmerised, we watched him.

I have since come to the conclusion that sex appeal is really only an inner energy, and star quality a mixture of talent and this same energy. It all has less to do with good looks or a splendid body. A few years ago, a friend and I went to the theatre to see Ian McShane in *The Witches of Eastwick*. When we got there we found that he was off sick. Disappointed, we almost walked away, but it was a wet, winter's afternoon and in the end we took our seats. I had worked with Ian for three glorious weeks not long before and found him a charming man with a wicked sense of humour. In the film we were making he had to wear a pair of black silk pyjamas and I teased him mercilessly whenever he wore them, telling him how sexy he looked (he did) and pretending to faint with repressed passion. One day I walked past his caravan and found him standing at the half-open door with a bare torso. I whistled appreciatively and carried on walking, but he called me back. As I turned, he opened the bottom half of the door and stood there in all his glory, not a stitch on! We fell about laughing but I stopped teasing him after that. So, Ian's non-appearance on that wet Saturday was a particular disappointment and the first half of the show, whilst professional and entertaining, never quite came alive. We regained our seats after the interval and something amazing happened. During the interval Ian's understudy must have decided to 'go for it', for, when the curtain went up he bounced on stage and made the part his. The rest of the cast responded and the whole show sparkled. 'Oh,' said Sue, 'I'm in love!' and I knew exactly what she meant. Energy equals sex appeal and both were there that afternoon. Ian had competition.

But to return to the Prince Charles: Frazer, my photographer friend there, had by now become a really good mate and she offered to help me solve the problem of my *Spotlight* photo. One sunny Sunday, very early in the morning, she took me up to Camden Passage and posed me against a brick wall. On the wall she wrote my name and statistics in thick chalk. I was wearing my precious suede coat and had a fur muff. This went into the *Spotlight* and caused much comment. Many years later Dick Clements was to ask if I was that same Anne Ibbotson and seemed surprised that I had not kept on acting.

Frazer and I began to spend more and more time together. Not only did she have a sharp mind but she was very funny and good company and had, like me, an over- developed sense of the ridiculous. We seemed to spend most of the time laughing and I do so love to laugh. Money was, as ever, a problem but it never seemed to stop us from doing what we wanted to do, and we were always together at the theatre. Then, suddenly, we were separated, for I got a job with a company taking over the Grand Theatre in Wolverhampton. I was offered a contract as one of two deputy stage managers – a small step up the stage management ladder and slightly better paid. So, it was back to weekly rep, and a different rhythm took over. I also met Graham.

There are some people you meet in life with whom you find

you have an instant rapport. Graham was one of these. Even when you first meet them you know they are going to be important to you, but not necessarily how or why. With Graham it started with our attitude to our work, but out of that a friendship grew and then something more. Our digs in Wolverhampton were landlady dreary and expensive too, so we hit on the idea of living on a houseboat on the Grand Union Canal. But even renting one of these was rather more money than we could afford and so we co-opted the other DSM, a girl, and moved in together. This, however turned out to be not the happiest of solutions, for Graham and I quickly became an 'item' while she, obviously a little in love with him herself, began to feel decidedly left out. But Graham and I were delighted with each other and took scant notice of her feelings, or anyone else's for that matter.

The houseboat was quite a way out of Wolverhampton and the journey to it involved a long bus ride and a tricky walk along the towpath. The idea of owning a car entered our heads and so, after trundling round a variety of second hand car dealers, we found a black Consul for twenty-five pounds. It turned out to be remarkably reliable and completely transformed our lives. Now, not only could we go easily to and from the theatre at will, but we could also take late-night trips around the countryside and away from the sighs and reproachful eyes on the houseboat. There was only one drawback, Graham couldn't drive and so it was all down to me. But I enjoyed the freedom that came with owning that first car, and also the fact that I had proved my father completely wrong.

Graham was as besotted with the theatre as was I and we worked hard and long in it. I was given occasional small parts to revel in and Graham was always fully supportive and helpful as I learned my lines and worked on their interpretation. In the middle of the season we had a free week while an Amateur Dramatic Society took over and filled the theatre to capacity – something we were never able to do. Somehow, by now, we had persuaded our other tenant to move out of the houseboat and back into digs (blow the expense) so Graham and I were free to take the boat up the Grand Canal, or Big Drain, as we had rechristened it. We were moored not far from magnificent reaches of the Shropshire countryside, all just waiting to be explored. But first we had to pay a fleeting visit to Graham's mum in Wigan.

So I drove and we went, returning somewhat unexpectedly with Graham's dog, Pucci, who had been living with Graham's mum rather longer than she found convenient. The visit over, we embarked on a delightful four-day trip with Pucci thrilled to be along. It was still summer and the sunlight dappled the water through the horse-chestnut trees, and moorhens, ducks, kingfishers and herons took flight ahead of the boat. In the early mornings there was a chill in the air, and a mist trailed in wisps across the still surface of the canal. Pucci took up her place on the prow while we drank hot coffee and ate buttered toast and warmed the chill from our icy fingers. Around ten o'clock we started the engine and puttered our way along the almost deserted stretch of water. This was country reminiscent of Laurie Lee's Gloustershire, and the occasional glimpses we had of villages and farms painted a picture of a rural England from a hundred years ago. At night we tried to moor by a waterside pub, food being the main attraction, but also the toilets added to our comfort, especially if they were located outside the pub and could be used during the night if required.

On one particular evening we had arrived early at one such mooring and decided to stay there, for the next stop was some considerable distance ahead. We ate, walked Pucci and then Graham suggested a séance. I'd never taken part in one before, though I and several of my friends had all visited clairvoyants by that time, desperate to know when we would become famous. I believed that you needed at least three people in order to work the glass and we were but two and a dog. 'I've been told I'm clairvoyant,' said Graham, 'and I think you might be too.' This was news to me then, and rather took me aback for I had never connected that 'instinct' I mentioned earlier with anything so grand, but it sounded a rather glamorous thing to be so I went along with it. Pucci and I watched as Graham cut out the letters of the alphabet, wrote 'yes' and 'no' and selected the most suitable glass from the rather limited selection on the boat. Then, as Pucci heaved a sigh and went to sleep, Graham and I put our fingers on the glass and I watched in amazement as it almost immediately started to move.

I really never have seen anything like it, before or since, and I certainly wasn't pushing the glass. You can argue that Graham was, well in the beginning anyhow, but when the messages started coming they were about people he had never known, and when the spirit finally claimed they were from my mother, 'their' and 'there' were hopelessly muddled and a lot of other spelling incorrect. At first it wasn't frightening, just fascinating. One of the first to 'speak' was my father's aunt, the one who had brought him up. There was news of remote family members and then some incoherent gobbledegook. My mother's arrival was a shock. She seemed mostly concerned about my welfare and warned of an accident to my foot 'soon', and she stressed I must be careful 'jumping'. We took note and she finally went away. My father's aunt returned and we asked about my future. She spelt out work in the West End in London and when we asked which theatre the answer was the Vaudeville on the Strand. Then the glass slowed and spelt out 'tired, want to speak direct'. 'How?' we enquired. The glass moved again, first to 'R' then to 'A' and on to 'D'. At that moment our portable radio that had been playing quietly in the background throughout the séance, suddenly cut out. Graham sent the glass spinning, breaking the circle of letters, whilst we just stared at one another appalled. Pucci whimpered softly and when we looked down at her, every hair on her body was upright. For some minutes we continued to sit in silence, the paper alphabet scattered between us and the radio switched off.

We were considerably shaken and it took a walk along the tow-path, hand in hand, with Pucci close at our heels, before anyone of us could settle for the night. Next morning found us still sub-dued and we turned the boat back towards Wolverhampton a day early, but suddenly wanting to be among things and people we knew. Once there, we cleared up after the Amateurs and set-tled back in to finish the season.

Our repertoire included the usual farces and whodunits but rather surprisingly also embraced, if only tentatively, a little of the avant-garde. An example of this was *Rhinoceros* by Eugène Ionesco. Its cast was large, and I was down to play at least two parts, with a quick costume-change in between. The director rose to the occasion and determined to use as many physical lev-els in the play as there were metaphysical levels of interpreta-tion. My contribution to all this consisted of a leap off the stage into the orchestra pit. It was quite a drop and I never actually did it until the dress rehearsal. They had prepared a soft landing for me, a single mattress and a huge soft cushion on top of it. We came to the moment in the play where I was to run across the stage and leap into the unknown. I hesitated, the director shouted at me and I finally ran and dropped into the orchestra pit. All should have been well, but they had been careless with my soft landing and I had not thought to check it myself. I fell with my foot on the feather cushion but right on the edge of the spring mattress. Something snapped and I passed out. I had bro-ken my ankle. Graham arrived back from collecting props and was angry to find me hurt. Then we looked at one another in a state of total shock.

I was taken to the hospital, my foot was encased in plaster, and I was returned to the theatre. I was in agony and I could hardly move, but there was no one to go on in my place that night, so, heavily dosed with painkillers but helped by adrenalin, I did my best. Unsurprisingly, I omitted the jump into the orchestra pit, though I could see from the director's face that he was almost on the point of suggesting that I try it.

After that first night we were left with the problem of getting me home. It was my right ankle, and although later I was to drive somewhat erratically back after the show, that night it was totally impossible. So Graham half carried me from the bus along the towpath and then took great care of me until the pain eased. In time, the ankle began to knit and I became my independent self again. It took a while, but I never missed a performance of the play.

Rhinoceros safely out of the way, *A Taste of Honey* took its place. I was not required to do much for this production and so was ordered to rest my leg. Of course we needed a black actor for Shelagh Delaney's popular play and the one who came up from London was a friend of Graham's. Johnny Worth was lovely, gay, and extremely extrovert. The three of us became good friends and sat talking in the green room whenever we could.

Around the middle of the week Johnny wanted to buy some shaving soap and other items from a chemist so we went out shopping together, with me leaning heavily on his arm because of the plaster cast – and it was then I discovered racial prejudice in capital letters. The broadminded people of Wolverhampton almost spat at us, and the comments, audible ones, were obscene.

'Come on,' said Johnny quietly, 'let's go back.'

I was deeply upset and embarrassed too, but Johnny made light of it and we tried to forget. The next week he got an enormous round of applause for his portrayal of the boyfriend of a white girl in the play. Black actors, it seemed, were fine on stage, but not in the street with a white woman on their arm. It had been my second experience of racial prejudice and this time I was even more appalled. Nor was it anything I could understand, for again, it had no basis in logic or any other form of rational thinking.

After *A Taste of Honey* the end of the season rapidly approached. The theatre was soon to return to its role as a venue for some of the main touring companies and it was time for us to move on. Graham and I returned Pucci to his mother in

Wigan (reluctantly but she had missed her and now wanted her back) and we went on down to London together. We sold the car for the same price we paid for it and set about sorting out our futures. Celia moved out of the South Hill Park flat and Graham and I became determined to afford it on our own.

Graham got a job working backstage at one of the more up-market strip clubs in Soho. I was a little perturbed but he assured me that it all meant nothing and that none of the girls were at all interested in a backstage technician on basic pay. The money was certainly not brilliant, but there was overtime and we could survive. In the meantime I went back to usherette work and my father announced his intention of coming to London for a visit. In fact he came twice, the first time to see Sheffield Wednesday play Everton in the Cup Final. This first visit was only for two nights and, once Graham had persuaded me to stop being a temperamental drama queen and just go with him to the match, it all went off rather well. Sheffield Wednesday lost, but even so I quickly gave myself up to the occasion and thoroughly enjoyed myself, for the atmosphere was sensational. With Tommy Steele singing 'Little White Bull' and other of his hits, and the massed bands of HM Royal Marines, we were soon clapping to the music. Only 'Abide with Me' brought tears to my eyes for it had been sung at my mother's funeral and brought back painful memories. We left a few minutes before the end, Dad, as always, erring on the side of caution and causing me the usual irritation. The roar of the crowd still in our ears, we made for the station and I couldn't help wishing that just for once in his life my father would try living a little dangerously. A few weeks later he telephoned to say that he would be returning in the summer to stay in London for 'a proper holiday'.

This second visit meant a more major adjustment to our living arrangements. To be unmarried and living together was in those days still close to a crime, certainly in Derbyshire' eyes, but I was determined to be honest about the situation. Graham had other ideas, however, and persuaded me that we should temporarily turn the flat into two bed-sits. If we didn't it would only hurt my father, he insisted, and it really was only for a few days and would be such a small thing for us to do. I reluctantly agreed and, if I am honest, there was a certain amount of relief once the matter had been decided. In any case, it wasn't a difficult exercise, for there was little furniture in the flat and Graham and I had been sleeping on rugs on the floor in the living room. The back room was rather damp and not particularly pleasant to be in, so we didn't use it much, we now made it look quite lived in but neither of us spent much time there during my father's visit. I don't think he was fooled for a moment but I'm sure he appreciated the gesture. He certainly seemed to take to Graham and they got on rather well.

After a few days in London he suggested that he and I went to the sea for a few days. Of course I baulked at the idea, but once again Graham persuaded me to go, so I agreed with a bad grace and we went to Eastbourne. It was an unfortunate choice for we had been there before when my mother was alive. Maybe that was why we went but it must have produced painful memories, though he said nothing. The weather was dreadful for most of the time we were there but there was one day when the sun shone and we headed gratefully for the beach. I stretched out on a towel and my father hired a deckchair. Things seemed to be going a lot better and, relieved, I fell asleep. I woke to find an almost black sky overhead, rain starting to fall and a chill wind getting up. I looked at my father, huddled in his deckchair, his coat collar turned up. The beach was deserted.

'Why on earth didn't you wake me?' I asked.

'I was afraid you would be cross,' he said.

Such was the gap in understanding between me and my father. He never came south again, and the memory hurts now more than it did then.

With my father returned to Derbyshire life settled back into its more normal routine and I continued looking for theatre work. In the meantime we had a 'happy event.'

After the season in Wolverhampton Frazer had come back into my life and with her appeared several members of her large family. Only one sister still lived outside of London. Married, she and her family had a house in Portsmouth. Her husband was in the navy and away a lot and she had just given birth to a new baby. She was determined to come to London for a few days and one brother had a car but only a provisional licence. They asked if I would go with him to share the driving and to make him legal. We set off early one morning and returned with Frazer's sister, two children, one baby, a cat and a boisterous dog. Frazer's mother's flat was small and situated just off the Holloway Road. This made a dog a major problem, so Barney (for such was his name) came to live with us for a few days and thoroughly enjoyed the freedom of Hampstead Heath. Trekking up and down the stairs from the attic flat was a bit exhausting, but it was only for a few days and between us Graham and I coped.

He was a delightful character, but full of energy. Frazer's sister had found him on a local farm where he was supposed to be the children's pet, but the farmer had taken a dislike to him and begun ill-treating him. He went to live in the house in Portsmouth but was proving himself to be an impossible addition to the household. They had thought him to be an elderly dog but in reality he was only about two years old and something of a ladies' man. But this we had yet to learn.

Barney quickly made himself a part of our little family and when it was time for him to return to Portsmouth I wept hard and long. Still, we were both working and life was a lot easier without a dog. About two weeks later I finished my evening shift at the cinema and came out on to the Haymarket where I found Graham waiting at the staff entrance.

'Come on,' he said, 'we have to go somewhere.'

'Where to?' I asked. 'It's late.'

'Surprise,' he said and grinned as he steered me towards the tube. We emerged at Waterloo and walked into the darker reaches of the station.

'Where on earth are we going?' I asked again, beginning to get cross.

'You'll see,' was all he would say.

And then, finally we turned a corner and found a large luggage container and tied to it one very small Barney dog with a label attached to his collar. 'Ibbotson, to collect', it read. The tail was wagging and he was almost grinning with the delight of seeing us.

A station porter approached.

'Oh, am I glad to see you. He's been waiting a long time but he's all right. He's had two meat pies and a bar of chocolate. I took his muzzle off as soon as he arrived, he didn't look a vicious sort of a dog to me. Oh, and he's got his water.'

I looked at Graham in disbelief and then with delight. Heaven knows how we were going to cope but Barney dog was back and that was all that mattered for the moment. I gave Graham a big hug, thanked, and tried in vain to reward the porter, and then the three of us set off back to Hampstead on the tube.

We had not been travelling for long when we realised our new family member smelt very badly indeed. The other passengers stared pointedly at us and moved seats. We changed carriages three times before we finally emerged into the fresh air at Belsize Park and walked thoughtfully back to the flat.

'I know it's late,' said Graham, 'but he's got to have a bath. We can't live with that smell all night.'

In fact the situation was worse than we thought. Barney looked like a dog that happened to have a disproportionately large rear end. He was shaggy cute, with a black curly coat and eyes almost invisible through his fringe. There was a grubby white vest, a tiny, black-button nose and an apology of a tail that went round and round whenever he was happy.

On closer examination, however, the large back end was found to consist of matted fur. It was like felt and I have no idea how we failed to spot this when he was with us before. Graham picked up the kitchen scissors and took his shirt off. Around two hours later a slimmer and sweeter-smelling hound was put to bed on an old eiderdown and we headed for dreamland ourselves. Next morning Graham woke up to find he was covered in flea bites from his waist to his neck, and I was dispatched for a flea collar.

Such was the arrival of one small dog with a personality the size of a large house. He was to fill our lives with love, devotion, companionship, comfort, exasperation and sometimes despair, for the next eighteen years. And when he finally died in his bed from old age he left a gap that could never be filled. From now on he features largely in these pages and you will get to know him well.

That next morning neither Graham nor I were working so, once the flea collar had been purchased we determined to take this bouncing lump of dog out on to the Heath and tire him out. It was a beautiful English morning, early summer and it was certainly no problem to go for a long walk on the Heath. So, fortified by some strong coffee and a renewed determination to start as we meant to go on, we set out, Barney straining on his lead and, like Scampy before, eager for whatever adventures lay ahead. We walked up to the top of Parliament Hill Fields, the sun warm on our faces and dappling the grass through the leaves of the plane trees. Once we reached the top of the hill I looked at Graham. 'OK,' said Graham, 'let him off, at least we can see what he's up to from here.'

I unclipped the lead and the small, black bundle of fur shot like a bullet down towards the Highgate ponds. Soon he was only a black dot in the distance, then there was a nanosecond's pause and we saw a huge splash of water sparkle in the sun. Women and children scattered and a cloud of geese, water fowl, seagulls and assorted winged creatures rose into the sky. Graham and I looked at one another and started to run down towards the ponds. We arrived in time to apologise to the parents of several rather wet children and to see a small, black head swimming happily towards us, tongue hanging out. He emerged from the water and shook himself and then looked up at us as much as to say, 'OK, what next?'

Graham and I made our apologies again and walked rather quickly away. We tramped for another three hours, round the Heath, up to Kenwood and down past the East Heath Road. Then all three of us returned to the flat exhausted. Graham and I collapsed on the floor and looked at the recumbent dog. 'We've done it!' said Graham, at which point Barney stood up and went to the door, asking to go out.

For about a month we tried to impose our will, and got nowhere. We took him for injections to the vet's where he earned himself the name of the Perambulating Hearth Rug and fought with every dog in the surgery. The vet advised a special diet of fresh meat and bowls of milk to build him up. We learnt by trial and error that he would only eat if the meat was cooked and served without gravy and in a separate bowl from biscuits; milk and water must be close by and we had to tell him the food was his. We tried to change this routine and starved him for two days until, terrified, we capitulated and for the rest of his life he ate the same way. We took him for long walks on the lead but the second he could he escaped and shot off on his own, disappearing for hours. These hours Graham and I spent looking for him, me often in tears, expecting to find his body at the roadside and increasingly frantic as night closed in. Then, in the pale light of morning he would return, pleased with himself and delighted to be home. This was a gypsy dog, like no other I've ever known. In the end we let him go, and from then on life was easy. If we took him for a walk he bounced along with us, never straying far and always watching to see which way we were going. We took him to friends' houses and he behaved perfectly, curling up in a corner while we ate and never asking for food. He sat calmly on buses and in the tube, loved children and looked like the most perfectly trained dog ever. Only if, by his standards, we left him alone too long in the flat, did he express his displeasure by systematically tearing up a box of tissues, or, once, cracking open a whole bowl of Christmas hazel nuts, the shells crunching underfoot for days. Well, we had finally learned to live together, but it was he who had trained us, not the other way around.

Chapter Ten

Then, just as life was back on an even keel, several changes happened almost at once, all of them to have an enormous impact. Firstly Graham had got himself another job. Our return to London from Wolverhampton had coincided with the time that British Television was moving into a new era. Technology was improving almost daily and a new breed of directors and producers were grasping the advantages and changing the production values of the media for ever. It was an exciting time, but I was still committed to the theatre and had a rather snobbish attitude to television. I was not alone, many of the better known actors and actresses refused to work in television at all, even though the money was far better than anything they could earn in the theatre. Graham, however, had no such qualms and he had secretly applied to the BBC for a post as second assistant director. He now heard that he had been successful and was rightly delighted. With our soon-to-be-improved financial situation we decided we should buy another car. And so it was that one Saturday morning we set out, dog-less, to do the rounds of the second-hand- car dealers. 'I don't mind what we get,' I said, 'as long as it is not a Mini.' 'OK,' said Graham, ever reasonable. But it really began to look as though that Saturday was not the day for buying a car. We found nothing in our very limited price range that we liked. Tired and fed up we were just about to return home when we saw one last dealer's yard tucked away down a side-street. We walked in and looked around and half an hour later left the proud owners of – a Mini! It cost a hundred and sixty-five pounds and we paid for it in instalments. It turned out to be an excellent buy, serving us faithfully and being spotted happily trundling through the streets of Hampstead long after we had sold it.

Barney took one look at it and decided we had bought it especially for him, which in a way I suppose we had, for it made life a lot easier. At any rate he leapt in and sat regally in the front passenger seat and Graham had to squeeze in beside him when we all set off for our inaugural ride. As neither Graham nor Barney had a licence, all the driving fell to me again, but at that time I really didn't mind, and for the next few weeks we exploited our new freedom to the full, seeing friends and going on mini-excursions whenever we could. Barney developed a taste for fish and chips and water from a plastic cup and we all dined al fresco, eating directly from the paper of course. Graham and I also discovered the Buckstone Club and spent some rather silly evenings there. The club was to be found in the basement of a building near the Haymarket Theatre but was not the rather glamourous establishment that its location implies. It was however open until very late and usually full of actresses, actors and anyone else connected with the theatre. We found it an exciting place to be and thought ourselves very much part of the theatrical scene by going there. Much later I learned that Ronnie Corbett had worked there behind the bar in his early days in London and before he became so well known and I was also to have my wedding 'reception' there – but there was no way I could have guessed that at the time.

Then we had a minor setback. One afternoon while Graham was working, Val came over from the Finchley road and we spent a pleasant few hours together. I remember cooking kidneys in a red-wine sauce for our dinner that evening and after Val left I laid the table. Graham returned and we sat down to eat. I took one look at the food, left the table and curled up on the mattress on the floor. 'Whatever is wrong?' asked Graham. 'I don't know,' I replied. 'I've got a pain and I just feel terribly ill.' He fetched Sally from downstairs and they both sat and looked at me as if expecting me to say, 'Oh, I'm all right now.' But nothing changed. Finally they decided to take me to the hospital, Sally threatening me with dire consequences if it turned out I only had wind.

At the hospital they put me into a cubicle and left me for what seemed like for ever. I could hear the doctor trying to deal with an hysterical women in the next bed but finally he came to examine me. I next remember hearing him shout at the still hysterical woman in the next cubicle. 'Just be quiet, I've got a seriously ill young girl in here and she's not making a fuss.' Then things started to happen very quickly. Graham was summoned and told I had acute appendicitis and must be operated on as soon as possible. Luckily I had not eaten any of the kidneys and rice. I remember signing a form and being given a pre-med injection. After that I ceased to care and was actually singing when they wheeled me down for the operation. A handsome, dashing registrar was waiting. 'What do you do in real life?' he asked. 'I'm an actress,' I replied. 'Well,' he went on, grinning, 'tonight you are going to star in my theatre! Now, this delightful young man here is the anaesthetist and he is going to give you another injection and I want you to count out loud from one to ten, backwards. And I bet you can't do it.' 'Bet I can!' I retorted. I think I got to eight. The next thing I remember is waking up with a great thirst and finding a nurse bending over me. 'I want some water,' I pleaded. 'All right,' she replied, 'I'll go and get you some but I'll just moisten your lips first.' I then passed out again. This happened several times. Every time I came round she was there, and always the same answer. Later, of course, I realised that I was not allowed to drink until I was properly round from the anaesthetic, but what a wonderful way to keep me reassured and feeling safe. Then there came the time when she looked at me, smiled and said 'Want a cup of tea?' It came immediately and tasted like nectar. The best cup of tea I have ever drunk.

Graham arrived next, clutching a brown-paper bag containing two semi-transparent baby doll-nightdresses belonging to Sally. (Later another friend sent two maternity nightdresses, complete with breast-feeding flaps.)With these I 'made do' my entire time in hospital, for I possessed nothing in the way of nightclothes as I always slept naked. These, while hardly ideal, at least came halfway towards solving the problem of what to wear now that my operating gown had served its purpose. Graham left quickly for the BBC promising to return that evening. Then I had a visit from my handsome doctor, bearing the news that I was a lucky girl. My appendix had been tucked behind my intestines and about to burst. I had been in real danger of peritonitis and I had been on the operating table for nearly five hours. I apologised for being so troublesome but he laughed it off and said that I had given him an interesting night and it had been far better than hanging around with nothing to do – the fact that he probably saved my life seemed to be of small consideration to him, though he must have been aware of it. By the time he left to continue his rounds I had fallen deeply in love in that age-old tradition of patients with their doctors.

For the first two days I had the luxury of a small room to myself but then another young woman was moved in. We got on well and shared our visitors. Visiting hours were the high spots of our days. I was in the old Hampstead General Hospital, now replaced by the Royal Free, and our days were strictly organised. Visitors were only allowed in for an hour or an hour and a half in the early evening, but the rules must have been bendable for Graham often popped in for five minutes on his way to the television centre via Belsize Park tube. Nevertheless as the appointed visiting hour drew nigh there was a veritable buzz out in the main ward and all eyes, mine included, became focused on the double doors soon to open and admit emissaries from the big world outside from which we had been temporarily excluded. I was lucky, for someone came almost every night; my friends, all working, made a special effort to be there for me and it meant a lot. But not for me the rich bouquets and musk-covered grapes. We were all poor, and if I remember correctly my gifts consisted of a sixpenny bar of chocolate, a copy of a day-old Guardian and a rather scruffy orange long past its sell-by date. Only my father came up trumps, sending flowers by Interflora and phoning several times to check on my progress. Pete of Pete and Carol came, sat illegally on my bed, and made us laugh so much that I had to hold my stitches and beg him to leave.

One morning I received a message from Graham via a friendly nurse. At three o'clock that afternoon I was to go to the end of the hospital corridor and look out of the window towards the main Hampstead road. Holding my stitches, and still half afraid that they would burst and 'everything' pop out, I hobbled along and peered through the window. Graham stood there waving, and with him Barney dog, staring hopefully in the direction of Graham's pointed finger. It made my day.

But then one evening, shortly before I was due to be released back into the big, wide world, a remote Graham arrived, stayed only a few minutes, and left. I was dreadfully upset, disproportionately so. All the old fears of rejection returned and I decided that he no longer loved me and was off out with someone else. No doubt I was still a little unstable after the operation, but that was really no excuse for my paranoia. Two days later Graham explained that Barney had been missing for thirty hours and he was anxious to get back to searching for him and, with luck, find him before I got back home. He had spent that night looking for him, only to hear him barking for someone to open the door just as the morning chorus started and dawn streaked the sky. He said he was so relieved he couldn't even shout at him.

Soon after that the doctor said I could go home the next day. That evening Graham arrived with my clothes and said he had arranged for Carol to collect me in the car. I should have been excited but I discovered I didn't want to leave. In the ten days I had been in hospital I had become institutionalised. Life was so easy there, the routine, the easy friendships, the knowledge that you were safe, all had worked on me. But of course I had no choice, and so next morning I dressed in proper clothes (for some reason I had requested my 'best' dress and shoes), and gathering the inappropriate nightdresses together, I said goodbye to the rest of the ward and left. Carol was indeed waiting, and with Barney in the car too. She tried to persuade me to go and stay with them in Putney for a few days but I wanted my home and my life back, so reluctantly she drove me to the flat and installed me safely there.

Graham came home early, released by a sympathetic director, and we set about getting on with life. I knew we were desperately short of cash so next morning, after he had left, I took the piece of paper given to me at the hospital and crept to Downshire Hill and the local unemployment office. It was packed with irritable clients and very hot. There were no seats anywhere so I held on to the back of a chair and steeled myself to wait. After about half an hour, the room started to swim and I passed out. I came to on the floor with a crowd of people around me, some sympathetic, some not. I explained about the operation and was rushed to the front of the queue, soon emerging from the building with a cash voucher and the assurance that from then on my weekly payments would arrive by post. I made it to the post office and back to the flat, where I put myself to bed. Graham was furious, but the rent could be paid and life was back on course.

A week later I returned to the hospital to have my stitches out. There, the doctor sent the nurse out of the room and asked me very discreetly if I had recently been pregnant. I admitted I had and he then said: 'I thought so, you were rather a mess inside; but don't worry, we've sorted you out and you'll be fine. Just know that for the next few months you could get pregnant again very easily.'

To this day I don't think I fully appreciated how serious that operation was but I certainly did know that I could not have received better treatment or more kindness than that so generously given to me by the staff at the hospital. They had told me I would start to feel better after six weeks, and that the operation would be really behind me after six months. Once again they were absolutely right. After six weeks I went back to work. Then, six months later, almost to the day, I woke one morning and felt really well. Suddenly all things seemed possible again. This was just as well, for shortly after that two other things happened that were to change our lives dramatically again; and this time life was, once more, definitely on the up. But in the meantime there were six weeks of enforced idleness, and I made the most of them. We were all right for money, just; it was summer, and there was Barney to drag me out for long walks on the Heath. Graham was ever attentive, and I had Sally and other friends for company. Life seemed like one long holiday, but as I got stronger my restless spirit began to long for action.

I was in the flat one morning, waiting to go to the dentist for the extraction of a wisdom tooth, when the phone rang. I was sure it would be Graham checking I was OK but it was a female voice on the end of the line. I heard her say something about 'film' and 'spotlight' and John Huston and Pinewood, and was convinced it was a friend winding me up. Then I heard her say something about it all being a great chance but I didn't sound very interested. I woke up to the fact that this was for real, explained about the dentist and asked her to start again. When I put down the phone I had a part in a film to be shot at Pinewood, John Huston was the director and I was to act with David Niven! Frazer's *Spotlight* photo had got me the part. I walked down the hill to the dentist floating on a pink cloud.

I was to remain on the cloud for several days and it was Graham who brought up the fact that I really had no decent clothes and what about my underwear for when I went to the costume fitting? We ordered lingerie from Frazer's pay-weekly catalogue, scraped some money together and hit Carnaby Street. We ended up with a very nice – but totally inappropriate dress, signed a contract for what seemed an awful lot of money and sat and waited for the phone to ring. Eventually it did, but only to explain that they were behind with the filming so they wouldn't be requiring my presence at the studio for several days yet, I would of course be paid for sitting at home. I nervously mentioned something about a script but was told that it hadn't been written yet. What strange people these Feature Film Companies were turning out to be. I was deeply disappointed and began to fear the whole thing would never happen, but one day I got my call and was informed that a 'limo' would pick me up at dawn the next day. How incredibly glamorous I thought, and hardly slept that night for fear of not being ready.

But dawn arrived safely and with it the 'limo' and we drove out through a sleeping North London and arrived early at Pinewood. So early in fact, that there was only a security guard on the main gate. Finally a woman arrived with a piece of paper. She told me off for being so early and sent me to, 'Sit over there and wait for the others.' So I did. The 'others' began to arrive and started chatting. By now it was getting quite late and I had understood that I was due in make-up about then. I approached the woman with the piece of paper.

'Excuse me, but I think I should be in make-up.'

She looked down her nose at me. 'You're a supporting artist, dear,' she replied, 'You'll be seen later.' 'No, I don't think I am,' I objected. 'I mean I was collected in a limo.' She looked at me suspiciously. 'What's your name then?'

'Anne Ibbotson.'

She went white and then red and then started apologising profusely. She grabbed the phone and told me someone was coming to collect me. I looked at the other people sitting there and began to understand something of the hierarchy that existed in the film industry.

A second-assistant arrived at a run.

'We've been looking for you,' he said rather crossly.

'Well I was here,' I replied. He took me to a luxurious dressing-room, fetched me a coffee and disappeared. I sat there for a very long time. Finally, I opened the door and looked into the corridor: it was deserted and silent. I went back and sat down. I had no watch and no idea of the time. I had nothing to read and the dressing-room was bare of ornaments and magazines. I continued to wait. I heard a noise outside and opened the door again, there was a man with a coffee trolley, to my delight the coffee was free and I wished I hadn't turned down his offer of a croissant, but I only had about ten shillings on me and I was nervous of spending any of it.

Eventually there was a knock at the door and the second-assistant came in.

'We've broken for lunch,' he said.' Would you like me to show you the way to the restaurant?'

'Oh no, thank you,' I replied. 'I'm really not in the least hungry.'

'Well, if you are sure?' He sounded surprised.

'Oh yes, really, thank you.'

He went. I was actually starving but sure that I wouldn't have enough money to pay. I mean 'restaurant'? I had hoped there might be a cafeteria.

I sat there for the rest of the day, hungry and thirsty and pretty miserable. At six o'clock the second-assistant popped back to say that they had broken for the day. 'See you tomorrow,' he called out as he handed me a call sheet for the next day and ran off down the corridor. I picked up my things and left. I walked out of the gates and down to the railway station and went home on public transport. I had just enough money to get back.

The next morning at dawn the limo reappeared and we set off for Pinewood, but this time I had with me a thermos flask, a packet of sandwiches and a thick book. Again I spent the day in solitary confinement but a little more comfortably this time, though I did eat the sandwiches in the loo for fear of being found out. The third day was the same, and the fourth, then they told me to stay at home until they phoned as they were behind schedule, etc, etc. I began to be really disappointed; all right I was being paid, but for me, like so many of us in the business, the object was not the money, but the work.

After another three days the limo turned up at dawn and I was back, only this time I was taken into make-up where they spent an hour making me look as though I wasn't wearing make-up, and into hairdressing where they spent another hour making me look as though I'd just got out of bed. I was then escorted on to the set. At last, the moment had arrived.

Unlike the area by the dressing rooms there was nothing silent about the sound stage, all was bustle and shouting. I was introduced to my stand-in(!) and escorted to a chair with my name on the back. I was brought a cup of coffee and the 'script'. This was a single sheet of paper with some dialogue on it and I was told not to let anyone else read it. I looked around and saw John Huston talking to some electricians and then, round a corner of the set, appeared the familiar figure of David Niven in pyjamas and dressing gown. Like, 'Wow!' Then he came across and introduced himself and I could hardly get a word out in reply.

At last I was asked if I would mind walking through my first scene. Mind, I'd been waiting for this moment for days. So I did as John Huston directed me to do, he declared himself satisfied, and I was asked if I would like to sit down again and rest.

'But I'm not tired,' I said. They then explained that now my stand-in would take over while the scene was lit and I should sit in my chair until they needed me again. They must have wondered what on earth they had booked but they were absolutely charming. David Niven returned and told long stories of life in Hollywood, many of which I was to find later in his autobiography. He was the perfect gentleman but I was still too much in awe of him to respond properly.

After about an hour we shot the scene a few times and moved on to the second one. Then it was lunchtime and everyone left the sound stage. By now I was feeling a little more confident so I followed my stand-in as she walked through the grounds to a separate building. I looked around, so there was a cafeteria after all. I queued patiently and got some lunch and then discovered that it was all free! I had starved for no reason. My stand-in came over. 'What on earth are you doing here?' she asked. 'You should be in the executive dining room, this is the canteen for the non-speaking players and they'll kill me if they find you here.' The hierarchy was still in place.

I had never realised that I was entitled to eat free in the restaurant along with the stars and the directors – and as there were four feature films being shot at Pinewood at that time, the place was full of stars like Elizabeth Taylor and Anthony Perkins. I had completely missed out on most of the pleasurable aspects of being involved in a major film. I finished my canteen meal glumly and went back to the studio. We set to work on the afternoon session and my stand-in came over to speak to me. Without thinking, she picked up my script and stood holding it. Someone saw her and fired her on the spot! I was appalled and tried to intervene. Then it was explained to me that we were working on a closed set. I knew by now that the film was *Casino Royale* but the title on the call sheet was *The David Niven Story*. Later I discovered that, officially, we were not there at all. The first version of the film had been little short of a disaster so other directors were called in to try and save it. At that time, I was told, there were no fewer than four units all shooting simultaneously with separate story lines in an effort to save the original film. It didn't work and when the film was finally released it was panned by the critics; my part together with several miles of other footage ended up on the cutting-room floor. But all that came later, for now I was given another stand-in and we shot the rest of the scene. John Huston then declared himself satisfied, the first-assistant called 'Wrap,' David Niven thanked me, John Huston shook my hand and everyone started to disappear. The second-assistant shouted after me that my limo would be waiting at the main gate and then he too disappeared. I went back to my dressing-room tidied my hair and put on my 'special' dress, worn so carefully every day and seen by no one, and walked to the main gate. My limo was indeed waiting, and, as the driver told me later, had done so every day I was at Pinewood.

And so we drove back into my normal life and I pondered the sad fact that through ignorance and timidity, I had missed out on a great experience and the possibility of more work in films. It was, of course, quite funny, especially for the film people who must have realised how hopelessly inexperienced I was.

Graham was in the flat when I got back and he did his best to cheer me up, but I was not happy. I felt a fool and there was also a great sense of anti-climax. A few days later a cheque arrived in the post. It was for a staggeringly large amount, by our standards anyhow. We were well and truly back in the black. But I was still not a very happy bunny and so I was delighted when I heard that the Oxford Playhouse Company was looking for a deputy stage manager for their new season.

The Oxford Playhouse Company (Meadow Players Limited) was formed in 1956, with Frank Hauser as artistic director, and a policy which at that time was extremely daring. This policy was to mount international plays which had not been seen, or had been rarely seen, in Britain, while at the same time engaging actors of high quality to appear in them. The Royal Court Theatre had been the first one to start a company with similar objectives, but no other companies were yet being so adventurous. The policy worked well, however, and the Oxford Playhouse had a fine reputation and Frank Hauser continued to be in charge. Pushed in the direction of the telephone by Graham, but nevertheless almost visibly shaking, I finally phoned Frank at his flat just off the Finchley Road. Within an hour I was ringing his doorbell for an interview and emerged shortly afterwards with the job and a promise of two acting roles during the season. I was thrilled and so was Graham. Life was obviously going to get complicated, but we'd cope somehow, at least the majority of rehearsals were to take place in London and we had the car. Then, two days later, Graham came up with some other good news. The people in the garden flat in our house were moving out and Graham had phoned our landlord and secured it for us. No more climbing up and down the stairs on the whim of a demanding mongrel, and the flat was much bigger, with a proper bathroom and a reasonably functioning water heater. We were to move in at the end of the month.

I loved being with the Oxford Playhouse Company and was very proud to be there. All new jobs are terrifying at first, but everyone went out of their way to be friendly and involve me in everything that was happening. I quickly settled in. I was not much a part of the first production as rehearsals had already started and there was another DSM in charge and I have no recollection what that play was, for the theatre programmes I still have, fail to reveal the title. Still I am reasonably sure that I worked on alternate productions and that 'my' first one was *Ardèle* by Jean Anouilh.

We held rehearsals in a large sunny room in Earl's Court (the White House Hotel, maybe?) and I used to trot off eagerly every morning, full of enthusiasms and a hundred new ideas for making the production 'better'. With infinite patience Frank usually explained why they wouldn't work, but then, very occasionally accepted one as being, 'rather a good idea'. When this happened my day became tinted with a rosy hue and I couldn't wait to get home to tell Graham the good news. The cast consisted of George Pravda, Patricia Jessel, Hugh Paddick, Heather Chasen, Philip Voss, Christopher Gable, Prunella Ransome, Paul Large, Anne Salingar and Helen Weir. To me they represented a formidable group and I started off addressing the older members as 'Miss' and 'Mr'. I was soon asked to stop, however, and over the rehearsal weeks we developed into a tight-knit and friendly group. The days also settled into a routine – rehearsals in London until about three o'clock, a quick sandwich for lunch, then into the car and off to Oxford for the evening performance. Then it was back into the car and the reverse journey to London in order to be in the right place for rehearsals the next day. Sundays, except for production weekends, were free and life seemed suddenly most civilised.

Graham completed the move to the garden flat all by himself and I simply came home one night to find the wood-burning stove happily ablaze, our few bits of furniture spread carefully around and a new acquisition of a bedside lamp made from an empty Chianti bottle filled with orange dye and a lampshade made from string. Barney dog was stretched luxuriously in front of the fire and there was a Nigerian student installed in the 'bedroom' as part of Graham's economic strategy to cope with the rather large (to us) increase in the rent.

All three of us grew very fond of Philip, our lodger, and Barney spent many happy hours with him while he was studying, though he never became reconciled to his gentle, but forceful ejection when Philip was entertaining one of his vast collection of girlfriends. Even Graham was stunned by Philip's reputation as a ladies' man but it never really gave us any problems and in every other way he was an ideal tenant, never complaining about the basic furniture and cheap curtains we had provided, and always paying his rent on time. I was delighted with the arrangement, for the two favourite men in my life seemed delighted with their new routines, had plenty of interesting company and the money to go out in the evenings if they so wished.

Graham had fitted a 'doggy' flap to our back door and a trip to a local market had produced a second-hand but proper dog bed. This latter would have been more appropriate for an Alsatian than our spaniel-sized mongrel but Barney was delighted with it and promptly moved in all his favourite possessions such as old bones, a (clean) pair of my knickers and some mouldy dog biscuits, obviously hoarded against a rainy day. Graham and I now had a 'proper' bed too, although we hadn't yet managed to scrape up the money for a pair of curtains, a problem that we solved by simply turning off the light before we got undressed. Life felt decidedly good.

And there were other advantages as well. Sally, the landlord's daughter, still lived upstairs and was a useful, extra hand to feed Barney if required, and Joe, until the arrival of Philip our 'token' black man in the street, was also a car mechanic with his own small mews garage. He was a warm, generous man and always happy to help if there was a problem with the Mini. He quickly got the car heater working and it provided much comfort on the journeys to and from Oxford in the cold winter months that lay ahead. But for the moment all was sunshine.

Ardèle opened in Oxford and played successfully there. Then we took it on tour. I think the Nuffield Theatre in Southampton was our first stop, but I'm not sure now. At any rate I remember arriving there, finding digs and helping with the lighting rig, as taught by Frank in Oxford. As DSM I was running the corner and had learnt by now how important this job really was. I was responsible for all the different cues, lighting, flies, music, etc., and it really was possible to add to the quality of the show with my timing. I was also rapidly developing a sixth sense for when an actor 'dried'; a clever prompt would rapidly get things moving again and the sharp stab of fear that came hurtling across to the prompt corner, once detected, was soon calmed.

I was looking forward to the evening's show on one particular morning and only wondering how to fill the middle of the day when I heard the phone ring in the hall of my digs. It was quite late morning for I was savouring the opportunity of staying in bed, a chance for some daydreaming, no doubt, and I certainly wasn't expecting it to be for me, but it was. On the other end of the line was the company manager. 'Pat Jessel is ill,' he said, 'you'll have to go on for her tonight. Learn the lines and come to the theatre about three o'clock for a rehearsal. OK?' 'OK,' I replied quite calmly and began wondering where I could buy some theatrical make-up. Learning the lines was not difficult, for the colonel's wife only appeared at the end of Act 3 and after being on the book for several weeks, I knew most of them anyway. I got dressed and headed into the town centre in search of make-up and managed to find the essential 5 and 9 sticks and a few liners, then I made for the theatre. It was silent and dark but just before three o'clock the company manager arrived with George Pravda. 'So,' said George, 'let's do it.' We walked together into the theatre and I switched on the work lights. I went backstage and climbed the offstage staircase to the door through which the Colonel's wife made her dramatic entrance. On stage I began to walk slowly down the stairs saying the lines in my head as I hit the various marks I knew so well from rehearsals.

'No,' called out George, 'you've got to do it for real,'

'Yes, I will,' I shouted back. 'I'm just marking it through first.'

'Oh, sorry.' came the reply.

I finished my walk through and returned to the top of the stairs. 'In your own time,' said George. I psyched myself up as best I was able, trying to become the older, bitter, slightly mad woman that the part required, and then I started my descent. George fed me my cues and we went through to the end of my 'bit'. There was a pause and I looked at George, expecting notes and help. He just stood there, eventually I heard him say, 'Just do it like that tonight.' And he walked out of the theatre.

I was completely thrown. Was I so bad there was nothing he could do? Or was I OK? I simply had no idea. I switched off the work lights and walked backstage to the green room; it was empty, in fact the whole theatre seemed to be empty, so somewhat at a loss I just sat there and waited for someone to appear. Eventually the other actors started drifting in and the theatre began to come alive. Everyone knew what had happened and they all rallied round and gave me lots of support. Heather helped me with my make-up. 'Just screw your face up and paint in all the lines,' she said, so I did. 'Goodness,' she exclaimed later, 'no one has as many lines as that. Take some out.' So I did.

They made me run the corner for the first two acts, something I thought was very unfair but looking back I think it was to stop me getting too nervous. But I wasn't nervous at all and felt completely in control and rather excited. Then came Act 3 and I went back to Pat's dressing-room to check my make-up and put on the wig, etc. The wig didn't fit and the nightdress was too long, and I simply gave up on the slippers. Then I sat there listening to the words over the intercom and nerves clicked in. I heard the stage manager call me on stage and I made my way backstage, ready for my entrance. I was shaking from head to foot and my mind was a blank. I suddenly knew that there was no way I could walk on stage, the play would end in a shambles and I would have to give up the theatre and go back to whatever there was to go back to. Then I heard my cue and the next thing I knew I was centre stage, my mind was clear and the words were there, I was in full control of every inch of my body and what is more I had the audience in the palm of my hand. It was like no other feeling I had ever known and I loved it. I started my descent and took the audience with me. I could sense them all out there, every one of them, and they were mine. I came to the end of my 'bit' and exited, standing in the wings for the final pages of the play. 'Not bad.' said the SM, but I hardly noticed. Then there were the curtain calls and the applause. The other actors, generous as always, pushed me forward for one of my own. It was a very special moment. Then it was all over. Back in the dressing-room I started to take off my make-up. People came in to say, 'Well done,' but I was still flying on adrenalin and my feet weren't touching the floor. I remember some of the cast took me out for dinner and I was still floating when I finally got back to my digs. Next morning I woke up and remembered. I felt as though the world would never be the same again, and I wanted more. I had been on stage before of course, sometimes playing a leading role, and I remembered one night at Wolverhampton playing a comedy there. I was on stage with Gerry Cowan and that night we got an enormous laugh, built on it, heard it grow and built on it again, until the whole theatre was roaring with laughter. That too was pretty special, but not like this. I can only explain it by saying that whereas then I had been stage-struck, that night in Southampton the theatre entered my blood and was never to leave it. I walked around in a daze for most of the day, just waiting until it was time to go to the theatre. Eventually I found myself in Pat Jessel's dressing-room picking up the 5 and 9. There were nerves this time but they were nothing like before and I was eager for Act 3.

I think I only played the part for three nights but I remember on one of them turning to deliver some lines to Hugh Paddick and finding him missing. It was a shock, but Nita Valerie's training carried me through and I simply turned and addressed one of the other actors. After the show Hugh came to find me and apologised. He had a cold and felt a coughing fit coming on, so he left the stage in order not to detract from the scene – Hugh Paddick, apologising to me? It was a gracious gesture from a gracious man and I felt very much a part of that production then. But Pat came back and I returned to the prompt corner and the tour went on.

Back in Oxford the cast fragmented and we moved on to the next production. This was to be *The Mad Woman of Chaillot* by Jean Giraudoux, and Elizabeth Bergner was its star. It was to be directed by Minos Volanakis, a Greek director friend of Frank's, and another landmark figure in my life, although, again, there was no hint of it on that first day of rehearsal. I had seen Minos's work before I joined The Oxford Playhouse, and he already had a considerable reputation. This fact had slipped my memory, however and I met him with a completely open mind. He was simply like no other director I had ever met, or, as it turned out, was ever to meet again. From him I learnt more about acting and directing for the theatre than I was to learn from anyone else and the lessons were to be with me for life. But he was not easy. With the value of hindsight I can say categorically he was very Greek. I grew to love working with him but alas the same could not be said for Miss Bergner. She was well known in the UK in both theatre and film and also a famous star in Austria where she had obviously been treated as such. Rehearsals were stormy. At one point Minos walked out, winking at me as he did so and informing everyone that I was in charge. For two or three days he and Miss Bergner communicated by notes, ferried back and forth by Mike the student ASM. We in the meantime struggled on in rehearsals as best we could. But eventually an uneasy truce was established and we got the play back on the rails. My memory of it is one of a riot of colour. The costumes and sets gave an air of magic to the whole production, though, in my case, they presented a considerable challenge every night. In this production I had my very own speaking role, that of the Second Red Lady. I relished my small role and threw myself into it wholeheartedly and I clearly remember that Minos said at one point, 'Watch out for the Second Red Lady, I think she's going to be very big.' I took this as a compliment and soldiered on; in any case he made no attempt to tone me down and seemed to find it all rather amusing. There were three of us and we each wore a skin-tight, red satin dress, high, white stiletto heels and a mask through which we could only see straight ahead. A long necklace of table tennis-balls and a very long cigarette holder completed our costumes. So far, so good but we had to make our entrance down a steep flight of stairs. Balanced precariously and seeing virtually nothing, we could only take a deep breath and trust to luck. How the Third Red Lady coped I have no idea, for 'she' was being played by Mike in an identical costume to mine – with the addition of a very firm jockstrap, I assume!

I don't think I appreciated the play as a great piece of theatre, for I was far too in love with the fact that I had a speaking role of my very own, and a share of a dressing room to go with it. My name was in the programme too, and I'm sure one was sent back to Derbyshire, thus increasing my father's conviction that I was well on the road to perdition. But Graham was as supportive as ever, and I could see great things lying just ahead. We completed our run at Oxford and set off on tour once again. We were at Guildford when disaster struck. I had made my entrance, said my lines, and turned to exit when I became aware that one of my stiletto heels was stuck firmly down a small hole in the stage. I couldn't move, and no matter how hard I tugged, it was to no avail. Then, aware that an unsuspecting and optically challenged Mike was rapidly approaching from stage left, I decided to abandon my shoe and limp off. But this was easier said than done, for the shoe was half a size too big and had been attached to my stocking clad foot with a tenacious heel grip. I struggled and struggled and at last there was a loud ripping sound and my foot came free. By this time the audience had latched on to what was happening and they were beginning to enjoy themselves thoroughly. I limped off to a round of applause and then watched in suspense as the still unaware Mike missed the resplendent shoe by a hair's breadth and completed his part of the scene successfully. I turned away in relief just as Chris Gable signalled to me that he was going on stage to retrieve my errant piece of footwear. 'Don't,' I hissed, trying to warn him that it was very firmly stuck indeed. But he was gone.

Chris, internationally famous as one of Britain's great ballet dancers, had recently sustained a badly torn ligament and had turned his many talents towards acting. But it was as a ballet dancer that he flew on to the stage, stooped elegantly down to the offending shoe and tugged. And tugged and tugged. The audience were now laughing long and loud as Chris found himself stranded there, not knowing what to do. But the shoe must have grown tired of being capricious, for it suddenly came free, taking its rescuer by surprise, and throwing him on to his back, legs in the air. Somewhat chastened, he picked up both himself and the shoe and left the stage to a thunderous round of applause. The play continued.

Minos was not in the theatre that afternoon, but when told what had happened, he seemed delighted with both the event and his actors' reaction to it. So much so that for a moment we were afraid he might say, 'Keep it in.' – we were beginning to understand the workings of our new Director's mind, and, what is more, we were beginning to enjoy it.

The rest of the tour passed without any more dramas (as far as

I remember) and we returned to Oxford to begin work on the next production. Meanwhile back at 99a South Hill Park life was progressing fairly smoothly. Graham was doing well at the BBC and often working on *Top of the Pops*. He began coming home with tales of meeting the celebrities, and of being offered first choice of the, apparently, willing girls who came each week to make up the audience. Their availability shocked both of us, and it was a sign of the times that none of the other production staff could understand why Graham politely, but firmly, turned them down. It was a happy time. True we didn't spend as much of it together as we would have liked, but my contract only had a few months to run, the new flat enhanced our quality of life considerably, Barney had settled in completely and we had more money than we had ever had before. And Christmas was approaching.

My next production, and the one that was to run over Christmas, was *The Rivals* by Sheridan. My acting career had come to what I hoped was only a temporary halt and I had returned to running the corner. John Cox was the director and I rather think we rehearsed in Oxford, for I have no memories of Earl's Court. I was also seeing quite a lot of Dawn and Dr David, for they were now living in Oxford as David was pursuing his career at the Radcliffe Hospital. But with Christmas looming, my immediate problem was my share of the planning of this event and somehow finding time to buy some presents.

As it was our first Christmas in the new flat we determined to make it a very special one. Graham had decreed that we should have a series of presents starting on Christmas Eve and running throughout the big day. There was also a Barney dog to be catered for and three stockings were to be hung over our newly acquired fireplace. So, when Christmas Eve finally arrived, we rose comparatively early, walked the hound and set about our various tasks. First we did all the market shopping and then Graham left to buy the turkey. He had decided to go to Smithfield fairly late in the day as he had heard that birds were sold off very cheaply then. He duly departed and I set about the finishing stages of the stuffing. I had found a recipe in *The Sunday Times* and was determined to give it a try. The first stage had been completed twenty four hours earlier as directed, and this involved soaking apricots in brandy and prunes in port. The two dishes stood ready in the kitchen and I began to assemble the rest of the ingredients. At this stage, Barney dog expressed a total lack of interest in the proceedings and left to visit a lady friend who lived a few doors away. I concentrated carefully and by now the kitchen was full of the most delightful smells. I reached the end of the mixing stage and then went into the living-room flushed with success and bearing a mug of coffee. I put some music on the stereo and settled down to await the return of my men.

Graham (unsurprisingly) was the first to return. And he was carrying the largest turkey I have ever seen. Apparently, only the big ones were left and it was very cheap. The fact that we didn't possess a roasting dish of an appropriate size and that there was a strong possibility we wouldn't even be able to get it into the oven were minor considerations for the time being. We then decided to get rid of the coal-burning stove and open up the proper fireplace. This took some time and we were both rather sooty by the time it was accomplished, but it was worth the effort, and when Barney returned he took up immediate residence in front of the fire and hardly moved all evening. Graham and I cleaned up and I considered the logistics involved in stuffing the turkey. This turned out to be less complicated than I had anticipated and we even managed to concoct a baking device out of our small roasting tin and a vast quantity of baking foil. We squeezed the turkey into the oven and turned to other things. At that point Graham pointed to the two bowls still sitting on the kitchen table containing the apricots and the prunes. 'What are these for?' he asked, not unreasonably. I grabbed the recipe and read it carefully; apart from the original order to soak the prunes and the apricots, there was no further mention of them. We looked at one another and shrugged, then, with considerable difficulty, we retrieved the turkey from the oven and extracted the stuffing, discovering in the process that I had forgotten to remove the giblets. I glared at Graham and he tactfully refrained from comment. Then we added the fruit to the rest of the stuffing and jammed the turkey back into the oven. We poured the brandy and the port into two glasses and joined Barney in front of the fire to work out how many hours our Christmas albatross would take to cook. It quickly became obvious that if we wished to eat dinner at the traditional hour then we were going to be up most of the night supervising it. A change of plan was therefore deemed necessary. Well, it wasn't difficult. We would have brunch in the morning, and eat everything else in the evening. That decided we opened our Christmas Eve presents and nibbled on a few nuts. My pressie was a packet of coffee beans. I expressed pleasure but thought Graham had made a mistake for we had no coffee grinder. Graham grinned happily, and crossed to put some music on. It was magic sitting there, all three of us, warm and happy and with so many good things to look forward to. We had a small Christmas tree with decorations that Graham had inherited at the end of one of the BBC seasonal pre-recordings, and we had found holly on the Heath. The fire flickered in the grate and threw romantic shadows across the room and whispered the possibility of peace on earth and goodwill to all men. I wanted it to go on forever.

'Let's go to the midnight carol service,' said Graham.

'Oh, yes,' I replied.

So we pulled on our coats and set off for the church at the top of Pond Street.

Somehow it made the perfect end to a near perfect day, and when we left the church we found that it had started snowing. Everywhere was white and a flurry of snowflakes swirled around as we shouted, 'Merry Christmas' to complete strangers and walked hand in hand back to the place that had become the first real home I'd ever felt was mine.

We dragged a reluctant Barney dog away from the fire and walked him quickly round the block. There were still people about, and down the road someone was having a party. We, however, wanted only to hurry back. It was time to go to bed and, like three excited children, dream of all the surprises that tomorrow was sure to bring.

I woke next morning to find my two men standing expectantly by the bed. One was holding two glasses of champagne, while the other was standing wet and soggy, his tail going round in circles.

'Happy Christmas, darling,' said the champagne holder. 'Come on, wake up, it's time to open your big pressie.'

I am never at my best when I first wake up, and, although I tried hard, the only word that came from my mouth was, 'Coffee.'

'Soon,' replied an unrepentant Graham. 'Quickly, open your pressie and drink your champagne.'

I struggled to do the two things at once, and then all became clear. My pressie was a coffee grinder! Graham laughed and went into the kitchen. I leaned back against the pillows and looked around the room. The fire was once again blazing in the grate. Three filled stockings hung from the mantelpiece (I had slipped out of bed to fill Graham's in the middle of the night whilst he slept soundly beside me. The other two were still empty then, but not so now). Presents lay piled under the tree and from the kitchen came the smell of fresh coffee and the spitting sound of roasting meat. Outside the curtain-less windows the snow was lying thick across the garden, only tiny bird footprints crisscrossed the vivid white and nothing disturbed the sound of silence. A squirrel ran up the fir tree near the window and a small avalanche fell from a branch, the snow seeming to float down to the ground in slow motion. Time hung suspended.

Graham returned with the coffee and we snuggled back under the blankets. Barney, sensing the way things were obviously going, heaved a long sigh and went off in a huff to spread Christmas greetings around the neighbourhood yet again. Later Graham cooked brunch, and Barney returned with consummate timing, just as the first piece of grilled bacon hit the plate. We all ate breakfast and opened our stockings, Barney insisting on opening his himself, burrowing his nose deep inside until he reached the smelly bone at the bottom. Mine was full of little goodies but we both had the traditional orange and nuts and silver sixpence. We started to open the packages under the tree, and I forget now what they contained, but we had a book and a record each and Barney excelled himself again by locating his box of Doggy Chocs and tearing off the wrapping himself. Then the sun came out and we put on our coats, tied a red ribbon to Barney's collar and set out to walk around the Heath. Everywhere families were sledging and building snowmen. Excited dogs raced across the snow and threatened to turn over speeding toboggans and tottering toddlers, but no one minded and the laughter and screams rang across Parliament Hill. We walked up to the quieter regions of Kenwood and Barney went mad following the badger tracks. Ice covered the still waters of the ponds and Kenwood House looked suitably majestic as the sun slipped down the sky leaving long shadows and our breath drifted white in the cold air. Hunger drove us back, it was time to retrieve the albatross from the cooker and put on the Brussels sprouts.

In memory at least, the meal was perfect. We had so much food we couldn't possibly eat it all. There was the turkey, of course, the sprouts and bread sauce and roast potatoes and roast turnips and carrots. For later I had made a trifle, homemade mince pies and even a small iced cake. It was all far too much ... never mind. We still had no table so we ate sitting on the floor, Barney's bowl, for once, allowed into the living-room. He seemed delighted with it all, though his red bow now hung limp and muddy from his collar. We finally took it off much to his relief, for he had been deeply embarrassed by it and obviously felt that he had lost face in the neighbourhood.

By the time we finished eating it was well into the evening and the day was reaching its end. Next morning I had to drive to Oxford for we had a Boxing Day matinee. We washed up and cleared away all the wrapping paper, but still we didn't want the day to end. We had no television and we had played our new records again and again. Then Graham leapt to his feet. 'Come on," he said, 'let's walk up to the top of Parliament Hill.' So we did.

It had started snowing again, and we had the Heath to ourselves. Barney leapt happily in and out of the mounds of snow and Graham and I looked down upon an ageless London spread at our feet as the snow eddied round us and clung to our eyelashes and melted down our faces. We stood there, our arms around each other and there was nowhere else we wanted to be. But it was now bitterly cold and we turned to walk back.

'Let's all go to Oxford tonight,' suddenly exclaimed Graham. 'I'm not working tomorrow and Barney and I can come back on the train.'

It was all perfectly possible. Celia and her husband were away and I had arranged to stay in her house in Abingdon. We had plenty of food and as it was really late now, there would be very little traffic on the road.

'You're on!' I shouted, and, calling Barney out of yet another snowdrift, we raced back to the flat.

It seemed no time at all before the car was packed, the boot stuffed with the leftover food and Barney happily installed in his bed on the back seat. We damped down the fire, locked up and were off. The journey passed quickly. I remember a large office building, its lights depicting a Christmas tree, and then we were leaving London behind, the sleeping countryside stretching away white and silent, the stars blinking in a clearing sky. We reached Abingdon safely, unpacked, and put ourselves to bed, happy to think that when we woke up in the morning, we would be exactly where we needed to be and still all together – for a little longer at least. It had been a day filled with happiness, and quite the best Christmas I had ever had.

The next morning we ate cold trifle from the fridge and then headed into Oxford for my eleven o'clock call. I thought the theatre would be empty but there were a surprising number of people around. Graham and Barney fitted in easily and were soon chatting away in the pub that was literally next to the stage door. I set up for the matinée and then we walked the hound and went for lunch. Later, while the hound slept in the car, Graham watched the matinée, and then we spent a last hour or so together before they headed off for London, heavily laden with cold turkey and I settled back into my other life for a couple of days before rejoining them. I don't remember New Year's Eve, but I expect we were working. I've never been any good at New Year's Eves, I remember once going to bed early on the 30th of December so as to be fresh for the great day, only to learn that I had got the date wrong and spent it asleep. I remember a row with Gary, and once, in London, setting off for Trafalgar Square only to get stuck on the tube and miss it again. This unfortunate trend still operates today!

Chapter Eleven

Back in Oxford we settled back into a sort of routine. *The Rivals* was playing in the theatre and we gradually became a company within a company and cast and crew got along well. It was an excellent cast comprising: Christopher Benjamin, Roy Marsden, James Laurenson, Bernard Hopkins, Barry Keegan, Ian White, Frederick Dannmer, Clive Merrison, Joyce Grant, Lynda Marchal (later to become known as the highly respected writer Lynda La Plante), Janet Nelson and Rosamund Nelson, with Michael Davies and Jessica Shaw, our student assistant stage managers as the servants. It was a popular production too, and when we finished our run at the Playhouse we went off on tour with it.

When we reached Southampton I was teased about what part I would be taking over this time. But lightning never strikes in the same place twice, so when the phone rang early on the morning of our third day, I stayed relaxed and cosy in bed. I heard my landlady call my name, and, still unsuspecting, ran down the stairs to take the call. It was the company manager to say that Lynda Marchal had a bad dose of 'flu. I was to start learning Lydia, as I would be going on that night. I did as requested for a couple of hours and began to look forward to the evening performance; rather to my surprise I was quite calm about it all. A couple of hours later, the phone rang again. Again it was for me and again it was the company manager. 'Forget Lydia,' he said. It seemed Lynda would go on after all, but Janet Nelson, who played Julia, had been diagnosed as having an ectopic pregnancy and was already in hospital undergoing an operation. At this I panicked. Lydia was one thing, her speeches were mostly quite short, but Julia was something else. Well, at least thanks to the previous two hours I knew a lot of my cues. I returned to my room and picked up the script, but it wasn't easy. Julia's speeches were long and styled and her character much more difficult to pin down, for me at least. After a while I collected my stage make-up (now always with me, just in case!) and headed for the theatre. I knew someone was trying to find Jimmy Laurenson (playing Faulkland) so that we could at least rehearse our scenes together, and I wanted to be there as soon as he arrived. The panic had receded for the moment; there was a job to be done and I wanted to do it as well as possible. At least this time I was pretty certain I would get on stage. Backstage at the theatre there seemed to be a lot of people around, all of them willing to help in any way they could. But of Jimmy there was no sign. My first priority was still learning lines, so I went to Janet's dressing-room and really got down to it. I felt better there and the lines started to go into my head more easily, but there were interruptions. Janet was petite whilst I, though slim, was not, so some hasty sewing went on and different shoes had to be found from a Southampton shop. Fortunately there were other people to sort out these problems, and someone else was found to help me with the lines. The wig would only just go on my head and was very tight. It was to give me a headache every night I wore it but little could be done about that. The afternoon wore on and there was still no sign of Jimmy. He finally arrived about six o'clock, full of apologies and eager to help. It transpired that he had spent the afternoon in a cinema constantly having to reassure himself that he wasn't missing a matinée, for he felt very strongly that he was really needed at the theatre. In those days any Equity member could have a free pass to any cinema matinée. It was a great idea, but Jimmy had chosen the wrong afternoon. We had about an hour to rehearse before it was time to go back to the dressing-room and start putting on some make-up. By now I was beginning to get really nervous but the make-up helped, and every member of the cast found time to pop in, tell me to 'break a leg' and assure me that I would be great. Well I was not at all sure I agreed, but when they called 'Beginners' my hands had stopped shaking and I remember thinking that at least there was no question of my having to run the corner this night. The curtain went up and the play started and then, as I heard the dialogue that signalled my entrance approaching, the adrenalin once again kicked in. My head cleared and the lines were there. I swept on stage exactly on cue and started to speak. As before, I remember little of the actual performance. The rest of the cast were brilliant and supported me as much as they could. They also diplomatically adapted their moves when I not infrequently upstaged them by accident.

We came to the end of Act 3 without my needing a single prompt and I left the stage, excitement and relief mingling in equal proportions. The stage manager was waiting. 'You've got to go back on and do the Epilogue,' he said.

'Oh, no!' I gasped. 'Well I'll have to read it, give me the script.'

'What a shame,' he frowned, 'you've done a good job so far, pity to spoil it.'

I grabbed the script and read it through once, went back on stage and delivered it clearly and word perfectly and then forgot it. But he was absolutely right to goad me into doing it that way, for as I walked back into the wings I felt good and really pleased with myself. I had done well that night and no one could tell me differently. Not that anyone appeared to want to. At the curtain call I had again been pushed forward for a bow of my own and turned to see the whole cast applauding me. I think I remembered to acknowledge them, I hope so anyhow. Back in the dressing-room there were flowers from Meadow Players, from the cast and from Graham. I had left a message for him at the BBC but had had no idea whether or not he'd got it. I went to the stage door telephone to call him at home but he couldn't get much sense out of me. I was laughing and crying and so high I was flying. Even writing about it now brings back some of the feelings I had that evening and it is very unsettling. Once again we all went out to dinner and afterwards, even though by then it was very, very late, I was still walking three feet off the ground, so Jimmy and Roy walked me round the deserted streets of Southampton until about two o'clock in the morning, at which time I reluctantly went home to bed. And then the next night I had to do it all again, only this time much more was expected of me.

I played the part of Julia for about ten days I think, and each night it became more and more of a challenge. No one appeared to help or rehearse with me and I felt very insecure. I had no idea of how good or bad I really was but I cannot believe I was so terrible, for the Oxford Playhouse had a fine reputation and I'm sure something would have been done if they felt that I was letting them down. In the event they gave me performance money and thanked me profusely. I went out and bought two new mini dresses on the proceeds and began to look forward to every performance. We moved from Southampton to Guildford, and one night after the final curtain, I heard a knock on the dressing-room door. I opened it and there stood Graham. I was so pleased. As always he had been very supportive but his work had kept him in London, now he had become a part of it all.

Then Janet returned, accused me of stretching her wig and took her place back on stage. I went back to the prompt corner, but it was hard not to envy her every night as she made her entrance in what I had come to feel was my part. I learnt a lot from those few days. I only dried once but my time with Nita Valerie stood me in good stead. It was near the end of a scene and I was having an argument with my beloved Faulkland. I caught a glimpse of the prompt corner as I turned upstage and saw that there was no one on the book. The words simply disappeared from my head, so I burst into tears and left the stage, all in character, but slightly leaving Jimmy Laurenson in the lurch. When I was then due back on stage, sniffing into a handkerchief, I went to the prop table to collect it and to glance at the script, but the handkerchief wasn't there. I hissed at the ASM standing close by – a real piece of superstar temperament. She pointed to the prop table and there was my handkerchief, exactly where it should have been. I simply hadn't seen it. Later I apologised to the ASM and realised I had learnt something about actors and actresses that was be extremely useful for all my years in the business.

We returned to Oxford and started work on the next production. This was *The Glass Menagerie* by Tennessee Williams, and Sheila Hancock was to make her debut as director. I don't have the programme for this one, but Joyce Grant played the part of the mother and Alan Lake that of the Gentleman Caller. The theatre critic, Kenneth Tynan, once said that there was a feeling of danger about all the great actors. This was certainly true of Alan. Perhaps it was partly a sense of the tragedy that was to fill his life only a few short years later and result in his suicide, but I think it was something else too. That energy was there, and although the part he was playing was a relatively low-key one, he dominated the stage when he was on it. I adored him, and we spent a lot of time together when we were not rehearsing. He loved the camaraderie of the local pubs and drank quite heavily, though never when he was rehearsing or before a performance. I remember spending just such a morning with him. The drinks were coming far too fast and furiously for me, especially as, for some reason, I had elected to drink sherry. So I started pouring them secretly into a convenient potted plant, much as I had done with my illicit cigarettes when I was teaching. I thus survived quite well, though I was relieved when they called last orders. At least I was until I realised that we were now to become honoured guests and, as such, allowed to stay on drinking all afternoon. At that point I left them all to it and went back to my digs.

Days later in rehearsals Alan slipped a disc and was in agony. He and I were dispatched in a taxi back to Sheila's house in Black Lion Lane. The journey was a nightmare for him and he swore eloquently every time we hit a bump or went round a corner – only to immediately apologise profusely for using such bad language in front of me. In the end I told him to stop. I was not in the least offended and fully understood.

Working with Sheila was great fun. She was, and is, one of the nicest people in the business and a professional to the core. Rehearsals were a delight and everyone fell in love with her. From the point of view of the prompt corner, it was a difficult show to run. It was rather a moody piece and the lighting and sound cues were very much an integral part of it all. So, although I longed to be back on stage, I enjoyed running the corner and felt very involved. I was also still learning more and more about my craft.

After *Menagerie*, Minos reappeared to direct *The Good Woman of Setzuan* by Bertolt Brecht, with Sheila playing the lead. But first I had two days to see how life was progressing back at 99a. It was good to be back, the memories of Christmas still lingered in corners and a happy hound was soon stretched as usual in front of the fire, successfully preventing the heat from reaching his elders and betters. By now we were beginning to really settle into life on the ground floor. Barney had made friends with an elderly lady who lived on the floor above us. Quite how this had been achieved I'm not sure, but for the rest of her life they were to meet on Sunday mornings and partake of a Vienna chocolate biscuit each. How Barney knew which day was Sunday was a mystery we were never able to solve, but only on that day did he go and sit patiently on her little balcony until she emerged with the biscuits. We were to get to know her well, but for now we knew only that she had been born in St Petersburg before the Revolution and had worked with Anna Pavlova. Her story was a fascinating one, and I was to spend many happy hours listening to it while I was also to develop a liking for vodka, drunk the Russian way. But all that comes later. For now we exchanged greetings when we met and went our separate ways. We had also become very friendly with Sally, the aforementioned one who lived upstairs and whose father actually owned the house in which we were all living. So for two days I cooked and cleaned and washed and ironed and generally played at being a happy housewife with neighbours. Graham and I also had some serious discussions over my future as an actress. Meadow Players had cast me in one small part so far and they had promised me two when I applied and got the job. I had twice saved the show by going on at short notice and both Graham and I felt that I was certain to get my own part in *Good Woman*. I headed back to rehearsals full of anticipation.

Once back inside the theatre I saw what appeared to be the cast list on the green- room notice-board. I scanned it eagerly but there was no sign of my name. Nearly in tears I phoned Graham in London and he told me I must go to Frank Hauser and resign. I was appalled, was it really necessary to leave this company where I had been so happy and become so much a part of something special? I didn't know if I could, but Graham was adamant that it was the right thing to do. I rang off and reluctantly went round to the production offices. Frank's door was open, and he welcomed me warmly. 'What,' he asked, 'is the problem?' Somehow I managed to tell him what I had come to say. He apologised profusely and admitted he had simply forgotten the promise he had made those long weeks ago. Regretfully there was nothing he could do about it now for the play was fully cast and it was the last one in the current season. He tried very hard to persuade me to stay but I kept refusing. He finally asked me to reconsider for twenty-four hours and go back tomorrow. I agreed to that for I wanted desperately to get out of his office and a part of me hoped that I could find some way of staying on.

I phoned Graham again, hoping against hope that he would say something along the lines of, 'Oh, never mind.' But he was more certain than ever that I shouldn't back down. The next morning Frank still seemed perplexed by my decision but regretfully accepted it. I walked out of his office close to tears, feeling as though my world had fallen about my ears. Well, I had to work a month's notice to work out and perhaps something could still happen to change things. The season only ran for three more weeks after that. My righteous stand was all beginning to look a little silly, and in retrospect it was, for over the years I was to come to regret it deeply. But for the moment hurt pride prevailed and I had to get on with the day-to-day business of a new production. I think it would be fair to say that no one understood my decision to leave and I became something of an outsider within the company. The four weeks I had left with this most special of theatres promised to become something of an ordeal. I rather dreaded going to work, for no one quite knew what to do with me. I would not be there to run the show and a replacement had been found, so how usefully to employ me? It was Minos who came up with the answer.

He came and found me one day in the theatre and asked why I was leaving. I explained, only to hear him answer that he had had no idea of the arrangement I had made with Frank and that I could have had the part of Mrs Mi Tzu in *Good Woman*. I was devastated, but it was all too late now. 'You should have come to me first,' He said, and I knew he was right. He went on to ask if I spoke any French, and when I replied in the affirmative, he said, 'Come with me.' We walked backstage and found a man I had never seen before. He was standing in the shadows of the wings trying to communicate with one of the carpenters. Minos told me that this was Nicos Stephanou, who had come from Athens to design the sets and costumes but spoke only Greek and French. I was to work as his assistant and interpreter. I looked across at Nicos and found a pair of twinkling eyes regarding me quizzically. This, I found myself thinking, was going to be fun.

Ever since I could remember there had been Greeks in, or around the edges of my life, their influence sometimes waxing and sometimes waning, but always there. I enjoyed their company and found them to be great fun. Minos of course, had already reconfirmed my first impressions. I had categorised him as 'impossible but irresistible', a lethal combination, and he was to go on to have a major impact on my professional life. Now I had met just such another one though I was not to realise this for a few days yet.

We spent that first day getting to know one another a little and resurrecting my imperfect French. I was a little nervous of this stranger who seemed to know exactly what he wanted and wouldn't settle for anything less. But my experiences backstage at Barrow-in-Furness Rep stood me in good stead, and my enthusiasm met with approval and gradually we became a team.

By the end of the first week we were getting along fine, and when Minos asked if I would drive Nicos back to London on the Saturday night, I was more than happy to agree. We talked generally on the way back, mostly about work. I discovered that he was an artist as well as a designer and he told me about some murals that he was working on in a big hotel in Crete. He lived in the Kolonaki district in Athens and he was married to a costume designer, but, he insisted, it was more a marriage of convenience, because at that time, as a single woman, she would be unable to work freely. It sounded an exotic life and I was fascinated. He was easy to talk to and there was that sense of fun in everything he said.

From the Monday onwards we were moving into the theatre in Croydon, where the play was due to open in two weeks' time, so I arranged to collect Nicos early on the Monday morning, dropped him at Frank Hauser's flat where he was staying and carried on home. There I slipped easily into my other life, receiving an ecstatic welcome from Barney and a delicious supper and all the warmth of a good relationship from Graham. But I found myself looking forward to the next week and working with my interesting new friend. I even slipped my French/English dictionary into my bag – just, I thought, in case.

The weekend passed happily; we spent hours on the Heath and cooked, played records and made endless cups of coffee for visiting friends. Nicos slipped into the back of my mind, and when I finally picked him up at some ridiculously early hour on Monday morning, I was surprised by how pleased I was to see him. Once at the theatre we found ourselves with plenty of work. Everything was waiting in the wagons that had come down from Oxford, and as there was no sign of Minos, I found myself stuck like glue to Nicos, for things were chaotic and without my somewhat original translations would have been a great deal worse.

By the end of the day the vans were unloaded and we had started to build the set on stage. Day turned into night and the carpenters worked on. Minos arrived and I was told to go home and get some sleep. I left reluctantly and was soon driving through the empty London streets, but I missed my travelling companion, and I missed the camaraderie of the setting crews. I was back in the theatre early next morning and found the theatre almost deserted. The crews had worked through the night and the set was up. I went backstage and found a weary designer bent over a hamper of props. I took one look at him and put the kettle on.

'Go home to bed,' I said.

'Are you crazy?" he replied, and made a weary sweep with his arm. 'There is much work to be done.'

So we worked on until early evening, painting and making some of the hand props. I liked working with him for he knew exactly what he wanted and was very clear with is instructions. And, although he must have been exhausted, he never minded questions and answered them with infinite patience.

Sometime in the early evening Minos arrived, twinkling and irrepressible. What was it about Greek men, or these two at any rate? They had such confidence and such genuine charm. Though impossible in some ways they had the ability to make you feel very special. I would have moved mountains for either of them. Minos eyed Nicos quizzically and then said to me, 'Anne, take him back to the flat.' Nicos protested but finally gave in. We set off in the Mini and within minutes he was fast asleep. A strange man in a strange land but he seemed completely at ease. Like everyone when they are sleeping, he looked very young and vulnerable. I drove carefully and woke him up gently when we got to his flat.

'See you tomorrow.' he said and climbed slowly up the steps to the front door.

I drove across to South Hill Park, suddenly at a loss and facing an empty evening, for Graham was working late.

It was strange to be working from home after all those weeks away. I should have been delighted to be back, but I was strangely restless and couldn't settle. The week progressed, sometimes I drove Nicos and sometimes I went to Croydon alone, the car seeming oddly empty on these occasions and the journey a long one. I continued to work solely with Nicos and the rest of the production passed me by. Minos was rehearsing on stage now and there were plenty of old friends around, but my leaving was growing ever closer and the knowledge of it seemed to throw a shadow around me. The last Sunday we had a long production weekend before the dress rehearsal on the Monday and the pressure was now really on. I was carving a small piece of wood with a scalpel when it slipped and the blade sunk deep into my knee. Blood spurted everywhere and I stared at the blade in disbelief. Suddenly Nicos was there, solicitous and anxious. It wasn't such a major injury and I soon recovered but I was touched by his concern and ended up having to assure him repeatedly that I was OK. I still have a small white scar today, proof, as if it was needed, that it had all really happened. Then the crew insisted on breaking for an hour's lunch around 3 p.m.

Nicos was astounded. 'But there is so much work still to do,' he said. He stayed working in the theatre and I stayed with him. 'You are the only one who understands,' he said. And he looked at me in a way he never had before. Something had changed between us and my mind went racing. I was used to half falling in love with the people I worked with – it was par for the course – but it didn't mean anything. You finished working together and it all faded gently away. Graham was my life and my future. I was happy, wasn't I? Suddenly I wasn't sure any more.

I drove home alone that night and gave myself a good talking to. In a few weeks Nicos would be back in Greece and I would be here in London. I was leaving the company at the end of the week and had to find a new job. I resolved to distance myself from whatever was going on and soon it would all be just a pleasant memory. But in the event, it wasn't as simple as all that. The next day I started as I meant to go on, but Nicos wasn't having any of that. He came across to where I was working. 'What's wrong?' he asked.

'Nothing,' I replied.

He looked at me with the question still in his eyes but I carried on working and he walked away.

For the rest of the day we stayed that way, suddenly my interpreter's skills did not seem to be needed very much, and I began to wonder if that had always been the case. I left the theatre early and drove back alone. Graham was at home when I got there and I was glad. But again I was restless and very irritable.

'What's wrong?' asked Graham, and I wanted to scream, 'Leave me alone,' but I didn't.

'I'm tired,' I said, 'and worried about finding another job.'

Graham said nothing more and we got through the evening without any upsets. Then I began to dread going back to the theatre the next day.

Anyhow I went and everything seemed fine. At one point Nicos made me laugh and the world turned the right way up and things got back to normal. The rest of the week passed quickly and suddenly it was Friday and time for me to leave Meadow Players. I was deeply upset and more so when, rather to my surprise, everyone made a big fuss of me. There were presents and cards and flowers and many good wishes and Sheila Hancock had bought me a beautiful coffee pot that I was to use for years. Eventually, alas, it got broken but I still have the note that went with it. And always in the background, that last evening, was Nicos, smiling and watching. I drove home alone and in tears that night, the car full of memories and gifts. An understanding Graham had cooked a delicious supper and an understanding Barney dog leaned against me for comfort. All this was for the best, I thought to myself, time to get back to reality.

I began looking for another job, and for once it seemed that I might be lucky. I heard of someone needing a DSM and understudy for a play due to start rehearsing almost immediately. I rang the production office and arranged an interview for the next day. I then took Barney for a long walk across the Heath and tried not to think of all the nerves, excitement and bustle that would be taking place a few short miles away. The next day I went for the interview and got the job. It was for a commercial company, and would begin on tour before, if all went well, coming into the West End. It was a light comedy called *The Man Most Likely To* and Leslie Phillips was the star. I rang friends with the good news but was surprised by their lack of enthusiasm. 'Commercial theatre?' they said. 'Oh, shouldn't think you'll like that very much after Oxford.' They were right.

For the moment, however, I was simply pleased that I had found work so quickly, and was delighted that most of my time was going to be spent in London. Nicos stayed in my mind but I gave myself stern lectures about it 'all being for the best', until one morning the phone rang and suddenly there he was. We met later that day and continued to do so for the few days he had left in London. I brought him to the flat and introduced him to Graham and Barney, but carefully avoided any information about my relationship with Graham. Nicos and I picked up easily from where we had left off. We talked for hours about art and theatre and love and life, and in some ways it was like the heady days of Oxford University and I realised how much I had missed that side of my life recently. Throughout Europe the Arts were taken far more seriously than in England and to be a part of that was something I longed for. Always something of a misfit, I really only felt myself among creative people and I loved the unconventionality and unpredictability of their way of life. The gypsy in me was always anxious to come bubbling up to the surface. Both Minos and Nicos seemed so much a part of this special coterie, and I longed to be there alongside them.

We started rehearsals for *The Man Most Likely To* but every spare moment I met up with Nicos, until, inevitably, we came to his last night in London. We went out for a meal together and then I drove him back to Frank's flat. It was late, but still we sat in the car not wanting the evening to end. Finally we had to say goodbye and I drove back home and parked. As I was getting out I glanced down and saw his passport lying on the floor of the car, and I knew that it expired in thirty hours' time.

We all wanted him to stay in London, for the Colonels were running a draconian regime in Greece and Nicos had taken a considerable risk coming to work here with a known left wing director; he had been warned that it might be dangerous for him to go back. He knew, too, that there were many ex-patriot Greeks here in London, some his friends – and that design work was available if only he would stay. But he had told me that Greece was his country and his inspiration as an artist was there and that it would be wrong to desert her when she needed his help against the oppression forced on her by the Junta. From our point of view it made so much sense for him to stay, but he didn't want to. I looked hard and long at his passport, but it wasn't my decision to make, and eventually I drove back to the house I had left only half an hour before and pushed it through the letterbox. I thought I would never see him again, but I wasn't quite right about that!

Graham was working the next day and I was grateful for some time alone. Also I had to drive up to Birmingham that same evening to prepare everything for a dress rehearsal in the theatre the following day. I got through most of the intervening hours somehow and then set off on the drive north. Getting into the centre of Birmingham proved a nightmare. Maybe I just wasn't concentrating enough but the ring roads and flyovers had me completely baffled and I seemed to be going round in circles. Eventually I made it, parked the car and headed into the theatre. First I had to take one of the phone numbers from the lower price range on the list of accommodation pinned on the notice-board by the stage door and then telephone in order to find digs for the week. I hated phoning for anything connected with my-self, and I usually felt quite sick at the very idea, but it had to be done. I don't understand this hatred of the phone, unless it is part of the fear of rejection that has stayed with me all my life but it is very real and has often caused me problems. Ask me to phone in the course of my work and I will do it gladly. On that occasion, the call I had to make presented itself as just another obstacle in a fairly dreadful day, but finally I did find digs, though I doubted these would add greatly to my comfort.

Theatrical digs at that time were mostly pretty dire, especially the cheap ones. Basic would be an accurate description. Usually clean, they did, however, condemn one to heatless bedrooms, limited hot water, and nylon sheets. One also ran the risk of an ex-pro landlady with a limitless store of her own past successes and a deep reluctance to part with a front-door key. Mine in Birmingham was no exception, though the house was near the theatre and the breakfasts were surprisingly good. Alas, in my lovelorn state I was unable to eat them, a fact that led to near rows every morning and the statement that I was not getting a reduction just because I only wanted coffee for breakfast. In the end, I just stopped bothering going into the dining room at all, and that didn't please her either.

I went into the theatre early and found the set up and fully lit. The props crews were finishing off the dressings and my relatively few hand props were sitting in their own separate hamper. I unpacked them, checked them and found myself with nothing to do until the dress rehearsal later that day. It was all very different from my experience with other companies. There was no friendly Frank Hauser to involve me in the lighting, no actors sitting drinking coffee and eager for a chat, in fact I don't think anyone even said good morning to me. I left the theatre and wandered around the city centre, ending up inevitably in the Bull Ring. I found it the most depressing city in which I had ever been. Doubtless my mood was partly responsible, but later I was to know it far better and never changed my first impression of it, though the people were not at all like their city.

There was no doubt that the ethos of commercial theatre was very different from that of the repertory companies. Money and success were the motivating forces and as DSM I had no part to play other than checking the props and running the corner. The actors, though always polite, stayed in a clique of their own, the production manager stayed in his office and the scene crews and lighting crews did their jobs and went home. I found myself very much alone. In some ways this suited my mood, and I wandered around Birmingham depressed and solitary with far too many empty hours to fill before I was needed at the theatre. True, I was supposed to be understudying the juvenile lead but no one seemed at all bothered about that, so I learnt the lines and the moves and left it at that. Twice I plucked up my courage and phoned the Athens flat but each time someone told me that Nicos was out. Once I came back from a pointless wander to find that he had phoned me. I hit a sort of rock bottom then and found it difficult to concentrate on anything.

I was obviously desperately unhappy and this almost certainly communicated itself to the people around me. So when, in self-destruct mode, I went to the Company Manager and asked to be released from my contract, he quickly agreed to find a replacement, saying I could leave as soon as one was in place. This happened faster than I had dared to hope, and in less than a week I found myself once again hopelessly lost on Spaghetti Junction until I finally managed to hit the M6 and head for home. I didn't know it then but I had just walked away from my last job in the theatre.

PART TWO

Chapter Twelve

It was a relief to be back in London, although there was little work around. I went back to being a cinema usherette and one weekend drove up to Norwich where *The Good Woman of Setzuan* was playing. I stayed the night with friends after sitting way back in the stalls watching a play I knew well, and seeing all the props that Nicos and I had made together. It was all deeply upsetting and I wished I hadn't gone. I didn't go backstage and left quickly before anyone could recognise me.

After that life slowly returned to normal. I watched the progress of *The Man Most Likely To* as it toured around England and eventually came into London. A few days after it opened in the West End the juvenile lead abruptly left the cast. If I had still been with the company I would have almost certainly have gone on in her place, and possibly have ended up playing the part – and *The Man Most Likely To* was playing at the Vaudeville Theatre in the Strand! Graham and I were stunned, remembering the messages from our séance on the boat.

Looking back now, I was definitely wrong to leave that production too. Apart from anything else it was the next logical step for me to make. I was not the archetypal juvenile lead still fashionable then, but make-up and hair styling could have turned me into one, and if I had gone on stage at the Vaudeville and been any good, I would have certainly got myself a good agent and possibly gone on to a full acting career. But I had let my heart rule my head, not for the first time, and certainly not for the last.

In the meantime, Graham was as understanding as ever. I never knew whether or not he guessed at the impact Nicos had made on our lives. Certainly nothing was ever said, and as the weeks slipped by the memories faded into the background and we moved on. Graham designed a set of stacking furniture based on a three foot cube and he began to build some for the flat. He never got very far with it though and the idea was put on the back boiler; only a very few years later someone else had the same idea and shops like Habitat appeared in London. We also got very excited with photography for a time and I began to write a play but we never followed anything through; ideas seemed easy to come by then and I think we were a bit in awe of anything that came under the heading of 'success'. I certainly was, back in 1959 I had written to Barney Colehan at Broadcasting

House suggesting a follow up to the series of *Top Town* using teams from different colleges and universities. I still have his reply thanking me and saying they would keep in mind my suggestion. In 1962, *University Challenge* appeared on TV and ran until 1987 and started again in 1994 and is still running.

Meanwhile work as a cinema-usherette was badly paid and in any case had become boring. To this day I have only to hear the music from *Around the World in Eighty Days* and I see myself standing at the back of the stalls, torch in hand. It was time for some sort of change, so when I saw an advert for people to work in Camden Play Centres, I applied and got the job. There were several of these centres in the large council estates in the Borough of Camden and at the time they were something of an original concept. They took the form of adventure playgrounds but had a permanent staff on duty as supervisors and quasi social workers. On the whole they worked well, for they kept the younger children off the streets and provided a social centre for their parents. We were encouraged to become involved with all our visitors and help wherever we could.

In some ways it was like being back in Hackney, but the idea of the family as a positive unit seemed stronger than there and I met some really good people. There was still poverty, for most people, if working at all, were in the low-income bracket. Still there was a great sense of survival and some hope for the future. But for me it was too much like being back in teaching and I was not to stay there very long.

One day we discovered that a small child had gone missing. We took to the streets to find him and after many hours the police phoned to say that they had him at King's Cross Police Station. I was sent to collect him and when I reached the police station found that the press had latched on to the story and were determined to report it in the next day's papers. The article with my photograph duly appeared and later that day I received a phone call at the Centre. It was from Colin. He had returned to England from Australia and was teaching in London. Two days later we met. It was a strange meeting. He seemed curiously philosophical about my failure to honour our engagement, and said cryptically that 'I was always cleverer than he was anyhow'. After that we rather ran out of conversation and I walked him to the gate of the Centre and watched as he strode down the Camden High Road and out of my life for ever.

The only other notable event from these days was the purchase of a pair of boots. They were brand new and offered to me by one of the mothers at the centre who often popped in for coffee. They were the most amazing boots I had ever seen. They were knee high, a pink-beige in colour and made from the softest leather imaginable. I coveted them dearly. The price to my astonishment was only five pounds, so I paid half then, promised the rest when I was given my wages, and took them home. It was there that Graham pointed out that they were almost certainly stolen and that I should never have bought them. I was mortified but secretly delighted when he finally admitted that nothing could be done about it now and I might as well keep them.

Meanwhile I longed for more theatre work, but I wasn't the only one unhappy with the state of my career. Graham, too, was beginning to feel very limited by the bureaucracy and the restrictions that governed the careers of production staff at the BBC. He had wanted so much to train as a director but, although he was regarded as highly eligible, it seemed that this was going to be a very slow process indeed, and in some ways he was as impatient as I was.

We read of the new franchises about to be bid for on the ITV network and we followed the stories with great interest. Then we heard on the grapevine that the new companies were desperate for trained production staff. There had been a considerable shake-up within ITV and one of the new companies bidding for the London weekend slot, (London Weekend Television) sounded especially interesting and refreshingly original. It had some rather impressive names attached to it, notably those of Frank Muir, Andre Previn, Ken Loach, Tony Garnett, Derek Granger, Alan Clark, Jimmy Hill and Humphrey Burton. It was also rumoured that many of the younger scriptwriters, currently making a name for themselves at the Bebe, (BBC) were also to join LWT if it got the new franchise and work on a new show with David Frost who was also involved and then riding high with *That Was The Week That Was*. Satirical comedy was just beginning to show its nervous head over the parapet of mainstream television and was already having an enormous impact. It was to have an enormous impact on Graham's life, and mine too, but there was no way we could have guessed that then.

Graham went for several interviews and soon ended up with at least two job offers. He accepted one with LWT as a freelance stage manager and astounded the Bebe by tendering his resignation. In vain did they point out the advantages of their pension schemes, the future possibility of training to be a director, and the, to us, perplexing advantages of job security. Graham was hungry for more and he moved into ITV eager for whatever it had to offer. Gerry Pearson, the friend from the Barrow-in- Furness days, was also at LWT and he and Graham began working on a plan to get me a job there too.

Whenever there is a shake up of company franchises there always exists a period of job opportunities. This only lasts for a few weeks and you have to move fast. But Graham and Gerry did, and I ended up with two interviews, one was for a job at LWT and the second was for a similar job at Yorkshire Television. They were for two specific productions and the dates ran concurrently. The YTV interview came first. My theatre work obviously impressed but I could see that they were a little nervous about my lack of television experience, so without actually lying, I implied I already had the job with LWT. The next day I went for an interview at LWT and repeated the process. I ended up with both jobs.

I still had reservations about working in television as opposed to theatre, but I was curious and determined at least to experience the medium before proceeding with my plan to be a theatrical superstar. But it didn't quite work out that way, without any planning from me my life had just swerved on to a new and exciting track. The road was still going to be bumpy, but it would lead to unique opportunities and I would do so many things that most people only dream of doing. Only much later did I regret that I never went back to the theatre for, if I had a natural talent for anything, then that is where I could have used it to its fullest advantage.

When I first sat down to write this epic, I thought its main theme would be that of my adoption and the effect it had had on my whole life. But then it gained a momentum of its own and as it did so I began to understand many things about myself that before had been something of a mystery. Being adopted was and to a certain extent always will be one of the major events of my life. The sometimes overwhelming fear of rejection that it generated has stayed with me and still creates major havoc with my day-to-day existence and long-term happiness. For someone living with this fear I chose a strange way of life, for professional rejection is endemic in theatre and television. But there was never anything else I wanted to do and so, following my school's advice to 'do what you want to do and don't blame anyone but yourself if you don't make it', I ploughed ahead. Once reasonably established within my profession I discovered most of the things that made for fulfilment. Not for nothing were actors once regarded with suspicion and thought to espouse a decadent way of life, but this was exaggerated and there was great discipline within the profession. There was freedom to work creatively, a constant challenge, and a commitment to something bigger than oneself. I made many friends, and often discovered that I was not the only one with a difficult past. Our love of the job united us and I began to feel like a member of a very special and exclusive club. I discovered, too, that people liked me for who I was, I was no longer the misfit, the one who was always in trouble for breaking the rules. My energetic and somewhat irrational self was accepted and even loved. Someone once told me that if I had not gone into show business I would have ended up in prison – they might well have been right.

In my experience, problems of adoption are almost always created by the grown-ups, most of whom are not adopted themselves. The birth of a baby into a family is regarded as a cause for celebration. The arrival of an adopted child into a family is often treated with secrecy and concealed as much as possible. The main reason for this is almost certainly because it implies a 'failure' on the part of the adopting parents to produce their own. In far too many instances the adopting parents have not fully come to terms with this, and where they have they have to face the fact that it still remains deep-seated in the psyche of society in general. What I was looking for, and to an extent I still am, were the facts that surrounded my birth and some knowledge of my blood relations. Such knowledge is a basic right of the non-adopted child. For us it involves a difficult and often expensive search and we are 'invited' to seek the help of a councillor. We seem to be regarded as some sort of threat, though I have never met an adopted child who has wished harm to either their blood parents or their adoptive ones. But read some of the pamphlets issued to the Social Services and you will find some interesting phrasing. One that I read stated that they had taken a survey into the incidence of crime in the lives of adopted children and 'natural' ones. It went on to say that to their surprise they had found no greater rate of criminality in adopted children than in 'normal' ones. For me a child is a child – race, colour, background, all are irrelevant, but all should have a chance to be brought up in a warm and loving family environment. To this end both fostering and adoption should be brought out from the shadows where they lurk and be embraced for the very positive things that they are.

At this point in my life, however, such matters were far from my thoughts. The ever- present fact of my adoption certainly remained, and sooner or later people close to me had to be told. The people I knew now professed interest but it did not seem to affect their opinion of me in the slightest, and so, it slipped slowly into the background of my life. I now found myself surrounded by intelligent, talented, famous and fun people, and not one of them wore hats. I was definitely on the 'up' bit of that roller coaster ride.

My first job was on a production of *Camille* and by a stroke of great good fortune John Frankau, the director, was a craftsman and a man with infinite patience towards someone who wanted to understand everything yesterday and had a hundred questions and an unlimited number of bright ideas. I must have driven him mad, but I cared, oh how I cared, and he was never anything but gentle and considerate. I was lucky with the cast too, although I don't remember all the names, but Genvième Page played the leading character Camille, and we became good mates, chattering away in a mixture of French and English. Cavan Kendall played Armand, and Edward de Souza was Bob, and Michael Barrington was the doctor.

We had a read-through in YTV's executive London flat, on a Sunday I think because a lot of the actors were still involved in other productions. This was nothing like any read- through I had ever experienced before. We drank real coffee out of china cups and the atmosphere resembled one you would be more likely to find at some sort of fundraising soirée. Everyone seemed to have chosen to dress in their best clothes and Edward de Souza in particular caught my attention. He was very good-looking and dressed in loose cream trousers with a matching Indian-style top. He sat quietly and seemed completely relaxed while the other actors chattered nervously around him. I began handing out the coffee and took a cup over to where he was sitting. I introduced myself and held out the coffee across the table in front of him, but something went badly wrong and I tipped the full cup all over his cream tunic and trousers. I was mortified, and there was a sudden silence in the room. He stood up and smiled across at me, 'It's all right,' he said. 'Perhaps we could do with a cloth and some cold water?' Somehow I managed to help him remove the worst of the stains and eventually we started the read-through. I have never forgotten his kindness that day, though I still go a shade of red when I think about it. We were to meet nearly every day for several weeks after that but he never mentioned the incident again and was always the perfect gentleman at rehearsals. He went on to my mental list of heroes and years later, when I found myself on the receiving end of a similar accident caused by another stage manager's nerves, I remembered him and tried to emulate his actions that day.

Although I was so scared those first few days in rehearsal, I quickly began to realize that the disciplines were much the same as those in the theatre and I just relaxed and got on with the job. In fact it was all much simpler than what I was used to; no longer did I have to trail round shops trying to borrow things for the actors to use as props, or spend hours at home working with pâpier mâché and wine gums. Now I simply wrote out a list and things magically appeared in the rehearsal room, or I gave another list to the designer, confident that he would choose whatever we had come to rely on in rehearsal, but in the right period and style.

The days passed quickly and the studio date came nearer and nearer. John began to look at the floor plans and make curious notes on them. Intrigued, I watched him until he looked up and smiled. 'Camera positions,' he said. I must have looked impressed because he burst out laughing and then went on to tell me something it could have taken me years to work out for myself. 'The camera is only a machine,' he said, 'it shows the audience what you want them to see. Find the truth of the play in rehearsals and that dictates the camera shots. True, you can use technique to speed up the action, add suspense or highlight a particularly dramatic moment, but always find the truth.' Then he winked at me, just like Minos before, and he added, 'it works in life too.'

I've never forgotten what he told me that day and I have often judged other directors on their understanding of this precept. It was a rule that the really good ones always applied, and their names often went on to become famous while the others have passed from my mind and mostly out of the public eye. Meanwhile we worked on, the actors too, bent on finding the truth in their performances, until inevitably the day arrived when it was time to clear out the rehearsal room and move into the studio. The next day I went in early to check the props and hand out the set and strike list to the prop crew. We were recording at the ATV studios out at Boreham Wood, for the Yorkshire TV studios were still being built up in Leeds. The ATV studios were once film studios and were set in a large complex with a canteen, many offices, scene docks, prop stores and plenty of free parking, but they had a rather dreary air about them and I suddenly felt friendless and found the crews preoccupied and rather world weary. I missed the sense of excitement that had always been there in the theatre. I struggled on but was glad when it was time to go home, and that evening I spent a lot of time arguing with Graham as he tried to reassure me and explain the different working practices that I was going to have to accept if I was to stay working in TV.

The next day I set off for work with a more up-beat attitude, determined to do my best. In the studio electricians were tweaking lights and the designer was working with the painters and prop crews, no one seemed to need me or indeed notice my presence at all. When I tried to check the hand props I was more or less told to get out of the way, so instead I went to check that the actors had arrived and found that someone called an assistant floor manager had already done that and taken them all into make-up. I ended up sitting alone in the canteen until I heard a voice on the tannoy system call the artists and crews into the studio for rehearsals. Not knowing what else to do I made my way back and stood behind a piece of scenery for most of the day while the recording went on around me. It seemed a slow business and there were quite a few re-takes but gradually we settled into a rhythm and the prop men began to check things with me and listen to what I said. At first I stayed glued to the script but quickly found out that I was not even expected to prompt; someone called a PA up in the recording area was now doing that for me. Occasionally one of the actors wandered over to check the words for the next scene but they were preoccupied and obviously 'in character' and mostly we just smiled at one another and left it at that. Finally the floor manager announced that it was a 'wrap' and gave out the starting time for the next day. The recording lights went out, the work lights came on and we all started to drift out of the studio. I walked back to the car determined to return to the theatre as quickly as possible.

The next day was Friday, 2 of August 1968. In the studio at ATV the day went on much as before but when the floor manager at last called 'That's a wrap everybody,' I rushed to my car and drove quickly home, for this day was to see the start of London Weekend's franchise and the word was out that we were in for great things. Their on-air time ran from six o'clock on Friday evening to the end of transmission on Sunday and I was anxious to see the start of it all; not least because Graham was at the studios and working on the first show to be transmitted live. Barney and I settled in front of the television set with minutes to spare and watched excitedly as the LWT logo came up on the screen. We then watched in disbelief as the screen went blank and stayed that way. Although we didn't know it for some hours, we had just witnessed the start of an indefinite strike organized by the union of the ACTT (Association of Cinematograph, Television and Allied Technicians) – the biggest union in the whole ITV network. At first I thought only that something had gone wrong with the set itself, for it was an old one passed on to us by more affluent friends, but Graham's eventual return brought home the seriousness of the situation. At a loss, we tried to work out how it would affect us. We were both members of Equity, the actors' union, which, as far as we could gather, was not directly involved in the strike.

In the morning I drove out to the ATV studios and was met by a row of pickets at the main gate. Unsure what to do, I stopped the car and got out. One of the men there was someone I recognized from our studio crew and seeing me he walked across to join me. 'Are you Equity, love?' he asked. 'Yes.' I replied. He turned to talk to his companions and then nodded to me. 'It's all right, love, you go on in, but don't touch anything in the studio. That way they'll have to pay you and we know you don't earn all that much.'

I drove in, not knowing whether to feel pleased or patronised. I couldn't see much point in being there, but once inside the main building, I found other people around and at least it was a chance to establish what was happening. Inside the studio everything was exactly as we had left it. The work lights were on and two or three people sat around drinking coffee and talking. I was suddenly filled with anger and frustration, how could they do this to us when we had worked so hard? Whatever had happened to the principle that 'the show must go on'? Surely they could at least let us finish the recording and then go on strike. I went across to a group of the men on strike, naïvely convinced that if I explained my feelings with enough conviction they would understand and let us work on. Of course it was a crazy thing to do but I had never experienced anything like this and thought it exceedingly unprofessional of them. They seemed stunned by my passionate plea for them to resume work but they tried to explain and then told me to go home. I would get paid, they assured me, but money was the last thought on my mind. Defeated, I went up to the office of the man who had employed me. Percy Welsburg was his name and later I was to get to know him well, but for the moment he was just a man who could tell me what to do. As middle management he was not a union member and so he was in his office and working. He also told me to go home and assured me that I would be paid to the end of my contract no matter how long the strike went on. Again, not exactly what I wanted to hear, but he also assured me that he would phone me as soon as the crews were working again. So the penny finally dropped and realizing at last that there really was nothing I could do to change the situation, I went home and sat there as the days passed and the last day of my contract came and went.

But the last day of my YTV contract also signified the start of my new one with LWT. Graham of course was already working there and he had been going in daily throughout the strike. He assured me that things were better there and insisted I went in to work in order to honour the first day of my contract. He was quite right on both counts, though as we drove past the LWT studios with the line of pickets, my heart sank.

In those days the new company was split between two buildings. The production staff worked out of Station House, a recently built, multi-storey building situated at Stonebridge Park and overlooking the North Circular Road, while the technical crews were based at the old Rediffusion Studios at Wembley Park, near to the football stadium. As Graham and I walked into Station House I found, to my delight, that there were no pickets parading outside, only a friendly security guard was there to say good-morning and nod us towards the lift. Inside the building the atmosphere remained welcoming, especially on the Light Entertainment floor where I was supposed to be based.

The offices throughout the building were nearly all open-plan ones, something that was thought to be avant-garde at that time, but given the current situation, it soon became rather fun and made for a very sociable atmosphere. People sat around chatting and laughing and everyone seemed to know Graham and like him. He introduced me to the people we came across as we walked to his office and they all smiled and said hello. We then went to another floor to meet the Percy Welsburg of LWT, a man called Martin Case. He was tall with twinkling eyes and he had an air of great warmth about him. He welcomed me to the company, assured me that I would be paid from the start of my contract and wished me well. I left his office perplexed by the fact that everyone suddenly seemed anxious to give me money for doing nothing again.

Back on the Light Entertainment floor the atmosphere had become more bustling and efficient. Typewriters clicked away and phones were ringing on several desks. Just visible through the open door of the corner office (the only office to actually have a door) was the shape of another tall man, the owner, as I soon found out, of another pair of twinkling eyes. He appeared in the open doorway and became Frank Muir, the new head of the department.

It was something of a shock to see him standing there, for he was already a popular and well-known personality and not one that I had ever thought to meet face to face. Perhaps I shouldn't have been so surprised for I knew that one of the bases on which LWT had secured its franchise was the list of talent that it had managed to attract to work in its production teams. Cyril Bennett was Controller of Programmes, Jimmy Hill was Head of Sport, Humphrey Burton Head of Music and Arts, while on the drama floor, Derek Granger (later to be famous for the wildly successful *Brideshead Revisited* drama series that he was to produce for Granada) tried, and often failed, to contain the enthusiasms of people such as Kenith Trodd, Tony Garnett, James McTaggart, Ken Loach and Alan Clarke. Andre Previn appeared in the lifts and the names of international stars began to be heard in snippets of conversation I caught as I roamed the open-plan offices looking for the ever-elusive photocopying machine; but I am slightly running ahead of myself. For me that day there remains only the image of a charming, courteous man who took the time to ask who I was and what programme I was to work on, and then to welcome me aboard the new flagship and urge me not to hesitate to come and see him if I had any problems or queries.

Alas, I never got to know him really well and in some ways he seemed an odd personality to be the head of a department. That he was one of life's true gentlemen was never in any doubt and he had an enormous amount of energy, talent and love for the business in which he was involved. But there was an air of innocence about him too and, reading his autobiography many years later, I was surprised to learn that he, too, had had a struggle to find work in the early days and that he had been a part of the raggle-taggle world that we had all joined in order to get started in the business. He generated great affection wherever he went, leaving behind the impression of a lovable RAF flight lieutenant who had somehow wandered into (and eventually escaped from) the corridors of the BBC Television Centre and worked his way up from there.

That first morning passed quickly though what I could have been doing to keep myself busy is now a mystery. Graham came to take me for lunch and we shot up to the top floor and the LWT staff canteen. There we found long tables standing in rows and delicious smells coming from behind the serving counter. Here, too, an easy atmosphere prevailed and as we sat eating our food Cyril Bennett came to join us, followed by Tito Burns. Tito was another large man, who, I learned later, had once toured Britain with his own accordion band. He was a very funny man too, with a seemingly endless store of jokes and tales from his years on the boards. Here was someone who really was at home in television and I detected a raunchy air of elegance about him.

Lunch was fun, and the afternoon passed quickly. As Graham and I drove home later that evening I found myself looking forward to the next day. I didn't know exactly what I had let myself in for yet but that first day had left me with an impression of Savile Row suits, champagne, laughter, and the sense of an enormous and exciting creative energy; and I very much wanted to be part of it all, if only for a while. Well, I very soon was; indeed I had just spent the first day of the next twenty-seven years of my life.

Throughout the rest of the strike things settled into some sort of erratic routine. Writers, producers and directors began to creep back into the building for a few hours and set up as much of the pre-production planning as was possible, ready for a quick return to work as soon as a settlement was reached. David Frost appeared from time to time to 'rally the troops' and keep our spirits up. I discovered the delights of the much-sought-after cherry pie in the canteen and met my soon-to-be new director, Keith Beckett. 'Keithy baby' as he was known to everyone, including himself, was an ex-dancer and very much part of 'showbiz'. I couldn't wait to start work 'proper' for it all promised to be a lot of fun. Then one day my wish was granted, the strike was over and we were 'off' with a vengeance.

Chapter Thirteen

Never one to live in the past, my memory of the next twenty or more years are now a kaleidoscope of vivid images. True, there were sporadic attempts to keep a diary but these soon trailed off into odd entries here and there which usually, around March, ended completely. I continued working in television and to begin with I was working on one of the Saturday-night light-entertainment spectaculars that were still popular in the 1960s and 70s. They included dance routines, stand-up comics, singers and, occasionally, a speciality act. I remember working with Dickie Henderson and throwing in his hat and cane as he tap danced his way through a routine. It was a trick I had picked in the theatre when we had done an evening of Old Time Music Hall. Dickie was impressed, for it needed timing, accuracy and a sort of act of will to put the hat and the cane into the hands of the performer. He seemed to appear in LWT shows a lot at that time and I often got a message from 'Dickie's hat and cane' asking if I could pop over to the studio for an hour or so. But mainly I was in the rehearsal room with the dancers, the other artists only appearing towards the end of the week. The choreographer was Paddy Stone. He was a Canadian who had come to Britain with his partner Irving Davies and they were both internationally respected in dancing circles. I had several old copies of Dance and Dancers with their names mentioned in featured articles and they were described as 'highly innovative'. Older now, they had turned to choreography. The magazine was one I had spent my precious pocket money on when I was still a schoolgirl, so I was thrilled at the prospect of working with Paddy, though somewhat nervous as he had a reputation for being a perfectionist.

That first morning I was in the rehearsal room with Gerry Pearson when Paddy arrived. Gerry was the stage manager and I his assistant. We had marked out the set the day before and a tape recorder was ready and the coffee was on. The dancers were called for later and we had a rehearsal script. I don't remember who the guest artists were for that first show but the dancers usually danced with or behind the singers for one number and also had a spot of their own. If the singers could also dance then the routines generally became more complicated. I kept rather a low profile at first and Paddy was charming, I think we were all just so pleased to be able to work.

As the weeks passed I found myself virtually running the rehearsals while Gerry worked in the office. Paddy was definitely cast in the Minos Volonakis mould but I was used to that so a few swear words and the odd explosion didn't really bother me, and anyhow it was soon over and we all settled down again. Paddy choreographed for the camera and put in his own tape-breaks in order to re-position his dancers. Mostly this wasn't a problem but our recording time in the studio was strictly limited and to go into overtime cost thousands of pounds and required the consent of the whole studio crew, something that could never be taken for granted. Paddy very much wanted to direct his own routines but he didn't have a union ticket, so although the directors he worked with involved him as much as they could, he simply could not be seen to direct in the studio as it could have precipitated another strike. This slowly built up into a big problem. Then Gerry Pearson left to work on another series and I took over as Paddy's stage manager. I think Gerry was relieved to go for the atmosphere in the rehearsal room could be on the verge of anarchy some days and I remember Gerry leaving the room one day, stopping at the open door and shouting, 'You are good Paddy Stone, and that is spelt with two o's not one.' It was a wonderful exit line and as the door slammed behind him we all burst out laughing. But the explosions continued and one day Paddy walked out of a production meeting and left the building. By chance I met him in the lift and he was obviously very angry. He told me he was going to sit by the Serpentine in Hyde Park and then swore me to secrecy about his intentions. I returned to the office to catch up on some paperwork and was eventually summoned to a meeting with Keith and Frank Muir. They asked me if I knew where he had gone, so I told them that I did but had promised not to say anything. That was all right, they said but would I please go and find him and talk him into coming back? If he was at work the following morning then the matter would be considered closed, but technically he had just broken his contract as he had told them he was resigning before he walked out.

I got in the Mini and drove down to the Bayswater Road where I parked the car (not a problem in those days) and walked across to the Serpentine. I quickly found Paddy sitting in a deckchair and glaring at the water and I slipped into an empty chair next to him.

'Oh, they've sent you have they?' he said.

'Yes,' I replied, 'but I didn't tell them where you are.' There was a long pause.

Eventually I was bought a coffee and we began to talk about his life in Canada and some of the shows he had danced in. I let him talk because I was fascinated by the stories and he slowly calmed down and began to laugh. There was another pause and then he demanded to know what 'they' wanted. He finally agreed that he would go back the following morning and I got up to leave.

'Don't go back too soon,' he said. 'Make it look like I needed persuading.'

'OK,' I shouted back and heard him add, 'and they were very clever sending you.'

I walked back across the park and then down Queensway to do some shopping in Whitely's department store. Finally, I went back to the car and discovered that I had somehow lost the keys. Panic! I phoned the AA and then sat for ever until they arrived. When the very nice man got there he simply looked on the ignition for a number, walked to the nearby petrol station and returned with a new key. This he handed to me and got into his van and left. Feeling rather stupid I returned to LWT where Keith and Frank were waiting. When I told them the good news I was thanked profusely and we all went home. Next morning things were back to normal.

Somewhere around this time we did a 'special' starring Cliff Richard. By now I was getting used to being around celebrities but Paddy was worried about Cliff. For one thing Cliff was known to be a very useful dancer and also another perfectionist. But the main problem was that he was also thought never to use even the mildest bad language. Paddy swore a lot but it never really meant anything and no one in rehearsal took much notice, in fact after a while you never really heard it. Still, he was worried and for the first two days of rehearsal we had a very subdued and ultra-polite choreographer. Then on the third morning Cliff was doing one of the routines and he made a mistake.

'Damn!' he said, and everything ground to a halt. But it broke the very uneasy atmosphere and I'm sure Cliff did it deliberately. After that everything got back to normal and Paddy relaxed, while Cliff continued to contribute the occasional 'damn' just to keep it that way.

One morning Cliff had another appointment and couldn't rehearse until the afternoon so I was ordered to stand in for him. I started to walk through the opening number to help the dancers but Paddy was not satisfied.

'Dance it,' he demanded.

'But Paddy, I'm not a dancer,' I protested.

'You've got two ******* feet, haven't you?' he shouted and proceeded to push me until I was dancing well enough to make the rehearsals worthwhile. I loved it, until the next day when I ached all over and was so stiff I could hardly move.

The routines for that show were special, even by Paddy's standards and Cliff looked great. The Shadows joined us and we went out filming. One evening we spent with them and the crew in Mini Mokes, driving round and round Piccadilly Circus and up and down the Mall. It was all great fun and hardly seemed like work at all. Arriving on location one day, Cliff pulled up beside me in his E-Type Jag and asked me if I was taking my car on location, my affirmative reply produced a smile and the statement that he would come with me and leave his car behind. So we spent a happy day trundling around Hampstead, stopping to pick up shots around the Heath and the village. We ended up at Marine Ices in Chalk Farm, filmed quite a long sequence there and then sat chatting while the rest of the crew left to set up the final shots. It was very quiet in the ice-cream parlour ... at least it was until just after four o'clock when the schools emptied and we were quickly discovered by hordes of wildly excited teenagers. Cliff and I made a dash for my car that was parked quite close on the main road. I tried to hold back the crowd of mostly girls and shouted to Cliff to get in the car.

He stood holding my driver's door open and said, 'After you.'

'Cliff,' I yelled back, 'just get in to the car please, this is not the time to be a gentleman.' He complied reluctantly and we shot off up Haverstock Hill, the screams fading behind us. He was obviously more used to vast numbers of adoring fans than I, but the situation had been getting out of hand and I was officially responsible for his safety. By the time we reached the rest of the unit, however, we were giggling happily and even now, whenever I pass Marine Ices I find myself half expecting Cliff to walk out of the door.

The rest of that summer passed quickly. Graham and I were both working and we suddenly found ourselves quite well off. We found a Greek restaurant in Camden Town and spent happy, silly evenings eating kebabs and drinking the retsina wine. We met up with friends and took picnics up to the summer concerts at Kenwood, lingering in the warmth of the summer night until Barney grew tired of our lethargy and began tugging at his lead, desperate to go adventuring. Then we would walk back across a Heath that was often bathed in moonlight while the intrepid hound chased deep into the woods, following the scent of the badgers and foxes that we knew lived there.

One day Graham and I were off work together and after a lazy morning Graham professed a concern that Barney had not seen the sea for a long time and was rapidly becoming an underprivileged dog. So we grabbed a towel, squashed, all three of us, into the front of the Mini and set off for Clacton-on-Sea. It was late in the afternoon when we started and the light was fading when we reached the coast. The beaches had emptied and we had them to ourselves, only the memory of the hot summer day still lingered, and the heat hung over the sand like a blanket. We went for a paddle, and then, stripping down to our underwear, we raced into the water, leaving Barney barking anxiously in the shallows. I think he was afraid we were leaving him behind, maybe heading for France, so finally he overcame his fear of the waves and swam out to join us. We played happily for a while then returned to the beach, taking off our wet underclothes and making ourselves superficially decent with the garments we had left behind. We went for fish and chips, all three of us eating them from the paper they were wrapped in. Graham and I shared a beer and Barney cleverly drank water from a plastic cup. We then returned to the car and sat damp and itching from the salt water through the long journey back. Once home we all had a shower and climbed happily into bed, Barney even forgoing his usual evening security check of the garden. It had been another happy day.

As the months passed we had become even more of a friend with our upstairs neighbour and by this time we had discovered something about her connection to Anna Pavlova. I very much wanted to learn more, but she seemed reluctant to talk about her life with that great artist and we were both too polite to press her. She would, however, talk about her own life and that alone was fascinating. She had been born in St Petersburg and trained as a seamstress. The family were not poor but neither were they rich and she had eventually gone to work at the Mariinsky Theatre where she met Pavlova. They became close and when she learned that Anna Pavlova was to perform in England she begged to be allowed to go with her. She was engaged to be married to an army officer at the time and he was reluctant to let her leave Russia, but eventually she prevailed and came to London for the first time. The trip was a success and they returned safely to St Petersburg. Then she heard that Pavlova was to tour in America, a country she had long wanted to see. Again she began to plead to be allowed to go with her and again she prevailed after promising to marry her fiancé on her return. They left, but while they were away the Communist Revolution broke out and they were advised not to return. They never did, and she never heard from her family again. She lived with Pavlova and Monsieur Dandre in the big house on the edge of Golders Green until Pavlova died in 1931. Allowed to stay in England as a political refugee, Manya's only official paper was her Tsarist passport. Graham delighted in surprises and in many ways spoilt me rotten. He knew that I was fascinated by her story and one Christmas asked her to make me a coat or a dress but she said her eyes now were too weak and she could no longer sew. Instead he bought me a book on Nijinsky and a ticket to see Nureyev dance at the Coliseum.

Another time he arrived home with tickets to see Judy Garland at the Talk of the Town. Judy was coming to the end of her career and there were rumours that she had become unreliable. So, with fingers crossed, we dressed in our finest and went down into the West End. It soon became apparent that something was wrong. Our seats were close to the orchestra pit and between us we knew most of the musicians sitting there. The show was very late starting but the first half finally went ahead. When we came back to our seats after the interval there was another wait and the musicians warned us that it was unlikely that Judy would appear. Then we heard that she was in the theatre and we began to hope. Suddenly the musicians picked up their instruments and began to play her intro. The house lights went down and a spotlight danced across the stage. There was another wait until finally a tiny figure could be seen by the edge of the wings. The audience exploded and rose to its feet. The figure moved into the spotlight and there she was. She was dressed in nylon ski pants and a rather dirty-looking white nylon blouse. She had slippers on her feet, her hair was a mess and she wore no make-up, but she was there. The band tried to help her, but at first she simply walked round the stage holding out her arms to the audience. We cheered and then she started to sing. She would start a number and then seem to lose her way and go into another song with the band desperately trying to follow. The audience ached for her but when she sang, sometimes only a few bars, the real spirit of Judy Garland spun across the footlights and we all fell in love with her. When she heard the intro to 'Somewhere over the Rainbow' she came to the front of the stage and sat cross-legged on the very edge. We held our breath. She sang loud and clear but never finished the song. Suddenly she stood up, left the stage and was gone. The front tabs swung to a close and the house lights came up. We cheered and cheered but to no avail, the evening was over. I suppose we should have been disappointed but we didn't feel like that. For brief moments we had seen the great Judy Garland as the star we had always thought her to be and there had been magic there that night.

That autumn Graham had worked on the Sunday series of *The Frost Programme*. This was primarily a comedy sketch show written around Ronnie Corbett and Ronnie Barker, with weekly guests and David doing the links. At the end of the series there was to be a big party to be held in the Alexandra Palace and Graham had been invited. The invitation said 'Graham plus one', so I was to go too. We searched hard and long for a suitable (cheap) dress for me to wear and finally found an all-in-one garment that looked like a long dress but had a skirt that was divided in to culottes. When we arrived at the party it proved to be a wise choice, for inside David had arranged for a complete working fun fair to be built in the big hall. There were dodgem cars and side shows, candy floss and hot dogs – and so many famous faces it was impossible to keep count. David and Jenny, his then girl friend, stood at the entrance to welcome their guests and, once inside, Peter Cook walked past with Judy Garland on his arm and the Bishop of London raced round the dodgem track bumping enthusiastically in to anyone who got in his way. The two Ronnies were there, Barry Cryer, the writers and most of the well-known guests who had appeared on the show. Happily Graham knew most of the production team so we soon stopped being over-awed and began to enjoy ourselves. In the early hours of the morning we reluctantly left for home, saying a big thank you to David and Jenny on the way out. As we walked to the car I turned and looked back to the palace and thought how lucky I was to have been there: I still do.

By the end of the next summer the new series of three, weekly Frost programmes began to feature in the autumn schedules and I longed somehow to work on one of them. I went to flutter my eyelashes at Martin Case and he promised to see what he could do. David had arrived at LWT with a very high profile indeed and he had only increased his popularity there. He also had brought with him some young and talented writers and performers. Two of them I had got to know quite well during the summer, for they were often to be found on the light-entertainment floor and frequently begged the use of my old, manual typewriter and persuaded me to provide them with a seemingly endless supply of free unit coffee. I don't think they were officially working for us then and eventually they threw their lot in with the BBC with spectacular results. Michael Palin and Terry Jones were great fun to have around; they seemed to be very much the new kids on the block at that time and, while the occasional arrival of Peter Cook et al produced a wave of excitement throughout the building, they came and went as they wished and quickly came to be regarded as part of the gang. Years later after the phenomenal success of *Monty Python's Flying Circus* I met up with them at YTV. I was working with Ian McNaughton, the *Circus*'s director, when they breezed into our office and settled in to drink coffee. As the clock ticked on to eleven o'clock they suggested a move to a nearby pub, and as it seemed a most logical move at the time, off we went for 'a quickie'. I had a dental appointment at 2 p.m. and as I was terrified of dentists I rather welcomed the opportunity to acquire a little 'Dutch courage'. We had a hilarious time until I glanced at my watch and realized it was 1.55 p.m. I leapt to my feet and found that my legs were less co-operative than usual, but with lots of encouragement from the other three and with promises that we would do it all again soon, I threw myself into a taxi and made it to the dentist only late by a few minutes. The treatment (I think it was for a root canal) passed in a haze of giggles and when I tried to apologise for the smell of alcohol on my breath the dentist told me to 'please do the same again' before my next treatment. Alas we never did.

One day while back working at YTV I received a phone call from Graham. He had been contracted to work again on the Sunday Frost series but the other two were still without a stage manager. Friday was to be the serious one, Saturday was to be more general and light hearted and someone was needed to work on both. I quickly phoned Martin Case, and a few days later was summoned to his office and offered a contract to work on the two of them together. I was over the moon and couldn't wait to start work.

Looking back now I believe that it was working on *The Frost Programme* that opened doors and provided opportunities for me that I would never have enjoyed otherwise. The programmes went on air live and created an adrenalin buzz of their own, but having worked in theatre I was used to that and thrived on it. The members of the production team were all highly talented and professional but most came from a journalistic background and only I was 'show biz' and so I was very useful in some areas and quickly sorted out where I could be most effective. I also discovered that a mention of David's name would open almost any door and make available knowledge and expertise from unusual sources. But I was certainly not prepared for the regularity with which I was asked to 'look after' some of the most famous and influential people in the realm, or in some cases, the world. I was to become extremely grateful for my mother's early insistence on politeness and good manners and for my school's teaching that all things were possible.

While I was working on the British shows David began to have his own series in America, these also achieved a similar level of success and he became a huge international star. He soon knew a phenomenal number of people in all walks of life – and most of them seemed prepared to appear on his show or help in any way they could. But to us he was always part of the team and was treated as such. One evening, leaving the studio after the show, I discovered that my car had a flat battery. At that moment I saw David and Bob, his driver and friend, emerging into the street. I shouted across to them and asked for a push. Strangers walking along the street were then treated to the sight of an international celebrity pushing a Mini round and round a traffic island in downtown Wembley. It took a while but eventually the engine caught and I waved cheerfully and drove off, leaving my helpers to cross to the far more appropriate pale blue Bentley that was almost certain to start on the first turn of the ignition key.

With David now often commuting to and from New York on a weekly basis we were left on our own for the first part of the week. The Friday-morning production meeting was the first chance to finalise the format for all the shows; David would arrive from the airport, and with coffee and croissant freely available in the conference room we would quickly begin to sort out the various ideas put forward by the producer and researchers. I would mainly listen and grab any information I felt was 'mine' as and when it popped up. Most of this information related to the Saturday show, for it was much broader in content and often included some 'props' – in the case of an interview with George Best, several footballs for instance. But I was also delegated responsibility for the musical items and that, on occasions, could make life complicated. I think David enjoyed putting a creative spanner in the works from time to time, perhaps he thought we enjoyed it too, and in a way he was right, though it never seemed like that until we had coped with the situation and come out of it successfully. I was in the office early one Saturday morning when the phone rang. It was David phoning from the car to tell me that he had just heard Rolf Harris's hit single 'Two Little Boys' on the car radio. He went on to ask if I would please get hold of Rolf and see if he could perform it on that night's show. He added that he had Rolf's home phone number if I would like it – I said I would.

I rang Rolf, only to be told that he was out, but when I explained the situation the voice on the other end of the phone said that he should be back in about half an hour and that they would get him to phone as soon as he came in. I left a message on the producer's desk and rang the director who said, 'Fine,' but went on to ask me to get him a copy of the recording as he hadn't heard it. Music Services were closed on a Saturday so I booked a car to go into Wembley, buy a copy of the record and deliver it to Derek in the editing suite where he was working. I then rang Music Services at home. Skip Humphries was the Head of Music Services and together with his wife Di ran a very professional department and all music items had to be dealt with through them. Luckily I just caught Skip before he went out. After checking that we were not satirising the number in any way he told me to go ahead if Rolf wanted to do it as it would be no trouble to clear the copyright retrospectively on Monday morning.

'What about musicians?' I asked.

'It shouldn't be a big problem,' said Skip, and added that Rolf should have his own arrangement and band parts for a four or five piece band. 'Let me know when it's a definite "go" and I'll sort it out with Rolf.'

I made one last phone call to warn Artists' Bookings and sat back to wait for Rolf's phone call. It came within the half an hour but he did not tell me what I wanted to hear. He was working out of London that night, he said, but how about pre-recording it? I looked up at the office clock, it was 11a.m.

David walked in and raised a quizzical eyebrow. I explained the situation. 'See if you can fix it, Annie.' he said, and disappeared into his office.

I told Rolf that I would ring him back in a few minutes and phoned the Wembley Studios. Yes, I was told, there was a machine available between 3 and 4 p.m. and they could crew the studio too. I booked it. I rang Derek. 'Good,' he said, 'keep going and I'll take over when I come out of editing.' I rang Skip. 'OK I'll phone Rolf and we'll sort all the music out and I'll let you know what is happening.' I spoke to Rolf, brought him up to date and asked that the musicians provide their own DJs and he brought whatever he wished to appear in, and I double checked that he would have the band parts. I then spoke to Make-Up, Wardrobe ,Props and Graphics. They were fine about it all and Props had music stands in stock and said they would have five standing by. A final call to Artists' Bookings and it was time to get over to the studio. I looked back at the clock, it was now five minutes past one; it was going to be tight but we were in with a chance. As I walked away from my desk the phone rang again. I considered ignoring it but couldn't quite manage to. It was Derek saying that he'd listened to the record and could I find him some pictures of toy soldiers and a rocking horse that he could use as captions? I simply didn't know how I was going to do that in less than two hours. I finally muttered that I would try, and phoned Directory Enquiries for the number of the Wembley Central Library. There the caretaker answered with the information that the library had just closed and everyone had gone home. I talked on, dropping David's name into the conversation as many times as I could. Eventually he offered to phone the chief librarian at home and ask him to call me. When the call finally came it brought good news. The chief librarian knew of two books that contained some good, large drawings that would fit the bill and he would allow us to use them provided we did not damage them in any way. I explained my time schedule and offered to send a car to his home to take him to get the books, bring them to us and take him back to his house. He agreed. I booked the car and fled to the studio. There, a quick peep through the main studio doors revealed Derek in full control and everything up and running. I returned to reception and waited for the books. At 2 they arrived and were perfect. At 2.30 p.m it was the turn of the musicians to begin to arrive, instruments in one hand and DJs in the other. Then Rolf walked in waving a folder containing sheet music. I began to believe in small miracles.

A few minutes before 4.00 pm Derek thanked everybody and wrapped the studio – with some luck and a lot of very professional help we had done it. True, we hadn't exactly changed the world but it felt like a victory of sorts. I parceled up the books, booked a car to return them to the library on Monday morning and wandered off to get a cup of coffee. David passed me in the corridor. 'Well done,' he said and I went all pink and fluffy. And there were to be quite a few more times like that.

I can't remember all the people who came on the shows now but some have stayed clearly in my memory. There was Paul Newman, kind, charismatic, a delight to meet and with the most amazing blue eyes. He departed leaving a trail of temporarily broken hearts behind him. King Hussein of Jordan was a perfect gentleman. I had been nervous of meeting him until one of the researchers told me that he loved model trains. When I mentioned this to him he smiled broadly and talked away for over an hour until David came to find him and more pressing matters swam into focus. Dr Kenneth Kaunda was another person who found time to be courteous at a moment when his country was collapsing into chaos. One of his bodyguards politely requested that I refill the jug of water for the studio in his presence, explaining that there had been threats to the life of the president and, whilst he was sure there was no problem, it was his job to take no chances. The then Prime Minister, Harold Wilson, joined us in Hospitality after the show and, together with Marcia, stayed for ages, delighting in a programme then being broadcast about naked witches in Surrey dancing round a bonfire. Norman Mailer, the controversial American writer, came and behaved impeccably, and there was an interview with the wife of one of the American presidents (Pat Nixon) who arrived with several security men, each showing a suspicious bulge in his left armpit. It had been my job to take them round the studio two days earlier and convince them that our security men were highly trained and efficient. As most of them were retired policemen or Ex-Terratorial Army and well into their sixties I'm not sure the Americans were totally re-assured but they said nothing and on the night of the interview simply lurked rather menacingly in dark corners close to the set. I think everyone was pleased when it was all over.

During the day I was often alone in the production office, researchers were out researching or interviewing people for the weekend programmes while the producer was in meetings. At that time the weekend slots were one of the hottest things on television and many people were eager to appear on them. But we had our own ideas of what we wanted and only rarely did we take such an offer further. One afternoon the phone rang and when I answered it I found the representative of a large film company on the other end. The film *The Magic Christian* had just been released to rather mixed revues and I suppose they were anxious for publicity. We probably wouldn't have been interested had three stars of the film not been in London and willing to do an interview with David. With Peter Sellers, Spike Milligan and Ringo Starr on board it began to look like an interesting proposition. I wrote down the details and promised that someone would phone them back, eliciting an agreement that we would have first refusal on the interviews. When, later, I passed on the details to the programme editor it was decided to go ahead, I received a list of props from the film company and set about organizing them. One item was a black briefcase that had to contain £1,500 in real money. They sent a photo of the briefcase that had been used in the film and one was purchased. The money, however, quickly began to provide enormous problems. The cash office at Wembley studios closed at noon on a Saturday and no one was available to stay around until the live evening show. After much discussion it was finally conceded that I could collect the money at noon, whereupon it would be checked into the briefcase that was then to be locked on to my wrist until it was required. An extra security man was to follow me around and take temporary possession if I needed to go to the loo. I was not to leave the studios and if any of the money went missing I would be liable for its replacement. So for many hours the wretched thing and I, and the security man, darted around trying to set up the rest of the show. As the studio canteen was also closed, I arranged for someone to bring us a doggy bag from the Chinese restaurant where everyone else was having a merry lunch. In the middle of the afternoon I began phoning around to confirm the car pick-up time for our guests ... and discovered that Spike Milligan had decided he would not be coming! I relayed the bad news upwards and it was decided to wait the hour or so before Peter Sellers arrived and consult with him on the best way to try and reverse Spike's decision. Peter spent a long time on the phone and eventually we heard that Spike would be coming after all. I rebooked his car and we all crossed our fingers. I showed the briefcase to Peter, told him I was only allowed to give it to him on the studio floor and jokingly added, 'I don't care what you do with it on set but don't throw the money into the audience at the end of the show.'

Eventually the audience began to arrive and I went down into the studio. I was nervous because there was still no sign of Spike. I gave the briefcase to Peter and David appeared and we went into the countdown. I became aware of someone behind me and turned round. Spike was standing there. I smiled and said, 'Good evening.' It was obvious that he wasn't happy.

'I don't think I want to do this,' he said.

Looking back I've no idea where my next words came from, but I heard myself say:

'How is the little statue in Kensington Gardens?'

I had read that Spike had recently surrounded it with little pottery figures of animals and gnomes and there had been photos in the press. He stopped and looked at me hard and long.

'Did you see it?' he asked

'Yes,' I replied, lying and crossing my fingers behind my back like a child.

'The vandals destroyed it.'

'Oh,' I sympathised. 'What a crime. It was so pretty.'

I saw the tension go out of his shoulders and he laughed. 'Peter and I are going on to Ronnie Scott's after the show, why don't you come with us?'

I was somewhat stunned. 'I'd love to,' I stammered.

'All right," he said. 'I'll go on just for you.' And he walked out on to the set.

The show was a success and Spike was very funny. As we came to the closing moments Peter stood up and threw the money into the audience. I stood open-mouthed. As soon as the LWT logo was on the monitor screen, I dived in and began to collect the notes. Members of the audience helped me and handed them over laughing and when I counted them nothing was missing. The security man and I checked the money into the studio safe and I went up to Hospitality for a well-earned glass of wine.

Peter Sellers came over to where I was standing. 'Don't you ever tell me not to do something again,' he said, and he wasn't smiling.

A little while later I sadly walked over to Spike and told him that I wouldn't be able to go to Ronnie Scott's after all, and then I drove home.

Another phone call that came my way was from two young men who had written a rock opera. They offered to send over an LP of the whole show and it arrived in the office just as I was leaving. I took it home and played it that evening and thought it terrific. Next morning, bursting with enthusiasm, I handed it over to the programme editor and continued to nag him until it was decided that the hit number should be used to open the Saturday show, that way it would be certain to be transmitted, for if we included it later and the show over-ran it could well be at risk of being cut.

Murray Head arrived at the studio shaking with nerves but he was terrific in front of the audience and made a great impact. Yes, the show was *Jesus Christ Superstar* and I was besotted with it. I kept the LP and tried desperately to interest some drama directors I knew well but no one shared my enthusiasm. I went to

St Paul's Cathedral and decided it was the perfect venue; I even talked to the Dean, who said that he was certainly open to the idea of staging it there, but I never managed to get it off the ground and I lost momentum and moved on to other things. Of course Robert Stigwood bought the performing rights and the rest is showbiz history. My first chance to become a millionaire had passed me by, but at the time I was simply thrilled that my original belief in it had proved correct.

With Graham working on the light-entertainment series, I often found myself out at the Wembley studios on a Sunday evening for the live transmission. There was a certain overspill between the three shows anyhow, and I got to know some of the writers and Ronnie C and Ronnie B rather well. The 'Two Ronnies', as they were always known, were great fun to be around and very professional. Two completely different personalities, they nevertheless were perfect foils for one another and had great respect for each other's talents. Barry Cryer was often around and became a life-long 'mate'. I used to meet him at most of the independent television studios where we would greet one another enthusiastically and catch up on all the gossip. I once walked into the ATV bar where he was chatting to someone whose back was turned towards me. He called me over and introduced me to his companion.

'Annie,' he said, 'come here and say hello to Bing Crosby.' So I did and spent a memorable and delightful lunch hour chatting to a legend.

McVinNob was our name for three other writers who often worked together. Peter McKellar, Peter Vincent and David Nobbs were their full names, David came from Yorkshire – Leeds I think – and he too became another 'mate' for many years.

Although there was a regular team of writers we often received work from other freelancers, which was accepted on merit and paid for at so much a minute. One name began to crop up quite regularly, that of Gerald Wiley, and his sketches were good. He wrote predominantly for Ronnie C and Ronnie became anxious to meet him. But the sketches were always submitted via an agent and Mr Wiley declared himself to be a very shy man who sought no publicity and regretted that such a meeting would not be possible. Ronnie C was doing a summer season at Brighton that year and he was anxious to buy the performing rights to some of the sketches, so he approached Mr Wiley's agent and was told that the rights were a gift and no money was required. Ronnie C then went out and bought a very expensive set of crystal wine glasses and dispatched them in lieu of payment. There the matter rested, but curiosity grew as to the identity of the shy Mr Wiley and rumours began to fly around the company. As the end of the season approached we heard that the whole production team had been invited to a meal at our local, and excellent, Chinese restaurant across the road from the studios. Our host was to be the mysterious Mr Gerald Wiley, who wished to meet us all at last. For several days there was a buzz of speculation and several well known names were put forward, though in the event no one guessed correctly. Graham and I were both invited and we found ourselves sitting at a long table with the rest of the team when Ronnie B stood up and revealed that he was our host! There was a stunned silence until Ronnie C saved the day by regretting the purchase of the expensive wine glasses and we all laughed and went on to have a very happy meal. The story was featured in several national newspapers and one or two people were rather put out, though most of us took our hats off to Ronnie B and thought it a great joke.

Meanwhile Graham and I decided that, once again, Barney was becoming an under-privileged dog and needed a day in the country. So we all piled into the Mini and headed for Brighton to visit Ronnie C for the show's Saturday matinée. Once in Brighton we set out along the beach with Barney running happily ahead. Alas, Barney was extremely racially prejudiced against small white poodles and large Dalmatians and at that moment we belatedly spotted a small white poodle ahead of us. Alas, too, the poodle was tied by its lead to the upright strut of a deckchair in which its master was sleeping peacefully. Even as we rushed forward, disaster struck. Barney and the poodle began a fierce argument, the upright strut was pulled from its notch and the occupant of the deckchair hit the sand with an audible thump. Graham pushed Barney's lead quickly into his pocket and we attempted to stroll past unconcernedly, but we had not counted on Barney racing up to us to tell us excitedly of what he had done and in the end, after checking that the man was being helped by several other people and appeared unhurt, we had to run for it.

Ronnie C was delighted to see us and declared that Barney's adventure was worthy of a place in his show. He also said that if he had known I was trying to find acting work he was sure he could have found me some in the sketches he was currently performing. But we hadn't been brave enough to approach Ronnie so we swallowed our disappointment, went to the matinée and laughed and applauded and cheered and finally drove back to London with a no-longer-under-privileged but still-in-disgrace Barney dog.

With Graham and I both, temporarily, out of work we were forced to take stock of our relationship, for, although there were still happy times, it had been slowly running into trouble. I was probably most to blame. Life had become very exciting and I went chasing ahead, always eager for the next experience and totally involved in what I was doing. Graham passed his driving test and began taking other people out for meals and drinks in the evening. As these other people were invariably young dancers from the shows he was working on I became resentful and deeply jealous. My rejection phobia clicked in and more doors were closed.

Then one day Graham announced that he was going to France as there was a theatre school there where he was hoping to study. He went, leaving a heartbroken dog who sat at the front door night after night waiting for him to return. As for me, I was determined not to show that I cared. I recently found a postcard from him saying that he had run out of money and asking me to send him twenty pounds. I did and later went over to France for a weekend, certain that it would turn out to be highly romantic and that we would get back together. But when I arrived I found that he had a new girlfriend and that nothing between us seemed to have changed for the better. A few months later I heard that he was married and back in England. Barney began eating again and life moved on, but one evening, walking along the Finchley Road with Barney on a lead beside me, I saw a young man in a green PVC raincoat coming towards us. I was sure it was Graham, and so was Barney. He began pulling me towards him, his tail wagging wildly, but it was someone else and the pleasure went out of the evening.

One evening I was talking to a friend of Graham's in the LWT bar. We began to talk about him and he said Graham had been deeply in love with me even after he had left for France. I never knew that because he had never told me and I had never told him that I still loved him either. Now it was all far too late and around the same time other things began to go wrong too and life entered one of its bumpy bits.

Chapter Fourteen

Just over a year after LWT went on air for the first time it was found to be losing ratings and the advertising contracts that were the lifeblood of the company. As a direct result the Money Men moved in with a vengeance and nothing was ever to be quite the same again. On 5 September 1969 the company directors sacked Michael Peacock, the managing director and replaced him with Tom Margerison. Today it still seems to me to have been an over-reaction to a serious crisis. Nevertheless it was one that brought about a radical change in the balance of power at LWT and one cannot help wondering if this was the ultimate aim of some of the people involved. At that time owning shares in ITV was widely described as being 'a licence to print money', and LWT had failed to live up to that part of its contract. Meanwhile the sacking of the company director caused chaos amongst the heads of departments and left us all feeling insecure. Several people resigned, among them our very own head of department Frank Muir. (See Frank's own account in his autobiography *A Kentish Lad*.) While we understood and admired Frank's loyalty and integrity we felt abandoned. Perhaps Frank never quite understood the impact he had had on the Light Entertainment floor at Station House. During the comparatively short time he had been with us we had grown to admire and trust him, and he had made us feel that we were all a necessary part of an exciting and forward-looking company. We had all worked hard for him but it had been a lot of fun. He, together with such people as Cyril Bennett and Tito Burns, had created a positive and creative attitude towards programme making and ensured that it spread throughout the company. It was something that was rare in the industry and we thought we would go on from strength to strength; now all that was threatened.

A few weeks before the crisis and before Graham had left the company we had heard that Frank had been invited to Buckingham Palace for lunch with the Queen and the Duke of Edinburgh. This was supposed to be a closely guarded secret but somehow it had leaked out. Once he had left the building his secretary proposed that we got Graphics to write a special scroll to mark the event. She approached Graham and me for help and we leapt into action. A quick trip to the studio prop store produced a cloak, an orb and a sceptre. We fashioned a crown from cardboard, cotton wool and the ubiquitous fruit gums and waited eagerly for his return. Security alerted us when he was back in the building and the whole unit lined up to welcome him, bowing or curtsying as was appropriate. A photographer recorded the 'ground-breaking' event and Frank loved it. There would be no more afternoons like that.

Now, over a period of years, the accountants moved in and budgets were cut. It was assumed that all production staff wanted only to screw the company for as much money as they could get, but, while there were a few people like that, the majority of the staff were dedicated to making good television. For a long time the effects of this new profit first policy were slow to take hold and many good and popular programmes were still made, but tighter budgets meant less imaginative scripts, less expensive artistes and lower quality production values. After the departure of Michael Peacock, both staff and freelance writers, producers and directors began to move away from LWT and seek their fortunes elsewhere, often with considerable success. During the next few years LWT turned down scripts that were to be highly successful for other companies, *The Good Life*, for instance, being only one of these.

Inevitably the shock waves subsided and the day-to-day life of the company went on; and mine with it. Pete and Carol were back in London too, having returned when Pete got a job with the BBC. By now they were a 'proper' family that included a son and a daughter and we had become very close again, our lives mingling over long phone conversations and weekend dinners when we explored the delights of Robert Carrier recipes and the newly arrived fish brick. Pete was the fish cook and he was excellent. I concentrated on meat and once was regarded with awe in my local butcher's shop when I requested a whole beef fillet. The resulting boeuf en croûte was good and I began to enjoy cooking again.

Then Pete applied for a job working abroad where the BBC was involved in helping to set up new TV stations. He was offered a posting to Benin, then part of Nigeria; not his first choice and one that many people had turned down. There was one other place on offer but that sounded even more challenging than West Africa and they decided to go to Benin. I was going to miss them dreadfully and there were tears when they left but we promised that we would meet up soon and I would join them for a holiday when I had a gap between contracts.

That first Christmas and New Year period without Graham

was a dreadful one. Friends invited me everywhere, but to be single in a room where everyone else was part of a couple was worse than being alone in the flat. At least there neither Barney nor I had to pretend that we were enjoying ourselves. One good thing was that I was working with friends, Derek, the director from *The Frost Programme*, was there together with Pauline and also Russell Harty (this was before Russell became 'the' Russell Harty) – and Russell, Pauline, Pauline's partner Alan and I used to play silly games over long Sunday lunches in Pauline's flat in Primrose Hill. The series we were working on was one that featured young, highly talented musicians who gave a new meaning to the phrase 'making music' and, in one case, was to provide my first acquaintance with a Stradivarius violin. The series ran into the New Year and New Year's Eve found us all rehearsing in a little theatre near to Swiss Cottage. We finished in the late afternoon and popped into a nearby pub for a friendly drink before we all dispersed to various parties. The pub was full of local people, all intent on enjoying themselves, and we quickly became a part of the crowd. Russell sat down at the piano and began to play some of the old music-hall songs and people began to join in until it became quite a 'knees up' with everyone having a great time. Then Derek looked at his watch and said he had to leave and the three of us trooped out after him, the pub falling strangely silent as the doors swung to behind us. Next day, back at rehearsals, all of us confessed to having spent a miserable evening after we parted company – we should have stayed exactly where we were.

I continued to work on a series of projects until, after about a year, a gap occurred and I became determined to make the long talked about trip to Nigeria. I booked a flight and set about the complicated procedure of getting my visa and letters began to fly between the two countries; those from Carol more and more resembling a shopping list. In England we were in the middle of the three-day week and a series of random strikes. Shopping was difficult and recording TV shows was difficult too. The electricity went off nearly every day and many shops closed their doors. I waded through the requests only to add more as the letters from Benin continued to arrive. The day of my departure finally came and I finally threw away the shopping list, Barney was taken to stay with a couple of his friends, my car was left with other friends and I was driven to the airport. I checked in, bought my duty-free goods and then everything fell apart.

Hostilities had broken out in the Middle East and I was flying with Egypt Air via Cairo. I chatted to an Egypt Air official and when we were told to go back into the departure lounge he told me quickly to hide my duty-free goods, so I did. We were given a form to fill in and my new Egyptian friend materialised at my side and told me not to use my London details as I would only be sent home. I wrote down my Derbyshire address and was given a room in one of the airport hotels. For a while I stayed in the departure hall not quite believing what was happening. A *News at Ten* film crew arrived with two trolleys of equipment; there was a famous TV news face with them, but I can't remember now who it was. They were quickly checked on to an El Al flight and disappeared, leaving the hall eerily quiet. I checked into my hotel room and phoned friends to tell them what was happening but it was impossible to get word to Pete and Carol. Later I went down to get something to eat and found my Egyptian friend in the snack bar. We talked for hours about the crisis. He was an interesting man and I suspect that he was part of the Egyptian Secret Service for he was remarkably well informed. It was late when I went back to my room and I slept badly. I hate violence of any kind and the thought of yet another war with its inherent loss of life depressed me.

The next morning brought little news. My Egyptian friend found me and told me not to leave the airport, so mid-morning I phoned my friends in Sheen and Martin came out for a while to help to pass the time. Mid-afternoon I heard I was to be put on that evening's Air Nigeria flight direct to the capital of Lagos, it was just a question of filling in a few more hours.

It was dark when we finally took off. The man sitting next to me was an Anglo-Indian who lived and worked in Africa. We chatted for a while, swapping all that irrelevant information that is obligatory on long flights, and when the stewards brought round the dinner he offered to buy me a small bottle of wine to drink with it. I accepted and chose the red, probably a mistake, as I soon felt very sleepy. I find it almost impossible to sleep on an aeroplane but this time the wine worked well. Two hours later I awoke to find myself draped across my travelling companion and was deeply embarrassed. I extricated myself, apologising profusely, but he claimed that it had been no inconvenience at all. As the plane began its descent into Lagos he invited me back to his house to have a shower and rest for a while. He lived close to the airport, he said, and would run me back there in good time for my flight to Benin.

I had been warned that Lagos Airport was one of the most difficult in the world to negotiate but nothing had prepared me for the noise and chaos that greeted me when we entered the arrivals building. Once inside the hall, I saw two men summarily dragged off by soldiers toting guns, and I found myself squashed in the middle of a group of screaming passengers. Suitcases were forced open and hand luggage spilt across trestle tables, tomato sandwiches were confiscated and bottles of whisky disappeared. My friend from the plane turned himself into a white knight and negotiated us quickly through all the formalities and out on to the concourse. I suppose now that he must have bribed us out but I never saw any money change hands, perhaps he just had contacts there. Whatever the reason I couldn't have been more grateful for I would have been vulnerable without him.

He went to fetch his car leaving me to my first taste of Africa. We had arrived in the middle of the night but the sights, sounds and smells were overpowering. Some images I recognised from newsreels and photos, well, recognised in a sense, but now they appeared larger than life. The big, brightly painted 'mammy' wagons roared past, their drivers shouting above the noise of the engine and the radios, their headlights spotlighting groups of people in brightly coloured clothes and the three dusty palm trees that stood like cardboard cutouts close by. The smell was one I had never smelt before, spices, petrol, earth ... later I was told it was 'just the smell of Africa', and that summed it up exactly. I was to find it everywhere and carry the memory of it with me to England, where the slightest hint of it would transport me instantly back to Nigeria.

When, later, I returned to the airport, it was to the domestic terminal. The scene that met my eyes there was one from a novel by Graham Greene; large fans were fixed to the ceiling turning slowly and barely disturbing the humidity, dusty potted plants sat in dusty corners and the obligatory three Americans sat drinking out of enormous bottles of Star beer. A group of Nigerians stood waiting to board a plane, bundles of possessions at their feet and a complacent goat on the end of a length of rope. Outside dawn was just breaking and I longed for a coffee. There was a counter that seemed to be serving drinks but I only had large-denomination notes and they had no change and I had to wait the interminable two hours until I was on the plane before that longing could be satisfied.

The plane was the smallest and oldest that I had ever flown on and the in-flight breakfast consisted of a paper cup of lukewarm coffee and a slice of dry bread; but it was delicious, and now I was excited at being on the final leg of my journey. That excitement grew as we bumped our way down the Benin runway and I could see Carol standing in front of the airport building. I was waving as I ran towards her but she gave no sign of recognition; later she told me that on the two previous days the plane had arrived, made two or three attempts to land and then returned to Lagos, She had simply not expected to see me and nearly had not driven out to the airport at all. We drove straight out to Pete's office and, for the moment, all was excitement, laughter and happiness, repeated when we went to their home and found their two excited children waiting to welcome me; only later did I become aware of tension and a feeling that all was decidedly not well.

It transpired that there had recently been an attempted coup. This had been a local one and had not made the newspapers, but for several days Pete had been confined to his office with a man holding a large gun positioned outside his door. Pete felt that the gun was not for his protection. Unsurprisingly he seemed very nervous and was obviously under a great deal of stress. He was also drinking steadily and probably more than he should. Meanwhile Carol had become close friends with a man from Beirut who was working out there too. The atmosphere at home was strained and we found ourselves eating rather a lot of Lebanese food but my first concern was with the political situation. This was not long after the Biafran war and Nigeria was not known to be one of the most stable countries in the world. Created by ex-colonists it was then, and probably still is, a series of indigenous tribes bundled together to form a new country. As I was later to learn at first hand, there was still considerable inter-tribal squabbling that escalated into more serious skirmishes from time to time. Meanwhile, my two best friends appeared to be locked into their personal problems and somewhat naïve about what was going on around them, so when Pete arrived home and said that he had to take their passports into work the next day, I insisted that he took them instead to the British High Commission for safe keeping. If the Nigerians wished to examine them, then they could go there.

The next morning Carol and I tackled the problem centering around her new friend; only to Carol it didn't seem to be a problem. She was obviously enthralled by it all and seemed unaware of the stress that it was already causing in her marriage and of the implications that it would have in the future. She talked of little else and seemed to be expecting my full support. Whilst not being completely unsympathetic, I was also not fully convinced of the genuineness of the motives of her new friend at present back in Beirut. In any case I was more concerned with the crisis at the TV station and of the considerable added stress that it was causing Pete – but this was something which, to her, appeared to be of a minor significance, and so we ended the morning with a fair amount of friction between us, until we finally decided to stop before we ruined a very important friendship and my holiday into the bargain. Instead we set about introducing me to Africa.

Benin City was small for a city and was isolated by the fact that it was surrounded by jungle and a long way from any other town. True, the bush was well populated with small villages of mud huts all linked by well-trodden paths but the ex-pat community never went there and so stayed in a tight enclave of their own making, which only added to their feeling of isolation. There were only two ways out of the city. One was on the plane that didn't always come, or if it did come, didn't always land. The other was by a highway that was modern and fast but went through an area populated by bandits. It was dangerous to stop, even if there was an accident, and I was told that for many weeks there had been an outline of a man lying in the middle of the road and run over so many times that he resembled one of the frogs I had seen years ago in the South of France. I was shocked.

Late on the first morning we went into the market. It was a big one, improvised stalls were selling all the local produce, together with a large selection of imported goods, and in one shady corner was a stall with voodoo dolls, dried frogs and pickled snakes. The dolls were male and female, hand carved with lines of colour on them. I thought them charming and bought several, hoping that they were still free of any curse! The market was noisy, busy and full of life, the different local dialects of the shoppers adding to an atmosphere that made me begin to understand that I was in a country that bore little resemblance to any I had ever known before. I also found that they were selling there at least half the things for which I had searched so desperately in London.

Insidiously, something of Africa found its way into my blood and the images have stayed with me, sharp and clear. It was hot and sometimes unbearably humid so we went, almost daily, to one of the two clubs. 'Ours' had a swimming pool and was frequented mostly by the foreign families. Officially there was no segregation in Nigeria but it was rare to see an African there. In the afternoons it was full of bored wives and their children and appeared to be the social heart of the ex-pat community. Here they upheld the tradition of 'Empire' and presented themselves as some sort of élite. The conversation revolved around problems with the 'servants' and who had been seen with whom; as I was of no interest to them at all, I read my book and delighted in the pleasure of immersing myself in the cool water of the swimming pool.

One Sunday we went out to a river for a picnic. It was supposed to be a popular spot and to Pete's horror had recently been discovered by a small group of Americans. He complained bitterly that their arrival had made prices soar – but there was nothing to buy there; only a frail-looking boat was moored at the water's edge with a 'For Hire' sign nailed to its prow, and we were the only people there that day. The jungle reached down on both sides of the river in shades of dark green, cutting out the sun and seemingly impenetrable, except for a small dirt track on our side of the water. After our picnic lunch I wandered along it and soon lost sight of my friends. The vegetation pressed close all along the way and there was absolute silence. I began to feel strangely disorientated and soon turned back towards the river, a feeling of panic starting to rise until I turned a bend and came out on the riverbank where everything was the same as I had left it.

Another day we were invited to visit a local tribal prince. He lived a little way outside Benin City in a palace that was made up of a large number of mud houses joined together by a confusing system of corridors. It was a fascinating building and we found it delightfully cool inside – a pervasive argument for the traditional way of building versus the breezeblock construction of the more modern houses. The prince greeted us at the entrance to the compound and we were taken into a small room with conventional Western-style furniture and where a bottle of whisky and three glasses sat waiting on a table. The formalities over, he showed us round his home. At every intersection of the corridors there was a small altar with bowls of herbs and dead flowers and often a human skull. These, he explained, belonged to his ancestors and were kept within the family home as a sign of respect and to provide a sense of ongoing inclusion to the long-dead person. We saw no other person during our time there but often heard the sound of women and children quite close to where we were walking. The drive back home passed in silence; we had been shown a glimpse of a way of life that in no way touched our own; we had been treated with great courtesy and for the first time since my arrival I felt I had briefly touched the heart of this intriguing country, but I also knew that I was a long way from understanding it.

My visit had coincided with Ramadan and the weeks of day-long fasting only added to the atmosphere that was a mixture of frustration and anger, one that I was rapidly becoming used to. At night there were the screams of the animals being sacrificed, often at crossroads, their little bodies still lying abandoned in the sunlight next day. I once saw what appeared to be a dead baby at the side of the road and it was explained to me that in Nigeria human life grew in value as a person grew older. Family members were buried under the floors of the huts or in the compounds and I was told of a funeral where the head of the deceased had been placed on a trestle table and covered with a blue sheet that lay flat around it. There was no sign of the rest of the body.

The longer I stayed, the more the days took on a rhythm of their own; the situation at the television station seemed to have calmed down, and with Carol's friend away in Beirut, things at home seemed to have improved too. There was a still an air of unreality about it all, but some of that was probably caused by the anti-malaria tablets we were all taking – they made you 'do-lally' and very forgetful, possibly not a bad thing in the circumstances. Carol told me I had to buy a 'native tea set' from one of the travelling Hausa traders and she put out the word that we wanted one to call at the house. I was intrigued but she would tell me nothing more. Eventually there was a knock at the door and a man with a sack stood there expectantly. Carol told him what we wanted and he produced a beautiful hand-carved Nativity set and laid it out on the step. It was made from balsa wood and everyone was there, including the animals and a tiny baby lamb. The faces of the people were dyed black, including that of the little baby Jesus, and it seemed so much more authentic than the sets back home, where everyone was white and blonde. I still have it and unwrap it with great delight every Christmas.

We began to plan a trip in the Land Rover up through northern Nigeria to the edge of the Sahara Desert, and once we had got out the maps the project took on a momentum of its own and we all became very excited about it. We were to leave ten days before I was due to fly home, and the end of my visit was rapidly approaching.

The night before we were due to set out there was an official drinks party at the British High Commission. Attendance was obligatory for residents and I was given permission to join them.

We went early, for the Land Rover was being serviced and Pete would have to leave to collect it before the garage closed. All the representatives of the foreign governments were there and the Nigerians were well represented. All in all it was a big, if rather provincial event. In true British fashion the alcohol flowed freely and the hors d'oeuvres were scarce and unimaginative and caused comment amongst the French and the Italians. I rather envied Pete when he made his apologies and left after about an hour, saying he would return to collect us, but I struggled on, trying to do my best to make polite conversation. Then something of a hiatus occurred when the wife of our host screamed across the room, 'Would you tell that bloody nigger to get me another drink.' So much for British diplomacy! The conversation tried hard to start up again but really the evening was lost and people soon began to drift away. It became an added embarrassment to stay, and Carol and I accepted a lift from another ex-pat, leaving a message for Pete to say that we had gone home.

Once there, we sat drinking tea and giggling about the evening, waiting for Pete. It was a long time before we heard the Land Rover and he burst into the room in a rage, only calming down when he saw the two of us. It transpired that he had returned to get us and had been told only that his wife had left with a man. Thinking the worst, he got back into the Land Rover and drove wildly round Benin and then up to the Nigerian High Commission where he had driven across the flowerbeds and into the sentry box, demolishing it completely. Seeing through the driving mirror that the sentry box was unattended he finally came home with a Land Rover that now had a badly buckled front wing. To me it seemed to be something of a crisis. I started to insist that we left on our trip at dawn and got as far away as possible. Pete and Carol seemed unalarmed but I eventually prevailed, and so it was with a great deal of relief that we crossed into Ibo territory before the sun was fully up.

We crossed over the bridge that had featured in so many news reports during the war, a strange experience for it seemed such an ordinary structure to have been the cause of the loss of so many lives. The countryside changed almost immediately, the style of the houses, the more open landscape and the clothes of the people walking along the edge of the road. For the first time I saw the plaited hairstyles of the woman, then far from being featured in the Western fashion magazines. I thought they looked so pretty. The road we were on was a good one and we made it to Jos by mid-afternoon. We planned to stay wherever possible in the old British rest-houses that had now been taken over by the Nigerian government. The one at Jos was set in a pretty garden and was clean and comfortable. For a small extra charge, dinner and breakfast could be included, so that evening we went happily to bed feeling that our adventure had really begun. Ahead lay experiences as yet unimagined and I was suddenly very happy to be there.

Next morning we set off for Kaduna in high spirits, driving through small villages where people waved, and stopping once at a tiny shop where we bought the last soft drinks on the shelves and felt guilty for doing it. My other memories have become a series of vivid images: the first was of an old European man pushing a cart piled high with firewood, his clothes hanging in shreds, his hair and beard long and uncombed, his eyes staring wildly. What was his story, I wondered, but he was dismissed by the others as 'having gone native', and was soon lost from view. I thought about this for quite a while. I had talked to both the Nigerians working in the house in Benin (all foreign workers were obliged to hire at least two people to work for them during their time in the country). Pete and Carol had three, a night watchman who spent most of his time asleep, and two others who cleaned and cooked. These two were both Ibo and seemed gentle and intelligent men. One was a war veteran and had been deeply affected by the fighting; the younger one had just got his girlfriend pregnant and they were deciding whether or not to get married. He explained to me that they thought they probably would not. Marriage was only one of the decisions open to them and it had to be something that they both wanted. If they decided against it, the girl would continue to live with her family or his and they would both be free to marry someone else. There was no shame attached to having the baby, in fact it was something of a plus, for the girl had proved herself to be capable of having children. I thought how civilised it all seemed and began to wonder if going 'native' was such a terrible thing.

We spent that night in Kaduna and then went on to Kano where we stayed for two days while the front bumper of the Land Rover was repaired. Pete had phoned a friend back in Benin and been told that there was a big fuss there and all the Land Rovers in the area were being examined for damage. Luckily no one had thought to connect him with the incident. When we left Kano we were again in high spirits, and with the end of Ramadan expected nightly, so was most of Nigeria.

The landscape was flatter now that we had left all traces of the bush behind, and it was mostly an area of low scrub and tiny villages; occasionally a solitary tree broke the line of the horizon, usually with someone sitting in its shade. There was little traffic on the road and we made good progress, only stopping once to stretch our legs and buy some water. About forty minutes later I discovered my bag was no longer with us: in it was my passport, money, keys and some jewellery. We remembered that the door of the Land Rover had not been closed properly after our stop and had swung open. We had closed it from inside and driven on. With a fair amount of barely concealed bad temper we drove back. As we approached the village we saw a small crowd of people sitting by the roadside. Spotting the jeep, they came running towards us waving my bag in the air, pleased that we had returned. Everything was safely inside and they would take no reward. Somewhat humbled we continued on our way.

On the outskirts of Sokoto we passed the main killing stone for the town; it was running red with the blood of slaughtered sheep and already the fires were lit and the smell of roasting lamb mingled with the smoke. A cloudless sky bode well for the celebrations that had been delayed for two days while the imam waited to see the moon. As we left our government house that evening the streets were buzzing with anticipation, and, when the moon rose finally into a black sky, the streets filled with galloping, fiery Arab horses, wearing harnesses and saddles dyed turquoise and maroon and heavily enriched with silver. Their riders were dressed in flowing robes and firing rifles into the air; excitement was everywhere.

As we left Sokoto the next morning the celebrations were still in full swing. We were on the edge of the Sahara now and desert tribesmen were still charging into the town after travelling all night under the stars. We passed many market stalls, but this was no market like the one in Benin, it was far too grand for that; this was a bazaar, with an array of beautiful handmade carpets, rich silks and cottons, silver and brass and the heady smell of incense and spices. A Tuareg caravan rested at the edge of the town before setting out across the desert. The woman were very beautiful, their eyes ringed with kohl and the deep blue of their robes a vivid streak of colour, the men handsome and proud, striding restlessly around the camp. The camels waited calmly, chewing cud and dreaming in the heat. We gave the children sweets but I think they had never seen such things before and they looked at them uncertain what to do until we showed them by eating some ourselves and their mothers laughed and waved their thanks. I longed to stay but we were running out of time and had to leave for the journey back to Benin. We drove on minor roads now, full of potholes and deserted. Here there were no villages or petrol stations and it was several hours before we saw someone on the road ahead. As we approached, he waved us down and we stopped, thinking he needed help of some kind, but he only wanted a cigarette and was soon satisfied – a naked man on a bicycle smoking a British cigarette.

It was evening before we reached a small town and found the only hotel there. The rooms were hot, there was no water and the sheets on the bed were grey and had known many bodies. We hardly slept and left at dawn, covered in mosquito bites; it was a long time before we found somewhere for coffee and we were all grumpy and sat in silence as we drove hard, arriving back in Benin late in the evening.

Two days later I left for Lagos. We knew that the situation in the Middle East had improved – well, the fighting had stopped – and naïvely assumed that the Egypt Air flights would be back to normal. Lucky, a friend of Pete's who worked with him at the TV studios, was already in Lagos and was going to meet me when I arrived – it all seemed to be well organised. We were all crying as I left for the airport; I had been with Carol and Pete for nearly five weeks and suddenly the problems, the arguments seemed pointless. We had always been such close friends; surely it would be that way again?

It was one of the plane's good days and we left on time. Lucky was at the airport in Lagos but he had bad news. There were no Egypt Air planes in Nigeria and it would be several days before one came. The luxury hotel in the town was already full but I had been found a room in a small one close to the airport. Lucky put me into a taxi and promised to be in touch with any news. I never saw or heard from him again. The Nigerian owners of the hotel were friendly and welcoming; the husband had lived in England for several years but had found it 'too difficult for a black man there' and had returned home. He said that no foreigner would ever be treated badly in his hotel and I felt shamed and embarrassed. I could only too easily guess at his treatment in my own country.

For a few days I had the chance to experience at first hand something of the African way of life, I was the only foreigner there and was expected to fit in. The food cooked in the hotel was African, very hot and served on a bed of sweet potato. Once I ate caterpillars I think, but they tasted like chicken and were delicious. At first I stayed close to the hotel but one day the owner of the hotel invited me to meet his father at his home in Lagos. His father had been an important man in one of the previous governments but had now retired – though the family was obviously still well connected, for they lived in one of the big colonial buildings in the centre of town and the flat comprised the whole of the first floor. It was huge with ceiling-to-floor windows, wooden floors and carved double doors leading to the main room. Inside were two very old, wooden framed sofas, a coffee table between them – and nothing else. His father appeared, dressed in traditional robes; he was a very tall man and walked with great dignity and when he clapped his hands someone appeared with the obligatory unopened bottle of whisky and three glasses. It was 9.a.m. and my heart sank.

After effecting the necessary introductions his son left, claiming urgent business in the town and saying he would return in an hour. My heart sank further for I was now familiar with the fact that an African hour bore little resemblance to one on my watch and conversation was already proving difficult. My host sat there, regarding me with polite interest and courteously answering my questions whilst voicing none of his own. So if I stopped speaking, then so did he – and the silences then became longer as I ran out of things to ask. I became increasingly uncomfortable. At last his son returned and it was possible to leave.

My escort now took me on a tour of the town that ended at the luxury hotel. Here he left me again, saying that he would return in the late afternoon. I was rather thrown by this but in fact it turned out to be a pleasant way of passing my time. I ordered a large pot of coffee and settled by a window with my book. There was a young man sitting close by and we soon began to talk. He was an American from the Midwest and was currently travelling round the world. He didn't look at all like an intrepid traveller and I was intrigued. It turned out that this was to be a once-in-a-lifetime experience, for his father had recently died and he had inherited the family business. He had felt it incumbent upon himself to see the world before he settled down, so, leaving his mother behind to find a suitable lady to marry him on his return, he had set off, flying from capital city to capital city and staying only in top international hotels. He had allowed three weeks for his epic journey. I asked what he had learnt of the world so far, and he explained, as to a child, that Europe was decadent, the Middle East unreliable and Africa 'very simple'. He had spent three days in Lagos, mostly in the hotel, and tomorrow was flying on to India, a country that he wasn't expecting to like very much. Left somewhat opened-mouthed by all this I attempted to describe some of my experiences during the last few weeks, but he was uninterested; already he had learned all there was to learn about Africa and his time there was finished. Rather to my surprise he suggested we took a walk on the nearby beach, it would be, he said, a way of passing the time. So we walked through a series of building sites and on to beautiful white sand. The Atlantic waves were pounding in, foaming and dangerous and their noise made conversation impossible. I looked across to where I thought England should be and knew suddenly that I was ready to go home. I was already several days late and people would be wondering where on earth I was.

When my Nigerian host returned to collect me he bore the welcome news that the Egypt Air plane would be flying in tomorrow and leaving for Cairo the day after. I was glad about that. For my last evening it transpired that I was to be taken to 'the best club in town'. Already mentally halfway back to London, I didn't want to go but felt it would be rude to refuse. We left the hotel very late and drove to a large concrete building. Inside it was packed with dancers and the music engulfed us in a wave of sound, the beat throbbing round the walls. My entrance caused a sensation, for mine was the only white face there but a chair was soon found, a drink pressed into my hand, and I was surrounded by curious, laughing faces. I was overwhelmed and felt completely out of my depth though there was nothing other than kindness there. We had arrived during an interval in the general dancing and now people were taking it in turns to provide a cabaret. The best dancers exhibited their skills and large banknotes were tucked into their waistbands and coins thrown at their feet. They were amazing but the rhythm was one I had never heard before and when, later, I was asked to join them in the dancing I refused, completely disorientated by it all. But I was happy to have been a part of that evening; it was something I was not likely to experience again. It was early morning when I got back to my room and began to pack; in a few hours I would have to leave for the airport.

The chaos there was the same I remembered from my arrival, only this time I had to survive it on my own. Passport and ticket in hand I approached the first desk and there I discovered I had to leave all my Nigerian money. This presented no problem as I had almost run out and I left several disappointed faces behind me. Next I came to Customs. They made me open my suitcase and I began to panic. Pete and Carol had persuaded me to take back a bronze sculpture from Benin; it was old but not, I think, very valuable. Nevertheless I was pretty sure I shouldn't be taking it out of the country and I wished I had refused. It was wrapped in one of my Laura Ashley dresses in the middle of my case. When we got down to it I lifted the dress out as though it weighed nothing and placed it gently on top of my other clothes. The Customs officer shouted, 'Stop,' and I froze, but he had only got bored and turned away, waving me on. I repacked everything and moved on to Emigration. I handed my open passport across the desk and again my heart skipped a beat. I looked up at the officer and knew that he had seen the same thing as I – my visa was out of date by two days. The scene that followed was worthy of someone's National Theatre. He shouted and threw my passport back across the desk. I screamed, 'Deport me then.' And everything stopped in the Departure Hall. We stood shouting at one another for a long time until someone walked past me and said, 'Cry!' So I did, in fact I sobbed, real tears streaming down my face. The officer reached for his stamp, stamped my passport and stood looking at it.

'Ah, you are an actress,' he said.

'Yes,' I replied.

'You must come back soon and star in one of our theatres.'

I looked at him incredulously, took my passport and moved on. In the departure lounge I sank into a chair as someone in an Egypt Air uniform pressed an ice-cold drink into my still shaking hand.

'Well done,' he said, 'and don't worry, we wouldn't have left without you.'

But I don't think I really stopped shaking until the plane was in the air. Later someone explained that I was supposed to bribe my way through the airport with dollars. It was something I had never thought of and anyhow I had no dollars with me, only three English pounds to get me from the airport in London. But I should have guessed.

Before long we were flying over the desert, mile after mile of golden sand, the dunes framed by a blue, blue sky. Nothing moved there except a Tuareg caravan moving slowly, the camels throwing long shadows and the deep blue of the Berbers' clothing clearly visible. I wondered idly if it was the same caravan we had seen in Sokoto and thought it quite possible that it was.

The sky darkened into night as we neared the Egyptian border. The plane began to climb and we were told we had to fly very high to make sure that no one fired at us. The lights were turned off and the window blinds closed, everyone fell silent and the atmosphere in the plane became charged with uncertainty. Then suddenly we were coming in to land and we all cheered. We crossed into a deserted airport building with blacked-out windows. The airport hotel had been turned into a standby hospital for the duration of the war, though happily it had not been needed. There were few travellers about for our plane had been the first international flight to land since the hostilities had ceased. One snack bar was open but all the shops were shuttered and security was tight, with armed soldiers strolling everywhere. I heard two British voices complaining bitterly to one of them that they were not being allowed to visit the nearby tombs and moved quickly away. I felt as though I was back in the West already. I sat and ordered a coffee at the bar and when it came I found that it had already been paid for by 'a gentleman'. I sat there for nearly two hours and drank three coffees; they had all been paid for too but I never discovered who my benefactor was and the barman explained that it was simply Egyptian courtesy towards a woman travelling on her own.

It was late when I went up to my room and I slept badly, my mind running over the conversations I had had during the evening. I had tried to find out something of the war and the feelings of the Egyptians, but they were reluctant to talk. The only thing that was repeated often was that they had nothing against the Jews and had many in Cairo who had not suffered in any way during the hostilities for they regarded them as Egyptians. It was the Israelis they hated. It was not a religious war they said but it was about land and the Palestinians' right to live in their ancestral homes. Even then it seemed an insoluble problem.

Next morning the sun was shining and the airport was returning to normal. After a slow breakfast I boarded the plane for Rome and London and soon found myself back at Heathrow. My Egyptian friend of before welcomed me back and I phoned a relieved Martin and Joanna who said they would come and pick me up. Back at their house we discovered the cat had stolen and eaten most of the meat for our supper so we went out to a nearby Italian restaurant. There I looked at the linen cloth and napkins, the ice-cold water in a jug and the long menu of delicious food and I nearly burst into tears. My friends laughed.

'You're suffering from culture shock,' they said. I supposed I was but it was a very strange feeling. The following morning I collected an ecstatic Barney dog and we went home. He rushed off to organise the squirrels on the heath and I began to readjust to the sophistications of a life that I had taken for granted only a few weeks before. The phone rang with an offer of work and Africa faded.

Pete and Carol came back to England a few months later. Carol flew to Cairo with the children and Pete was to cross the desert in the Land Rover and join her there. He invited me to fly to Lagos and drive back with him but the situation between Carol and I had become more complicated since I returned and Pete said she was still very angry with me. Not wishing to make things worse I reluctantly refused – needlessly as it turned out for our friendship never recovered and we lost touch. I did, however, meet the Lebanese gentleman who had been causing some of the problems in Benin. He rang me at home in Hampstead one evening and suggested we met for dinner. Curious to discover more about him I was told to join him at The Hilton Hotel in Park Lane where he was staying. When I arrived I was sent to his room by Reception and there offered a drink from a large bottle of whisky. As this was still the one spirit I really disliked and would only drink when good manners made it impossible to refuse I declined his offer, something that seemed to confuse him somehow. He then produced a large wad of pound notes and asked me where I wanted to eat. I suggested various restaurants but it quickly became obvious that we were to go to a Lebanese one just off Trafalgar Square and he insisted we went there by taxi. By this time he was beginning to annoy me with his ostentatious references to money and the fact that he had a lot. We soon got a taxi and on arrival at the restaurant he pushed a five pound note into my hand and asked if it would be enough. I was pretty sure he understood English currency very well and the fare on the meter was just over a pound but I decided to play him at his own game, so, smiling sweetly I told him that that would be fine and handed the money to the driver, telling him to keep the change. He began to protest that it was too much until I silenced him with a look. The look on my escort's face then told me that he knew exactly how much he had paid for the short ride but he said nothing and we got out of the cab and went in to the restaurant. Once inside it became transparently clear that he was very well-known by the waiters and that I was just one of many girls that he took there. It finally dawned on me that he was making a pass at me and I was furious. I waited calmly until he went to wash his hands and then got up and asked for my coat. I ignored the waiter's attempts to keep me there and walked outside where I hailed a passing cab. It turned out to be the same one that we had arrived in! Once in the cab I was quickly driven back to my car, the driver refusing any further payment. Still furious, and very disillusioned, I drove home and cooked myself some supper. And there my reluctant involvement in the matter ended.

But my friendship with Pete and Carol never did recover from my trip to Nigeria, something I regret to this day – for they were my closest friends and very important to me.

My life slowly settled back on to a more even keel and, with another Christmas and a new year rapidly approaching, I became determined to enjoy the festive season. Christmas was spent pleasantly enough with friends, leaving only the problem of New Year's Eve. LWT were staging a huge, live variety show on New Year's Eve and although I wasn't contracted to work on it one of the producers asked if I would go in on the night and keep an eye on things. Not being too sure what that would involve but nevertheless being rather flattered by the invitation I happily agreed. After all there was to be a late bar set up in the small studio, plenty of food and some rather famous names taking part so it all sounded a pretty good way to spend the evening. And it was.

During the day I had a chance to meet many of the guests and had a great chat with Anthony Newley who was also currently appearing in the West End in *The Good Old, Bad Old Days* – one of his musicals created together with his long term writing partner Leslie Bricusse. He was good fun, but I was sad to learn that business at the theatre wasn't so hot and he confessed to being puzzled by the fact that he could fill one of the huge theatres in Las Vegas for weeks on end but never seemed to do well in his own country. I resolved to go and see the show in the New Year. It was something I had been planning to do anyhow, for my old mate Paddy Stone had done the choreography and I was sure I would know most of the dancers.

All live TV shows are great – well I think so. There is always an element of danger about them that gets the adrenalin flowing and it is this adrenalin that keeps you bouncing along. That night was no exception. As we were about to go on air the director suddenly demanded an opening shot of all the stars standing centre stage. We were missing some but at that moment Tony Newley walked back into the building and I grabbed him, threw him into his evening clothes and on to the set, helpfully zipping up his flies with just time to clear myself out of the shot. It got us off to a good start and went on to be a great evening.

A few days later I decided on impulse to go and see Tony's

show. The only tickets still available were for the front stalls, so I chose a seat as far back as possible and felt that I would be safely incognito there. Alas, when the curtain went up there was a lighting overspill from the stage that lit up a large area just in front of me and I quickly realized that I had been recognised by most of the dancers. That night was a Monday night and the audience was a sticky one so the dancers began to direct most of the show into my lap. It was all rather embarrassing and got worse in the second half when Tony came on, dried completely, looked directly at me, said 'I know you are in tonight', and left the stage. There was a long pause and then the show continued. I shrank back in my seat, appalled at having stopped the show.

I didn't go backstage that evening, though now I wish I had. I did write a complimentary note though, for I loved the show and still think it should have been a long-running hit.

Chapter Fifteen

After Graham left I had advertised for a new tenant in the local paper and an American girl came to live with Barney and me. It was the time of the escalation of the war in Vietnam and it quickly became apparent that she was involved with a group of American ex-pats who were energetically opposed to it. Concurrently it was still the time of the right wing military dictatorship in Greece (the Junta) and I was in contact with a small group of Greek ex-pats who were having some success in helping their fellow country men and women avoid house arrest or prison in Greece by bringing them to live in Britain. So there were times when several young American boys (introduced to me as hitchhikers) spent an uneasy night on the floor of the flat en route for Sweden, while I tried unsuccessfully to convince my contacts in television that the Greek Junta was backed by the CIA in Athens – something which at that time and for many years after was vigorously denied by the American government. The phone in the flat developed a strange, hollow quality and there were always a series of clicks whenever we picked up the receiver. Technology was unsophisticated then and there was a number you could dial to check if a line was tapped; thus did we discover that ours almost certainly was.

While my flat mate was politically involved with her group, I was motivated on humanitarian grounds but it was with no small sense of satisfaction that, only a few years ago, I was watching Greek television and saw and heard the then Americam President, Bill Clinton, apologise to the then Greek Prime Minister, Costas Simitis, for his country's involvement in the coup that imposed that Military Dictatorship on Greece.

Meanwhile somewhere in the middle of all the good times there was another union strike and again ITV went off the air. This time I was not currently under contract to any of the TV studios and so was effectively out of work for the foreseeable future, so when someone suggested I took a temporary job as a waitress I decided it was probably a sensible thing to do. I was given a phone number and next day went along for an interview. To my complete surprise I discovered that the 'restaurant' was situated in a strip club in Baker Street. Even more to my surprise I got the job. So I donned my longest mini skirt and a blouse that fastened high on the neck and started work the next day. I was very nervous at first but it all turned out to be rather proper. We were heavily chaperoned throughout, escorted to our cars at the end of the evening and in many ways the work differed little from that in more conventional surroundings. In fact I now remember it as one of my better fill-in jobs, for the strippers were very friendly and most of the punters were rather sad, lonely men who came for the companionship. Many made a regular weekly visit to see the same girl, and more than one left in time to get the last train home. They weren't short of money, however, for the club was expensive and one of the top in London, and they bought champagne for the girls and often for me too. I got to know some of them quite well and felt sorry when I left them behind to go back to work in TV.

We had a mad chef who served bought in, pre-cooked meals from a microwave oven, drank a lot, and was highly temperamental. He would throw dishes and food around his tiny kitchen and sulk for hours if he ran out of the parsley he used to garnish the plates. I thought he was a hoot, but it was best to keep out of his way once the red wine had been opened.

Unfortunately I was no expert in my particular line of work for I was incredibly bad at opening the bottles of champagne – something I was supposed to do with a flourish – so the drummer of the live three-piece band began to give me a drum roll whenever I took the foil off the cork. I was rarely successful and someone had to give me a hand until there was a 'pop' and the band broke into a lively fanfare to celebrate. It was all good fun. Every evening I would walk down the stairs to the club to the sound of Nina Simone singing 'Marriage Is for Old Folks' and the slight smell of stale champagne. That song still brings back the memory of those evenings and I have never once regretted taking the job.

Eventually the strike was settled and my phone began ringing again. Purely by chance I soon went back to work at ATV for while. We were coming up to Christmas once again, and the evening before I was due to start work on my new contract was also the evening of David Frost's Christmas party. This year it was to be at his home in Kensington and Santa Claus was quickly recognized as Ronnie C in a rather large red 'frock'. We all had a great time and the sky was lightening when I left, so I was not at my professional best when, only a very few hours later, I drove out to Borehamwood.

This was the time of the big co-productions between Britain and America and most of them were recorded out at ATV. They had to be recorded twice as America had a different line system to us and only one machine existed that could convert from one to the other. The machine belonged to the BBC, but they categorically refused to hire it out and so we recorded the British version in the afternoon and the American version in the evening of the same day. They were done on a weekly basis and usually as a series, with a single big name fronting the whole run and different big names as guests. I think the Tom Jones series was the first but I was to work with Engelbert Humperdinck. Both he and Tom were with the same management company; it was one in which many people at LWT had been offered shares in hundred pound stakes, but alas at that time neither Graham nor I could raise that amount and so another opportunity was lost to make a considerable amount of money. Engelbert and I never did get on particularly well but he had some amazing guests on the programme, most of them from the States, and there were some magic moments. The other exciting thing about these series was that there was nearly always a live thirty-two-piece orchestra in the studio too.

Both LWT and ATV had their own musical director. At LWT it was Harry Rabinovitch and at ATV it was Jack Parnell. By the time I went to ATV I had got to know Harry Rab, as he was always known, quite well. Copyright laws or the fees demanded for payment to the featured musicians were so high that they prevented the studios from using existing recordings; it was cheaper and better to use a live band or put down our own backing tracks. LWT usually pre-recorded. I loved these sessions and went to them whenever I could. I was often first in the studio and watched, fascinated, as the musicians began to arrive. They were a motley bunch and you would never have guessed that they were among the best and most highly paid members of their profession. The double-bass player was nearly always the first there, easing himself and his instrument carefully into its allotted space and heaving a sigh of relief when he had done so.

All the musicians were booked in a block of three-hour sessions and a minute of overtime at either end meant prodigious overtime claims – but oh, did you get value for money during those three hours. Around a quarter to the hour the rest of the band wandered in and took up their positions. They sat around drinking coffee, doing crosswords or telling whispered, and I suspect rather risqué, jokes. At two minutes to the hour a 'Good-morning, ladies and gentlemen' announced the arrival of Harry with his baton and the coffee cups and newspapers would disappear. Someone had already put the necessary sheet music on the stands and so, as the clock ticked on to the hour Harry raised his baton and you were surrounded by sweet music ... or so you thought. But this wasn't always so. When Harry tapped his baton on his music stand it meant that something was wrong and the orchestra ground to a halt, then Harry would say something along the lines of, 'Second violin, bar eight, have you got an F in there?' The reply was invariably, 'Yes'. 'Ah,' frowned Harry, 'make that an F sharp, please.' And off we would go again. I could detect no obvious difference in the sound but Harry could and no wayward un-sharp F was going to escape his professional ear. I once saw him re-score sixteen bars for the full orchestra off the top of his head. I was stunned. Harry came from a classical-music background whilst Jack Parnell came from the big band tradition. As people they were completely different but as musicians they both shared the same expertise and were at the very top of their profession.

At ATV the 'orchestra' became the 'band', although many of the same musicians were present in both. With a permanent band area set up in the big Light Entertainment studio, the music seemed to be much more a part of the whole programme, one that came startlingly alive when Jack walked quietly on to the podium, bringing with him an atmosphere of late-night jazz clubs and sense of dusty variety theatres. He hunched himself over the podium and almost seemed to will the music out of the band. One day we were rehearsing with Ray Charles when one of the cameras broke down. Ray stayed at the piano playing softly. Engelbert walked across to him and began to sing but Ray segued into another song. Engelbert followed, but again Ray changed the song. They went on like this for a little while, Ray obviously enjoying his musical jokes, but Engelbert got fed up and moved away. Then I heard the double base come, in followed by the drums. Soon the whole band had joined in and for nearly a whole hour while the camera was being repaired, the crew were treated to an amazing jam session. When the floor manager finally called us back to rehearsals, cheers and a spontaneous round of applause came from the audience seating that had slowly filled up with ATV staff as word had got around about what was happening.

We soon adjusted to the American 'invasion' and though we still found them a pampered bunch there were lots of good times too and some became friends. Paul Anka spent hours chatting and invited me to go back with him to Hollywood. I didn't take him seriously but now I think he was serious. He had just recorded 'My Way', and talked of Sinatra and Sammy Davies and Dean Martin as though they were great mates of his. Well of course they were, but it all seemed too unreal for that small person from Derbyshire who still lurked somewhere in my psyche. Jerry Lewis spent a lot of time chatting too, telling us of his early days with Dean Martin and how he became 'insufferable' (his word) until he got his 'comeuppance' and work disappeared. Now he felt he had been given a rare second chance and this time he wasn't going to blow it. I liked him enormously and he helped us by searching the London stationery shops for a particular file that contained a large clip. This could be used for holding the idiot boards together and made our lives a lot easier. He also often stood holding the wretched boards as I flipped them.

Those idiot boards took over my working days for several months. Known as cue cards in America it began to look as though no artist from the States ever worked without them and I thought it unprofessional of an entertainer to rely on them for a few words of dialogue or, in some cases, the words of a song that had taken him or her in to the Hit Parade – especially as they were being paid an enormous amount of money to appear. We didn't use them in England except for a name difficult to remember or a phrase that had to be delivered exactly, but with the arrival of the Americans we began to put the entire show on large and heavy sheets of cardboard. It was hardly stimulating work but the money was very good and you did get a chance to watch some of the top international names in the business and, in many cases, that was enormous compensation. Still, to me they remained idiot boards and I always refered to them as such until I was approached by the director of the show who told me, grinning, that by doing so I was upsetting some of our guest artists and they were insisting I called them cue cards. As I rather believed in calling a spade a spade I objected to this, so I began to start saying 'idiot boards', stop myself halfway through, apologise and hesitantly utter 'cue cards'. This made the situation worse but I felt I had made a point, all-be-it a childish one. Still, there were a lot of days where I had to regularly hold up a small card that read 'Good evening, welcome to London, my name is ...' and I found myself wondering what sort of a person had difficulty remembering what time it was, where they were and what their names were.

Meanwhile other famous names continued to appear. Tony Bennett arrived and dreamed his way through a series of his hit numbers, so laid back that he scarcely seemed to have crossed the 'pond'. Lena Horne, Donald O'Connor, Ethel Merman, Tony Curtis, Phil Silvers, and many more brought a touch of showbiz magic while Sammy Davies Jnr left us open-mouthed at the sheer talent of the man. For a few days our arrival at ATV coincided and we would walk together into the studios from the parking lot, chatting away… it was the highlight of my day.

Many of the artistes were only in London for a few days and they came alone with only a member of the British branch of their agency to look after them, so we in the immediate production team were often invited to join them for dinner in the evenings. Thus did I begin a nodding acquaintance with five-star hotels and renew my knowledge of top London restaurants – it really was another world.

But there is one memory from this time that remains unique. Someone had decided that it would be really 'cute' if Sir John Gielgud and Sir Ralph Richardson were to sing and dance 'Tea for Two' in a guest spot. The particular show in which they were involved was a one-off special and seemed to spend its preparation days in chaos. A Sunday was the day of the final rehearsals and mid morning saw the arrival of the two 'Sirs'. I introduced myself and left them sitting in the audience seating where they seemed intrigued by everything that was going on around them. A while later rehearsals ground to another halt when it was seen that one of the sets had an American flag as a backdrop. This ended up draped on the back of the stage area and it transpired that there was a danger that someone could walk on it inadvertently. Apparently that would be an act of desecration and could not be permitted. From past experience I knew that the hiatus was going to be a long one and so I walked across to the canteen for a coffee. Alas, it was closed but sitting there in the huge, chilly area were two rather sad figures, Sir Ralph and Sir John.

'What on earth are you doing here?" I asked.

'Oh, dear Anne,' replied Sir John, 'everything does seem to be so disorganised. We rather wondered if anyone would need us today.'

It was mid-afternoon by then and we were due to finish at 6p.m.We were also a long way away from their spot in the running order.

'Would you like me to go and ask?' I replied.

'Ooh no, I don't think so; we don't want to be a bother,' said Sir John.

'This is extremely unprofessional of the producers', I went on. 'Let me go and ask.'

'Well, dear Anne, the Americans can be very unprofessional sometimes,' said Sir John as if this explained everything.

'Oh yes indeed,' said Sir Ralph, with a small but heartfelt sigh.

There was a pause.

'Do they really have all the words on those pieces of cardboard?' enquired Sir Ralph.

'Well, yes,' I said.

'It's most odd,' said Sir John.

'Most odd,' confirmed Sir Ralph.

I thought of all the leading roles my two companions had played, many of them Shakespearian.

'Yes,' I said, adding, mischievously, 'would you like me to write up "Tea for Two"?'

'Oh dear,' said Sir John, 'I don't know about that.'

'When in Rome …' murmured Sir Ralph.

'Well, one doesn't like to offend,' continued Sir John.

'I'll do them for you,' I said. 'It will only take a few minutes.'

There was another pause.

'You see,' said Sir Ralph hesitantly, 'we were wondering if anyone would notice if we went home.

Sir John brightened up.

'We thought, well, that as Ralphy has his motorbike here and I have my car and driver, well, perhaps we could go to Ralphy's house and sit in front of his fire and have a chat. It would only take us fifteen minutes to get back and, dear Anne, we thought you might phone us when it looked as though we would be needed and we would come straight back. Wouldn't we Ralphy?"

'Oh yes, indeed, straight back,' confirmed Sir Ralph.

I thought it highly unlikely that they would be needed at all, but …

'I can't actually give you permission to do that,' I said.

'Oh no, dear Anne, goodness, we wouldn't want to get you into trouble; we wouldn't say we had talked with you, it would be just our little secret. Ralphy and I can be very difficult sometimes and I don't think anyone would say anything.'

I looked at them sitting there like two naughty schoolboys – impossible to imagine them being 'difficult', but then they were two of our finest actors. Two pairs of eyes looked at me hopefully, they knew they had won.

'Go,' I said, laughing, 'and just let us hope we get away with it.'

I left them sitting there and went back to the studio where the discussion over the American flag was still going on. A few minutes later when I crossed back to the canteen on an impulse, I found it deserted. No one ever noticed that they had gone, and they were not needed. When they finally came back on the day of the recording they rehearsed their 'Tea for Two' song-and-dance routine, recorded it on the first take and never looked at the idiot boards once. I loved them both.

I stayed working out at Boreham Wood for many months, surrounded by superstars and the more friendly faces of people such as Barry Cryer, Des O'Connor and Dick Vosbrugh. They were busy days, good ones and bad, but the bad ones soon got forgotten and were more than made up for by those chance meetings with Gene Kelly in the corridor (my knees went again) or Bing Crosby in the bar. The money continued to be good too.

During one of my first weeks back there I had received a message from Percy Welsburg asking me to go to his office, as there was a problem with my time sheet. In those days everyone had to fill in a weekly sheet listing the hours you had worked. It was a nuisance but as you didn't get paid unless you submitted them, they somehow always got done. Percy was sitting in his office when I arrived there; inviting me to sit down he pointed out that there was no claim for overtime on my sheet. I explained that that was because I hadn't worked any. Percy told me that ATV expected and totally accepted that a reasonable amount of overtime would be claimed each week as stage managers worked on an Equity Union agreement that was considerably less generous than those of the other unions. It still didn't sink in. Finally he simply added several hours overtime to my time sheet, signed it and put it in his 'out' tray. 'Oh, thank you,' I stuttered, as the penny finally dropped. Whether this was due to ATV's generosity or that of Percy, I have never been sure, though I strongly suspect it was the latter.

Over the months I began to give Percy a lift back into town whenever we were leaving at the same time and I got to understand a little of this intriguing man. In 'real life' he was an Hungarian Count. When you knew that it explained a lot. He was a tall, slim man with the chiselled features of a European aristocrat. He had a slightly melancholy air about him but was always charming and his manners were impeccable. I was intrigued by him, and wanted to know more of his history but any attempts on my part to draw him out were always politely rebuffed, until one day when he suddenly began to talk.

When he was a young man he had worked in the film industry in Hungary but the Second World War had interrupted his career and he had returned to the family estate. There he slowly found himself involved with a group of partisans. They obviously were in contact with the Allies and became so successful that they had to take to the hills. When the Germans and Russians began to advance his family buried the family silver under a tree in the nearby forest and closed down most of the house. As the war progressed the group must have become pretty successful at both espionage and sabotage for Percy was warned by the Allies that his name was at the top of a Gestapo wanted list. Eventually they successfully got him out of Hungary and into Britain where the War Office told him that he could never go back to his own country. He settled in England and knew only that the rest of his family had 'disappeared'; he had been told not to try and contact them and never had. I suspect that Percy Welsberg was not his real name but I never found out for sure. I eventually heard that he had retired from ATV, had married a nurse, and together they had had a son. Then I heard that Percy had died. His death had coincided with the collapse of the Berlin Wall and if only he had lived a little longer he would have been able to go home. I sometimes wonder if the silver is still buried under that tree in the forest, and in my imagination I can see a château bathed in sunlight with trees surrounding it, but I never knew where in Hungary it stood or who he really was.

I was also spending some of the long summer evenings chatting to Madame Manya. As I gained her friendship she told me more and more about her life with Anna Pavlova. Forced to stay in London by the Bolshevik Revolution of 1917, Anna Pavlova, Monsieur Dandre (her companion and manager) and Manya had moved into the house in Golders Green. It was, and still is, a large house standing back from the Hampstead road and set in a large garden with a pond on which at that time there lived a pair of swans. Pavlova continued her ballet career, much of which consisted of tours throughout South America and Manya went with the company and told delightful stories of all-night poker games with the stage crews where she smoked and drank vodka until the sun rose. Looking at this rather gentle and genteel lady who sat calmly at the kitchen table, it all seemed an unlikely story, but I'm sure that it was true. She also spent days and nights sewing new costumes for Pavlova, and told tales of journeys over rough roads and bandit-ridden heartlands. In my imagination I travelled with her and it all seemed impossibly romantic, though she assured me it wasn't. I asked her if she had liked South America and she replied: 'But, darleeng, it vos so very difficult. Everywhere zere is bang bang and ze revolution.' But I still envied her those journeys.

Both at work and at home I found the days to be full of fascinating people and one of these was to become a great mate for a number of years and we had a lot of fun together. Though very much a person in his own right, Nick Daubeny was the son of Peter Daubeny (later Sir Peter Daubeny) – the man who had introduced the World Theatre Season to the London audiences and who for ten years treated them to a series of productions staged by high-ranking companies from all over the world, including some from behind what was then the Iron Curtain.

Nick had been brought up in a world I hardly knew existed, one that seemed to be full of great restaurants, excellent wine and long conversations centered on anything connected to the Arts. He was also something of a rebel and we quickly established a rapport that made for exciting evenings and a lot of laughter. He took me to eat in places like Rules or Simpson's on the Strand where he turned up in a Graham Green style suit of cream linen, the obligatory tie in his pocket, while I wore my only Laura Ashley dress, freshly laundered for the occasion. In Simpson's the wine waiter treated us with ill concealed disdain, until, that is, it quickly became obvious that Nick knew as much about good wine as he did and ordered one of the rarer and more expensive bottles listed there. At once our waiter's manner changed to one of respect and we began to receive excellent service. I was very impressed.

We went to productions of the World Theatre Season, staged at the Aldwych Theatre while the Royal Shakespeare Company was on its annual summer break. Usually arriving there in my rather battered Mini a few minutes before curtain up, I was always in a panic about finding a parking place, but there was never a problem. The commissionaire, seeing Nick in the car, would simply remove the 'no parking' signs in front of the theatre and we left the car there and raced inside. The tickets were always complimentary and in the interval and after the performance we mingled in the green room with the cast and visiting celebrities, all of whom seemed to have known Nick for years.

We also talked for hours on anything that took our fancy, politics, life and anything connected with theatre or the arts in general, meeting in the Savoy bar, Yate's Wine Lodge, and the Freemason's Arms or the Magdala pubs in Hampstead. Brecht, Mayakovsky, Sartre and Genet filled the conversations, together with names of artists and sculptors I had never heard of before.

I was embarrassed by my ignorance and often found myself rushing to Foyle's bookshop in the Charing Cross Road or searching the shelves of the local library for more information. He also introduced me to The Colony Room, a club in Soho where Lucien Freud, Francis Bacon and Jeffrey Barnard seemed to be permanently in residence, sitting on bar stools that are probably the ones there today and surrounded by their own works of art. The club is famous now and in many ways unchanged, still with the original painted walls of an industrial green and with a slightly risqué atmosphere; but the owners and the clientèle have changed and the more valuable paintings have been sold. No longer does Muriel Belcher glare suspiciously as you walk in, or the talking stop as eyes from the bar assess your potential as a person interesting enough to be granted admission to that eclectic circle, and something has been lost. When Nick first took me there I thought it to be the most thrilling place in town, anarchic and dangerous – and I delighted in being there. Going back recently, and reunited with Nick after more than thirty years, I was saddened by the threat of closure that now hangs over it and I very much wanted it to live on.

Vodka was always the drink at The Colony Room but Nick introduced me to Beaujolais Nouveau when we discovered that it arrived from France on my birthday and, in honesty, I always preferred that. For several years after Nick married Nina and we somehow lost touch I would return home after celebrating my anniversary and I would find a bottle of the wine sitting on my doorstop or perched outside the living room window – a reminder of a very special friendship and a time still remembered with great affection.

But I still had to earn a living, and so there were also the early morning drives in to the centre of London or out to Boreham Wood, the car windows open in summer, closed in winter, singing along to some pop station as it crackled and buzzed out of a small portable radio. You sometimes saw people you knew and there was nearly always the lady in the Rolls Royce trying to park it in Golders Green. She was something of a hazard until you became familiar with her, for she invariably signalled left when she was turning right and vice versa. She also preferred to drive in the middle of the road, and so common sense dictated that you crawled behind her until that magical parking space appeared and she dived in bonnet first.

Manda (who became one of my best friends until her tragic death a few years ago), Tony, John and Carl were frequent visitors to the flat and soon became very useful Barney minders if I was working late. Carl's father was a well-known cellist and I sometimes found him out at the studios playing in the orchestras and bands .

I now always had a car of my own and changed it periodically for a slightly more up to date model; necessary for work, it also meant that I was free to roam, visit friends, or race off to a late night-cinema on the other side of London, with Barney often sitting in the passenger seat contentedly watching the world go by. Once the car was towed away from Hampstead High Street with Barney in it and I was really worried for him, but, when I arrived at the pound I found him in the Fine Office being fed chocolate biscuits, none the worse for his abduction and delighting in his new friends.

I worked hard and played hard and I made many new friends. Some friendships only lasted the length of my contract but some are still there today, and there was always a social life for the taking if you fancied it. I was offered a last-minute chance to go to Greece for two weeks but no regular Barney sitter was available. As I phoned to turn down the offer a friend at ATV said that she would have him; she shared a house with three other girls, and as all of them worked different hours, they could offer a twenty-four hour minder service. So Barney went off to Kew Green and I flew to Greece. We stayed on Crete but had to fly there via Athens. With several hours to wile away at the airport there I phoned Nicos's Kolonaki flat. He wasn't there but a message was taken, one that included the phone number of the villa where we were staying and two days later he phoned. By chance he was on Crete walking in the mountains around Chania; my message had travelled from taverna to taverna across the country until it finally caught up with him. The next day he travelled across the island to Iraklion and we met. (See my book about Greece, *Coming Slowly*.)

Not long after I returned from Greece the news came that my grandmother had had a fall and ended up in hospital with a broken hip. I went up to see her there and stayed for most of the afternoon. We talked of my childhood and other things until she suddenly asked if I was happy in London and had the life I wanted. I said yes. Then she told me that she was so tired of living. Her daughter was dead and she had no wish to see men landing on the moon. She said the world she understood had horse-drawn carriages and values that were fast disappearing. She was ninety-two and I sensed that I was going to lose her soon. I loved her very much and thought I knew her well; she had always been my champion and had encouraged me to live life to the full. She was a strong, independent woman and she hated being old.

She never really got going again but died quietly in her sleep a few weeks later. Her hip was mending well and there was nothing really wrong with her; she just gave up. The day before her funeral I went down with a flu virus. I tried hard to get out of bed for the drive to Bamford, but knew I was never going to make it, so I never got to say a final goodbye. I was very sad but knew she would understand. For many years I thought about her often – the grandmother I thought I knew so well – until last year, by accident, I learned that she had had an illegitimate child when she was very young. The father had been the local bank manager. Nothing more was really known but it was thought that the child had been a girl and had been adopted or had died as a baby. It seems I didn't actually know my grandmother very well after all but that information explained a lot. All those years she had lived with a secret, knowing that others in the village knew it too. Was that why I always seemed to matter so much to her? Why she often spoilt me and provided me with opportunities that would have been beyond the financial limits of my parents? Indeed, was it one of the reasons I had been adopted in the first place? It also explained why we had so little contact with her sisters and her brother. All the people who could tell me more are dead now so I will never know the full story. I wish she had told me though for the knowledge would have drawn us even closer.

My Father and I stayed in touch. I wrote regularly and went up to Derbyshire for an occasional weekend, but I never felt close to him again. He seemed fine; he had a lady who came in to clean and went every Saturday to his football or cricket matches. There was always food in the house and he still helped his old ladies with their income-tax forms and they continued to bake him cakes and scones. I knew he missed my mother desperately, and I think he was still very angry that she had died but we never talked about her. After he died, someone in the village told me that they used to see him every Sunday walking up to the public call box at the top of the main road. He told them he was going to phone me in London. On the way down he would tell them how I was and what I was doing – but in London my phone never rang. I once asked him if we should buy a house together in London, one divided into two flats. Then he would be able to come and go as he pleased and perhaps spend the worst of the winter months with me. He replied that he 'didn't have money for that sort of thing', and I let the matter drop. I suppose I always knew that one day there would be a phone call and that things would change for ever, but when it came I was completely unprepared.

It was Cousin Iris who left a message for me to call back, and I knew that something was badly wrong. It seemed my father had had a fall and had been found at the bottom of the stairs in the hall. There was some talk of a suicide attempt and sleeping pills but I didn't really take it all in. She simply said that I had to go back to Derbyshire and I knew that she was right. At that time I was working back at LWT and I had the weekends free, so Barney and I set off on the Saturday morning afraid of what we were going to find in Hathersage.

Until that phone call I had been still sure that my father was doing fine. I had seen him about three months earlier and was not worried, but something had happened during those three months, for the man I found looked and talked like a stranger. He was a tiny little old man and seemed confused and uncertain about everything. The house was cold and his clothes were dirty and there was no food in the pantry. I tried to ask him what had happened but he didn't want to talk about it. Well, for the moment there was plenty to do. I went out and bought some food, found him some clean clothes and made him change into them; then I set about cleaning the house.

Our hot water had always come from a coal-burning stove in the kitchen; it was efficient and also went a long way to warming the whole house, but this I discovered had been broken for a long time. Hot water was now boiled in a kettle. There was an open fireplace in the living-room and plenty of coal but my father refused to let me light a fire and he sat huddled over a one-bar electric heater that he switched on and then switched off again as soon as it got red. This went on all day until I wanted to scream. As the weekend wore on, I realized that I no longer knew the man that had been my father. I had always been a little afraid of him, afraid of what he would think of me too, and as I said earlier, my mother had always been our interpreter. Now it was obvious that he was not coping on any level and I simply did not know what to do about it. He told me that I had to come back home to look after him, that I would have to get a job in the village and give up my life in London. He said he had no money except his pension and so I would have to keep myself.

That night I lay in bed listening to him talking to my mother and periodically thumping the bed-head with his hand. Over the weekend it became clear that he went to bed when it got dark and got up when it got light; the day was spent in front of that wretched one-bar electric fire, but at least when I cooked some food he would eat it and thank me politely.

On the Sunday evening I left to drive back to London, promising that I would return next weekend. I left him clean and tidy and with food to last him the week, but the reproach in his eyes as I closed the door stayed with me all the way down the motorway. I felt so guilty, not least because I didn't want to do what he asked of me.

Back in London I talked to friends and contacted the Derbyshire Social Services. His cleaning lady had stopped coming to the house; something had obviously happened between them but I never found out what. No matter, he could get help from the DSS, he was eligible for Meals on Wheels and someone would be available to visit and check on him at regular intervals. If I continued to visit at weekends it seemed like a positive solution, at least for the moment. I made plans to install an immersion heater for hot water and to try and sort out a better way of heating the house. There were, apparently, grants available to help. There was also a good old people's home in the village, but I knew instinctively that I could not even broach that subject for the moment. I also made enquiries about teaching jobs in the valley and in Sheffield but there was nothing available, not even in supply teaching. There was no work in the village and I had no idea how else I could earn a living. For the moment I shelved that problem and we staggered on.

In Hampstead I learned that Madame Manya had been taken to hospital. When I visited her there I found the same elegant old lady sitting up in bed in a diaphanous nightgown and full make-up. She told me she had diabetes, but would be home soon. I could see she had lost a lot of weight and I suspected she had cancer. She also told me that she had two new Australian friends who had the key to her flat and were very interested in the ballet. Something didn't sound quite right and I was a little alarmed. There were many momentoes of Anna Pavlova in the flat. Once she had shown me a small line drawing of 'her Pavlova'; it was exquisite and I warned her not to show it to too many people. She seemed puzzled by my insistence, but the name on the bottom of the paper was Picasso and it must have been worth a lot of money. As I had got to know her better she had also told me many stories of Pavlova, including information that surrounded her marriage to Monsieur Dandre. There had recently been a renewal of interest in the dancer, and although she had claimed to be married, no one had been able to find a copy of the marriage certificate. When I asked Manya about this she told me that she had been sitting in the garden of the Golders Green house when the pair of them had returned in very high spirits. They said they had just got married and that Manya must celebrate with them. As she pointed out to me, she had lived with them for many years unmarried so there was really no reason for them to say anything unless it was true. This fact I was allowed to talk about but for the other stories I was made to promise that I would not repeat them. It is a promise I have never broken, but I was not at all certain of the integrity of Manya's new acquaintances.

I knew that she still had long-standing friends in the ballet world for I had often helped her by going to the shops for her and was invariably rewarded with 'a leetle vodka, darling'. This vodka always came from either Russia or Poland and was unlike any other vodka I had ever tasted. She would produce two tiny vodka glasses and taught me to drink it the Russian way. You had to swallow it down in one go and savour the after taste, like oysters. It was delicious and quite lethal and the journey back down the steps to my own flat became hazardous in the extreme! She was particularly close to the Marks sisters, one of whom was of course Alicia Markova, so I phoned their house and told them of the two new friends and of the Picasso line drawing. When I returned from Derbyshire the following weekend I learned that Manya had died.

Manya had told me once that when she died she did not want anyone to wear black at her funeral; we were to be happy for her life and remember the good times. So Sally, the landlord's daughter, and I went to the Russian Church in Kensington wearing the 'pretty dress' that she had requested. The great of the ballet world were there, all dressed in black and purple, and we received some very strange looks, but we held our heads high and stood quietly to one side of the church. The music was unaccompanied voices and very beautiful and the coffin was an open one. I was a little afraid of drawing close but found it all very cathartic. Manya looked at peace and I was glad to have a chance to say goodbye. So much so that later, when they started to close the coffin lid and nail it shut, I wanted to scream out, 'Stop.'

A few days later most of her things were taken from the flat to the Pavlova Museum in the house in Golders Green, but I was told that there was no sign of the Picasso drawing. The night before the things were moved, Sally and I went and stood in her bedroom to say a final farewell. There was Anna Pavlova's bedroom furniture, many photos and a thousand of Manya's memories. We touched nothing; it was enough just to have been there. The next evening I found an old hat and two half-empty silver rouge boxes in the rubbish bin. I still have them.

My London Weekend contract ended and I was phoned by the Head of Drama at Yorkshire TV and asked to work on the next series of *The Main Chance*. I knew David well and had worked with him when he was directing at LWT. I respected him both as a director and as a person and we had become good workmates. Part of me very much wanted to accept the job but I simply didn't see how I could. I explained about my father and reluctantly said no. The next day he phoned back. He asked if I would reconsider and promised that in the event of another crisis involving my father I would be released from my contract immediately and a fast car and driver would be standing by to take me wherever I wanted to go. It was a kind and understanding offer and I said I would think about it. The series rehearsed in London with a thirty-six-hour break before we reconvened in Leeds to record. I would still be able to stop off in Derbyshire but now Barney was an added problem. I discussed the situation with a friend and she told me that her boyfriend had boarding kennels situated just off the M1. Why not drop him off there on my way to Leeds and pick him up on the way back? Life was going to be hectic but, again, it seemed like a solution for the moment and so I said yes.

I was still waiting to hear from the Derbyshire Social Services about the help I had requested for my father. After writing several times I finally phoned them and managed to speak to the lady who was dealing with it. She told me that there had been quite a few attempts to contact my father but he refused to open the door to the health visitor and had simply shouted at them to go away. Meals on Wheels had met with the same reception. When I tried to talk to him about it, he answered in half sentences or simply walked away. I had no idea what to do next; he was still my father, the man I had been brought up to respect and, to a certain extent, to obey. I found it hard to accept that our roles had changed and that I was the strong one now. Nor did I understand that what I was trying to deal with was a progressive form of senile dementia and that the rules had changed. On one visit a neighbour stopped me in the street and said that all the food I was so carefully providing was being thrown out as soon as I left, that my father was rarely seen outside the house and that, even for people he had known all his life, the door was never opened or the curtains drawn back. He, meanwhile, had been complimenting me on my cooking and telling me of his continual trips to football matches. I took a long, hard look at my father that weekend and could see that he was getting weaker. This man that I was trying so hard to get going again had simply given up.

My time in Leeds had been an escape – I was doing a job I loved, staying in a good hotel and I was surrounded by people whose company I enjoyed. Now I found I was slowly shutting myself off from all this and spending more and more time alone in my hotel room. This is never a good idea when you are very much part of a team and I knew that some people resented it. No one was aware of the situation with my father except David and there was no one I felt I could confide in, until one night I did start talking with a member of the crew who was staying in the same hotel. He was very supportive and I spent more and more time with him. This only seemed to increase the resentment towards me but I was at a loss to know why. Then I was told that until recently he had been involved with a member of the production team and I finally understood. Somewhat at a loss I went back to staying in my hotel room, trying to deal with a situation that I felt had become impossible.

Every weekend in Derbyshire I cooked a roast-chicken dinner on the Sunday. This had always been a favourite of my father's and it also provided for two more meals after I had left. One weekend there were no chickens to be had in the village so I simply leapt into the car and went to a shop on the outskirts of Sheffield. My father seemed stunned by this and protested that it wasn't necessary, but I went ahead and cooked as usual. I always put our meals on two trays and we ate from these in the dining-room. I called my father to collect his tray and walked ahead with mine. As he reached the doorway he simply dropped his tray and stood there looking like a lost child. We gazed at one another for a long time; no words were spoken but I still swear that he said to me 'Let me go.' I finally cleaned up the spilt food and tried to persuade him to eat another plateful but it was no use and there didn't seem anything else to say. Driving up to Leeds I knew instinctively that we had passed a point of no return and I felt so guilty that I had failed him. I resolved to go back to Hathersage at the end of my contract and stay there, at least for a while.

Unbeknownst to me David had ordered that all phone calls to YTV for me should be put through to his office, so it was he who took that final call from Derbyshire. We were out filming that day, standing in half-melted snow and ice when I saw David walking towards the camera. I thought nothing of it until he beckoned me to join him. Then time stood still and the noises of the film crew faded into silence. My father had been found in a coma, an ambulance had been called and he had been taken to hospital in Sheffield. David emphasised that he was safe and being cared for but I should go immediately to the hospital. Did I want the car that he had promised me? I said that I would drive in my own car because I was going to need it later to drive between Hathersage and Sheffield. I assured him that I was OK to drive for I had become very calm and seemed to be in control, though I'm sure I wasn't. Reluctantly he let me go, telling me to leave everything and that he would sort it all out. He had fulfilled his promise to the letter and continued to be a supportive and caring friend for the rest of my time at YTV.

I don't now remember that drive back down the motorway. As I didn't know the hospital to which they had taken my father I went straight to Hathersage, parked the car and crossed the road to the houses and the people I had been forbidden to talk to for so many years. They were amazingly welcoming. I was not to go to our house but I should stay with them they said. They gave me directions to the hospital and I set off straight away. There I was taken in to a ward and directed to a bed near the door. There was a man lying in it but he looked nothing like my father. The nurse gently assured me that it was he and I looked again. They had cleaned him up and shaved him and he lay there warm and cosy in brown-and-white-striped pyjamas that must have belonged to the hospital. He appeared to be sleeping peacefully but the nurse told me that he had been found in a state of hypothermia and was in a coma. She warned me that he was very ill. I sat for a long time looking at him and then began to talk softly. He grew restless and seemed to be trying to talk back but when the nurse passed by she said he could not possibly know I was there. I didn't believe her then and I still don't. I sat there for a long time and then left the ward telling the nurse that I was going outside for a cigarette and that I would return. I meant it at the time but once outside I got into my car and drove away from the hospital. I found myself driving back to Hathersage and once I reached the moors I stopped the car and got out. It was bitterly cold but I needed that and I walked for nearly an hour. As always, the moors calmed me and gave me the strength to go on. I finally drove on to the village and went back to my newly found relatives. They told me that there had been a phone call and that my father had died a few minutes after I had left. At that moment I could only feel relief that he was at peace at last and I hoped desperately that he was reunited with my mother, somewhere, somehow.

Next morning I awoke to a strange world, even the weather added to a sense of unreality. As I crossed that main road to our house I looked down towards the bottom of the village. Once again, as at the time of my mother's death, the houses and shops were shrouded in a mist that blurred their outlines and deadened the steps of the few early villagers walking along the pavements. There was a light on in the post office and the bank was just opening its doors. Inside Westmoor it was desperately cold and already the house felt abandoned. I went upstairs to my father's bedroom and stood in the doorway appalled by what I found there. It had only been ten days since I had last been home, how could everything have happened so fast? I started wandering aimlessly around the house until I heard a knock at the door. Cousin Eric was standing there. He must have known the state of that bedroom because he had brought his tractor and trailer with him. Together we went back upstairs and cleared bed, carpet, curtains, everything really except a chest of drawers and two chairs, and he took it all away to be burnt. I boiled a kettle, found some disinfectant and started scrubbing.

After that things began to happen all around me. Someone must have phoned our family solicitor for I was given a message that he was coming out from Sheffield later that morning. I was to touch nothing in the house. I lit a fire in the dining-room and made a cup of coffee. When the solicitor arrived he was a kind, understanding man and I liked him from the start. I told him that my father had always said that he had made a will and we began to look for it. I took him into the 'best' bedroom with the chest of drawers that had always been locked; that day it was open, one drawer full of official-looking papers. He began going through them, then opened an envelope and handed the papers to me. 'Those are yours, I think,' he said. They were all my adoption papers, the ones for which I had searched for years. At that point I sat down heavily on the bed; then I put them to one side for later.

After an hour we had still not found a will and the solicitor asked me to go to the bank to see if they had it there. Inside the bank I queued quietly until it was my turn. The bank was busy and full of people I knew. When it was my turn I asked politely if they had any papers in the vaults belonging to my father and I explained about the missing will. The cashier said quietly that she was not allowed to tell me the details of my father's account but that I would get the money when his affairs were cleared officially. I was outraged. 'F*** the bloody money,' I shouted. 'I just want to know how he wants to be buried.'

There was complete silence in the bank and then the manager's door opened and I was ushered into his office. He sat me down and quickly produced a glass of sweet sherry, obviously kept close by for just such an emergency as this one. Then he told me that they had held a wooden box of documents for my father but he had taken it out of the bank a few weeks earlier. I had the information I needed and I left, leaving the sherry untouched.

Back in the house we eventually found the wooden box, but it was empty. Then I remembered my mother's sewing cabinet, another place that was often used for important things. There was no will but there was a wad of five-pound notes, amounting to just over five hundred pounds, a lot of money then. The solicitor handed it to me. 'I haven't seen this,' he said. 'You are going to need some ready cash so take it.'

He left shortly after that, taking with him a lot of the papers we had found and telling me that I could live in the house if I wanted to and to let him know if I ever found a will.

I went back into the dining-room, built up the fire and took my adoption papers out of the envelope. In fact there wasn't much I didn't already know. The papers confirmed that I had been born in that house just off the Old Kent Road in London. The name of my biological mother was there and the details of the adoption. That was it, but now it felt like a start, a beginning to discovering a real identity and to finding out what had happened to me during the first five months of my life.

I crossed the road and stayed with my 'new' relatives again. There had been many kind phone calls from YTV and friends in London. For some reason Barney was staying with friends in Ealing and they, too, had phoned saying that he was fine and could stay there as long as I needed him to. Our local funeral director came to the house and took over all the funeral arrangements. I had been good friends with his sisters once and trusted him completely. A member of the British Legion came to ask if I wanted the Union Jack to be draped over the coffin as my father was entitled to that. I agreed. Suddenly there seemed a lot that had to be done and I was grateful. The final message was one telling me that in two days' time I had to go into Sheffield to the morgue to identify my father's body before a necessary inquest. I didn't quite know how I was going to deal with that and pushed it to the back of my mind to be faced up to later.

Back at the house the next morning I began to clear out some cupboards and drawers. The wardrobes were still full of my mother's clothes and in a kitchen drawer I again found her purse with the last shopping list and her housekeeping money still in it. In fact everything still seemed to be as it had been when she died; her embroidery was sitting half finished under a cushion on a chair in the lounge we rarely used, her music still in the piano stool. Only then did I begin to grasp how desperately my father had missed her and how he had been finally unable to go on without her. I took all her clothes and hats into a charity shop in Sheffield; we had one in the village but I couldn't bear the thought of seeing them around on someone else. My father's clothes I mostly burnt. That night I slept at home.

Inevitably the two days passed and it was time to go to the morgue. I was shaking when I arrived but forced myself to walk into the building. I reported to an office and was taken straight into a room where a body lay, naked, on a trolley. They asked me formally if it was my father. It looked like no one that I had ever seen before but I supposed it was and said yes. Then I was thanked and shown politely out of the building. I wanted desperately to sit down, to be offered a cup of tea, to have an arm put round me and to be told that it was 'all right'. Instead I got into the car and drove aimlessly for a while. Finding myself in the middle of the town, I parked the car and walked into the shopping centre. I had to buy something suitable for the funeral and I needed a change of clothes too. I had the five hundred pounds from the house in my pocket and I decided that it was acceptable to spend some of that.

I soon found a black suit for the funeral; there was an identical one in a rust colour so I bought that too. I then must have flipped for I spent several hours buying anything else that took my fancy – clothes, shoes, books, records, make-up. When I couldn't carry any more, I went back to the car and crammed everything into the boot. Finally I drove home, waiting until it was dark to take the things into the house. I felt despicable; how on earth could I go shopping with my father lying dead and unburied?

The next morning I left to drive back to London, the funeral was arranged but was still five days away. For the moment there really wasn't much else I could do and I wanted my dog back and my friends around me. Once there I collected Barney and for two days was surrounded by all the warmth and support that I needed. Then, with Barney sitting happily in the car, I set off back to Derbyshire.

I now remember little of that visit home, but one afternoon I heard someone at the door and found a woman standing there. I had no idea who she was. She gave me her name and then went on to ask if I would give her first refusal when I sold the house. I looked at her in disbelief and finally demanded to know how she dared to ask that. My father was not yet buried, I did not know if the house would be mine and I certainly had not considered what I would do with it if it should be left to me. I finished by adding that I would never sell it to her even if she were the last person left in the world. I then closed the door and went back to what I had been doing. I felt good about that.

The time for the funeral arrived and the chapel was packed. I remember the drive to the graveyard and wondering idly if it really was the body of my father in the coffin. The children again stood silent and still in the school playground and we passed the little road to the cottage that had once belonged to my grandmother. As the coffin was lowered into the grave I felt glad that it was joining the one belonging to my mother, and I felt that at least I had got that right. Then it was all over.

I simply had not thought to provide any sort of food and drink for the mourners and so I just went home. I was reading my book when there was a knock at the door. It was Nurse Jackson, our district nurse who had gone with my mother to bring me back from London all those years ago. She had been one of the few regular visitors to our house and I knew her well. I was pleased to see her. Sitting in front of the fire with mugs of tea we talked, and she began to tell me of that day. She said that they had met my birth mother, though they shouldn't have done. She had been late bringing me to the office and she should have been long gone but wasn't. Nurse Jackson said that she was very beautiful, with dark hair, and that she was desperately upset at parting with me. Finally she told me that perhaps it was time for me to try to find her, that she could be a lonely old woman in need of a daughter to look after her.

I'm sure she meant well but it was not what I wanted to hear at that moment. When she had gone I remembered a lot of questions I still wanted to ask but the opportunity had passed and in the event there was never to be another.

Later I went upstairs to the airing cupboard where I had glimpsed a large cardboard box half hidden at the back. I pulled it out and opened the lid. It was full of old photos, all of my mother and father in their younger days. There were many with friends, often in fancy dress, and there were others at the seaside. In all of them they were laughing and having fun. I had never known my parents like that and apart from our annual holiday we had rarely done anything as a family. At that moment it seemed I had never really known them at all and now it was too late. Barney came and sat close to me and did his leaning act to comfort me, licking my hand and wagging his tail. Eventually it worked and we both went back downstairs. The next morning I rang a plumber and asked him to come and install that immersion heater, and finally we went back to London.

Chapter Sixteen

Yorkshire TV had been so kind and helpful, phoning regularly, offering to come to Hathersage for a few hours, and sending flowers for the funeral. They had also told me that my job was still waiting for me or I could choose to be released from my contract. I chose to go back to work. Everyone in the London office was friendly and concerned and back in Hampstead my friends were there for me. I thought I was coping well. We came to the penultimate episode of the series and for some reason I had to go back to the house on my way to Leeds and so I took Barney with me. Early on the Sunday morning he found a way out of the garden and disappeared. I searched round the village but couldn't find him. Finally he reappeared, dragging himself back and barely able to walk; he must have been hit by a car. There was no vet in the village so I decided to drive straight to Leeds and find one there. I filled the back seat of the car with pillows and an old eiderdown and we left. In Leeds I soon found a vet. He agreed to keep Barney in his kennels overnight as he needed an X-ray on the Monday morning; at least he was now safe and in good hands. I spent the evening talking to a friend and drinking too much wine and on the Monday began recording the show. Mid-morning the vet phoned with the welcome news that Barney had fractured his pelvis, but there was no other damage and he would make a good recovery.

Back in London I carried on working on *The Main Chance* and Barney began eating again. Inevitably we approached the end of the series and the rehearsals for the final episode went smoothly. We came to the technical run and afterwards I began to clear the rehearsal room. One of the camera crew shouted, 'Goodbye, see you all in Leeds.' I remember thinking, 'No, I can't go back.' And the next thing I remember is coming back to consciousness and finding that I was lying on a hospital trolley.

The PA was with me and she was wonderful. She told me I was in hospital because I had collapsed on the rehearsal-room floor and they couldn't bring me round. They had phoned for an ambulance and when it came the ambulance man found that my left arm was twisted and locked rigid behind my back and they thought it was a birth defect. I had lost four hours and still remember nothing. A doctor came and wanted to admit me but I didn't want that; they offered me a psychiatrist but I said no. Finally I told them of my father's death, promised to see my own doctor the next day and they let me go. The PA took me home where I found that someone had driven my car back and parked it outside my flat. Manda came over and stayed most of the evening, and the next day I went down to see my doctor. The waiting-room was crowded and I began to feel like a cheat. He asked me what was wrong and I told him that I would be as brief as possible. 'You will take as long as you need,' he said, so I told him the whole story. When I had finished he smiled. 'I'm not a bit surprised that you passed out,' he said. 'You just couldn't take any more so your body and your brain called a halt. We're all still like children really, we need someone to say "well done" from time to time and there was no one to say that to you.'

Over the days that followed, Barney and I slowly mended together and the world began to turn the right way up. Eventually the day came when Barney was climbing trees again and dropping down in front of little old ladies, scaring them half to death; the squirrels were being organised on the Heath and one day the phone rang offering me a new series. When I had a free weekend I went back to Derbyshire and carried on clearing out the house. Sometimes a friend came with me and we took time off to drive around the Hope Valley to places I knew so well but hadn't visited in years. Occasionally, someone would ask me when I was going to take back and run the post office, but that was never an option, though I knew that it was something that had been expected of me for before he retired my father had asked me to do just that, offering to buy me a car if I would do so. To a certain extent I had been trained in the running of the business from a very early age but I had long known that it was not the right job for me and I had refused. Hidden among my father's official papers after he died I had found a cutting from the local newspaper. The small heading declared LOCAL GIRL REFUSES TO CARRY ON TRADITION and the following article was about me. I realized then how disappointed both my parents must have been.

One day while in Hathersage I phoned an estate agent in Sheffield and asked him to come and value the house. I emphasised that I had not made up my mind whether to sell or not and had only to know its value for probate. The next time I went back I found For Sale notices stuck to all the windows and a board in the garden. I was furious, tore down all the notices and phoned the agent. I made it quite clear that the house was not on the market, and that if it ever was, they would not be involved. They wrote a letter of apology and that was that. But I knew that I was going to have to decide about the house. My 'new' relatives across the road had asked me to let it to their son, but the market rent was tiny and the house needed work done on it. I said no and we more or less went back to not speaking, except for the matter of the tea service. This was supposed to be a very old and valuable one that had somehow got into the clutches of our branch of the family. Rightfully it should be theirs apparently and was one of the reasons we had all stopped speaking. I found a tea service, but it was of rather thick china and covered in brightly painted red roses. I thought it very ugly, but I took it across to them and they seemed delighted with it. After many years the matter was finally closed. Certain friends of my mother came to the house and asked for a 'keepsake'. They almost invariably chose a piece of silver, but there seemed more than enough 'keepsakes' for me, and so I let them take what they wanted. In Sheffield the solicitors were still ploughing through the paperwork, so I had time to make some decisions.

Then Cousin Eric paid me a visit. He asked that if I did finally decide to sell the house, I would consider selling it to him. He named a price considerably above that of the probate evaluation and told me that there would always be a room for me whenever I wanted to stay. It seemed like a good solution but there was one problem. Years ago my mother had told me that the house would be mine one day and that the only thing she asked was that I never sold it to Cousin Eric. I have never found out all the things that went on in the various bits of my family; there must have been the usual petty jealousies but it seems it was often more than that. Then I wasn't really interested, now I am intrigued but it is too late. In the event I told Cousin Eric that I would think it over and left it at that.

By the end of that summer I had inherited everything from my father's estate including the house but felt that I should have none of it. I very seriously considered giving it all away, but my friends were horrified and finally persuaded me to do nothing for the moment. For those days it was a lot of money; I could easily have bought a house or flat in London, left the rest invested and need not have worked. But I loved my work and giving it up was not something I wanted to do. I had heard of a house for sale in the next road to South Hill Park. It needed renovation and had sitting tenants, but at sixteen thousand pounds in Hampstead it was a good buy. The old lady who had owned it had died and her flat was vacant so I went to look. Her daughter was handling the sale and she wanted me to have it, for she said I reminded her of stories of her mother when she was very young and she thought she would have wanted me to have it too. I discovered that the family who occupied the top two floors was leaving to go back to Ireland but the people on the ground floor were rather aggressive, said they had no intention of moving and hated dogs. But the timing wasn't right either, for at that time my father's estate was still being processed, and I was also frightened of the commitment. Reluctantly I pulled out and away went another opportunity to become a future millionaire.

It is fortunate that I have never been particularly interested in making a lot of money for I have certainly had chances to do so but money always came second in my considerations and I never stopped to think about it very much. Of course a certain amount is necessary and life with it is certainly better than life without but beyond that the matter doesn't interest me very much. That is not to say that I don't enjoy spending it because I do.

Meanwhile, my adoption papers, so relentlessly sought for over the years, stayed in their envelope in a drawer. Like Scarlett O'Hara again, it seemed that I was going to 'think about it tomorrow', only those missing five months continued to haunt me.

After my father's death my friends were all very supportive, both at work and in my private life. London had become the centre of my existence by then and in many ways it was comparatively easy to put my life back together again – only the memories from my father's death took a long while to come to terms with. There was even a marriage proposal, but he didn't seem to have that special 'something' that I had found with Graham and I was not prepared to settle for anything else.

Over the years the flat had slowly acquired more furniture, pictures and antiques; there were shelves full of books and records, curtains, carpets and cushions too. I now added some other things from the house in Derbyshire (finally sold, with a considerable amount of guilt, to Cousin Eric) and it became a really cosy place to live. I began to spend long winter evenings in front of a blazing fire with a Bruckner violin concerto on the record player and a contented dog curled up beside me, or singing and dancing along with Sammy Davies Jnr, Frank Sinatra, Liza Minelli or the latest pop hit on the radio ... no back line of the chorus line stuff for me! In summer I moved out to the garden, often joined by friends, with a bottle of dry white wine slowly emptying as we listened to John Williams practice his classical guitar repertoire from the balcony of his house two doors away. With the back gate of the garden opening directly on to the Heath, so convenient for Kenwood and long summer strolls and with the village atmosphere of South End Green or that of Hampstead itself, both of them only a few minutes walk away, I thought myself lucky indeed to live there.

While I had been at YTV I had met Peter; he worked there more or less permanently but had a flat in London only two roads away from me and we became friends and often met for a drink in one of the local pubs. He and a partner had started a cleaning firm and had the franchise to clean the ICA (Institute of Contemporary Arts) building in The Mall. They also had permission to stage a short play there and were looking for a suitable script. Pete asked me if I would help them and then go on to direct it. I was thrilled and plunged into the preliminary work with enthusiasm. Then one evening he came round to my flat and said there was a crisis in the cleaning of the kitchen floor at the ICA. The hygiene inspectors had paid a visit and unless the floor was properly cleaned within twenty-four hours they would close the restaurant. He asked if I would go down straight away and, together with a mate of his, help him out by spending a few hours cleaning the floor. I agreed and we set off for the West End. The floor was tiled and the problem was the gunge that had become embedded between the tiles. The only way to get it out was to scrape it up with a small knife. Pete wisely disappeared and his mate and I set about the job. It wasn't a big kitchen but it took all night to clean it well. We finished as dawn was breaking and as I sat back on my heels with a sigh of relief I heard a voice ask if I wanted a coffee. I looked up and saw an extraordinarily good-looking man standing in the doorway. I clearly remember thinking that if that was the sort of person who frequented the ICA then I should start going there more often.

As we sat drinking coffee it became clear that this was Pete's partner, Phil, who worked at the ICA arranging the exhibitions there, and was also the man who would design and build the sets for the play we had yet to find. I arranged to meet him in a couple of days' time and to discuss the venture further and went home to get some sleep, rather pleased by the thought that I would see him again.

I went back to work at Yorkshire TV, though I have no memory of the programme I was working on. We worked and played hard, and on the days we were in London we took great delight in crossing Regent Street and diving into one of the small alleys behind the shops where we frequented a Spanish restaurant known for its magnificent paella. It was also known for a drink called *sol e sombre* – sun and shade. This was made half with Spanish brandy and half with anis and was not to be partaken of unless work for the day had been completed well in advance. It was traditionally drunk at a bull fight and sometimes, after a particularly hectic morning in the office, it seemed to be a not altogether inappropriate choice. Having spent one such enjoyable lunchtime I walked through a brilliant summer afternoon down to the Ice (our nickname for the ICA) to meet Phil for our production meeting. But he wasn't there. Crossing into St James's Park I spent a carefree hour before going back to see if he had returned, but again he was not around. This went on for a little while until someone informed me he was at a wedding, and I began to get annoyed. By the time he appeared, slightly drunk and full of apologies, I had gone off the whole idea, and if it hadn't been such a lovely day for sitting in the park, I would have left long before. I started muttering something about letting me know he had intended to go to a wedding, but was stopped in my tracks when he explained he had not heard about it until that morning, and as it was Pete's wedding, he simply had to go. I was somewhat surprised for I had no idea that Pete was getting married or even had a girlfriend. When Phil suggested we repair to a pub to have our meeting I trotted after him eager for more details.

We met several times after that and it was always great fun. Phil was one of those people who could turn any day into Christmas Day, and frequently did. Meetings that were supposed to be about work turned into long social evenings that were full of laughter; and Barney thought Phil was great. He told good stories of his work at the ICA, including one of a German artist who was to have an exhibition there. The day for its opening was rapidly approaching and they had received no exhibits. Then one morning Phil got a phone call telling him to go out and buy thirty small, framed blackboards – the kind used by children, several packets of white chalk and some fixative. He complied and left them on a trestle table in the empty gallery. The next morning the artist arrived, drew a variety of squiggles in white chalk on twenty-four of the blackboards, signed them with an illegible signature and left, telling Phil to use the fixative and hang them as he wished. Less than impressed by all this Phil nevertheless did as he had been told and then, seizing a spare blackboard, drew some squiggles of his own and added them to the exhibition. No one appeared to notice, and when the 'paintings' were packed and sent on to New York, Phil's went with them. There the exhibition was a success and every exhibit was sold for an impressive figure. So someone somewhere does indeed have a unique drawing, for Phil was never again known to exercise his talent for creative art.

Then one day he went missing. I phoned Pete but he couldn't find him either and this went on for days. My anger turned to concern and finally to a feeling of resignation. The plans for our play faded, though Pete and I still talked of going ahead in the future. Life went on and I found myself temporarily out of work. Friends started persuading me that I needed a holiday and I went up to the travel agent on Haverstock Hill to enquire about a trip to Barbados. There the young man sold me on the idea of Brazil instead and when I returned to the flat I was booked on a flight to Rio de Janeiro. Suddenly there was a lot to fill the few days I had left before my holiday.

While I was packing my suitcase Pete called round to say that Phil had been found wandering around Cornwall and was safely back with his parents. There seemed little I could do about that for the moment for it was far too late to change my plans, so, mentally leaving him there, I concentrated on my trip. I nevertheless hit on the idea of contacting the Brazilian Embassy to see if I could find any new plays from that country, and they were very helpful. They gave me a list of addresses for people who worked in the arts in Rio and I wrote to all of them, giving my hotel phone number and the dates I would be there. Finally I set off on what was to be a twenty-two-hour journey to South America. The plane was small, we went via Switzerland and the woman next to me had halitosis and insisted on talking at me. It was a most unpleasant journey and by the time I stumbled off the plane I really wished I had gone to Barbados. I soon changed my mind, however, for driving from the airport I had an intriguing first glimpse of Rio and the hotel was by a beach of golden sand and there was superb and unlimited coffee available on request. There was also a list of messages and phone numbers from the contacts I had been given by the Embassy in London. Things really were getting off to a good start. I showered and collapsed on an enormous bed, promising myself a quick nap before I got on with things.

It was early evening when I awoke and I was still tired, so I settled for eating in the hotel instead and vowed to start in earnest the next day. I dressed and went down into Reception and sat reading my book while unobtrusively people-watching. When a man came and sat near me with his newspaper I smiled and went back to my reading, but we soon got chatting. He was a business man on his way back to Sao Paulo, but he had missed his plane connection and was stuck in Rio until the next morning. He told me he was married with two children and he was interested in learning about life in England and curious to know more of my work in theatre and television. He seemed a very genuine person, and when he hesitantly enquired if I would allow him to take me out to dinner and show me a little of Rio, I agreed to go, but only if I paid for myself.

I have no idea where we went but it was a beautiful restaurant. He introduced me to caipirinha, the local drink made from white cachaça rum and one which went perfectly with the live samba music and the knowledge that I really was in South America. Afterwards he drove me round the city, a mixture of wide roads, neon lights and tree-lined squares of tall Portuguese houses where people sat on balconies in the warm night air. We returned to the hotel after an evening that had been a wonderful start to my holiday; he had been delightful company and insisted that everything would go down on his expenses. It was my first taste of Brazilian hospitality, often to be repeated. Next morning the girl at the reception desk handed me a note from my benefactor of the night before, thanking me for an enjoyable evening. He had already left for the airport. After several cups of that fantastic coffee and a croissant I walked out to the beach and sat in the sun watching the waves pounding on to the sand. The city was shrouded in mist waiting to be explored while to my left and right on the sand there were stubs of black candles and stems of dying flowers. High behind the hotel I could plainly see a *favela*, one of the makeshift Indian towns for which Brazil was so regrettably becoming known. I thought about all the untouched food that was even now being cleared from the dining-room of the hotel and hoped that there was some sort of system in place for it to be taken across for the children in the shanty town. But it was a forlorn hope, and one that died quickly when a little while later I saw the food being burnt in a special area by the kitchens.

Back in the hotel there was a message from one of my Embassy contacts. I returned his call and readily accepted an invitation to dine with him in his flat that evening. I then leapt on to the courtesy coach into the centre of town and went exploring. It was to be several days before I found my way to Copacabana Beach but I delighted in the older parts of town. It felt like I'd always imagined the whole of Europe to be in the twenties and thirties, the tiny bars, the cafés filled with people where, in my imagination perhaps, I saw business deals being sealed, great works of literature being written and philosophy and politics being discussed by the hour. It was all hopelessly romantic of course, but that was how I saw things then and maybe a little of it was real.

That night I went to dinner at the flat of the art critic. The walls of his home were painted white and original paintings covered all of them. They had mostly been gifts from aspiring artists and they provided a fascinating hint of a lively arts scene and my hopes of finding a play rose considerably. It was late when I left with an invitation to spend the following weekend at his house in the country, where I would meet several of his friends. Meanwhile I continued exploring. One day I set off to visit the new art gallery for I had been told that it was something very special. Indeed it was, light, spacious and airy it was unlike any other art gallery I had ever seen, but, alas, almost all its entire contents had left for an exhibition in Spain and only one tiny picture hung in its enormous main gallery. Later, on the courtesy bus, I was telling one of the other tourists about my visit and we began laughing. The driver, who until then had led us to believe that he didn't speak English, suddenly turned around and told me off for making fun of his country. I began to consider more seriously what I knew of the political situation in Brazil. I knew that North America backed most of the regimes in South America, many of them right-wing dictatorships, and I had been warned to keep a low profile, but I was not there for any reason other than to have a holiday and find a play. I also felt that I had the protection of the Brazilian Embassy in London, but so far the only one to phone me since I arrived had been my art critic friend and I had not heard from him again about my weekend in the country. Also, once or twice I had felt that I was being followed but had put it down to local curiosity; now I wasn't so sure. Not wishing to cause anyone any problems I ceased the phone calls and re-planned my days.

There was plenty to do and see and my early-evening sojourns in Reception continued to yield someone to talk to, only now I concentrated on the other tourists. These were mainly rather rich North Americans and one couple especially became my friends. They had vouchers for meals in various expensive restaurants in the centre of town and one night we went to a large samba hall. The food consisted mainly of huge joints of meat roasted on an enormous spit with potatoes and salad and you could eat and drink as much as you liked. The music was live and there were singers and dancers. The evening started off slowly and the band seemed slightly off-key, but as the atmosphere built the samba rhythm grew faster and faster and the dancers whirled in a rainbow of colour. By the end of the evening the music was swirling in my head and it was impossible not to join in the dancing. I was high with the excitement of it all and stayed that way for several days afterwards. When they left, my American friends gave me their remaining vouchers and I continued to eat well and cheaply for the rest of my holiday. This was extremely useful as I had only been able to take a limited amount of money out of England and I was fast running out. I had already abandoned my plans to go to Brazilia and Bahia. The plane fares were far too expensive and to go by bus was simply impossible in the time I had available. Brazil was a much bigger country than I had ever imagined.

Every morning my stroll on the beach revealed fresh evidence of voodoo practices and I was curious to learn about them. They had been brought from Africa during the years of the slave trading and had taken firm root in their new land. Officially banned by the Christian churches, voodoo rituals still took place but were surrounded with secrecy and no one I talked to about them admitted their existence. Alas, I just didn't have the courage to walk alone on the beach at night and I never did find out more.

During my final week I was befriended by yet another North American, this one a man who was living and working in Rio, and, more importantly, owned a car. My evenings could now be spent driving away from the hotel and into the fringes of the rain forest. Here was a different sort of beauty. The narrow roads wound through a tent of dark-green foliage formed by the tallest trees I had ever seen. Occasionally the sunlight leaked on to flowers of crimson or briefly trapped a multi-coloured bird in its rays. When we stopped the car there were noises all around us, hinting at other wild life too busy or too shy to make an appearance. Once we found a roadside shack selling drinks. We stopped and bought one each. They consisted mainly of fresh fruit juice with a shot of alcohol. Though I was warned that they were very strong they were delicious and I insisted on having a second one. At that point my legs simply stopped working and it was quite a while before I could walk again. Another time we drove to a deserted beach just as the sun set, the moon rose and the sand turned from gold to silver in the moonlight. Another small shack served us with a huge plate of freshly grilled prawns, and we were the only people there, the sound of the lapping waves our orchestra and the now fully risen moon our only source of light. Later we drove back into Rio and up to the Christos where we sat in the car with the doors locked. Most of the town lay at our feet and a large, rat-like animal dashed in front of the car lights. Again there were rustlings all around us but this time they were dangerous, and there had been a murder up there a few weeks before. Finally we drove to a small café in a run-down part of the town. Here a would-be songwriter had penned 'The Girl from Ipanema' and made himself a fortune.

My North American friend disappeared to Los Angeles and would not return until after I had left. We made promises to keep in touch and I was condescendingly told that I was one of the few women he would consider marrying, but that was not something that I was considering at all. I had always insisted on paying for myself when we went out and had never thought of him as anything other than a pleasant companion. His place was quickly taken by a much younger and more handsome acquaintance, a Brazilian this time and someone who loved to laugh. With only two days left of my holiday I had little time to get to know him well, but he tried to persuade me to return to Rio very quickly and held out promises of a job and an introduction to the theatre and television worlds of his country. I was tempted to miss that plane home and take him up on his promises, but reluctantly I admitted to myself that even I couldn't do that.

The flight to London took off in the evening. I had heard of an arts and crafts market that took place every Sunday in a large square in the centre of Rio, and that day was a Sunday. I packed early for the flight and set off for the last time on the courtesy bus. It was busy in the market, full of Sunday couples, children and dogs. There were many things I wanted to buy but I had so little money left I despaired of finding anything I could afford. Then I saw an elderly Indian sitting surrounded by large woodcarvings made from tree branches. They were all the same figure, a rather alarming animal with gaping red mouth, but they were truly original and I wanted one. A passing local who spoke some English acted as my interpreter and informed me they were of one of the Indian tree gods and that he was definitely benign. He negotiated a very reasonable price for me and I chose one of the smaller ones and left. As I walked away I saw a stall of oil paintings that I had somehow missed. They were painted in pastel colours, each of a figure doing some mundane domestic task, and they were full of light and character. I stopped. By using the money I had saved for a last lunch and emptying my purse of everything except my bus fare back to the hotel, the artist and I reached an agreement that I am positive was very much in my favour. Then I fled away from further temptation. From where I sit typing now I can see both the carving and the painting. They have given me, and others, enormous pleasure over the years and I have never regretted going hungry that day, or the difficulties of getting them safely to London. I don't remember the journey back, only the feeling of sadness at leaving so much behind. I was sure then that I would return but, so far, I never have.

A friend was waiting for me at the airport, a hitherto unknown luxury, and I was soon back at the flat where Barney threw me a cold look of total disapproval and went back to his patrol duties on the Heath. My bathroom had been turned into a darkroom, my living room into a studio, and there were several items of feminine clothing in the bedroom, but none of it mattered for Barney had obviously been well looked after. There had, apparently, been a slight muddle over the date of my return, so we went to find the hound and persuade him to join us at our local pub.

A few days later Phil, too, returned to London, initially to apologise for his sudden disappearance and to repay the small debts he had left behind. He began to spend more and more time at the flat and soon got a job. A few weeks later, to the shock of family and friends (and myself), we got married. (See *Coming Slowly* for details.)

It took a while for everyone to get used to the idea but I rather revelled in my new role of married lady and became very left-handed for a while. We didn't have a honeymoon, though inexplicably I went to Spain with our best man for a few days. It had been a trip that had been arranged before I got married and we stayed with Carl's married brother, (I was heavily chaperoned.) and Phil was working very long hours, but ...? Once back I took to cooking enormous three-course meals until Phil, finally overfaced by yet another chocolate pudding with fudge sauce, asked if we could adopt a simpler way of eating. Secretly relieved, I abandoned the puddings, produced starters only when we had guests and concentrated on providing just a main course – with Barney's favourite dish of take-away fish and chips as a standby when all else failed.

Then Phil got a job as a master carpenter at the National Theatre. At that time its home was still at the Old Vic and Sir Larry, as he liked to be known, was firmly in charge. Soon Phil was coming home with news of chats with his new boss, who had become an avid daily reader of Phil's *Manchester Guardian*. He was obviously happy there and I was thrilled by the fact that he was working in a theatre I loved and where I had sat enthralled through so many exciting productions.

Although the new building was slowly coming into existence, the company at the Old Vic had a vibrant identity of its own. Over the years I had been a regular presence in the queue for balcony seats (available on the day of performance only and very cheap) and I had been swept up enthusiastically in the thrill of each new opening. If the clientele had changed a little from Lilian Baylis's early days, it was still a theatre that catered for the public at large and everyone felt that it was theirs to enjoy. Some of the plays are still vivid in my memory. *The Royal Hunt of the Sun* by Peter Shaffer I saw five times, each time witnessing the silence that preceded the applause as the red curtain covered the stage before the interval, symbolising the mass slaughter of the South American Indians. Rare for me, I even bought a copy of the play and sent it, together with a stamped envelope, to the stage door to be autographed by members of the cast. It is still one of my prized possessions. I sat twice through Sir Larry's *Othello*, mesmerised by the sheer brilliance of a technical performance I have never seen bettered, and during *The Crucible* by Arthur Miller I heard a member of the audience cry out in protest against the injustice of the witch hunt – and realised that it was me and sat embarrassed and blushing in my front-row balcony seat.

Now I was getting the daily gossip and details of plays in rehearsal, it was all great fun. With two good wages coming in, Phil, Barney and I began to enjoy a more liberated life-style. With little thought for the future we spent as fast as we earned: we discovered a Greek restaurant in Camden Town and spent many a silly evening there when we couldn't be bothered to cook, long-stemmed red roses kept appearing and at the flat there was an open-house policy and a lot of laughter. I bought Phil a camera for his birthday and he and Barney, his eager assistant, went for long walks together. When the first roll of film was developed it revealed photograph after photograph of empty grassland or bare branches of trees. This was put down to over exuberance on the part of the assistant, but they still went off together. One weekend the three of us went down to Box Hill in Surrey with two friends, Joanna and Martin. We walked for miles, with Barney running free, until we saw a sign for a café and decided it was time for tea but when we called Barney he had disappeared. For nearly two hours we searched and whistled but to no avail. The light was fading fast and we were seriously alarmed; we told our two friends to go home while, knowing that we could never leave him there alone, we decided we would try to find a shop where we could buy a couple of torches and return to the search. But back in the car park where our two cars were parked side by side, we found a disgruntled hound waiting patiently for us to return, a look of 'what-kept-you' on his face. Our dog had proved to be more intelligent than his owners.

By now I owned my third Mini and it was showing signs of old age. Seeing an advert for the new MGB sports car I jokingly suggested we buy one. Phil looked incredulously at me but the idea stayed hanging around and when I checked our finances it suddenly became a possibility. The next day I phoned the sales office and found they had a burgundy one coming off the production line that week. Not long after I drove out to the Welsh Harp showroom to collect it; it was the start of the long hot summer of 1976 and for weeks we never put up the hood. We all adored it. Phil and I bought special jackets (mine was silver) and the compulsory sunglasses, and Barney had a new collar that he hated until he had reduced it to the same state as his old one. We called her Lily, because LLY was part of the registration, and she definitely had a feminine personality. Driving acquired a new, exciting dimension, but there was one disadvantage. Barney developed a penchant for trying to leap out at traffic lights when he saw a particularly attractive female 'pooch' on the pavement, but we soon learnt to cope with this – nothing was allowed to spoil the pleasure of our new toy. All told there were many happy days then and the once all-consuming issue of my adoption stayed well in the background. Phil knew about it, of course, but it seemed to matter little to him and with my new persona as a married woman, I, too, consigned it to a 'pending' file and lived in the present.

Then, slowly, things began to move on. The first changes began at the National Theatre. Amidst a great deal of controversy its new home was nearing completion on the South Bank. From outside the building looked to have little charm but much was promised for the three theatres now being finished within the concrete outer walls.

By now Peter Hall (as he then was) had pretty much taken over the running of the company and Sir Larry was seen less and less at the Old Vic. There were rumours of 'problems' and the two men were known to have conflicting views on much of the policy connected with the day-to-day running of what was fast becoming an enormous enterprise. I knew neither of them but they seemed to be vastly different characters. Sir Larry was essentially a man of the theatre while Peter Hall came from a more academic background and was, to many people, very much 'the new kid on the block'. As observers, we waited to see what would happen. There was to be one last glorious evening at the Old Vic. Because it was very much an 'invitation only' event Phil had been unable to get me a ticket, but afterwards he discovered that someone had made a sound recording of the whole evening and I still have a copy of that. Presented as a homage to Lilian Baylis, it was entitled *Tribute To The Lady* and was the story of the theatre from the time she took over the running of the Vic. In parts it is very funny, in others very moving. That evening the auditorium was packed with some of our greatest actors, actresses and directors, and many more appeared on stage. Only one was missing, for Sir Larry was not there. Even on the recording the knowledge of his absence adds a prevailing sense of loss, for if the evening was a tribute to a great lady of the theatre, it was surely a tribute to him too,

The Vic closed and the struggles to complete and open the Lyttleton Theatre went on. Phil came home only to sleep for a few hours and I rarely saw him. There were stories of meetings about meetings and budgets that were broken, re-estimated and broken again. To the people struggling to get the theatre running, and far removed from the decision-making, it seemed that there was no one really in over-all control or understood what was needed to make the technical and backstage machinery work. Expensive decisions were made, only to be reversed a few days later, and there were times when the colour of the seats in the auditorium took precedence over the facilities necessary to fly the scenery and open and close the front tabs.

The company had grown prodigiously and Phil now found himself working with many new faces. He told me that it was slowly becoming apparent that many of the new backstage crews lived locally and had criminal records; in one case for GBH. It was never clear whether this was a deliberate policy to give ex-criminals a new start or whether the people responsible for them were simply unaware, but they certainly added a new dimension to life backstage. In the Borough of Lambeth things began to 'fall off lorries' at an alarming rate. Fortunately undamaged by their experiences, they were then sold on quickly and cheaply via the props stores. For a long time Phil and I did not participate, but he was showing an increasing reluctance to go to work, and when he came home one night with a deep cut on his forehead, caused by a metal chair that had been thrown at his head by one of his workmates, we hastily reversed our policy and became the owners of a large new colour television. After that things started to get better.

Phil eventually became good mates with one of the props guys from work and Tony became a frequent visitor to our home. By now the walls of the flat were becoming covered in paintings, most of them bought cheaply from market stalls, but all of them originals or limited print editions. Seeing a book about L.S. Lowry on our coffee table, Tony remarked that the Vic props stores was throwing out what looked like one of his pictures and he asked if I would like it. Assuming that it was a mass-produced print, but not wishing to offend, I said yes. Several days went by but it didn't appear and he finally told me that, alas, the head of the props stores had taken it. I felt rather relived until I learned that the picture had turned out to be an original work and had now quietly disappeared from anyone's memory. But what on earth had it been doing in a theatre's props store?

Phil was still working long hours and I was in the middle of a long series of *General Hospital* and working out at Boreham Wood, so we decided to complicate our life further by buying a house. This decision had been triggered partly by seeing a picture of some Filipino twins in the *Evening Standard*. They had been found abandoned and somehow touched our hearts. Although, as far as we knew, we could have had children of our own, we talked longingly of adopting them, but couldn't see that we would be eligible with our gypsy life-style and far from luxurious flat. Over dinner one evening with Tony Adams and Caroline Mortimer, we somehow began talking about the twins and Caroline revealed that she worked as a volunteer at the orphanage to which they had been taken. They had had trouble finding a suitable home for them and she felt certain that we would have been considered an ideal couple. Both Phil and I felt disappointed for a long time after that.

Meanwhile the Lyttleton Theatre had its grand opening and the National Theatre of Great Britain was now a reality. Phil couldn't get me a ticket, but we went down to the South Bank and joined in the party afterwards. It really did seem a momentous occasion and just to be there made you feel that you were living through a piece of history. Later, however, when the Olivier Theatre finally opened, Phil somehow did manage to get hold of two tickets. It was another great night, and as before just to be there was all. Twirling round the foyer in my feather-trimmed evening dress, bought in a sale for twenty pounds, I felt I was one of the luckiest people on earth that evening, and I was floating high on adrenalin and champagne. I also reflected that I was getting rather good at these events for I had also been at the opening of the Barbican and standing in the Art Gallery when the Queen walked in and said, 'Good-evening.'

With our feet firmly back on the ground, Phil and I continued looking for a house or a large flat, but nothing we found ever quite seemed to have our name on it. We were already living in a near-perfect location with friends around us and, in retrospect, I'm not sure that we really wanted to move at all.

The decision was taken out of our hands for the moment when I was offered a job working on a series of Alan Bennett plays for LWT. I had long been a fan of Alan's work and anyhow we had mutual friends and I felt I already knew him. The series producer and part director was to be Stephen Frears, soon to become highly respected on both sides of the Atlantic and already making a name for himself here. I was to work on three of the plays, the first one, *Doris and Doreen* was to be shot in the studio while the other two, *Me, I'm Afraid of Virginia Woolf* and *All Day on the Sands* were to be shot mostly on film, and that meant a trip 'up north'. It would be the first time I had returned there for any length of time since the death of my father and I remember having rather mixed feelings about it. The first play of the season was being directed by Lindsay Anderson and was already in rehearsal when I joined the team. It sounded a somewhat exotic production with a high-profile cast, and stories of bursts of temperament came trickling back to the office, but when I gave Lindsay a lift back to the Finchley Road after a meeting he was extremely charming and very interesting to talk to.

Doris and Doreen was a virtual two-hander, with Prunella Scales and Patricia Routledge in the title roles and a then unknown Peter Postlethwaite appearing briefly somewhere in the middle of it all. Stephen was directing. We rehearsed in Camden Town very close to Alan's house. It was still winter and we were all very grateful when Alan invited us back for some hot soup one lunchtime. I clearly remember creeping past 'the lady in the van' and being aware of a pair of eyes watching our arrival with disapproval. Very few people outside Camden knew about her then and I really admired Alan for the way he coped with her presence in his driveway. I still do admire him for his generosity of spirit and practical acceptance, and I'm not at all sure that I would have been so philanthropic if it had been my driveway that Miss Shepherd had chosen to settle on. She was, however, well known in the area even then, a fringe personality in my life and that of many others for several years; for anyone who shopped regularly in Inverness Street market was bound to come across her from time to time. Once you were within range of her radar it was impossible to ignore her, though sometimes she went to enormous pains to ignore you. However much you tried to be warm towards her – by buying one of her tracts for instance – she always managed to antagonise you at some point and left you feeling angry; and guilty for feeling angry as well. We were to return to Alan's house several times and walking past that van to his front door was always a journey fraught with hazard as far as I was concerned, and I didn't envy the regular postman one little bit.

Over the rehearsal period we became a tight little group and very much enjoyed our days together. Stephen lived near me and I used to pick him up early in the morning, nagging him to finish his coffee or we would be late. It rarely worked, for he pointed out that as I was with the director and producer of the show no one would tell me off, and we often had another cup of coffee before we left. Alan was always in rehearsals, occasionally changing a word here and there, sometimes sighing quietly to himself or delighting us all with funny stories in the breaks, until one day it came to the crew-run on the day before we went into the studio and we almost resented their intrusion into our little world. Then we moved to the studio and the production grew up and left home.

Next came *Me, I'm Afraid of Virginia Woolf*. Large parts of the script were to be shot on location in and around Leeds and it had a much larger cast. It was completely different from working on *Doris and Doreen*, not least because Thora Hird was a member of the cast. I had never worked with her before and was totally unaware of the impact she was to make, especially over a cup of tea in the evenings back at the hotel. Thora, born in Morecambe, had grown up in show business and, with a career that stretched back to the last days of the music hall, was now one of the leading character actresses of her generation. She was also a gifted raconteur whose stories have been written up in her autobiography but to have them related personally by the lady herself was priceless fun. Sitting at a small table in the hotel bar, we would laugh until our sides ached, while Thora, like any true professional, revelled in the attention and treated us to more. In the play she was taking the part of the mother of the central character, played by Neville Smith. They made a perfect double act, and I remember every detail of a scene we shot in Leeds town hall, where Thora's character was trying to discover the details of her son's love life. We shot it at least five times from five different angles and each time the crew was in agony with suppressed laughter until Stephen called 'cut' and we could all let go. It was a rare evening, and our spontaneous laughter was a tribute to some fine writing and acting from a group of professional people not always so affected by what they are shooting. After Thora's contract ended and she was returned safely to London, we heard that she had written to Alan, saying how much she had enjoyed working with us all and asking that he write her a part in one of the other plays. She added that it didn't matter how small the part was, she just wanted to be in it. And she was!

All Day on the Sands was to be shot in Morecambe, so with Thora's stories still ringing in our ears we set out to film the story of a family summer holiday on the a beach where, even though it was by now late spring, we could only shoot the long shots in one direction because of the snow lying white on the nearby hills. It was bitterly cold, and the cast were truly heroic as they gambolled on the sands in swimsuits, while wardrobe stood by with blankets and hot-water bottles. Then one day our lighting cameraman returned from lunch to continue filming on the beach and decided, in what can only be described as a flash of human error, to take the quick way back to the sands and leap over the railings on the promenade. It was a considerable drop and we watched in horror as he landed heavily, broke his wrist and turned green with pain. I had never seen anyone turn green before and he must have been in agony. He was rapidly dispatched to hospital and his assistant took over until a replacement could be rushed up from London.

At the end of filming in Morecambe, I was left behind to do a final clearing up while the unit moved across to Hartlepool to start filming *Afternoon Off*. This was not one of my productions but I was to follow on to join them as an extra member of the crew and general 'gofer'. I finished early on my last day and wandered along the promenade where I noticed that Gypsy Lee's caravan appeared to have opened for business. I plucked up my courage and wandered across and she called me inside. Having negotiated a fee, she leaned forward and tugged a hair from my scalp. It hurt and the action made me very nervous, but she was remarkably accurate about many things in my life and I was beginning to enjoy myself when she suddenly told me that I would marry twice.

'But I could never leave my husband, I said. 'He needs me.'

There was a pause, and then she told me that when I married for the second time there would be no divided loyalties.

I left shortly after that convinced that something bad was going to happen to Phil, and the premonition stayed with me for a long time, making my heart skip a beat when I suddenly remembered it.

Back with the film unit, I found I was staying in a tourist area named Seaton Carew. This was a small holiday area just outside Hartlepool and featured a few houses, a perfectly acceptable hotel, an antique shop, and a desolate windswept beach that was littered with sea coal collected on a daily basis and sold in the town. It should have been a depressing place but somehow wasn't, so, having decided that the name was better suited to an out-of-work repertory actor of dubious sexual persuasion than to a northern holiday resort, I settled in with the lighting crew for company and trotted off to find the rest of the unit who were staying in a hotel in the middle of Hartlepool.

I think it was in the middle of this production that we went to shoot a sequence in Scarborough and to my great delight I found we were to stay overnight in that very same Grand Hotel that I had gazed at so longingly as a child. Alas, that once great hotel that had seemed to me to be the very epitome of elegance had fallen on hard times. Used now mainly for one-night stays by coach parties, the rooms were falling into disrepair and the service ran along the lines of holiday-camp rigidity. I went down to Reception to see if I could change my room for one with a sea view only to find half the unit there complaining that they had no hot water, or their room key wouldn't work, or the windows wouldn't close ... I tiptoed away feeling that lack of a sea view was a minor hardship and one that could be borne with fortitude. Later, when we went to eat, a man wearing too much sallow make-up and a shiney pale-blue suit tried to tell us where to sit and was most upset when anarchy broke out within our ranks. The final straw occurred when he refused to serve us potted shrimps unless we paid the fifty pence surcharge up front, at this point most of us left and went to eat in town with the blessing of the unit manager. It was all very funny but sad too and we were glad to leave.

Once back in Hartlepool there really wasn't very much for me to do, so a phone call to London elicited the promise of a visit from Phil the following Sunday after a friend of his had been coerced into driving him up. They arrived late morning, the three of them, for Barney was squashed happily into the front seat of Paul's sports car, his tail going round and round in delight when he saw me through the windscreen. We all followed a racing dog across the sands and caught up on all the latest gossip, and later Paul tactfully disappeared, leaving us alone. I was so thrilled to see my 'family', but couldn't get Gypsy Rose Lee's prediction out of my mind. This was my husband I was with; I had believed my marriage was for a lifetime; I thought that the only way I would ever marry twice was if Phil was to die or be killed in some dreadful accident and therefore I was very afraid. I couldn't possibly tell him what was going on in my head but it caused a distance between us and the visit was not the success I had longed for. I had looked for reassurance, confirmation that all was well, but I hadn't found it. Instead we played with Barney until they set off early for the long drive back to London, leaving me feeling desperately insecure – a feeling I had not experienced since my marriage and one I had hoped had gone for ever. There were several phone calls the following week and all seemed fine between us, but I couldn't quite shake the conviction that something had changed, as when the sun disappears behind a cloud on a hot summer's afternoon.

A few days later we finished filming and I returned to London bearing various items bought in an antique auction and happy memories of a job well done and a series that had been a real pleasure to work on. Life settled back into a routine and I pushed my insecurities to the back of my mind, for they seemed out of place now that I was home again.

With Phil's life seemingly sorted for the moment I turned my attention to my own, and soon became aware that changes were happening there too. With the accountants more and more firmly in control of the budgets, and with management starting to battle with the unions, my phone was ringing less frequently than it had in the past. To add to the complications the British film industry was dying on its feet and freelance film technicians were increasingly taking jobs in television, something they would have never considered before. I was offered a contract by Southern Television filming a children's series in the New Forest, and, after discussing it with Phil, I accepted. The series was based on the Enid Blyton 'Famous Five' books and was something of a feather in the cap for Southern. It meant living down there for at least five days a week, and there was the problem of Barney. We solved this by borrowing a caravan from friends and parking it in the grounds of a pub in the heart of the forest; Barney would spend his days at a local kennels and his nights with me. Once we had all settled into a routine it worked well. Most weekends Barney and I drove back to London and occasionally Phil spent the weekend with us. It was not the happiest of jobs though, as most of the crew were ex-film and very 'blokey'. The unit manager in particular seemed rather aggressively to object to my involvement. I was told that this was partly because I was not a man and partly because I drove a new sports car and he didn't. I gathered he had no reservations about my professionalism but that didn't stop him from making my life miserable whenever he had a chance. Eventually the antipathy between us became mutual, but there were actors and other freelance crew around who went out of their way to be friendly and we worked hard and had some laughs.

The unit was based in a beautiful old house on the Rothschild Estate; it had been empty for some time and we had the run of the whole house apart from a couple of rooms packed with antique furniture. It was a lovely place to be and exactly right for our series. On the final night the family threw a big party for us all and the house came alive again. Phil travelled down and thoroughly enjoyed himself, spending most of the evening chatting to Enid Blyton's niece and from time to time offering her cocktail-sized pickled onions from his jacket pocket. Next morning when I apprised him of this fact he denied it strongly, until he put his hand into his jacket pocket … and produced some rather fluff-covered pickled onions!

Chapter Seventeen

I was so looking forward to being home again and hopefully staying there for a while with my little family but it was not the happy place I had left and Phil was obviously once again finding his situation at the National Theatre to be increasingly frustrating. Neither of the two theatres was functioning properly while new and ambitious productions were coming up thick and fast. A sense of elitism was invading the South Bank and the company was now so vast and made up of so many new faces that it had become impersonal, with no proper sense of cohesion. I continued to take advantage of the complimentary tickets, welcome because the ticket prices had risen dramatically, changing the audience and the front-of-house atmosphere too. Now twin-sets and pearls were seen more often than jeans and leather jackets, and the matinées especially were full of tourists. Something was missing from the days at the Vic, and when I found myself sitting in the front stalls for a performance of the Scottish play, wriggling in my seat and glancing secretly at my watch, I decided to stop going for a while. For a long time I puzzled over what was missing from that new building. Only finally did I come to understand that the spirit and dreams of Lilian Baylis, fought for throughout her years at the Old Vic and protected and embraced by Sir Larry, had not and perhaps never would make that short journey from the Waterloo Road to the South Bank. There have been many fine productions in the three theatres there and only an ever diminishing number of people will know what I am talking about. I never knew the Old Vic when Miss Baylis was alive but I certainly did while Sir Larry was there and I knew that I was experiencing something that was unique in the British Theatre.

I still visited the new building though, usually to meet Phil for a few hours in a break between the shows. Both front and back stage it was an impossible building to negotiate and I invariably got lost on my way to the Green Room. I wasn't the only one, there always seemed to be people searching for somewhere and there were endless corridors with closed doors that never looked familiar. Eventually someone put down coloured tape and a few signs appeared and life got simpler. One evening I was sitting in the Green Room in my black velvet trouser suit waiting to go out to dinner with Phil when Peter Hall came in. he looked around and walked across to where I was sitting:

'And who are you?' he asked.

'The wife of one of the chippies,' I replied.

'Oh,' he said, and losing interest, he walked away.

It was many years before I saw him again. I was living in Greece where I took great pleasure in visiting the summer season of classical plays at the Epidavros Theatre in the Peloponnese. One of the best preserved ancient theatres in Greece, it is renowned worldwide for its acoustics. Within the circular acting area no microphones are needed, for every word can be clearly heard from every one of its fourteen thousand seats, but step outside this area and voices carry no farther than normal. To this day no one knows how it has been achieved, or indeed whether it was created deliberately or by chance. One summer I read that the, by then, Royal National Theatre of Great Britain would be performing there for two nights. The two plays were to be by Sophocles: *Oedipus the King* and *Oedipus at Colonus*. They are both long plays and I assumed that one play would be performed each night and I booked a ticket for the first night. I had seen them both many times but earlier that summer there had been a particularly impressive performance of *Oedipus the King* by the National Theatre of Greece and I thought it would be fun to compare the productions.

The week of the British company's arrival in Greece a storm of controversy broke out in the Greek media. The British set required a large number of wood-fueled braziers to be situated at the edge of the acting area and they were to burn throughout the performance. Justifiably, in my opinion, the Greek Archeological Society woke up and registered a series of protests. They feared that the not inconsiderable heat that these would generate would have an adverse and maybe permanent effect on the acoustics. The British company was offered every facility to modify the braziers to an electric source of power with a flame effect or to make whatever other change they deemed appropriate. It was then reported in the newspapers that Sir Peter, as he was by now, had categorically refused to modify the set in any way, claiming that it was an essential part of the concept. He had also added that if the braziers were banned he would have no option but to cancel the productions. The controversy went on. Meanwhile, I discovered that the two plays were to be performed together each night. Unless they had been heavily edited this meant that we were in for around four-and-a-half hours of theatre and it was clear that none of the British company had ever perched on a rather small piece of marble with no back rest and little leg room for that length of time. I made a mental note to take a cushion.

On the opening night I arrived at Epidavros not a hundred per cent sure that the plays were going to take place but all seemed normal there and I made my way to the auditorium. It had rained that morning and was quite cool high up there in the mountains, so I was glad of my sweater and the small thermos of hot coffee I had smuggled into the theatre in my handbag. I walked past a considerable number of the controversial braziers (unlit) that ringed the outer edge of the acting area and noticed a large and steeply raked ramp that had been built upstage centre. I then settled to watch a few arriving celebrities being photographed for the newspapers. Traditionally the play starts when it is dark, and already the light was fading fast. The Greeks love their theatre and usually come in family groups, grandpa relating the story of the evening's play to excited children. But, perhaps because of the controversy or of the knowledge that it would be performed in English, many people had been deterred, for the seats were less than half filled when a spotlight appeared centre stage and a figure walked into it. This turned out to be Sir Peter, holding a microphone! A small ripple of laughter ran through the rows of seats near me and we settled back, intrigued, to see what would happen next. Using the unnecessary microphone, he told us that the leading actor playing Oedipus had fallen off the ramp during the dress rehearsal the day before and broken his ankle. He would, however, be performing this evening, and he asked for our understanding. There was a small round of applause and if only he had stopped there, all would have been well. Alas, he didn't, he went on to say that as there had been no dress rehearsal the day before(!), he would be treating tonight's performance as a dress rehearsal and would be stopping it to give notes and redirect the actors when he felt this was necessary.

The audience – well, certainly those members of it near me – were obviously upset. We had paid full price for our tickets and we had come to see a first night of a world-renowned classical play performed by an important foreign company; not a working rehearsal. When Sir Peter added that there would be no photographs taken or reviews written for the papers, a photographer standing near me uttered a series of Greek swear words and walked out of the theatre, followed by a few members of the audience. Finally the play began with the lighting of the braziers, something that further unsettled us all; they looked impressive but I think we were all more comfortable when quite early during the play they slowly went out one by one and were not re-lit.

It is difficult now to be objective about what I saw that night, for in a sense the evening had already been lost. In the event, Sir Peter did not interrupt the performances, but I found myself distracted by the belief that he might do so at any moment. There were other distractions too, for you could clearly see hesitant actors being led by torchlight into their opening positions at the top of the ramp – one they were obviously nervous of descending. Furthermore, the new English translation was in rhyming couplets and I found myself trying to guess the word that would complete the second line; the Greek language does not translate easily into English and I felt that the added discipline of rhyming couplets was a complication too far. Lastly, and more prosaically, it was decidedly chilly after the morning rain.

Following *Oedipus the King* there was an interval, but it was already late and a lot of people did not return to their seats. In many ways this was a pity, for I enjoyed *Oedipus at Colonus* far more. There was a feeling of cohesion to it and a clear sense of the tragedy that had preceded it in the first part of the story; we began to feel back in familiar territory and relaxed. When the evening ended there was warm applause, but it had been a very long night and I was glad when I could finally walk back to the coach for the two hour journey to Poros. As I left the auditorium I passed Sir Peter standing with his assistant and heard him say that he thought the boys and girls had done rather well. Alas it was not a feeling shared by many of the audience and I felt so very sorry for the actors.

It was nearly 4 a.m. when I finally got to bed. The newspapers later that day had mainly obeyed orders and not reviewed the show, but the controversy surrounding the visit of the British company continued for several days and it was said that they would not be invited again.

Years later I saw a thrilling production of *Hamlet* in Athens. It had been translated into Greek and was performed within the parameters of classical Greek theatre.

The actor playing Hamlet (Konstantinos Markoulakis) was outstanding, for here was a prince you could warm to, one full of life and mischief and not always overwhelmed by events, until destiny slowly overtook him and, in the final moments of the play, tragedy swept across the stage, leaving the audience breathless at witnessing the awful power of the relentless gods. The audience rose to its feet, grandfathers and children together, proving that great theatre has no frontiers and a good story is always a good story.

But I digress.

One evening Phil came back from the South Bank with the news that he had been offered a job as a technical director with the National Company. I was thrilled and proud for and of him, but as we talked it became obvious that he didn't want to accept. In the end, after several days of discussion, Phil decided that it was time for him to leave the National Theatre and he went to work for a small independent company run by mates of his and there he rapidly became much happier. One of my more outlandish daydreams at this time was to become a theatre 'angel'. But that meant having the money to invest and a suitable vehicle in which to invest it. Phil announced that he had solved both problems and arrived home with a script to prove it. It was of the musical *Bar Mitzvah Boy*, from the book by Jack Rosenthal, successful playwright and Maureen Lipman's husband to boot; the songs were by Don Black and Jule Styne. Its parentage was impressive and I read the script with excitement. The show was not yet in rehearsal and I knew things could change at any time, but I thought it fun, and when later I heard a tape of the music I picked out the 'show stopper', enjoyed the rest and thought there was a good chance of the show turning out to be a popular success. But what about the money we needed to be 'angels'?

'No problem,' said Phil, 'leave it to me.'

We were finally liable for a hundred pounds. I think the production office where he now worked had bought a larger stake and divided it up; anyhow we signed the contract and became 'angels' overnight and thought ourselves very grand.

I was offered another job down at Southern TV and, after checking that there was a different production manager in charge, I accepted. Then Phil walked out of the marriage and disappeared. Everything seemed to go on hold and I remember little of the next few weeks. I did try to honour my contract with Southern, but in the end I gave up, explained what had happened and asked to be released. They were very understanding and agreed so I returned to London and waited for the phone to ring. When it did strange voices told me that Phil was ill and needed me but rang off before telling me where he was. This happened several times until someone told me that it was probably a joke – some joke.

When I told friends and Phil's family what had happened they were stunned. We simply had no idea where he was or exactly why he had gone. Then Phil got back in touch and we began seeing one another quite regularly, often spending a whole day together. On my birthday we met in our local pub where he arrived bearing a card and a present. Sometimes he talked of coming back and we even began to plan a holiday together, but by now I had discovered the presence of a tenacious 'other woman' and nothing ever quite worked out. Eventually friends persuaded me to move on, and they were right, for after so many weeks of uncertainty and a very real feeling of betrayal there was little of the marriage left to save.

There remained one complication to solve, however: the opening of *Bar Mitzvah Boy* was looming and two complimentary tickets for the first night were sitting on the dining-table; to go or not to go? That was the question. And if the answer to that question was to go, then who to go with? While I was working down at Southern I had become good mates with a member of the Art Department there; he knew why I had left and we had kept in touch. When he phoned one evening I explained about my dilemma and was surprised and touched when he asked if I would allow him to escort me. I was also delighted, for he was easy to be with, very good-looking and thoroughly charming. In fact, a perfect escort for the evening. I was sure he would look terrific in a dinner jacket and he promised to pick me up in his vintage sports car in good time for the show.

By now, alas, I had begun to hear rumours that all was not going well in rehearsals. It seemed to be a case of 'too many cooks' and there had been a lot of changes made to the original script and the musical number that I had identified as the 'show stopper' had been cut from the show completely; so it was with mixed feelings that I began to get ready for the theatre that evening. Rob phoned from the motorway to say he was running late and could we meet at the theatre – how awful that I can now no longer remember exactly what happened that evening but I think it involved the last-minute hiring of another car at considerable expense and rather a lot of hard driving.

Phil was outside the theatre when I arrived. He was working backstage running the show and said he would meet me in the bar during the interval. He seemed to assume that I was there on my own so I said nothing. Rob arrived with minutes to spare and we took our seats. Alas, it quickly became obvious that this show was not going to be the long-running success we dreamed of. It wasn't bad, it just didn't have that something that made the hairs on the back of your neck stand up and trumpet 'hit'.

In the bar at the interval I saw Phil walk in and became very nervous.

Rob stood resolutely at my side.

'Just introduce me,' he said. 'I'll handle the rest.

The look of astonishment on Phil's face when he saw I was with someone was quite something and he didn't stay talking long. Rob stood a little behind me and I felt safe and protected and very special. Later the two of us went out for dinner and then we went our separate ways. I don't think I ever saw him again, but I will always remember that evening, for Rob gave me back my pride and nothing was ever so terrible again. It was a generous thing to do, a warm gesture from a kind and considerate man and one performed with enormous charm.

Bar Mitzvah Boy ran for a few weeks and then quietly closed and we lost our money, somehow I never got round to being an 'angel' again. Not all dreams come true.

The next few years were to be a confusing mixture of good times and bad. The National Theatre disappeared out of my life completely, and though I worked mainly in London, I saw little of Phil. Once, in a particularly gloomy period, I seriously contemplated suicide. I worked it all out, told no one, and then couldn't make up my mind whether or not to go ahead. For want of a better solution to this problem I gambled on winning two tickets for the premiere of a film. The competition was in the *Evening Standard* and I remember feeling vaguely annoyed when I won the tickets and was stuck with going on living. I have no doubt that I was serious about the suicide at the time but a deal was a deal. I went to the premiere and carried on from there, and it was an outcome I have never regretted.

I'm sure there was another strike by the ITV unions about now. Certainly there was a good deal of unrest around. A large number of young people were coming into the industry, many straight from university. Employed as researchers and assistant producers and thus not requiring an ACTT union ticket, they represented a new departure for the media. Television needs young blood and they should have been welcome, but many were arrogant and did not understand much about the mechanics of programme making, nor did they particularly wish to learn, and the phrase 'sort it out in editing' became far too familiar. It began to look as though a second-hand Porsche and a large and far from mobile phone were all that was required for a successful career in TV.

The production crews bailed them out many times, of course

they did, but it began to cause a certain amount of friction. I remember working with a young director who had just gone freelance from the BBC. Ex-BBC people were usually well trained so I was surprised when our film editor arrived on location one day and asked me for a quiet word. He came with the news that the day before, our young and very pleasant director had failed to shoot enough footage for four scenes to be edited together. I looked at the list of shots we still needed, saw that we had the same actors with us that day, and guessed we could knock them off in about half an hour, but there was one major problem – that of the ever-present producer. Already past retirement age he was desperate to keep working and very much a member of the old school. If I told him of the problem our inexperienced director would not have worked for the company again; the film editor knew that too and that was why he had come to me. I wandered inconspicuously around the set and chatted to each section of the crew, and before long we had a solution. At the end of that day's filming we would start to 'wrap' the unit until the producer and the director had left the set and headed off for home, then with a skeleton crew and two willing actors, we would quickly pick up the missing shots. No one would claim overtime and no one would talk about what had happened. This we did and all was well. It was a generous gesture by the members of three unions, a gesture that I saw repeated in other ways when the circumstances required it, often at a time when we were all being reported in the press as 'greedy' and 'hard liners with extreme left-wing tendencies'. In my opinion the union agreements at that time should have been re-negotiated completely for they were often out of date, large profits and a rather weak middle management had often taken the quickest and easiest way out of a dispute and undoubtedly some of the more radical members had to be contained. But some protection was needed, especially in the areas of safety and crewing for they helped to keep production standards high and provided a period of training for younger people entering the profession.

The low spot of this period of my life was when Barney died. It was obvious that he was getting old but a trip to the vet reassured me that he was in no pain and so we just went on from day to day. Then he stopped eating and a few days later he stopped drinking until finally, one day while I was at work, he went to sleep in his bed and didn't wake up. That morning I had carried him out to the Heath and he stood for a few minutes sniffing the air and wagging his tail. I could swear that he was remembering the wild days of his youth. He was nearly twenty years old and had had a great life, but oh, he left an enormous gap and it was to be a very long time before I could put my key in the lock without waiting for the welcome that invariably came hurtling towards me at the sound. That evening Sally and I buried him in the garden under a tree. Ho, Sally's cat, came into the garden with us and sat in the tree until we had finished, then she disappeared for a while. For many years they had been 'pretend' enemies but could often be found in the garden together, neither admitting that the other was there. I got very drunk on red wine that night. He had been so much a part of my life for so many years, good times and bad. I knew I was going to miss him dreadfully. But all was not quite lost.

Several months later I was walking down to the shops in South End Green and noticed two ladies ahead of me chatting together by the flower stall. One of them held a lead, attached to which was a puppy-sized version of a Barney dog, perfect in every detail as far as I could see, from the little white shirt front and curly fringe to the tilt of his head … and the look of barely contained impatience as he waited for his walk on the Heath. As I reached the place where they were standing the ladies ended their conversation and the puppy, realizing that finally freedom was becoming reality, stood up and stretched; his little tail going round and round in happiness. Then I was convinced that I was looking at a great, great, grandson of Barney's, for the puppy even walked like him too. So in some ways my dog lived on and something of his spirit would continue to chase across the Heath. I was delighted by the thought – but not sure whether I envied or sympathised with the puppy's owner!

I was working at the time on a play set in Brixton, a play that had a predominantly black cast and dealt in some measure with immigration. Before we started filming I had been dispatched to the borough to meet a gentleman who, I was told, could help us considerably with any facilities we needed. Not too sure what I was letting myself in for I set off to find his office one day, armed with a copy of the script and some company money. He was a large man, as were several others who sat in an outer office, but I was treated with great courtesy and my offer to make a contribution to the funding of a local project, such as the building of a children's playground, brought smiles all round and I was assured we would have no problems while filming in the area. And indeed we didn't – film cameras and all our equipment showed no inclination to walk away, and even parking was easy with no hassle from passing traffic wardens. It was a really pleasant few days. It also started me thinking about that trip to the Caribbean previously sacrificed for Brazil.

One of our advisors on the play also worked as a travel agent so I rashly booked a fortnight in Barbados and flew off two days after we had finished filming. The holiday began badly for the flight was delayed by several hours and I arrived in Barbados in the middle of the night. Half asleep I walked round the airport looking for a courtesy bus to the hotel and avoiding a man who kept asking me if I wanted a taxi. Finally, however, I decided to take a taxi even though I was sure it would cost me a fortune, and I approached a driver sitting in his cab by the airport doors; but he sent me back to the man I had been avoiding. He asked where I was going, and a figure was written on a piece of paper. This I was told was the amount I was to pay and not more, and he explained he was employed by the government to protect visitors from having to pay excessive fares. I need not have worried in the first place however, for my taxi driver was totally honest. He was concerned only for my wellbeing and disappointed that my first impression of Barbados was being tainted by my late arrival. At the hotel he woke up the night porter, carried my bags to my room, refused a tip and disappeared.

Next morning the sun was shining and a knock at the door heralded a breakfast tray which included a huge pot of coffee; I sat on the balcony in the sun while a tiny humming bird hovered over the bougainvillaea and I began to think I had landed in paradise. In fact I wasn't far wrong – that morning set a pattern that never changed for the two weeks I was there. I had actually arrived at the start of 'millionaire's fortnight', but although there were a few big yachts around and Mr Winner was probably dining somewhere, the island was far from swarming with tourists and it was rare to hear an American accent. I found a tiny silver sandy beach not far from my apartment and went there most mornings. A coral reef formed a perfect pool of crystal-clear sea, and there was one tree, half dead from some forgotten storm, that gave me enough shade to lie in and dream the hours away. No boats came, there were no mysterious footprints in the sand and the only sounds were the gentle lapping of the ocean swell and an occasional burst of birdsong.

After a few days I hired a Mini Moke and went exploring. Observing the top legal speed limit of thirty miles an hour, I trundled round the island and began to appreciate how unbelievably laid back the Barbadians really were. One morning I drove to the far side of the island, through the old sugar plantations, and down to the beach where I found a tiny bar and ate my customary fish-sandwich lunch. On my way back to my apartment I found two men and a woman sitting at the side of the road; I guessed they were waiting for a bus so I stopped to offer them a lift. They accepted gratefully for the next one was not for two hours, and they piled in, surrounding themselves with various baskets and packages. We set off but after about a journey of only five hundred yards they shouted for me to stop. They pointed to a small cluster of cottages across the road and said that was where they lived. There we parted with good wishes all round and promises of meeting again soon.

It was so easy to meet the local people and become friends then. There was such a kindness there, with everyone wanting to show you a special welcome; and when I asked if they didn't resent the British for their colonisation of the island, they said no, because when they finally left they gave Barbados the traditions of democracy and enough money to set up the schools and the hospital. And indeed every morning you would see groups of schoolchildren, their uniforms freshly laundered, walking hand in hand in tight crocodiles to school, and passing the red pillar boxes with the royal crest that looked so odd standing in the brilliant sunshine.

The days passed slowly and it began to seem that they would drift on to eternity, but inevitably the day of my departure began to loom. On my last evening I sat on the balcony waiting for the green flash at sunset and drinking something long and cold, and an overwhelming sense of loneliness and sadness came over me. Then I wept – for the deaths of my parents and Barney, for the end of my marriage and for the fact that I was alone on this beautiful island. I sobbed my heart out for a long time, and then went inside to begin to pack. It was the end of an era in so many ways, and though I wasn't at all sure what the future would bring, I was determined that there was going to be some laughter in there somewhere.

What it did bring was a chance to go filming in France and Italy. Frazer rang me with this proposition and it all sounded too good to be true, which in a sense it was, for the movies could best be described as 'blue' and there was no way I wanted to be involved in that part of the media. Apart from anything else, it was thought to be run by the 'hard' boys of Soho and the East End, and some of those hard boys were reputed to be very hard indeed. I did agree to meet with the producer/director however, for I was curious to see what they were like. This particular one was a softy and only making the films as a way of getting into the industry and eventually becoming eligible for that elusive ACTT ticket that I, too, was chasing after. He seemed a very nice, well-educated young man, and he assured me that the films would really only consist of striptease with a decent storyline. I was close to broke at the time and there was no other work around. Against my better judgement I agreed and a few days later, at the crack of dawn, a rather odd assortment of people climbed into a fourteen-seat minibus and set off for Dover.

Any lingering doubts about my decision to take part in the project quickly disappeared, together with any thoughts that the girls were being exploited. I think I had rather seen myself as being there to protect them in some way but it soon became clear that they knew exactly what they were doing, regarded themselves as professional artists, and thoroughly enjoyed the work. It soon became clear too that the films were remarkably innocent in a way, and as far as eroticism was concerned, less was definitely more, or perhaps 'tease' was more than 'strip'. In any case they contained images that were hardly eyebrow raising and ones which are now frequently viewed without comment on broadcast TV and in many feature films.

That first day we drove hard through France, arriving near to the French/Italian border late in the evening. A second early start saw us quickly at the border where we eased our way through customs with the help of a bottle of whisky, a carton of cigarettes and by having the girls get out of the minibus to 'stretch their legs' before we continued on our way. They were a very pretty bunch of girls, and great fun to be with. The crew was a professional one and everyone behaved with great decorum. By the time we arrived at the château where we were to stay we had bonded into a film unit and only the remarkable briefness of the girls' mini-skirts gave a rather rakish touch to the project.

My room in the château had once been a private chapel. It was huge with a balconied sleeping area and a walk-in sized fireplace. It opened on to a small courtyard in the centre of which was a neatly stacked pile of canon balls. Every morning as I walked to breakfast the canon balls were spread across the yard, and every evening as I walked back to my room, they were neatly stacked again. It became a running gag on the unit, but no one ever seemed to know who was guilty of knocking them down. As for why, well we all had our theories about that. The other unit joke was that I never got to have a full meal. Some crisis always prevented me from sitting down with the others and by the time I arrived in the dining-room everything had been eaten or cleared away. I began to complain noisily, so one evening I was told that I was to be treated to a 'proper' meal in a trattoria in the nearby village. We were a small group, one that included the writer for he had claimed to speak good Italian back in England and that was one of the reasons we had brought him with us. It was a pretty little restaurant but it was early spring and there were not many diners when we walked in and managed to cause rather a stir. The menus appeared and I opted for fish while the others chose mainly steaks. Our writer boldly ordered in Italian, and though the waiter seemed slightly puzzled by my fish, he eventually nodded and went away. It was pleasant sitting there, drinking the good, local wine and anticipating a delicious meal, and the time passed quickly. The boys' food began to arrive and they waited politely for my fish, but nothing happened. We called the waiter over and he seemed surprised that I wanted to eat at the same time as the others but he went away and came back with a small portable gas ring on a trolley. Ah, we thought, the fish was a separate course and had to be cooked at the table. I told my companions to eat their food and sat back expectantly. The waiter then took a large and beautiful peach from the fruit bowl, covered it with brandy and put it on the heat. The penny dropped. Our fluent Italian speaker had confused 'peche' and 'pesche' – peach and fish – and my longed for dinner was being sautéd before my very eyes. It was a perfect peach, beautifully cooked, but it was late by now and the restaurant near to closing. Quite obviously I wasn't going to eat that night either. I began to laugh and the laughter spread round the table and then the restaurant. Tears streamed down my face and I was still laughing when we left. I was probably close to hysteria but I had the sensation of breaking through a plate-glass window and all the pain and depression of the last months suddenly counted for nothing. I was alive and life was good and there was more to come. Chewing on a piece of bread, I giggled my way up to bed. Tomorrow, I felt, was going to be a memorable day. And it was, for at breakfast we heard that Britain had invaded the Falklands. That glimpse of Utopia had been brief.

Our last night in Italy we decided to take the whole unit out for dinner in nearby Florence, so we all dressed in our finest and drove in the minibus to a car park close to the centre of town.

There we set out on foot for the restaurant but had not gone very far when we began to cause a riot. We had become surrounded by a large crowd of very excited young men, all enraptured by the presence of our actresses; in fact obsessively so. Then we realized why. The girls were wearing their usual tiny mini skirts, but, something we had never known before, they were not wearing any panties. Apparently no one did these days, or so we were told later. The Italians had discovered this fact almost as soon as they had discovered us, and now things were rapidly getting out of hand. Dinner quickly forgotten we fled back to the minibus and drove to one of the small villages we had passed on the way in. Next morning we left early for France.

Originally we had been scheduled to spend a week in Paris, but several late night conversations about the Camargue area in southern France had brought about a change of plan. Both the director and I knew the area well and we loved it, so it was decided to indulge our dreams and shoot the second film in that area. The previous day I had got on the phone and found us an almost empty hotel with enough rooms for the whole unit and the rest we decided to play by ear. By now I was used to driving the fourteen-seat minibus though I had never discovered why it caused so much amusement among the crew. I was a good, experienced driver and I began to get rather irritated by the nudges and winks that always went around when I was in the driving seat. That day I finally exploded and demanded to know what was going on. Then it was explained that, used to driving a sports car, I revved up the engine and double declutched when I changed gear thus giving everyone a bumpy ride. After learning that I drove more casually and we all relaxed.

Again we arrived late at the hotel and this time found the staff on strike. This did little for my temper and I had a fierce row with the director, grabbed the keys to the unit car and drove around the countryside for half the night until I had calmed down. Next morning we woke to find that the strike was still on and breakfasts were not being served. We took over the kitchens and found the coffee, slowly waking up to the fact that we only had a vague storyline with which to start filming, and no locations. At least I spoke some French, so I volunteered to go into the nearby village and see what I could do. The production manager left me at the little bar there and drove away, under orders to return two hours later to collect me. I entered to find it half full of men, all of whom looked at me in total astonishment. In the middle of a profound silence I sat at the bar and ordered a coffee. The silence continued. I took a deep breath and decided to 'go for it'. I introduced myself, mentioned the film unit and offered to stand a free round of drinks. This seemed only to increase the astonishment surrounding my arrival but it still didn't prevent anyone from ordering a 'marc' (brandy) to go with their coffee. Slowly the conversation restarted and we were soon chatting freely. By the time the production manager returned I had found the locations we needed, secured the full co-operation of the village and ended up far from sober. I retired to bed enjoying the satisfaction of a job well done and woke up with an incredible hangover. For the rest of the week we ate cold, raw bacon and hard-boiled eggs for breakfast, made our own coffee and filmed happily in a selection of houses and barns without anyone ever guessing what we were up to. We then drove back to England and I severed my connection with the sex industry for good, though I remained friends with the director for a long time afterwards and watched with pleasure as he moved into more orthodox areas of the business and made a success of it all.

Back in London two jobs stand out in my memory around that time. The first came out of the blue and with a casualness that made me wonder if it was all for real. It seemed that Paul Hogan was in town to make a TV special and did I want to work on it? I said I thought I did and waited for the follow up phone call that never came. What did come was an enquiry as to why I had not appeared at a meeting the day before and when I had explained away that one, I was invited to lunch in a restaurant in Kensington in an hour's time. We went on from there and it was quite the most unconventional contract I was ever to have – or never to have, for in fact there wasn't one. It transpired that a substantial amount of money was owed to Paul from royalties and was held in a bank in London. Alas he was unable to take it out of the country for some reason and so he had come to spend it in London by making a one-off TV special he would then be able to take back to Australia and broadcast there. It was also explained to me that the second priority was to have a fun time spending it all and this we proceeded to do with alacrity. I don't think we ever talked money. We had some lovely lunches and one or two dinners, rehearsed fleetingly and recorded the show successfully. I was then handed a large bundle of sterling, asked if that was enough and then thanked profusely, and that was that. They had paid me way over the union rate and in cash and it had all been a laugh really; I never quite came across another job like that one.

The second job started more conventionally, Blake Edwards the American director was in London filming a Pink Panther movie. His wife, Julie Andrews, was with him and keen to make a TV Easter Special. The line-up sounded fun and included the Muppets and Leo Sayer, while Paddy Stone was to do the choreography. We began rehearsing in the usual chilly Territorial Army hall in South London and all was going well until Paddy dropped a paper cup of scalding black coffee into his lap and had to be dowsed with cold water, removed from his trousers (settling once and for all the ongoing speculation as to whether or not he wore underpants) and dispatched to hospital. (Gentlemen reading that sentence have been known to go white in sympathy.) This caused a hiatus, one that quickly turned into a crisis when Julie Andrews said, very politely, that she was unable to continue rehearsing in the drill hall as the damp air was having a bad effect on her voice. She asked if it would be possible for her husband to find and pay for somewhere warmer. LWT had no objection provided they were not footing the bill and so I packed up the rehearsal room ready for a quick move. I was told that the details of our new rehearsal space would be given to me at the sound recording next day.

They were. I was told to go to the Dorchester Hotel in Park Lane where someone would be expecting me. It was a Sunday morning and parking was no problem, and I wasn't expecting to be there for very long, so I was somewhat taken aback when I was politely escorted to the Dorchester ballroom and asked how much of the carpet I needed taking up. While a small army went about this task I was served delicious coffee from a silver pot and sat trying to adapt to the change in circumstances. It really wasn't very difficult and we spent a very happy week there causing a considerable amount of chaos. I had been provided with a parking space in the forecourt of the hotel and I remember dashing into the foyer to find that every phone at the reception desk was off the hook with a call waiting for me. It nearly went to my head and I certainly decided it really was the only way to rehearse.

By the end of the week Paddy had been returned to us more or less restored to his usual self, Leo Sayer was charming to have around and Adam Faith, then his manager, told us silly stories of life as a pop star. Julie Andrews, meanwhile, remained her very pleasant and professional self and so it was a happy group that moved into the studio one morning and found The Muppets milling around in their specially made Easter bonnets. My favourite Muppet was Animal but of him there was no sign. I talked to the others and eventually found out that Animal had not been brought to the studio because it had been thought that he was too disruptive and sometimes his language was a little too strong for a family show. I swallowed my disappointment and got on with the camera rehearsal. Next morning I felt a tap on my shoulder and heard a gruff voice say: 'Who am dis sexy woman here den?' I turned round to find Animal, complete with a ridiculous Easter bonnet, gazing up at me, his head cocked to one side. His 'owner' had brought him as a surprise for me, and someone, I was told, had sat up late making him his bonnet. I was so thrilled and thanked everyone profusely, though after a day being pursued by an over excited puppet I was not at all sorry to wave goodbye when he finally left the studio.

By now I had got pretty used to living on my own again. I still had lots of friends in Hampstead and there was still that social life attached to working in television, though many of the familiar faces were not around anymore. Some people had gone freelance or moved to other companies and some were beginning to take the early retirement packages offered by the big studios. I don't remember feeling particularly lonely, though I continued to miss Phil and Barney and had no desire to get involved with anyone new. There were opportunities but I skipped hastily away from any form of commitment; there was a genuine dilemma too, for relationships within the 'business' were not well known for their stability and those outside it suffered from a lack of understanding that the job invariably came first. Alone was best, for the moment anyhow.

I became friends with another count, a half Belgian one this time and, again, someone who worked in television. His mother lived in France, in a keeper's cottage on the edge of the Forest of Fontainbleau. We were to spend silly weekends there, rushing to the airport to catch a last-minute plane to Paris, and once taking with us all the food we had just bought for an Easter weekend in Hampstead. On another occasion we drove down to Provence with his cousin and stayed in her house in the middle of a vast field of lavender, far away from any hint of civilization and where we could play music at a volume so loud that it made the windows rattle alarmingly. Phillipe was a happy addition to my life at that time. He was good looking in an aristocratic sort of way, with blonde hair and a stylish way of dressing; something that made it easy for us to get into all the best clubs. He also used his good taste to search through my wardrobe and come up with an outfit for me that was original and stylish too. In some ways he was highly irresponsible, but I enjoyed his company greatly until finally he complicated both our lives to such a degree that we were better off apart.

Financially I must have been going through one of my 'up' periods, for I owned some rather nice clothes. A pair of red-satin overalls still stand out in my memory and one or two good leather jackets that were soon to be stolen by a drug addict who lived upstairs at South Hill Park and who came to apologize for the theft after he got out of prison. He told me that his addiction had left him with no choice and seemed to expect me to understand. I didn't.

I began to visit Catherine in France and once, after an indulgent evening in a fine sea food restaurant, I treated the Ile Saint Louis to an energetic performance of Singing in the Rain, complete with umbrella and in the middle of a thunderstorm that had taken us by surprise. I visited other friends in Italy and Spain and I went to four of Frank Sinatra's concerts, lucky to get tickets and thrilled to be there. However controversial his private life, he sang like no other entertainer I had ever heard and was a great showman. One evening, sitting close to the stage in the Albert Hall, I watched and listened as he played musical games with the orchestra and 'The Lady Is a Tramp'. After several false endings as he tried to fool the band and failed, he lost interest and walked off stage, only to turn round suddenly and go into yet another reprise. The entire band came in one beat behind him and together they swept on to a long, last note. The audience, fully aware of what was going on, rose to its feet cheering. As with Judy Garland, I knew half the members of the band, and Carl's father was there with his cello, so it almost felt like being with family. Work continued via the telephone, some rather run-of-the-mill but all welcome, for the money was needed for such essentials as the Sinatra tickets and the leather jackets.

When the *South Bank Show* rang with a job working on a profile of one of our more avant-garde playwrights I accepted eagerly, remembering the pleasure of the days with Alan and Stephen. But, apart from the freezing cold weather, this job bore little resemblance to the carefree days in Leeds and Morecambe. The programme was to contain excerpts from the writer's plays and these we were to rehearse for several days before the recording. The plays were left-wing and political and the actors were all people who had worked on them before so it should all have been straightforward but it wasn't. The first setback was the rehearsal room. This turned out to be an abandoned sugar warehouse in a then deserted part of docklands. Successfully designed to maintain a cold temperature, it felt like walking into an icebox and seemed even colder than outside where the ground was covered in snow and ice. There was no electricity, we were without toilets, heating or running water and the nearest telephone was on the road outside the dock gates. Convinced that it was in no way suitable as a rehearsal room but willing to admit that it would serve well as a location for the filming, I stared in disbelief when the writer/director announced that we would move in at the start of the rehearsals so that we could all absorb the ambience and 'live' the conditions that were the lot of the characters in the plays. I thought longingly of Sir Larry's alleged comment to Dustin Hoffman: 'Try acting dear boy.' But I said nothing.

Back at LWT I managed to get permission for a simple electrical rig and a space heater. Then I ordered a dozen chairs, a table and an electric kettle and set out for my own little Siberia. The first few days we sat and talked, and froze, and talked. My only comfort was the presence of Kenneth Cranham as a member of the cast. We had worked together before and I knew him to be something of a rebel and good for a laugh. At first he kept my spirits up but when he began sitting opposite me next to the director, pulling faces and rolling his eyes, he had me in agony trying not to laugh. The days dragged on and it really was a struggle in those near zero conditions. I kept inventing excuses to go back to LWT and one day I stomped through the artists' coffee bar in moon boots and ski gear and someone asked me what on earth I was working on. I heard myself reply: 'I'm wanking in a warehouse in Wapping.' And the whole coffee bar fell about laughing. The next time I went back to the building the phrase had become immortalised in the annals of LWT.

By now we were only a few days away from Christmas and at last we started proper rehearsals. I ordered some hand props, among them some mock-up handguns and one fake Colt.45. I hate guns of any kind and even these rough copies could be a nuisance to have around, especially with the holiday coming up; but the director was adamant so I arranged for them to be delivered asap. They arrived late on Christmas Eve, and were nicely packed in a box when I took them off the props van. Then Paul handed me a separate package. 'Be careful with that, Annie,' he said, 'you've got a real shooter there.' And then he was gone. I thought he was joking but when I opened the package there was a full working gun inside. I guessed it had been adapted to fire blanks only but even so it should not have left Bapty's (the suppliers) without a firearms expert accompanying it. I stashed the props out of sight and dashed off to the telephone. Nobody was answering the phones at LWT and the switchboard told me that the building was virtually empty. I phoned the firearms firm but there was no reply there either, so I set off back and then remembered the little Docklands Police Station tucked away near the river. They would have a solution to my quandary I was sure, but they, also, had locked up and gone home. Back at the warehouse I found everyone had already jumped ship there too, so much for the 'we are all one team' spirit that we had spent hours talking about. With no other options I hid the guns next to the spare wheel in the boot of my car, locked up and drove fearfully home. I was breaking the law big time and I just hoped I would get away with it.

The day after Boxing Day was a Saturday and still no one was working at LWT except us rehearsing in our Siberia but I saw with relief that the Docklands Police Station had reopened too. I parked outside the warehouse, put the Colt .45 into my pocket and strolled casually across to 'give myself up'. There were three police officers inside drinking coffee and chatting. I walked up to the counter, put both hands in full view on top of it and smiled cheerfully.

'I'm from the film company across the dock and I had some fake guns delivered for rehearsals, only one of them is a real gun, and I have it here in my pocket.' I said calmly.

The three policemen sprang to their feet.

'Can you put it slowly on the counter?' they asked as though talking to a very young child.

I did, stood back and told them the whole story. They were, of course, extremely helpful and confirmed my suspicion that the handgun had been adapted for blanks only but was very dangerous, they then offered to lock it up in their safe until Tuesday when it could go back to Bapty's. Finally they christened me Annie Oakley.

On Monday morning all hell broke loose at LWT and Bapty's. Interpol was alerted, people lost their jobs and the gun's details were faxed off in a general alert ... but no one contacted me. I froze innocently in rehearsals as usual, giving myself a pat on the back for the sensible way in which I thought I had handled the situation. It was only on Tuesday when I phoned to try and get the gun back to the suppliers that I became aware of all the fuss. The Docklands Police were separate from the main body of the Force and they, too, had been unaware of the panic. The gun was quickly collected and I got a telling off for taking delivery of it in the first place, something I thought very unfair in the circumstances.

Ken Cranham took me to the Thirties Exhibition at the Hayward Gallery as compensation and we finally filmed the programme inserts successfully. Meanwhile I discovered that my enthusiasm for modern, alternative drama had suffered something of a setback and I swore to avoid it in the future. It was to be some time before I was provided with a chance to do so, but when the phone finally rang with an offer of something I felt was out of the same stable I found that my resolution had not weakened and I turned it down.

But it simply wouldn't go away. With the declared aim of winning a BAFTA award, LWT had commissioned a series of plays by the highly successful playwright Dennis Potter. The series came with Kenith Trodd as its producer and for the last few weeks the building had been buzzing with the stories of mild anarchy that were filtering back from the film unit. Certainly Mr Trodd had made a noticeable entrance at the beginning of the series when he arrived to find that he had not been allocated a place in the underground car park that was reserved mainly for management and rarely full. He had quickly brought the matter to the attention of Stella Ashley, the person in charge of directors and producers, by parking his car so that it blocked the entrance to the car park, locking it and disappearing into the wilds of Waterloo. When 'the suits' began to arrive somewhat later there was mayhem until Mr Trodd returned mid-afternoon and was given his parking space. Stella told me this story herself, a half-smile playing around her lips, for she had been involved with the more creative characters of TV for many years and had a soft spot for most of the rebels.

However, the play they wanted me for was not by Dennis Potter. It was one that had been included with the others and was very much a part of the whole deal. In fact there was no actual script then, just a few pages of rather random dialogue by writer Jim Allen and classed as 'work in progress', and it was to be directed by Roland Joffé, who was described to me as a young, controversial director, someone already making a name in the business having been trained at Granada TV. Everything I had learned about this production screamed 'avoid' at me. So I did.

I had just finished a long series and it was easy to plead that I was pretty much exhausted and really needed a break. I was told that it would be shot on film somewhere in the north of England and so I also confided to Stella that I was not happy about returning to an area that was close to my childhood and about which I had mixed feelings still, after the death of my father. That I thought was that. But it wasn't.

Stella continued to try to persuade me to accept the contract and I continued to dodge my way out of the situation. In the end she almost begged me to allow her to give Mr Joffé my phone number so that we could resolve the matter ourselves, once and for all. I gave in and one evening on the jot of the appointed hour, the phone rang in my flat. I had decided that the easiest way to disqualify myself from the situation was to present myself as a rather dizzy, pretentious, spoilt brat, so I embarked on my performance with enthusiasm and was unprepared to be taken as a serious contender for the job. A phone call I had expected to take five minutes went on for an hour and a half and only ended when Roland apologised for having to end it as he was late for a dinner engagement – and he asked to be allowed to ring back the following evening. Somewhat thrown by the way things had gone I determined to be even more outrageous and agreed. Next day, when the phone still hadn't rung thirty minutes after the appointed hour, I congratulated myself on a final victory and let down my guard. It was then that the call came, with Roland again apologising, this time for being late. I tried to keep up my act but I sounded so preposterous to my own ears that I started giggling. 'I thought so,' said Roly, 'but I just wasn't sure. So you'll do the show then? I really want you to and I think you'll enjoy it.' I knew I was beaten and, after squeezing a few days off, I capitulated and braced myself for a bumpy ride.

The first time I met Roly in person I was confronted by someone who seemed perfectly normal, extremely polite and organised – and was the owner of an amazing pair of hazel eyes. Within a few days he had won me over completely and it all became rather exciting to be involved in something to which everyone concerned seemed to be so committed. We were obviously going to be working very hard but that was nothing new and I began to be glad that I had ended up as part of the production team after all.

As I worked in our office at the studios more stories continued to filter back to LWT from the crews who had been working on the Dennis Potter plays and these had woken up and upset a company that, in my opinion, had become far too complacent. Many of the people in positions of responsibility no longer seemed overly committed to good, innovative programme-making and were perhaps rather too concerned about protecting their own survival. Now it seemed as though things were changing for the better. Slowly we continued the usual process of putting the production together and Roly went into rehearsal with two of the leading characters and began to work on a series of improvised scenes that were to be built on as the play developed. I was not required in rehearsal and was ordered to take a few days off and rest as I would be very busy very soon.

Then things began to go wrong. It became very difficult to get a decision from anyone in a position of authority at LWT and Roly put the rehearsals on hold and moved back into the office. Ken Trodd joined us and together we tried to move things along. By now I felt I knew Roly quite well, we were both Scorpios and we seemed to have an easy rapport and think alike on many aspects of the job. Ken Trodd, too, was easy to work with, despite a reputation for being difficult. True, there was that sense of danger about the pair of them and neither suffered fools gladly, but that was something else I was used to and very much a part of the job. We struggled on with setting up the film shoot. A location had been chosen near to the town of Huddersfield and one of the LWT designers was up there on a recce. One Friday I was sent to join Roly and the PA and the small team now working from there too and beginning to sort out all the major locations. Roly and the PA were returning to London for the weekend and Roly wanted me to stay behind to continue liaising with the local people. He left me the keys to the unit car 'in case you need to get away for a bit' and we arranged to meet up again on Sunday.

In the middle of the next week we were all called back to London and the start of filming was put on hold. I was not present at the initial meeting between LWT and Ken Trodd but no one seemed very clear as to what was going on; there were rumours of course and I began to think about these rather carefully. The Dennis Potter plays had been commissioned because LWT was very keen to win a BAFTA award. They had been forced to take *Commune* (our play) as part of the deal and had never really wanted it. It was to be written by Jim Allen, a known writer committed to left-wing causes, and it was to be directed by an innovative director who did not work from a formal script. The alarm bells must have been ringing before we had shot a scene. But perhaps also relevant was the fact that the Dennis Potter plays were now shot and edited and had gone way over budget; was someone wondering why not recoup that overspend by cancelling a production no one had ever really wanted or felt they needed in the first place? I believed there were people at LWT who did want *Commune* cancelled but for them to cancel it would be to break the contract that had given them the Dennis Potter plays and probably they were very nervous about the reaction of its producer and director. Were they perhaps hoping that in face of so many obstacles these two would walk out and break their contracts, thus saving LWT the rest of the budget and placing the blame very firmly in their court? I went in search of a few favours, but no one was talking. From the head of one department I got a few kind words and two bottles of wine from his personal store, not much help but accepted graciously; then I went to a middle management friend and told him my suspicions, fully expecting to be laughed out of his office. He stopped me before I had gone very far.

'Anne,' he said, 'I can't say anything – I work for the company.'

I just looked at him.

'All right,' he went on, 'tell me exactly what you think and I'll tell you how wrong you are.'

I told him how things seemed to me and when I had finished there was a long pause.

'Well?' I asked.

The pause continued until finally he looked at his watch. 'I'll have to go or I will miss my train,' he said, and left the office.

I was stunned, until that moment I had not really believed my own suspicions. I regarded LWT as 'my' company and felt enormous loyalty to it. It had been very kind to me in the past and had always treated me with respect and consideration. I couldn't take in the fact that it was not playing fair, and that it was prepared to behave in what I considered to be a shabby and dishonest way, but it seemed it was, for I could think of no other explanation to my friend's silence. I walked slowly back to the production office and told my sad story. At first neither Ken nor Roly felt that I was right, but after a while we decided we had nothing to lose by pushing ahead with the pre-planning, contracting artists and generally spending as much money as possible so that we passed a halfway point and it became more productive to finish the film than to stop it and end up with nothing. It didn't work, but perhaps it did call the management's bluff for they quickly moved to cancel the production and pay off the contracts. Roly said he would donate his fee to Shelter. I asked to be released from my contract. Stella tried to persuade me to stay on and promised that I would not be attached to any other project, but that rotten old 'integrity' got in the way and I persuaded her to let me go. Eventually *Commune* went to the BBC where, with a few changes, it became *United Kingdom* and, with the same writer, producer and director, was nominated for a 1981 BAFTA award. Ironically the Dennis Potter plays were not.

Before the awards were publicised I was invited to the preview at the BAFTA screening cinema, and found it to be an outstanding piece of work and only wished I could have been a part of it all.

I stayed in touch with Roly for a while and on his urging applied yet again for my ACTT freelance first assistant director's ticket. It was my third attempt and when the reply envelope popped through my letterbox, I took it back to bed to read the polite rejection I was sure it contained. Only it didn't. I had been accepted at last. True it had on it a two-year restriction to non-broadcast television but that seemed a minor handicap, for freelance tickets were almost impossible to obtain and two years would pass very quickly. I was on my way – though quite where I was going I was not too sure. There was plenty of non-broadcast work around at that time and the money was good, so I set about adapting to my new title and discovered that I was encouraged to use all my acquired experience and even direct from time to time.

Chapter Eighteen

It didn't seem very long before the end of my two-year restriction was in sight. I hadn't worked in broadcast TV for the majority of that time but most of my old contacts there were fully aware of my ACTT ticket, so I was rather surprised when an old mate from ATV surfaced via the telephone (if one can do that) and offered me a job working as a stage manager on a puppet show. I was less than enchanted with the idea, explained my position and forgot about the whole thing. But once again, it was a job offer that simply would not go away. Finally I sat down and examined the logic of the situation. The contract would take me up to the expiry of my two-year restriction, the money was good, and what could be difficult about a puppet show? I decided to make life easy for myself for once and signed the contract.

It was 1985, I was to work on the second series of the show and I knew nothing about *Spitting Image* when I arrived in Docklands for my first day at work. I had not owned a television set for quite a long time and so I knew nothing either about the pedigrees of the people working on it, and, although a director friend had seen the first series and described the puppets as brilliant and the show as patchy but very funny in parts, I really had no hint of the phenomenon the programme was to become. Ignorance was indeed bliss, for of all the TV projects in which I have been involved the 'puppet years' were the most demanding and the ones that were to have the greatest impact on my life.

The private dream of Peter Fluck and Roger Law had, against all the odds, turned itself into something that was, and still is, unique in television history. As the television series progressed it became apparent that a diverse group of very clever people had come together at the right moment and filled a gap in the programme schedules that no one had realised existed. But it didn't happen without a struggle and a phenomenal amount of hard work, and there were many days when it all seemed like a form of madness.

The puppet heads are, at worst, very clever, and at best, simply brilliant, but the fact remained that when they were handed over to the puppeteers and the production team we were dealing with something that was still essentially a lump of foam rubber. The initial ten-second impact was terrific but there had to be more to hold the attention of the viewers and make a satirical point.

The writers were, of course, the starting point but more was still needed. Somehow we had to create a puppet person with a character and life of its own. And it happened. The puppets really did come alive and became so successful that they almost literally took over. But that first day at work I had no intuition about any of that.

The offices were pretty deserted when I arrived and I spent the morning reading a copy of the *Guardian* that I had had the foresight to bring with me. I had asked for a script but no one seemed to know anything about that, and when I approached a rather large man with a beard he just shrugged and said I should ask John Lloyd. I wasn't too sure who John Lloyd was exactly but it seemed he might be in later that afternoon. At lunchtime I went for a walk round the desert that was still Docklands. It was all rather depressing, even though the sun was shining, so I returned to the office regretting the uncharacteristic streak of common sense that had brought me here. But during my absence the office had transformed itself into a hive of bustling activity. The person known as John Lloyd had arrived and seemed to be directly responsible; the large man with the bushy beard turned out to be Roger Law; and a tall thin person with twinkling eyes identified himself as Peter Fluck. These last two people had been around all the time, upstairs in the workshop, the heart and soul of *Spitting Image* and a place of which I had been totally unaware all morning. John Lloyd stopped by my desk to ask if I was all right, but when I replied that a script would greatly improve my wellbeing he looked alarmed and quickly disappeared. Eventually a few pages of script found their way to me, but with them came a warning that we probably wouldn't be recording them until they had been rewritten, so I marked them up, piled them on a corner of my desk and sat trying to look busy. At six o'clock I looked around the office still populated with a wide range of dust-covered, overall-clad puppet makers. I put on my full-length cream leather coat that matched my cream leather boots and thought ruefully that someone was going to have to change. Instinctively I knew it would have to be me.

By the end of that first week we were almost up and running, I don't think it was ever possible to say that all was under control but there was a sort of order amid chaos and if we survived it was totally down the brilliance, expertise and enthusiasm of every member of the team. We were a disparate group of people but there seemed to be comparatively few egos, (not strictly true but I thought it so at the time), though I did avoid Roger as much as possible. I was used to people shouting but Roger roared, and if the roaring took place anywhere near to me, my brain simply froze and I became a stuttering mass of incompetence. Peter was the mediator, the soft-spoken man of reason – and interpreter for Roger's more complex demands. I thought him a lovely man and was delighted when I found out that he was to come to Birmingham with us to record the show, leaving Roger in London to handle any crises that affected the workshop.

Once the shows began being transmitted it became a crippling schedule, one that involved working on three episodes at once. We recorded and transmitted from Birmingham and did most of the setting up from the Dockland's office. I quickly became big mates with the Art Director, for only by working closely together could we just about contain the demands made by the last-minute scripts and meetings that often took place on the telephone and involved script changes that rarely made it on to paper. Happily we got on well and between us we ran an unorthodox system by production standards but one that really worked, i.e. we played it by ear and didn't panic.

Ken always provided realistic sets for the puppets and I began to give them personal props, which, hopefully, added to the character. These were many and varied and there was a certain misplaced logic to them and, although some of the props were carefully thought out, many arrived randomly on to the set and became permanent by chance. For instance Melvyn Bragg's 'snifter' was a baby's bottle found in the props stores in a desperate search while the studio held up the recording of the initial sketch. It became a constant, so much a part of the puppet that, years later, when I travelled in the lift with Mr Bragg at LWT, I found myself staring at the breast pocket of his jacket trying to work out why it looked so odd. When I suddenly realized I had to get out of the lift before I started to giggle. I also (and for no good reason) thoughtfully provided David Attenborough with a battery-operated miniature fan to keep him cool when he was reporting from the jungle, and a small hot water-bottle when he was in a cold climate. There were to be many more examples of my generosity.

One of the early sketches in the first series I worked on had Colonel Ghadaffi playing Scrabble with his aides. At that time the newspapers seemed to spell his name a different way every time they wrote about him, so without saying anything to anybody I took the board and glued on to it all the different variations, gave the aides the difficult letters to get rid of and the

Colonel all the easy ones. Then I waited to see if anyone would notice. John Lloyd did and a few days later we got one letter from a viewer saying he had spotted it too. Encouraged, I began to think up more. Then we heard that many members of our audience had started recording the show as they watched it so that later they could play it back and freeze frame from time to time to see if they could find more throw away jokes. My props lists got longer and Ken joined in, bringing me back anything he thought appropriate (or, more accurately, inappropriate) when he went round the hire companies.

Our mail increased in volume, most of it protesting over our portrayal of the Royal Family. But we only ever really regarded them as a dysfunctional middle-class family rather out of touch with the modern world and a little while later they were to generate far bigger headlines than their puppets ever did. The biggest fuss was over whether or not we were going to have a puppet of the Queen Mother. For a long time this was never on the cards but eventually, when the fuss would not go away, it was decided that perhaps we should. One was made under conditions of great secrecy and a little sketch was written for her but the final decision about whether to use her on the show or not was left to the last minute. I don't think she came up to Birmingham on the van with the other puppets but was probably escorted personally by Roger or Peter. But the press somehow received a tip-off that we had made one and the phones in the Birmingham office rang off the hook and one or two people who answered them reported being offered money if they would only confirm her existence. On the Sunday morning when we always recorded what we named 'the topicals' for that evening's show, no one was still sure what was happening, and when the show went out it began to look to anyone watching as though she would not appear. Then, after the credits had rolled, the camera cut to a caption bearing a quote in the style of one issued recently by the defence in the Ponting secrets case. It denied all knowledge of something and ended in 'and I was on holiday at the time.' Ours denied the existence of the Queen Mother puppet, and at that point she appeared on screen and said, 'Oh what a pity, and I was so looking forward to appearing.' Then the Central logo came up fast and it was all over. Throughout the world wars were being fought, people were dying of drought and there were countless other horrors going on but for several days prior to the show nearly every newspaper had carried headlines about the Queen Mother's puppet appearing on *Spitting Image*. We found it bizarre. On the Monday morning after the show many of the newspapers missed the point completely; some felt that we had been censored by the big bosses at Central, others thought we had lost our nerve, only a few grudgingly conceded that we had had the last laugh. After that the fuss quickly died down and she appeared regularly and we always thought of her with great affection too.

As prime minister, Margaret Thatcher was one of our main targets but when Mark, her son, was lost in the desert we never used her puppet until after he was found safe and well – then we went for them both. Cecil Parkinson was another target for quite a while. We were not really bothered by the news that he was having an affair and had apparently fathered a child with his mistress, nor did we mind that, even so, he was to stay in office (as someone said at the time 'if they fired every politician who was having an extra-marital affair we'd be left with no parliament'); but we minded very much that he denied the whole affair and claimed the child was not his, only to admit later that he had not been totally honest about it all. So his puppet began to stir its tea with a vibrator and was often found with frilly pairs of panties hanging from its jacket pocket.

As the series grew in popularity so we preserved the idea of the puppet 'family' and stretched the boundaries of the puppet world. Everyone remained involved, the writers, the workshop, the puppeteers, the production team; ideas came from everywhere and were backed by the goodwill to make them work. When I joined I had been told that the Central Television Board did not censor the sketches but that the Spitting Image Company censored itself and, naturally, we were subject to the laws of the land and every script was read and passed by the company lawyers before we started to work it in to the show. As I said before, it became the most demanding show I had ever worked on, but it was also the most fun and I loved every minute of it.

By the start of the third series everyone felt that in *Spitting Image* we had created something very special indeed. We were told that pubs were emptying just before we went on air on a Sunday evening and that people were setting the alarms on their wristwatches so as not to miss the start of the programme. We were also now getting an even larger amount of mail, some of it written in pencil on small sheets of lined notepaper and generally unsigned. Quite often the writer accused us of being traitors and expressed a strong desire to see us lynched or incarcerated in the Tower of London. We felt we must be getting something right!

One morning when the series was not in production I walked down to my local newsagents to get the Sunday papers wearing a *Spitting Image* sweatshirt with my jeans. I was actually mobbed by people demanding autographs and asking for stories about the puppets. Back in production it was almost impossible to work in the studio, for every time we turned round we bumped into a hand-held camera filming a documentary about the making of the programme and behind that camera there was usually a highly frustrated sound recordist complaining about the language used by the people he was recording when they turned round and tripped over him. But somehow the series got made, and though not infrequently the second half was still being sent down the line whilst the first half was being transmitted, it never missed its broadcast slot.

Looking back now that word 'unique' still seems to apply, and when it came off the air for the last time it left an enormous gap in the lives of a lot of the people who had been involved; but it also left behind a trail of troubled relationships, broken friendships and some people close to collapse, and their was an element of relief, certainly for me, for it had sometimes seemed that working with the puppets had swamped any possibility of a private life. Nevertheless by the time my days with Central TV ended the puppets had brought some profound changes in that private life. I had been taken on as a producer with the Spitting Image Company, and bought my flat in Hampstead. While no one begrudged me my flat, my appointment as a producer caused widespread consternation, especially in the Birmingham studios where my old 'mates' on the team refused to work with me on our Election Special. I was told that a great many people had believed themselves to be in the running for the job that had been given to me. It didn't help that I had believed myself to be working as an assistant producer with John Lloyd, only to be informed by Roger on my first day that John was having some time off and I was producing an advert for the cinema that was to be shot that same week, and what did I require from the workshop? Nor did my popularity improve when I was sent to Los Angeles with the final tape of a show that was supposed to produce an offer for an American series. Sadly the American series was not optioned, and with no more British shows in the offing, the company diversified and the television part of it declined for the moment. When I went to work as live producer on Network 7 I thought I had left the puppets behind for ever, but once again I wasn't quite right about that.

Network 7 was one of Janet Street-Porter's 'youf' programmes, so I found myself surrounded by young producers with wild ideas, some were good and highly innovative but there were others that were entirely unrealistic, if not dangerous, to stage. One involved a metal arrow being fired from a high tension bow into a live television set. The main attraction of this stunt seemed to be that it had never been done before. I thought it highly dangerous and contacted several technicians for a second opinion but no one would commit themselves. On the day of the programme, as Live Producer, I was asked to make a decision about its inclusion and, convinced I was right, I finally I said no. The very young assistant producer, whose idea it had been, begged me in floods of tears to allow the stunt to go ahead as all her family and friends would be watching, but after we came off air, every member of the crew came up to me and said thank you and backed me to the hilt. Further research revealed how very dangerous it would have been for all of us in the studio.

I had made myself pretty unpopular by making that decision but I had the full backing of LWT. Not very long before that incident someone had been killed during a stunt on a BBC programme and it had, rightly, received a lot of condemnation in the press. Stunts always contain an element of risk but usually are fine if properly staged by fully qualified professionals working in controlled conditions; the one on *Network 7* did not begin to come within that category.

When *Network 7* ended I went back to Greece and for several months made that my base, while continuing to return to London to work from time to time. I have forgotten the job sequence of this period but I did work on three Telethons that were broadcast live and very exciting to be involved in. On the last one I was one of three assistant directors and at the opening of the show I had to cue Michael Aspel from the top of a high, off-stage staircase. As I stood there my hands were shaking and I was terrified, then suddenly and thankfully, the adrenalin hit and I went off on a high that was to last until we came off air the next day. In the final moments of the show I sat with my shoes off watching the band as it played us out. We were a few minutes early and Laurie Holloway, the musical director, had to reprise the final chorus of the closing number several times. I caught his eye and we both grinned happily, it had all gone 'awfully well' we thought.

There are other snapshot-like memories too, like standing on the studio floor in rehearsals and hearing a voice from someone beside me say: 'Hello, I think you may be expecting me, my name is Nigel Kennedy. Will you please hold my violin while I go and park my car? Oh, don't drop it, it's a Strad.' And so another Stradivarius came briefly into my life. Later we listened in delight as he rehearsed with the studio orchestra – another person who made music rather than simply playing it. Then Gloria Gaynor and the Tabernacle Choir walked casually on set and suddenly produced a volume of perfect harmony that shook the rafters and stopped the sound technicians in their tracks; and I was there when a well-loved Jazz singer was brought in to rehearse in a wheelchair, for she had had a stroke and was no longer able to walk. But she so wanted to sing in the Telethon and give something back to the business that she loved that we had arranged for her to be lifted on to a bar stool during a commercial break so that she could perform from there. But on the night, in the middle of her number, she suddenly got off the stool and began to walk. Her doctor, who had accompanied her to the studio, seemed unsurprised, but to us standing near by, it was like watching something close to a miracle.

Alas there was tragedy too. During a series of *London's Burning*, our Fire Brigade advisor was called away to a fire, a bad one. It was the one at King's Cross station and although it filled the news media for several days it was really only when Nobby (Clarke) came back to us that the full horror of it smashed into our consciousness. There had been a picture of him in a newspaper, a man exhausted, drained of emotion and so very alone. But that was only a part of it for he told us that once the fire was finally out he went down into the Underground to check that it was safe for the reporters to take their pictures. He kicked at a bundle of burnt-out rubbish to make sure that it was no longer smouldering and belatedly realised that it was the body of a baby. He said that there were no words to describe how he felt then, but it was as though something had changed forever.

By now, back on the little island of Poros and at the start of a summer I decided to stay for several months and got myself a little job working in one of the small tourist offices there. The work was not difficult and there was plenty of free time to enjoy the advantages of a life in the sun – in some ways it seemed like all the holidays I had never taken were being rolled into one. I began to feel really settled and relaxed ... and then a friend sent me an advert from one of the trade papers for TV personnel with 'knowledge of Greece'. It said nothing about the project itself and I was less than enthusiastic for I assumed that it would involve working back in London, still I sent off my CV. Three days later I received a phone call inviting me to Athens for an interview.

In Athens I found the beginnings of a new TV broadcasting company called Skaï. It had nothing to do with the other Sky and was a completely Greek venture but its Greek owner had been at Oxford University where he had become a fan of the *Spitting Image* programmes. When setting up his new company he had decided that the puppets were something he wanted to introduce in Greece and he had already ordered six puppets of Greek politicians from Roger Law at the Limehouse workshop. I also found a small group of British TV people who had been working there for several weeks and who cheerfully informed me that I was too late as no more foreigners were being taken on. Nevertheless I went to see Mr Spanolios, the man seemingly in charge of everything, and after a short but delightful chat he looked at me and said, 'So, can you start tomorrow?' I eventually signed a nine-month contract as an advisor and moved to Athens at the end of July – just as everyone else went on holiday!

A new studio and office block were being built in Faliro and we were temporarily housed in a pretty but very old building off Syntagma Square. The rooms were small and office space was at a premium so I found myself sitting in the conference room of a luxury hotel close by, where the air-conditioning was so fierce I had to wear a thick sweater as I sat there for most of August in solitary confinement. From time to time someone would pop in for a coffee, but mostly I occupied myself by reading up on recent Greek history, while trying to unravel the political complexities prevailing in Greece at that time. I knew only that a General Election was looming.

At the beginning of September people began to reappear. I met a brilliant young impressionist (Costas Mitzicostas) and that was one major consideration happily solved. I requested studio space, puppeteers, writers, – and a director maybe? The director arrived (he was also an excellent editor) and was to become a great friend and ally; writers drifted into the conference room, a producer ... then things went quiet again. I had from the start assumed that Skaï wanted the full *Spitting Image*; only months later did I discover that that had never been the intention. The programme was to have been built around Mitzicostas with the six puppets making brief comments direct to camera. Our lives could have been so easy.

There must have been many meetings of which I was unaware for suddenly everything began to move at an alarming rate. An empty warehouse was found and people began knocking large holes in walls and floors. Three security guards, an out of work bouzouki player and someone's cousin arrived in my conference room and announced they were to be the new puppeteers; there was one other young man but he declared himself unhappy with the job-description and quickly left. Of the five survivors not one had been anywhere close to a puppet before and knew nothing of *Spitting Image*. I couldn't help feeling that Roger would have been delighted with that.

I asked for, and eventually got, a puppeteer from England to train them; they worked hard while still continuing their various 'day' jobs and I was surprised how quickly they adapted to the new skills we demanded of them. One day we all moved down to our new home in Faliro and I swapped my luxury conference room for an empty warehouse, copious dust and the constant sounds of demolition. Sets and props started to appear. I flew to England and returned with some of the puppets and a few spare heads. (Weeks later I was to realise that one of them was an old version of Jeremy Paxman. We were to use him often, mainly as our philosophising waiter, and someone must have seen him in our nightly transmissions for word got back to Mr Paxman, who was not amused. He rather went down in my estimation after that). A member of our team returned too, after spending time with the *Spitting Image* workshop learning to repair and repaint the heads. By this time we had a rudimentary studio with a basic set and a few props. People were heard talking about going on air and the puppets were to be a part of the opening programme. By chance I heard that a date had been fixed – it was two days away. I asked Steve, one of the English technicians, if it was possible and he confirmed that it was, but only to a small area of Athens. Even so I was pretty sure that our boss would do it and I put the pressure on our little team. Somehow we began to record some simple sketches, and we sent them off to be edited and dubbed. In the event Skaï went on air twenty-four hours late and without a licence. The puppet slot was dreadful, but we had done it and it was something to build on. Suddenly it was all very exciting.

At the time we went on air Greece had a right-wing government, one that seemed decidedly opposed to giving us that licence, so the channel was taken off air or blocked more times than I care to remember. But situated in our warehouse studio we were removed from all the political battles and free to concentrate on recording the ten minutes of edited material required for our five-nights-a-week slot. Ten minutes a day was something we had not always achieved in England where we had been backed by all of Central Television's back-up facilities and crews. In Athens we had a tiny crew consisting mostly of people who were somebody's relative and had never set foot in a TV studio before. For a time I found myself becoming more of a Roger Law than a Peter Fluck and quickly learned enough Greek to shout 'It matters – not it doesn't matter', 'It can be done – not it can't' and 'We haven't got time for slowly, slowly, I need it now!' We had to work long hours and often six or seven days a week but somehow we did it. We were also becoming better and faster. It was all coming together and one of the most rewarding things was seeing the puppeteers taking great pride in their work and gaining self-confidence for themselves as a result. And we really did begin to match the standards of the British programmes.

The title on my contract was still 'Advisor' but as the weeks passed more and more pressure was put on me to direct some of the sketches. I resisted firmly. Directing satire in England in English would have been challenging enough, directing satire in Greek, when I barely spoke the language and was only just beginning to understand the country, was simply out of the question. Mitzicostas's voices were superb but I had no real knowledge of what he was saying beyond a rough translation given to me by one of the puppeteers who had lived in Australia.

Then one morning Nikos, the director, didn't arrive at the studio and the pressure on me to take over was palpable. I held out until midday, by which time the situation was becoming desperate. Reluctantly I agreed to direct the one-puppet-to-camera bits and we began to work. By six o'clock in the evening we had recorded all the available material, including the multi-puppet sketches, and the tape was sent off to editing. About an hour later Nikos strolled into the office looking remarkably fresh and energetic.

'It's all fine,' he said. 'I've just seen the tape.'

I glared at him. 'Did you disappear deliberately so that I would have to direct?' I demanded. He grinned.

'Yes,' he admitted.

Many weeks later I asked him why.

'I thought you needed something for yourself,' he replied.

'But what if I had let you down?'

'I didn't think you would.'

I stopped wanting revenge.

So we developed a new regime. Nikos directed Mitzicostas, the musical numbers and did most of the editing while I continued with the sketches. A second team of puppeteers was trained and another lighting cameraman employed. I simply worked a double shift until, what seemed like many weeks later, another director joined us too. The madness of 'Spit' was back, but not like anything I'd experienced before. Nevertheless, the programme got made, though, as with its counterpart in England, the edited and dubbed tape often arrived at the studio for transmission seconds before it went on air. Technically we began to improve daily. I began to take the puppets outside and that added another dimension to the show. The light in Greece is so fantastic that we needed no electrician and we took no back-up team with us either. We just went, found somewhere appropriate and pointed the camera. It was all very challenging but strangely liberating and I loved it. By the day of the Election we had shot some memorable footage.

That Election evening the owner of Skai threw a huge party at the Grande Bretagne Hotel in Syntagma Square. It was a great evening, not least because we knew that PASOK, the left-wing party, was going to win and that meant that our transmission problems were over. A licence to broadcast was to be a reality at last. As I walked through the hotel reception that evening I was confronted by a video bank of screens with everyone showing something that I had directed, and it all looked just like *Spitting Image* should. I stopped in astonishment and remember thinking, 'Oh my goodness, we've done it!' I must admit I felt pretty good about that.

Many weeks later, back on Poros after nearly a year away, I slept and ate my way through days that stretched into weeks. Then, slowly I began to look at the world around me. What, I wondered, was I going to do next? I spent time with friends, travelled around Greece, and visited Athens, but something was not right and I missed that sense of purpose and commitment that I had always had in the past. So what to do about it? Finally one day, complying, but metaphorically kicking and screaming against the idea of a friend back in London, I picked up a pen and began to write. And that, I quickly realised, was going to keep me busy for quite a long time.

Postscript

From the time I got married I had stopped being so curious about the facts surrounding my adoption. It was almost as though my married status had given me a completely new identity, one that required no background details. I came across my adoption papers from time to time, usually when I was looking for something else and when I was working on *London's Burning* I frequently drove past the end of the street where I knew I had been born. I promised myself that I would make a detour down there one day, but that day never came. My move to Greece meant that I thought about it even less, it was almost as though I had given up on the situation.

Then one day I collected my mail from a friend's office in Poros town and opened a letter from someone who claimed to be my half brother. I went very white and the world swam out of focus. A large brandy was pushed into my hand and for a while I sat very still, hardly able to breathe. Reality hit hard that morning – so much, I thought, for 'giving up' on the whole situation.

It turned out that the letter really was from a half brother of mine. In fact there had been three of them but one had died as a young child. Slowly now I began to fill in those missing five months of my life, or at least partly fill them in. All four of us had the same biological mother – the woman named Violet I knew of from my adoption papers – but only two of us had the same father. Most of the information came from Violet herself in a letter written to John, her youngest son, not long before she died, but it was quite a while before John sent me a copy of this letter and so I started to put things together in dribs and drabs.

Violet had been married and had two children, both boys, but the younger one, Andrew, had died very young and the marriage had drifted into trouble and she claimed her husband was violent and had an affair. In the end Violet left and went to London and then to work in Harrogate, where she became involved with someone she doesn't name. Meanwhile her eldest son was being brought up by his grandmother and grew up believing his mother was dead. According to Violet the situation in Harrogate began to 'get out of hand', and she left and went back down to a job in London but the man followed her down and she got pregnant with me and tried initially to get an abortion but couldn't afford one. She ended up living off her savings until she may have gone into hospital to have me; at any rate she appears to have been persuaded to go into a Church of England home at some stage, maybe by a family member and in order to give me up for adoption. She may also have had some idea of claiming that her husband was my biological father for, around the time of my conception she had been back home in an attempt to reconcile with him – alas my arrival with bright red hair had rather put an end to that but she says in the letter that she never told my biological father that she was pregnant. Well, maybe, but in the final column of my birth certificate there is that reference to the affidavit signed by someone named John Kelly, one that requires all reference to John Chamberlain (her husband) to be deleted from the records. This was signed shortly before my adoption took place. So, again, I wonder, who was John Kelly if not my father? In the letter she goes on to write that she was disgusted and deeply ashamed, but once I had disappeared to Derbyshire, she returned to her family and 'picked up the pieces', though this did not include any contact with her son. In time she fell in love with a man who was killed in a road accident one night on his way to meet her. She says that he was the love of her life and after his death she felt that nothing much mattered. She was very ill but after some months began working in the Services where she met and had an affair with a married man. This affair also resulted in a pregnancy and it seems that maybe there was another attempt at reconciliation with her husband for when the baby, a boy, was born she was allowed to keep him. But she and her husband never did get back together and eventually they divorced and he left to live in Australia, while their only son, now a teenager, stayed behind with his grandmother still believing his mother to be dead. At this point she met another man who wanted to marry her and bring up her last child as his own son.

The letter is significant in that she expresses no concern for her first three children and writes almost solely about her continuing misfortunes. Indeed, when John, having finally learned of my birth all those years ago, asked her if she would like him to find out what had happened to me, she forbade him to make any enquiries and did not even want to know if I was alive or dead.

I had never had any illusions about my early background, never seen myself as the daughter of a rich father or had dreams of celebrity. In fact I had seen my biological mother as being trapped in a pregnancy very much as I had been and I felt I understood why she had put me up for adoption. But to learn that later she had not even wanted to know if I was alive or dead was a second rejection and hit me hard. She also denied me the one thing I really wanted from her; the name of my biological father.

My two half brothers and their families could not have been more kind and welcoming and there were hints of fatted calves to be slaughtered, but I felt I was being steamrollered into too much instant family. It was overwhelming and I began to pull back. John claimed that I was bitter about it all, but I didn't feel bitter; my main problem was a feeling of disloyalty to the two people who had brought me up as their daughter and given me so much. I still have those feelings and I think I am something of a disappointment to my new relatives; but we stay in touch and I have met them both and we are slowly filling the spaces left by circumstance in our very different lives.

But who was I really? Well it took a long while to answer that question, but one day, not long ago, I went back to Hathersage. I was with my brother and sister-in-law and the visit was an impetuous one. We parked the car near The Gables and walked through the chapel grounds to that familiar main road and the old building that still housed the post office. It was another grey, rainy day and the light was on inside. I pushed open the wide, heavy door that I remembered so well and crossed the granite flagstones to the counter. Very little had changed, and there was a man standing there holding a bunch of keys in his hands, a man who looked familiar. I guessed he was the son of the man my father had sold the business to all those years before and I asked him for postcards. He stood to one side to reveal a rack of them and then said, 'Is it Anne?' It had been many years since I had walked along that main road or stood in the post office, and I was hardly the same person who had left as a young girl eager for whatever life had to offer, but at that moment all those years fell away and it seemed like I had never left. And in a sense perhaps I never had.

Later we walked up to the Scotsman's Pack Inn for some lunch, past the entrance to my school and the spot where I had first asked my mother who was adopted, past the barbed wire fence where I had nearly ripped my face open while sledging; past the village school where the children stood silent when a funeral went by and past the little road to the cottage where my grandmother once lived. I was surrounded by a thousand memories, sights, sounds and images that I had carried with me for years, and I suddenly knew with absolute certainty that whatever blood ran through my veins and however many surnames I could legally claim, there was only one that was truly mine. I was Anne Ibbotson, the daughter of the postmaster and his wife from a small village in the Peak District of Derbyshire – and at long last, that was fine with me.

First published in Great Britain by:

Ashgrove Publishing

an imprint of Hollydata Publishers Ltd
27 John Street
London WC1N 2BX

ISBN 978 185398 155 5

First Edition

Book design by Brad Thompson

Printed and bound in England